A Celebration of Young Poets

West – Spring 2006

Creative Communication, Inc.

A Celebration of Young Poets
West – Spring 2006

An anthology compiled by Creative Communication, Inc.

Published by:

CREATIVE COMMUNICATION, INC.
1488 NORTH 200 WEST
LOGAN, UT 84341

ISBN 10: 1-60050-051-X
ISBN 13: 978-1-60050-051-0

Foreword

Welcome! Thank you for letting us share these poems with you.

This last school year we surveyed thousands of teachers asking what we could do better. We constantly strive to be the best at what we do and to listen to our teachers and poets. We strongly believe that this is your contest. Several changes were made to this anthology as we adapt to what was requested.

In this and future editions of the anthology, the Top Ten winners will be featured on their own page in the book. Each poet that is included in this book is to be congratulated, however, the Top Ten Poets should receive special recognition for having been chosen as writing one of the best poems. The Top Ten Poems were selected through an online voting system that includes thousands of teachers and students. In a day and age where television programs use viewer voting to determine which contestant is the winner, it is appropriate that our poetry winners are chosen by their peers.

Over the years we have had many parents contact us concerning the privacy of their children. The comments focus on the fact that publishing a poet's name, grade, school name, city and state with each poem is too much information. We want to address these concerns. In the Fall 2005 edition of the anthology, we made the decision to only list the poet's name and grade after each poem. Whereas we received many calls and letters concerning the issue that we were publishing too much information, we received thousands of calls and letters requesting that we again publish more information to include a student's school name and state with each poem. Therefore, for this and future editions we will publish each student's name, grade, school name and state unless specifically instructed not to include this information. Just as this information is included in a school yearbook, we provide this information in this literary yearbook of poetry. This decision hopefully makes it easier to find classmates in the book and brings appropriate recognition to the schools.

We are proud to provide this anthology. In speaking to the poets in our anthologies we have found that our anthologies are not stuffy old books that are forgotten on a shelf. The poems in our books are read, loved and cherished. We hope you enjoy reading the thoughts and feelings of our youth.

Sincerely,
Gaylen Worthen, President
Creative Communication

WRITING CONTESTS!

Enter our next POETRY contest!
Enter our next ESSAY contest!

Why should I enter?

Win prizes and get published! Each year thousands of dollars in prizes are awarded in each region and tens of thousands of dollars in prizes are awarded throughout North America. The top writers in each division receive a monetary award and a free book that includes their published poem or essay. Entries of merit are also selected to be published in our anthology.

Who may enter?

There are five divisions in the poetry contest. The poetry divisions are grades K-3, 4-6, 7-9, 10-12, and adult. There are three divisions in the essay contest. The essay division are grades 4-6, 7-9, and 10-12.

What is needed to enter the contest?

To enter the poetry contest send in one original poem, 21 lines or less. To enter the essay contest send in one non-fiction, original essay, 250 words or less, on any topic. Each entry must include the writer's name, address, city, state and zip code. Student entries need to include the student's grade, school name and school address. Students who include their teacher's name may help the teacher qualify for a free copy of the anthology.

How do I enter?

Enter a poem online at:
www.poeticpower.com
or
Mail your poem to:
    Poetry Contest
    1488 North 200 West
    Logan, UT 84341

Enter an essay online at:
www.studentessaycontest.com
or
Mail your essay to:
    Essay Contest
    1488 North 200 West
    Logan, UT 84341

If you are mailing your poetry entry, please write "Student Contest" at the top of your poem if you are in grades K-12. Please write "Adult Contest" at the top of your poem if you are entering the adult division.

When is the deadline?

Poetry contest deadlines are December 5th, April 5th, and August 15th. Essay contest deadlines are October 17th, February 15th, and July 17th. You can enter each contest, however, send only one poem or essay for each contest deadline.

Are there benefits for my school?

Yes. We award $15,000 each year in grants to help with Language Arts programs. Schools qualify to apply for a grant by having a large number of entries of which over fifty percent are accepted for publication. This typically tends to be about 15 accepted entries.

Are there benefits for my teacher?

Yes. Teachers with five or more students accepted to be published receive a free anthology that includes their students' writing.

For more information please go to our website at **www.poeticpower.com**, email us at editor@poeticpower.com or call 435-713-4411.

Table of Contents

Spring 2006 Poetic Achievement Honor Schools

* Teachers who had fifteen or more poets accepted to be published

The following schools are recognized as receiving a "Poetic Achievement Award." This award is given to schools who have a large number of entries of which over fifty percent are accepted for publication. With hundreds of schools entering our contest, only a small percent of these schools are honored with this award. The purpose of this award is to recognize schools with excellent Language Arts programs. This award qualifies these schools to receive a complimentary copy of this anthology. In addition, these schools are eligible to apply for a Creative Communication Language Arts Grant. Grants of two hundred and fifty dollars each are awarded to further develop writing in our schools.

Acacia Elementary School
Vail, AZ
Claire Jacobson*

Acme Elementary School
Acme, WA
Jon Anderson
Diane Leigh

Albuquerque Christian School
Albuquerque, NM
Dawn McKenzie*

Aurora Quest Academy
Aurora, CO
Kim Meyer
Roger Schafer

Barbara Bush Elementary School
Mesa, AZ
Christopher K. Roche*

Barratt School
American Fork, UT
Vickie Marrott*

Bates Elementary School
Colorado Springs, CO
Michele Comfort*

Bella Vista Elementary School
Salt Lake City, UT
Diane Shenosky*

Bright Beginnings School
Chandler, AZ
Barbara Jones
Carole Slaybaugh

Brush Creek Elementary School
Eagle, CO
Ms. Givens
Elizabeth Ronzio
Jenna Walsh

CLASS Academy
Portland, OR
Teresa Cantlon
Justice Evans
Leslie Huffman*

Coal Creek Elementary School
Louisville, CO
B. Arnold*

Colbert Elementary School
Colbert, WA
Don Hartvigsen
Connie Ramsey*

Copper Canyon Elementary School
Scottsdale, AZ
Jan Gaio*

Copper Creek Elementary School
Tucson, AZ
Ms. Boyd*
Mrs. Wall

Corpus Christi School
Colorado Springs, CO
John Eaton*

Eagle Point Middle School
Eagle Point, OR
Sammie Eaton
Lee Shupe
Rick Taylor*

East Evergreen Elementary School
Kalispell, MT
Michelle Mitchell*

East Middle School
Grand Junction, CO
Ann Hanson
Mr. Mantlo
Nancy McFarlin*

Eton School
Bellevue, WA
Dr. Debra Gessert*
M. McGrath
Patty Sorenson*

Evergreen Elementary School
Cave Junction, OR
Tammy Griffis
Mr. Linnemeyer
Ms. Wiley

Fox Creek Jr High School
Bullhead City, AZ
Tina Moore*
Laura Workman*

Frontier Valley Elementary School
Parker, CO
Patrick Allen
Carrie Merrill
Carol Sotebeer
Sue Sporer

Gause Intermediate School
Washougal, WA
Jim Schroeder*
Connie Vernon*

Gold Canyon Elementary School
Apache Junction, AZ
Michelle Sobkoviak
Judy A. Youngren*

Greenwood Elementary School
Greenwood Village, CO
Adrienne Jaycox*

Greybull Middle School
Greybull, WY
Carol Kestner*

H Guy Child School
Ogden, UT
Mr. Johnson*
Mrs. Young*

Hafen Elementary School
Pahrump, NV
Ms. Andresen
Michael Gogerty

Hamilton Middle School
Hamilton, MT
Ms. Solander*

Hazelwood Elementary School
Lynnwood, WA
Sally Bjornson*

Heath Middle School
Greeley, CO
Charla Jerome*
Mrs. Kanagy

Hidden Creek Elementary School
Port Orchard, WA
Shannon Mackie*

Jackpot Combined School
Jackpot, NV
Cindy Champlin*

Kendallvue Elementary School
Morrison, CO
Connie Berry*

Khalsa Montessori Elementary School
Phoenix, AZ
Keerat Giordano*

Kingman Academy of Learning
Kingman, AZ
Mrs. Blackburn
Mrs. Lucier*

Kyrene De Las Brisas School
Chandler, AZ
Ruth Sunda*

Larkspur Elementary School
Larkspur, CO
Janet Whetten*

Lewis & Clark Elementary School
St Helens, OR
Maria Heath*

Lincoln Elementary School
Prescott, AZ
Vicki Makela*

Meridian Middle School
Meridian, ID
Donna Castillo*

Mohawk Valley School
Roll, AZ
Heather Stepp*

Morgan Middle School
Ellensburg, WA
Sara Eubanks*

Mt Olive Lutheran School
Las Vegas, NV
Mr. Rosenbaum*

New Emerson School
Grand Junction, CO
Michelle Hooker
Paula Martin
Terry Schamlz
Carrie Wertz

Patton Middle School
McMinnville, OR
Beth Downs*

Phoenix Metro Islamic School
Tempe, AZ
Fatima Abdel Hag
Alia Al-Taqi
Hind Hania
Mootaz M. Koriem
Badrun Nahar
Veronica Ramirez

Pinnacle Charter School
Federal Heights, CO
Mrs. Ladouceur
Mrs. Spencer
Zack White

Pope John XXIII Catholic School
Community
  Scottsdale, AZ
    Mrs. Medhus*

Presentation of Our Lady School
  Denver, CO
    Ms. Healy*

Reid School
  Salt Lake City, UT
    Kim Aulbach
    Meagan Black
    Paulette Evans
    Jill Gammon
    Cheri Israelsen
    Mindyn Mullinix
    Rose Palmer
    Michelle Peterson
    Shauna Tateoka

River HomeLink Program
  Battle Ground, WA
    Tonia Albert
    Ryan Anderson
    Sherri Gassaway
    Julie Sperry

Robert Frost Elementary School
  Silverton, OR
    Paula Cross
    Cindi Schmitz*

Sally Mauro Elementary School
  Helper, UT
    Katie Barker
    Michelle Tatton

Sangre De Cristo Elementary School
  Hooper, CO
    Lorrie Jacobsen*
    Sandy Rogers

Scenic Park Elementary School
  Anchorage, AK
    Cindy Forsyth*
    Mrs. Hill
    Mrs. Kueter

Sedona Charter School
  Sedona, AZ
    Joette Burke
    Deborah Williams

Sequoia Village School
  Show Low, AZ
    Robert Hesselton
    Mindy Savoia*

Skyline Elementary School
  Ferndale, WA
    Mr. Diffley*

Somerton Middle School
  Somerton, AZ
    Sylvia G. Barba
    Pauline R. Bratt*

South Middle School
  Aurora, CO
    Debbie Reed*

Southern Hills Middle School
  Boulder, CO
    Sharon Nehls*

Spring Creek Elementary School
  Laramie, WY
    Sherilyn Berube
    Andrea Hayden
    Mark Williams

St Anne School
  Seattle, WA
    Shannon Sifferman*

St Cyril Elementary School
  Tucson, AZ
    Sarah Unger*

St Patrick's Catholic School
  Pasco, WA
    Michelle Good
    Ms. Lampson*

St Vincent de Paul School
Phoenix, AZ
Kyle Metzger*
Mrs. Rogers

Summit Elementary School
Smithfield, UT
Carla Cox
Mrs. Shaffer

Sundance Elementary School
Sundance, WY
Connie Green
Tammy Needham

Syracuse School
Syracuse, UT
Aimee Ottley*

The Colorado Springs School
Colorado Springs, CO
Mrs. Gutierrez
Jennifer Whitehead

Thomas Edison Charter School
North Logan, UT
Tanya Bidstrup
Mr. Packard
Mären Wendel*
Lee Ann Wilkins*

Uplands Elementary School
Lake Oswego, OR
Betsy McCarthy
Maria Strycker*
Ned Williams

Vikan Middle School
Brighton, CO
Penny Heiserman*

Walker Middle School
Salem, OR
Amy Baldwin
Lisa Hughes
Susan Lovelace

Wallace Elementary School
Parker, AZ
Miss Davies
Christina Olague*

Walt Clark Middle School
Loveland, CO
Dianna Croft*
Patty Kimball*
Amanda Robertson

Washington Intermediate School
Walsenburg, CO
Albert Galvan*

West Mercer Elementary School
Mercer Island, WA
Julie Hovind
Julie Langley*

Wilson Elementary School
Spokane, WA
Amy Barton*

Language Arts Grant Recipients 2005-2006

After receiving a "Poetic Achievement Award" schools are encouraged to apply for a Creative Communication Language Arts Grant. The following is a list of schools who received a two hundred and fifty dollar grant for the 2005-2006 school year.

Acushnet Elementary School – Acushnet, MA
Admiral Thomas H. Moorer Middle School – Eufaula, AL
Alta High School – Sandy, UT
Alton R-IV Elementary School – Alton, MO
Archbishop McNicholas High School – Cincinnati, OH
Barbara Bush Elementary School – Mesa, AZ
Bellmar Middle School – Belle Vernon, PA
Bonham High School – Bonham, TX
Cool Spring Elementary School – Cleveland, NC
Douglas Elementary School – Liberty, KY
Dumbarton Middle School – Baltimore, MD
Edward Bleeker Jr High School – Flushing, NY
Emmanuel/St. Michael Lutheran School – Fort Wayne, IN
Floyds Knobs Elementary School – Floyds Knobs, IN
Fox Creek High School – North Augusta, SC
Friendship Jr High School – Des Plaines, IL
Gibson City-Melvin-Sibley High School – Gibson City, IL
Hamilton Jr High School – Hamilton, TX
John F. Kennedy Middle School – Cupertino, CA
John Ross Elementary School – Edmond, OK
MacLeod Public School – Sudbury, ON
McKinley Elementary School – Livonia, MI
Monte Cassino School – Tulsa, OK
New Germany Elementary School – New Germany, NS
North Beach Elementary School – Miami Beach, FL
Paradise Valley High School – Phoenix, AZ
Parkview Christian School – Lincoln, NE
Picayune Jr High School – Picayune, MS
Red Bank Charter School – Red Bank, NJ
Sebastian River Middle School – Sebastian, FL
Siegrist Elementary School – Platte City, MO

Language Arts Grant Winners cont.

Southwest Academy – Baltimore, MD
St. Anthony School – Winsted, CT
St. John Vianney Catholic School – Flint, MI
St. Paul the Apostle School – Davenport, IA
St. Rose School – Roseville, CA
St. Sebastian School – Pittsburgh, PA
Sundance Elementary School – Sundance, WY
Thorp Middle School – Thorp, WI
Townsend Harris High School – Flushing, NY
Warren Elementary School – Warren, OR
Washington High School – Washington Court House, OH
Wasilla Lake Christian School – Wasilla, AK
Woodland Elementary School – Radcliff, KY
Worthington High School – Worthington, MN

Young Poets
Grades 4-5-6

Note: The Top Ten poems were finalized through an online voting system. Creative Communication's judges first picked out the top poems. These poems were then posted online. The final step involved thousands of students and teachers who registered as online judges and voted for the Top Ten poems. We hope you enjoy these selections.

Top Poem Grades 4-5-6

The Moon and Nighttime

Busy, busy, are the streets,
Illuminated as the moon meets,
Glistening off the never-ending sea,
Rays of light beam on me.

Lonely is the blank walkway,
We all sleep until the next day,
Crying, sighing, in our sleep,
Broken dreams are what we weep.

I am the one likely to see,
The only dreams filled with glee,
Because my dreams are filled with fun,
Unlike the moon, I'm with the sun.

Felicia Chaidez, Grade 5
Hidden Hills Elementary School, AZ

Top Poem Grades 4-5-6

Apple Blossoms

Summer is here, but not to stay,
It's to and fro in a flash.
So before it's over please let me say,
Take keepsakes for winter's cold blast.
Pick apple blossoms, press them tight,
Save them for a stormy night.
Maple leaves, press their looks,
Between some paper and a couple of books.
Drink orange juice, freshly made,
Or maybe some sugary lemonade.
But let's get off the subject of fruit,
And talk about those little green shoots
That grow to give us beans and corn
We eat those under winter's scorn,
And I hope that when, in winter, things go amiss,
You'll see apple blossoms and be reminded
That further ahead lay summer's warm bliss.

Linnea Englund, Grade 4
River HomeLink Program, WA

Top Poem Grades 4-5-6

Imagination

ZZZZZZ
In my imagination,
there is so much to see.
There's saggy, baggy elephants,
and flying chimpanzees.
There's no such thing as homework.
The movies are always free.
Every kid has their own pool,
don't forget the Jacuzzi.
I don't have to take a bath.
I don't have to clean my room.
Purple cows give purple soda,
not milk, Ewwwww!!!
I don't…
Johnny get up now!
5 more minutes, Mom…
No, now!!!
ZZZZZZ

Kristen Hastings, Grade 5
Cottonwood Elementary School, AZ

Top Poem Grades 4-5-6

Nature's Pride

A simple seed inside your hand
Drop it in the muddy land.
First, a root and then a sprout,
Its leaves are pursed into a pout.
Next a stem and then a bud,
And then (gasp) up from the mud,
Rose a plant of great creation.
The beauty that has made a nation,
Its sight and smell has great power
It could be nothing else —
A flower.

Jessica Hillis, Grade 6
Phoenix Advantage Charter School, AZ

Top Poem Grades 4-5-6

Butterflies in Your Horse's Stomach

Striding around the Winner's Circle, the trainer screaming in your ear,
you nod your head, but like you said, you cannot even hear,
the oohs and ahs, and whoops and screams, all cheering just for you,
just then you realize, all at once, you're cheering for you too.

Too bad, don't care, they seem to say, about the way you feel,
you'd better win, you cannot lose, it's just part of the deal.
Around to the gate, you try to feel, full of pride and greatness,
unfortunately, you cannot help it, you're full of butterflies and fakeness.

You're number four, not bad for a rookie,
but the others look fine, a big smile on their faces, while you just want to play hooky.
The gates fly open, the deafening bell rings,
your horse surges forward. With a glance to your right, you realize with fright, the others look like kings.

Earth flies everywhere, as your horse kicks up his heels, leaving others in the dust,
you grin, you smile, you wonder why, you doubted your own trust.
Up comes the line, with big fat F-I-N-I-S-H letters, and once again,
all over again, you smile you grin, at your horse's big accomplishment.

Makenna Johansen, Grade 5
University Park Elementary School, AK

Top Poem Grades 4-5-6

A Plea for Nature

On the delicate wings of a butterfly,
Nature's sweet magic will dazzle the eye!
The bright smiling flowers, the soft song of birds,
That indescribable feeling for which there's no words.

For Nature is graceful, so very unique!
Warm calming sunsets, emerald leaves, crystal creek.

But Nature will always have to comply,
With the ever ongoing public outcry,
For all kinds of building! One *billion* new things!
And the craze will keep going through newborn offspring.

Can't we see all the beauty of Nature?
The love of Earth that we all must nurture!
Do we need to play Gameboy? Or Nintendos, or TVs?
Couldn't we choose to go play in the trees?

Nature is pleading, please listen hard.
If we want to play, let's go in our backyard!
Turn off the TV, head out the door,
And Nature will slowly appear more and more.

Jennifer Johnson, Grade 6
Foothill School, UT

Top Poem Grades 4-5-6

Dance of the Flowers

Resting on dew of moonlit showers,
Gazing at clouds for hours and hours,
The rose petal glistens with shimmers of light
Keeping me warm and beaming with delight.

I surrender my soul to the dance of the flowers,
This, by far, is their finest hour.
Swaying in the wind with the greatest of ease,
Petals take flight, joining fluttering leaves.

I will join them as well, and as you can see,
I'm light as a feather and I can fly free.
I won't fall on the ground, or ever be wary,
For you see, my friends, I am a fairy.

Savanna Jones, Grade 6
Tucson Country Day School, AZ

Top Poem Grades 4-5-6

My Name

My name is my most prized possession,
Something that will never get old or boring.
I might wish it was something else,
But it will always be a special part of me.
I like to say it,
Feel it rolling off my tongue.
The smooth sound it makes,
Takes lots of practice.
When I hear my very own name,
I know someone is talking to ME!
Not the person next to me,
Or the person across from me.
That is why I like my name.
It's my favorite gift.

McKenna Keller, Grade 4
Brush Creek Elementary School, CO

Top Poem Grades 4-5-6

The Ways of Spring

As the black raven wings of night
Fly from the fiery face of the sun
Spring chases away
The grumbling clouds of winter
Bringing a glistening blue to the sky
Then sun yellow and sky blue
Bring grass green anew
White flowers and clear water
Frisk in a calm, lulling breeze
The grey tumbling clouds of rain
Strike and roar
But the wind chides them on
And birds sing their evening songs
As the raven takes flight
Once more.

Annie Whittier, Grade 5
Patterson Elementary School, ID

Top Poem Grades 4-5-6

The Ocean's Jewel

Orca waving
path engraving
carving in the ocean blue

Water spouting
children shouting
for the Orca swimming below

The ocean's jewel
black and white
a glistening gem
on clear, placid nights

A graceful being
a massive sight
the ocean's jewel
black and white

McKenzie Woodral, Grade 6
Blaine Middle School, WA

Cars

Cars roar like thunder,
cars are as fast as
the speed of light,
with a V-8 engine
cars are at the top line.
They come in so many colors
it's like a color wheel.

Riley Bache, Grade 5
Sangre De Cristo Elementary School, CO

The Glen Canyon

I hear the running water.
I hear it going farther.
The water is so clear
That I saw a reflection of a deer.
It was getting dark.
I heard a bark.
I saw a road.
I saw a toad.
I smelled the air.
It was water.
I felt like I was in the air
on the teeter-totter.
I looked and heard and saw…
a waterfall.
I felt like I was going to
fall, fall, fall.

Haley Hinojosa, Grade 4
Great Expectations Academy, AZ

On the Other Side

On the other side,
where the eagles glide,
is where I want to be.
Where the river meadows wait
is where I want to be.
Where the water isn't shallow,
with the fish and the minnow,
is where I want to be.

On the other side
mountains and city collide.
The song of the bird
is not often heard.
Cars rumble by
and the birds don't fly high.

I look out my window
at the wind and the willows
so far away.
And I wonder why
I can't be lifted into the sky,
and be taken to that place far away.

Richelle McDermott, Grade 6
Colbert Elementary School, WA

Mom

Your smile is A's on a 4th grade
report card.
Your voice is saying "let's have
hot and toasty chocolate brownies
after a cold winter day."
Your love is popsicles on a hot
summer day.

Branden Lahman, Grade 4
Hunters Glen Elementary School, CO

Holidays

Labor Day's so boring,
That groundhog's pretty dull.
And when Thanksgiving comes around,
I fill myself too full.

12/25 is better,
But it's just not the best.
Just subtract 20 days from that,
I think that beats the rest.

December 5th is my birthday,
The day the numbers grow.
Balloons and parties, growing up,
I wish it would never go.

And then comes ol' Valentine again,
The Easter bunny too,
And every year we strain to hear
The New Year bell anew.

The 5th again…my birthday,
I wish it will never go.
But when I get to 50,
I'd wish that it would slow.

Ian Greer, Grade 5
West Mercer Elementary School, WA

Hurst

H uggable, lovable, and hyper too!
U nhappy when I leave,
R eally energetic every day.
S uper tired after jumping on the
T rampoline.

Jereth Beck, Grade 5
Thomas Edison Charter School, UT

A Dirty Way

Pink and white like a blooming rose
Wrinkling like my grandpa's nose
Like the lips and teeth
Of my great uncle Keith
A pink horizon in the sky
Bumpy like my gravel drive

Jennifer Moreno, Grade 6
Morgan Middle School, WA

Among Us

In trees,
Underground,
Beneath your feet,
Flying among us.
Tigers smell them,
Fish see them.
Birds hear them.
The cruel don't know them,
The sweet believe in them,
But those unknown
Feel, hear, and see
The spirits everywhere.

Katie Heisel, Grade 5
Lewis & Clark Elementary School, OR

A Pencil

A pencil is interesting,
A lovely, long, round little thing,
Sometimes yellow and often blue,
It is a handy tool for you!
With your head's help it can tell a tale.
And with your hand, it can draw a whale.

Wynelle Dueck, Grade 6
High Valley Christian School, CO

Wind

The wind blows softly.
The trees move back and forth s l o w.
The leaves do not move.

Bronson Morgan, Grade 5
Gold Canyon Elementary School, AZ

I Wish

I wish
I was famous

I wish
I was rich

I wish
my sister felt better
for the next week

I wish
I could fly

I wish
I could sleep
as long as I want

I wish
a lot of things
but I am glad
for what I have.

Ana Toledano, Grade 5
Edgewater Elementary School, CO

Walking Thunder

Dark branches cover the field.
There is no sound, not even a bird.
Soon a slight breeze makes the branches move.
It grows stronger each minute.
Soon God says run and make a joyful noise to me,
my animals, my wolves, my raccoons, mountain lions,
serpents, birds and horses.
Come and live your lives.
Be free.
We all need to be free.
Horses run and make a noise of thunder,
and shake the ground as you run for joy and freedom.
Run to the mountains,
Leap to the sky,
Fly over the cruel world.

Terilee Waltenbaugh, Grade 4
Olympic Range Carden Academy, WA

Animal Inside Me

There is a kangaroo inside me
Just waiting to come out
It loves to play with all the joeys running about

Energetically jumping around inside me
Waiting to be released

Living in Australia where it's nice and hot
That's where kangaroos are
And where I want to be

Surrounded in company
That's how kangaroos travel
Talking and communicating sharing ideas all the time

There's a kangaroo inside me
Just waiting to come out

Kelsey Lang, Grade 6
Walt Clark Middle School, CO

The Only Sounds I Hear

The only sounds I hear
Are the pitter-patter of rain,
Tick-tock of a clock,
And a scratch of a cat's nail.

The only sounds I hear
Are crackling wood in the fireplace,
Beep-beep of a car horn,
And the hum of a radio playing a soothing song.

The only sounds I hear
Are my dad snoring in slumber-land,
Now finally some peace and quiet,
Now it's time for me to sleep.

Makenzie Blake, Grade 6
Home Choice Academy, WA

Pickles

Puckered lips as I sip pickle juice in a jar.
I'll taste the sour in an hour
as I go to the Eiffel Tower.
I'll pay a nickel for a pickle
so I'll pucker all throughout the day.

Amelia Burnett, Grade 4
Edmonds Homeschool Resource Center, WA

The Titanic

On April 10, 1912
The great unsinkable ship is ready to sail.
Friends wave goodbye,
Little babies wail.

The ship is off and sailing,
Everyone is having fun.
Everything is quiet,
Their trip has begun.

On the night of April 14,
An iceberg hit the ship.
Water poured in,
The ship snapped in two with the crack of a whip.

Many fell into the chilling waters,
Some got into a lifeboat.
Only few were lucky,
The ship could no longer float.

The survivors were rescued,
What had happened to the Titanic was unthinkable.
Now everyone knew,
No ship is unsinkable.

Zhiming Zhong, Grade 6
Enterprise Middle School, WA

True Love

True love is more than a brilliant red rose
It's something you feel deep down inside your heart
It smells so beautiful under your nose
But you feel true love even when you're apart

True love just never seems to go away
It's like a picture in your locket
It stays on your mind every single day
Whether it's around your neck or in your pocket

True love can make you feel your very best
True love makes you feel as light as air
True love can make your heart be filled with zest
A feeling of true love is very rare.

Let's say you suddenly get set apart
Your love will remain forever in your heart.

Abigail Luchs, Grade 5
Reid School, UT

My Horse Blue

My name is Sue
I ride my horse named Blue
We once were on a trip
And I lost my grip
And never again did I ride Blue

Tyler Baumunk, Grade 6
Bright Beginnings School, AZ

Hockey

Hockey
Intense, rough
Hitting, fighting, checking
Goalies, pads, book, classroom
Studying, testing, listening
Horrible, long
School

Emerson Ehrlich, Grade 6
Heath Middle School, CO

Where I'm From

I'm from my mom,
I am from the apple cider,
That my family makes,
Every year.
From comedy,
Making jokes,
Every day,
Every week of my life.
I'm from the mountains,
Adventuring, climbing,
From the pigskin of a football,
All 7 laces.
I'm from my father,
Growing up on the farm.
I'm from the beginning,
The beginning of my life.

Josh Strobel, Grade 5
Namaqua Elementary School, CO

Swimming in the Ocean

Swimming in the ocean
Swimming in the sea!
Swimming in the lake
Come and swim with me!!

Splashing up the river
Sliding down a stream!
You're my friend
And you swim with me!!

Jumping out of the pool
Sliding down a slide!
Smiling under water
With you by my side!!

Irene Aplan, Grade 5
M A Lynch Elementary School, OR

Spring Baseball in Colorado

I like standing in the outfield and hearing the crack of the bat
And hearing the ice cream truck behind me.
I love spring ball in Colorado.
I hear the birds chirping and flying low on the field.
I love spring ball in Colorado.
I smell the grass and the dirt, it is warming with the warm weather.
I love spring ball in Colorado.
Oh no, the ball is coming toward me, I better stand up.
I love spring ball in Colorado.
I run, I catch, we win the game, the crowd is screaming.
I love spring ball in Colorado.
We go for pizza to celebrate our victory, I eat a whole pepperoni pizza.
I love spring ball in Colorado.
As we head for home we see the sun slip under the mountains.
I love spring ball in Colorado.

Clay Billing, Grade 6
Corpus Christi School, CO

My Magic Box

In my box I hear,
The quacks of ducks on a crystal clear lake,
The crash of waves, breaking upon the white sandy shore for the first time.

In my box I find,
The sounds of the green rain forest, waiting to release its magic,
The roar of a jaguar when it has triumphed.

In my box I find,
Early buds,
waiting to open again and again, to unleash their beauty.

In my box I find animals,
growing and growing,
like a fawn just learning to walk,
or a bird learning to fly.

In my box I find nature,
nature to the eye,
nature to the ear,
And nature to the heart! Nature.

Nick Carter, Grade 5
Mesa Elementary School, CO

Beauty

Beauty isn't always a size three for a dress or a head full of thick blond hair
Sometimes beauty is your heart in which controls your emotions
Or beauty is how people think about you bad or good
Or maybe beauty is a newborn child being treated with care by its parents
And beauty even is a flower that's different from all the others
Or could beauty be laughter from a young child
Beauty is a leader in a room full of followers
Beauty's also a quiet nerd who gets all the answers on the math test right
And beauty is a kid whose purpose is to do good deeds for no expectations afterwards
After you think about it beauty isn't always a size three for a dress or thick blond hair

Kegan Mengel, Grade 6
Walt Clark Middle School, CO

March

March reminds me of clovers
Clovers remind me of St. Patrick's Day
St. Patrick's Day reminds me of the color green
The color green reminds me of shamrocks
Shamrocks remind me of March

Hannah Rocke, Grade 4
Clarkmoor Elementary School, WA

What Are My Flowers?

What are my flowers?

Red and yellow
So beautiful they make the stars glitter
A beauty of the Earth
Made by a goddess
The spring's diamonds
From the heavens
More lovely than the sun
Make light and day
Demeter's smile
Jewels against the grass
Rubies on a ring
Sparkles in Persephone's eyes
Hera's secret garden
So sweet they stop wars
So beautiful Aphrodite has them in her hair
So delicate they're softer than clouds

Those are my flowers.

Chandler Williams, Grade 4
The Meadows School, NV

Hot and Cold

Hot…
A devastating fire
Lava melting into your skin
A burning desert, no oasis in sight
The sand shimmering in the harsh sun's glow
A star to which we cannot travel
Our sun that can melt us in only mere seconds
A house burning to the ground
A brush fire in the woods
A black coal flaming in the fireplace
To set foot on Mercury's warm side
Cold…
The icy planet Pluto
Liquid nitrogen
A day in the freezer
Snow in which a child loves to play
A swim in the Arctic Ocean
An air conditioner
Frozen metal
A stream with chunks of ice in it
A frozen lake during winter

Glenn Elms, Grade 6
Khalsa Montessori Elementary School, AZ

Handcuffs

Handcuffs
Shiny, silver
Arresting, tightening, clicking
Don't run in handcuffs. Ouch, these hurt.

Darren Hester, Grade 4
Jackpot Combined School, NV

I Am

I am beautiful
I wonder what it feels like to lose a friend
I hear baby birds chirping
I see a nest with baby birds hatching
I want more friends
I am beautiful

I pretend I am a cat
I feel jumpy on my horse
I touch my old, old dog
I worry my mom is going to get in a car wreck
I cry when my cats get hurt
I am beautiful

I understand happiness
I say I am cool
I dream I am a movie star
I hope I'm good
I am beautiful

Danielle Bennett, Grade 5
Kingman Academy of Learning, AZ

Smelling the Delicious Smell

Walking in the door smelling the tremendous smell
Looking and smelling the fluffy chocolatey cake
Down in the hall
Smelling the red frosting and the sprinkles too.

Walking in the hall smelling it even more
I can already taste the delicious cake
I walk in the kitchen
And my brother ate it all

Alyssa Harris, Grade 6
Pope John XXIII Catholic School Community, AZ

Snowflakes

Corkscrewing — faster! — Through the air
Like echoed footsteps that aren't there
Descending through the blackened sky
Are freezing needles, brushing by
Feathery flowers, dancing 'round
Sailing to the now snow-strewn ground
Swirling, plunging, twirling, floating
Hints of silent faeries, gloating
Cascading through the open night
Snowflakes convolving, shining bright.

Bryn Reinstadler, Grade 6
Lolo Elementary School, MT

Happy Day

Dark clouds fade away
Promising a better day
Now sun shines on us

Ciana Gastelum, Grade 6
St Cyril Elementary School, AZ

I Am

I am creative and smart
I wonder if God is real
I hear voices at night
I see pale figures
I want my grandpa back
I am creative and smart

I pretend to love our new dog
I feel the love of my parents
I touch the top of my dog's head
I worry my grandma might die
I cry over death

I understand math
I say the truth
I dream of bad things
I try to do science
I hope God is real
I am creative and smart

Hanna Brown, Grade 5
Elger Bay Elementary School, WA

Red

Red is the color
Of strawberry jam,
The cherry cheeks
Of a very cold ma'am.

The color of blood
Dripping off roses thorns
The flame breathing dragon's
Fiery horns.

A Huskers jersey
And raspberry pie,
Your face when you laugh
So hard you cry.

The licorice ropes
Little kids eat,
The pudgy toes
On my sisters feet.

Valentine hearts
And a cardinals tummy,
Appley tarts
And a twizzler that's yummy.

Zoe Kreft, Grade 6
Kendallvue Elementary School, CO

Spring Is Hatching

From its inner
It reveals
A baby bird
That squeals and squeals.

Its mother laid it
With tender care,
To make sure
That it stayed there.

It was silent
'Til that fateful day,
When the white shell cracked
And out it came.

Like a groundhog
Out of its hole,
Squinting, adjusting to the light,
Not sure, feeling lots of fright.

It came into the
World full of
Wonder and love.
It came from above.

Maddie Giles, Grade 5
Barratt School, UT

White

What is white? Is it a color
or is it just the empty space
of what used to be a color?
The blank emptiness of something
that was once so beautiful.
It's like you squeezed all the color out
and all you're left with is white.
Just dull plain white.

Connor Dedrick, Grade 6
Eagle Point Middle School, OR

An Old Friend

It seems like only yesterday
That you were here beside me.
I loved the way you looked at me,
With those big eyes.

I miss your fur as soft as clouds.
Your cheerfulness like spring.
But in a blink you were gone.
I miss you, my dog, my friend.

As dogs go there are many good ones
And many more will come along.
But in my heart you'll always remain
My sweet dog, my old friend.

Kyleigh Carter, Grade 6
Beacon Country Day School, CO

Basketball

About basketball,
To get the ball
Around defenders
To pass it
Near the half
Under some pressure
Up with the ball
to the center
Below the hoop
In the key
Up with the easy shot
Near the end
Up by 12
With a big win!

Trevor Johnston, Grade 6
Fox Creek Jr High School, AZ

Hockey the Game

He shoots he scores
The buzzer screams
The crowd goes wild
We start to cheer
We won we won
We're the champs
We know that the game is over
We won we won

Marcus Jordan, Grade 6
Corpus Christi School, CO

Sounds

Rustle, rustle, rustle
Sighs the wind in the trees
It sends cold shivers
From my head to my knees

Howl! Howl!
Sing coyotes at night
Although they're not fierce
Their sound gives a fright!

Listen, listen
To the sounds heard at night
Sometimes the sounds
Are better than sight

Morgan Tholl, Grade 5
Firwood Elementary School, OR

Spring

Beautiful sunset
Walk in the park
Calming cloud in the sky
River that never dries
Starry night that never ends
Picture being painted

Isabella Davis, Grade 4
Lincoln Elementary School, AZ

Come Back to Me

Left alone, to waste away
Left with thoughts of you
You said you'd be back someday
Isn't that day here yet?
What am I supposed to do
I'm lost without you.

I can still remember the day we met
Just like it was yesterday
You smiled, I smiled.
I couldn't help myself
Your gaze made me feel like I was just a child
My heart melted at that moment.

When you come back
I can stare endlessly into your eyes
And drown helplessly in your love.

The thought of you every day
Tugs endlessly at my heart
Wanting to be held in your arms again
Is tearing me apart
While I'm waiting,
Waiting for your return.

Kim Jackson, Grade 6
Blaine Middle School, WA

I Am Clumsy

I broke my mother's plate,
I crushed my sister's doll,
Ran into a metal gate,
And made my brother fall.

I'm very sorry for stepping on the cat's tail,
And for hitting the dog with a rake.
You see I tripped over a water pail
When running from a snake!

I am very clumsy as you can see,
I know that I am clumsy…
Or maybe it's just me?

Zoe West, Grade 4
Gause Intermediate School, WA

The Whirlpool

A whirlpool spinning round like the Zephyr of Arabia
Twisting and turning like the sea
As a ship goes by
A whirlpool is blocking their way in the light of day
But as soon as the gray mists come spinning up like a tornado
And the ship goes under the water and below the waves
Where the fish bubble and burst
No one will ever know the land that they seek
For a whirlpool blocked their way.

Sophia Litwin, Grade 4
West Woodland School, WA

Flowers

Flowers, oh flowers, so wonderful so bright,
They sing a sweet melody that makes me dance all night.

Flowers, oh flowers, so beautiful and bold,
When I look at them they refresh me and do not make me cold.

Flowers, oh flowers, so soothing so pink,
They have an amazing color they really makes me think.

Flowers, oh flowers, you see them in May,
You should plant your garden, I planted mine today!!

Caroline Federici, Grade 4
Double Eagle Elementary School, NM

Peace Is Mysterious Indigo

It sounds like jazz music played on the streets of Chicago.
It feels like my hand running through an ocean of fog.
It smells like fresh, cold air on a snowy morning.
It tastes like hot cocoa on a cold winter's day.

Christopher Canopen, Grade 6
Cadwallader Middle School, NV

Feeling Green

Green is calm and relaxing,
and wild and attracting.
Green is the taste of grapes fresh off the vine,
cools down your mouth and is the smell of wine.
Green is the sound of a rushing river,
and the generosity of a loving giver.
Green is the color of fresh cut grass,
and of algae in a very large mass.
Green is the feeling of having the flu,
green is me, how about you?

Tyler Gaumond, Grade 6
Sequim Middle School, WA

The Shot

7, 6, 5, 4, 3, 2, 1…shoot! Nick Ambuul shoots the ball!
A miss…but the ref calls a foul! He has 2 free shots!

Ambuul taking his time…ready to shoot.
Ambuul shoots and makes the shot! The game is now tied!

Nick hoping to shoot again to win the game.
Dribbles…dribbles some more…he shoots he scores!!!

Wait the ref calls a violation…it's a lane violation.
Nick has to shoot again.

Ambuul is very nervous. He takes his time once again…
Nick pumping up the crowd.

Nick Ambuul shoots…it goes in once again!!!
Nick Ambuul and his team win the game!!!

Nick Ambuul, Grade 6
Corpus Christi School, CO

The Hat

Sloping and curving,
Right down to the brim,
The hat band gleams in the light.
Black as night,
Softly shaped from felt.
Thin leather straps
Hold it on when we go.
I pick the horse up
And ask her to run,
My hat flies behind me,
As we soar beneath the sun.
The thudding of her hooves,
Are the only echoing noise.
We stop and turn towards home,
With my hat flying behind me.

Jessianne Wright, Grade 6
Monforton School, MT

The Sea

The sea, the sea, it calls to me
A mad, aggressive mountain lion.
It rolls and thunders, yells, and roars.
It whispers and cries, floods and sighs.
The sea is a warrior fighting the wind.
It calls a sad, lonesome cry,
An owl calling for its mate.
It is filled with love and filled with hate.
It is full with beauty and compassion,
It is filled with living sight,
But filled with a living fright.
Calling, calling, crying, crying
Nobody knows why it calls or sighs.
The sea, the sea, goodbye, goodbye.

Hannah Hogan, Grade 4
Roy Moore Elementary School, CO

Tigers

Tigers are a deadly race
And when they see you they give chase

You can see them with their stripes
Running through the Inky night

And see them with their glowing eyes
And your body they soon will spy

And they do have those very sharp teeth
Which any other animal cannot beat

And they do have those very sharp claws
Which they keep inside their paws

Tiger are a deadly kin
So run away to save your skin

Timothy Hurson, Grade 6
Morgan Middle School, WA

Flower

A small seed, which becomes a bud.
Next it becomes a soft little sprout,
cuter than you ever could imagine.

The compassion flowers have for care, sun, and water.
Soon it unfolds into a clear vivid blossom.
The vision you see on this blossom will take you to another world.

The fragrance will make you think
about what and why you've missed this beautiful beauty that you are smelling.

Arda Alev, Grade 4
Eton School, WA

Grandpa Jake

He stayed awake
For 92 years
Yet he shed no tears
Except when his first child was born
He went to World War 2
His family knew what he had to do
21 trips to the hospital
A soft but full heart
Last night I cried my grandpa had died
From beginning to end his life lives not on Earth but in my heart

Emma Guzman, Grade 5
St Mary's School, ID

Dirty Jobs

It was night time for me,
Suddenly the fluorescent sun lit up.
I was tired because I had one minute of sleep in the bathroom.
Then I was picked up,
I was put in a long tunnel with white and yellow tooth-shaped rocks
Running through the bottom and sides of the tunnel
I was feeling kind of grossed out,
By the wet gooey stuff pushing against me.
There was a pink fast-moving figure,
Like a worm, but faster,
Then I was put in a round cylinder with a the top cut off,
It was night again.

Katherine Gallion, Grade 6
Blaine Middle School, WA

One Scary Night

I find myself in a dark, damp alleyway.
I feel the icy wind upon my back.
It seems as though I am being watched,
      from inside the old, wretched warehouse.
I feel a large bony hand on my neck.

I turn around, nobody is there.
Suddenly, an eerie specter appears out of the shadows.
It is my pale-faced uncle.
He is here to take me home.

Gregory Nowicki, Grade 6
Pope John XXIII Catholic School Community, AZ

Useless Things
cat without fur head without a hat
birds without wings pencil without lead
sink without water

door without a doorknob soup without a spoon
light without electricity money without value
mud without dirt

swing without a seat shoe without laces
flowers without wheat tree without roots
popcorn without pop

guitar without strings people without clothes
fan without blades TVS without television
music without sound

hunting without any fowl fishing without any fish
video games without tv pillow without feathers
window without curtains

Zack Wynn, Grade 6
Walt Clark Middle School, CO

Brain Waves
I realized my brain is like jelly when I sit in that desk,
and find that I did not study for that test!
My brain was all squirmy it just wouldn't sit still.
I'm losing my mind, I've gone over the hill!
I managed to write some answers, the ones I could think of.
My eyes glanced at my teacher with dismay.
I think I might study before the next test day!

Karina Guzman, Grade 6
Meridian Middle School, ID

Flowers
The bright petals on the flower smiled at the sun.
Their beautiful color attract the bees.
The petals are so smooth and silky.
The flower balances on the long stem.

Catherine Wetter, Grade 6
Pope John XXIII Catholic School Community, AZ

The Outdoors!
Springtime
Summertime
Anytime
It's fun
To be
Outdoors
Go crazy
Go wild
Explore
Galore
With crisp sun, fresh air
It's the outdoors!

Olivia Driscoll, Grade 4
Edmonds Homeschool Resource Center, WA

My Teacher
Ms. Musselman was my 5th grade teacher,
She inspired my life,
She inspired me about school,
It seemed like all we did was play games
But we didn't,
You learned in those games.
I would stay after school to set up parties
For the class, and get help from her.
Ms. Musselman inspired me about art
And inspired me about life.

Jessica Weese, Grade 6
Hazelwood Elementary School, WA

A Mystery
Silent shadow, slinking through the dark
With a hiss and a scratch, I make my mark
I never falter, I'm the master of the night
Unlucky are those who feel the wrath of my bite

I'm fearless and sly, you can't scare me
If you think I can be tricked, you shall see
I may be small, but I sure pack a punch
It only takes one claw to snag my lunch

My strategies are many, my enemies few
If I do get threatened, I've got that covered too
Those who chase me do it at a cost:
I turn right around and show them who's boss!

I have all this power, I own all this land
But I've not yet told you who I am
I have many nicknames, hundreds at that
Some call me evil, but most call me cat!

Laura Wisniewski, Grade 6
West Jefferson Middle School, CO

Love
Love is as beautiful as the sun and the sea.
And the flowers and their petals, love is beautiful to me
Someday I will find that heartwarming man
I can think, I can dream, I know I can
The roses of the red and the violets are blue
All things beautiful make me think of you
'Til then stay true,
Because heaven only knows when I'll find myself with *you*

Baily A. Phillips, Grade 5
Discovery Plus Academy, AZ

Wildness
Wildness is a scribble of light brown and emerald green.
It sounds like kids screaming and running at Chuck E. Cheese.
It feels like playing laser tag with all of your friends.
It smells like the burning of the wick of fireworks.
It tastes like a full three pound bag of sugar.

Ryan Jenkins, Grade 6
Cadwallader Middle School, NV

Competitive Business

In the town of Albuquerque
there is a kid who makes beef jerky
out of smoked ham and turkey.
He likes the money that he's making;
he's going to make more
with the cake he's baking.
A couple days later,
he has a fear
that he's going to
lose his business
to a kid selling bottles
that are shiny and clear.
He did not lose his business,
in fact,
he's rich,
but the kid selling bottles,
is now digging a ditch.
Josh Hedderig, Grade 5
Frontier Valley Elementary School, CO

War

We hear some rumbling
We hear something rattle
We get our guns
And get ready for battle
We go outside
To get ready for war
We see our enemies
By the seashore
We load our guns with ammo
Then we cock them
Then my friend yells,
"Let's sock them!"
We shoot at them
They shoot at us
How can this be?
They killed my friend Gus
We won the war
Some of us started to shout
Some other people
Just ran about
John Paul Nuez, Grade 6
Queen of Angels School, WA

Tree

Package of leaves,
barked branches,
ladders
waiting for me to climb.
In the rain I smell rotten wood
In the sun I smell fresh air,
from my perch
I am surrounded,
trapped in a leafy prison.
Brittnie Fawbush, Grade 5
Carrolls Elementary School, WA

When I'm Lost in My Mind

When I'm lost in my mind I don't know
What to think
I don't know what to do
I feel I have the flu
I get so lost in my mind
I don't have a clue
I feel like a clown I just want to lie down
If only I could turn my frown
Upside down
I'd be happy
Michael Alessi, Grade 6
St Anne School, WA

Sausage Pizza

Sausage pizza is bumpy,
rough, jagged layers
of sedimentary rock.
Tyler Inlow, Grade 5
Lake George Charter School, CO

A Small Fish

A small fish in a large ocean
Bigger fish just waiting
Hiding in an anemone
Just to stay happy.
Cody Ray, Grade 4
St Andrews Episcopal School, NM

Paintballs

I am red, green, and blue
The color of splat on you.
I soar through the sky
Until I hit a guy.
I can fly so high
That sometimes I cry.
I would not like to die
But that guy,
Ah,
There's his eye,
SMACK!
OUCH!
Chad Minnick, Grade 6
Cottonwood School, MT

We Still Live Free

We still live free.
Where there is no slavery,
While the soldiers fight for freedom.
So we can live free.

We still live free.
Because of men's bravery,
As the flag still waves,
We still live free.
Cody Nate, Grade 4
Cokeville Elementary School, WY

My Favorite Dragon

My favorite dragon
Shiny black scales
Sharp white claws.
Dragons are fierce beasts.
Dragon riders have long silver swords.
Dragons are dangerous.
Dragons can be gentle
And harmless.
Nate Richardson, Grade 6
Orient Elementary School, WA

Desire

Sunshine's warmth comes
in rays and beams
water surrounds me
currents pump from my tail
I bump off the reeds
Searching for a meal
The first day of spring
I am hungry for a meal
I swim faster covering yards of the lake
Glimmer and glitter
Pink and gold my meal waits
In my vision another fish
The food is mine, I am a faster swimmer
So competitive I am for a taste
So worried about the other fish
without noticing the hook
my mouth opens wide
I swallow — as I come out of the water
the last thing I hear is "Fish On!"
Dolan Adams, Grade 6
Meridian Middle School, ID

Smiles (and Memories)

It happens night and day
It happens when people say

Smile!

When your picture is about to be taken
When the scrapbook is maken

You will be able to hold
Smiles and memories in your hands.
Bethany Baker, Grade 4
New Emerson School, CO

Dragons

Dragons
Blue, scaly
Flying, walking, clawing
A must for me
Dragons
Robert Woodland, Grade 5
Cottonwood Elementary School, CO

That's What Love Is

Doing little deeds,
That's what love is
Standing up for them,
That's what love is
Not being embarrassed for being with them,
That's what love is
Knowing what they do and do not like,
That's what love is
Remembering their anniversary,
That's what love is
Actually loving them, and willing to commit,
That is what love is all about.

Mary Sewright, Grade 6
Pope John XXIII Catholic School Community, AZ

My Cat

My cat has eyes ever so keen,
they are a black pupil surrounded by green,
and when they see a fly,
oh how he zooms by!
Then he sticks out a claw,
and eats it all raw,
but he can be lovely,
and so so fluffy,
and when I start to scratch,
oh he does attach,
he is so cute,
and never ever mute,
'cause when I try to sneak,
he always takes a peek,
my cat is so clever,
he could even work a lever,
my cat is sooo good,
MY CAT!!!

Shannon Zhu, Grade 5
Lister Elementary School, WA

Caesar

There once was a city named Rome
Many people called it home
His name was Julius Caesar
He wasn't such a pleaser
That Rome killed him on their own

Jacob Wagner, Grade 6
Pope John XXIII Catholic School Community, AZ

The Sea

The sea
Beautiful dazzling blues and greens
An underwater world of marine life
Free to swim, free to be
Inside the sea alone
Except for the beautiful, swimming creatures
In the sea

Isabella Brown, Grade 5
Eton School, WA

A Rainbow of Friendship

Take two cups of sugar,
Add three cups of laughter,
Add one cup of sweetness.
Sprinkle a slumber party,
One cup of pool parties.
Cook until you hear laughing.
That's how you make a rainbow of friendship.

Lana Smith, Grade 5
Desert View Academy, AZ

Tigerwind

With its strong gusts of black and orange wind,
Its roars and howls surround and start to claw at you,
And the trees shaking with the great power of tigerwind,
It pushes you over with its large, large, paws,
It roams the forest and plains,
Capturing the small creatures it finds,
So now I will warn you that you must never ever go out
When a tigerwind has begun.

Neha Kumar, Grade 4
Kyrene De Las Brisas School, AZ

Dogs

Dogs lick of love.
They bark and beg.
They don't see color but that's okay!
They have yellow, orange or brown hair.
We love our dogs because they are everywhere.

Alexa Boliba and Abby Albrecht, Grade 4
Frontier Valley Elementary School, CO

The Beauty of the Wood

A gorgeous wood,
A wonderful wood,
Of radiant colors so true.
A wood of peace and wildness too,
The wood I'll explain to you.

Pillars of pale light,
Dim, yet bright,
Fall smooth as a dove,
From the white sun above.

Many beautiful trees, and bushes and things,
All blended colors of light blues and greens.
None are alike; they're all different ways,
Growing ever upward toward the sun's bright rays.

To walk through that wood is to fly way up high,
With rainbows and eagles and stars in the sky;
And in that wood the most wonderful thing,
Is if you listen real hard, it's so quiet, it sings.
And although these sights seem too good to be true,
They are real and are waiting for you.

Dillon Jarrell, Grade 5
Mount Carbon Elementary School, CO

Construction

Construction site building.
Paper folding.
Cars waiting.
Ships stop.
Drawbridge stuck.
Huge mess up.
Crashing cars.
Draw man angry.
Late for work.
People getting angry.
Ronaldo Varela, Grade 4
Acacia Elementary School, AZ

Tigers

Tigers are little kittens
When they play
They may look fierce,
With their stripe body,
And sharp teeth,
But they are kittens
Which are not tame.
Monick Cornejo, Grade 5
Ames Elementary School, CO

On the Road

Life fading past,
Everything's so flat,
Like a giant stretched it out,
By tugging at its sides,
Lush and green,
The sky so blue,
Darker and darker,
Until,
Black,
Then,
Flashing lights,
No more taken breath,
Zooming past me every step,
Until I can't keep up,
And then,
I find it,
Just in between,
The comfort and happiness,
With the exhilaration,
The home.
Katie Schmidt, Grade 6
Walt Clark Middle School, CO

Old Arizona

The old and out of date Arizona
Is quite amazing and marvelous
With a route that is well known.
I am here with all my passion
For the old fashioned Arizona.
Elena Tassinari, Grade 5
Kingman Academy of Learning, AZ

Mislead

Robins sing out loud,
With the misfortune of snow,
Come at the wrong time.
Trevor White, Grade 6
Recluse Elementary School, WY

A Hummingbird

Inside of me there's a animal
that's waiting to burst out
I have another side of me
that's far from hyper and loudness
The only sound it makes
is a sweet humming sound
What is that animal you say?
A hummingbird, that's what's waiting
to burst out of me!
Krista Matuszek, Grade 6
Walt Clark Middle School, CO

Sweet

Sweet
Chewing, biting
Soda, lollipop, gum
Buying, amazing, crying, licking
Pain, lemon, lime
Stinging, melting
Sour
Eduardo Flores, Grade 4
Jackpot Combined School, NV

Freedom!

Big eyes glaring, staring
Strong, stripy, invisible, beautiful
He is powerful
Prowling the night
He'll win the fight for food
He has no freedom
Oh Tiger

Hunters shoot Bam! Bam!
Will they kill her too
Her green evil eyes glow
Boy, does she love snow
Spots! Disguised! Watch out guys!
For here Leopard comes.

Leopards and Tigers running free
That dream it is hard to see
But we have to try
Before they die
Imagine no tigers no leopards
Please! Freedom is needed.
Before they are extinct
They need you they need me
Josie Anderson, Grade 5
Greenwood Elementary School, CO

Haley

H umorous is what I am.
A lways out of my seat.
L ike to read
E ating yogurt is really good for me.
Y elling is what I do too much of.
Haley Duran, Grade 4
Mills Elementary School, OR

Bad Luck

There once was a man from Peru
Who lost, in a stream, his shoe.
"For crying out loud,"
He said with great sound.
Bad luck! He stepped in some goo.
Andrew Kraemer, Grade 6
Patton Middle School, OR

Warm 'n Cozy

In the night
You turn out the lights
Snuggle in tight
In your bed toward the warmth
Away from the cold and storm
Under the sheets
You will hear a small little beat
When you hear it
You will know that you are
Warm
Cozy
And safe from harm.
Julia Lu, Grade 4
Double Eagle Elementary School, NM

My Soul

I awake and my body is really stiff
so I have to lay there until
someone comes.

3 days I lay there by myself
but no one comes.
Faithfully I'm still alive.

7 days no food, no water, no energy.
I notice my soul is weak and gone.
Now it's harder to move on.
Ashley Hayes, Grade 5
Enterprise Elementary School, OR

If I Could

If I could come back after I die
I would come back as a tear,
I would start in your heart,
Drip down your cheek
And gently fade at your lip.
Marty Mazzara, Grade 6
Green Valley Christian School, NV

Inside Me

Inside me there's a deer
Ready to spring out
Soft, gentle, shy, and quiet
Afraid of loud commotion, but very social

Fast and slow, but confused
Active and lazy, but should be on the go
Worried and panicked, but relaxed and calm

Afraid of the spotlight,
But afraid of the dark
There's a deer inside me.

Briana Merrick, Grade 6
Walt Clark Middle School, CO

Midnight Sky

Black is the color of the midnight sky,
The color of space that is very high,
At night it is frightening,
It is also chilling,
A bloodcurdling sentence goes through my head,
And now I just want to curl up in bed,
I don't know what to do,
I'm scared; I'm weak, yes that's true,
Finally, I find where I'm going,
But then I see a crow crowing,
It takes me so high into the clouds in the sky,
That's why I'm scared of the midnight sky.

Tasha Jones, Grade 6
Bright Beginnings School, AZ

Sadness

Sadness, a blue tsunami lunging in,
Salty tears capturing my taste buds,
The aroma of dead animals destroy me,
As brokenhearted songs pierce my heart,
I experience loneliness when nature hurts people,
A downpour is an opaque sheet of rain.

Abbey Emery, Grade 6
Lolo Elementary School, MT

Pets

I wish I had a puppy.
I wish I had a dog.
I wish I had a puppy to play with me all day.
I wish I had a kitten.
I wish I had a cat.
I wish I had one to play with balls of yarn.
I wish I had a pony.
I wish I had a horse.
I wish I had one to ride on a bumpy course.
I know I am all alone,
With nothing else to do.
Then I got a puppy, so now I'm not alone!

Emily Love, Grade 4
Wilson Elementary School, WA

In You…

In your eyes I could see the bright blue sky.
In your smile I could see the brightness of the sun.
In your nose I could see the moon looking at you.
In your face I could see all of those things
working together to make your life way better.

Wendy Ayala, Grade 5
M A Lynch Elementary School, OR

Is This the End

Freedom opens a door
that leads to a grassy meadow
Captivity shuts the door behind you
while walking into an abundant house
Will freedom fight back and open the door again?
Day
when the sun
hauls up the curtains
releasing its light
Night
when the moon
closes those curtains
Will the sun be able to roll them up again?
Summer is a star shining brightly
and in winter a black hole
Will the star dust
form a new or even brighter stars
The beginning is a growing wave
that builds higher and higher
until it crashes on the shore
Is this the end?

Amanda Smith, Grade 5
Khalsa Montessori Elementary School, AZ

Basketball

Basketball is my favorite sport,
I like the way you dribble up and down the court
I get the ball,
Shoot the three,
And I see it go down the drain.
Next time we have the ball,
I go down and get the rebound,
Everybody in the crowd goes wild,
I take it back,
Fake the pass,
Then I go down the lane,
With 3 seconds left,
We're down 1 point,
I step back and hit the fade-away,
Then there is 1 second left,
They get the ball,
Pass it in,
But their hopes are crushed, as I reject the shot.
We won the game, and it's all over.
My dreams are accomplished!

Deuel Meadows, Grade 5
West Mercer Elementary School, WA

8777

88788

After Effects

In the morning
the air was sparked with tension
and unseen radiation.
I was blind to what had occurred.

At school
we were robbed of outside.
All day we sat within.
They wouldn't tell us why.

Our teacher told us
to hasten home after school.
No lingering.

I saw firefighters bullet down the road
to the nuclear power plant
south of town,
where father works.

Chernobyl
was never the same after the explosion.
Kara Diemer, Grade 6
East Middle School, CO

Tests

Tests
Long, short
Listening, no helping, quiet
Some are boring, some are fun.
Antonio Torres, Grade 4
Jackpot Combined School, NV

Leprechauns

L ittle green men.
E veryone's after them.
P ots of gold await.
R ainbows mean there's riches.
E lusively camouflaged.
C areful where you step.
H iding in the grass.
A lways wearing green.
U nder the rainbow you go.
N ever give up their gold.
S t. Patrick's the king.
C.J. Fuentes, Grade 5
M A Lynch Elementary School, OR

Star

The stars in the sky
Sometimes want to make me fly
They make me happy
They twinkle down in my heart.
I'll never forget
The way they shine in my life
Breanna Shaw, Grade 6
Morgan Middle School, WA

Summer

Summer
Very hot sun
Playful on the beach lots
Joyful, burning, water, sprightly
Joyful

Beach fun
Love to play, waves
Run, dig in the sand, play water
Cold, hot, food, happy tanning in sun
Excite

Bright orb
The sun is bright
The star radiates
Blind, happy, the sun out today, glad
Amuse

Season
Fun in the sun
Going swimming, lots of fun
I feel summer is the best thing
Content
Erika Hoglund, Grade 5
Olympic Range Carden Academy, WA

Laneah

L oving
A lways excited
N ot unhappy
E ver so kind
A lways happy
H appy at two years old
Kathryn Turley, Grade 5
Thomas Edison Charter School, UT

Fall

F alling leaves on the ground
A ll the children making piles
L eaves turning orange and red
L ovely breezes every fall.
Feddiena Young, Grade 4
Gause Intermediate School, WA

Just a Bird

Just a bird spending the afternoon
On a sunny day
In the shade of an oak's branch maze

The wind makes a swish and a swoosh
Through the old tree's branches
When a storm takes the day away

And just a bird flies home
Aubrey Powell, Grade 6
Monforton School, MT

Little Puppy

A little puppy
in New York City
walking on the streets
on Sunday morning
was looking for a home
Ileana Martinez, Grade 4
Jackpot Combined School, NV

A Great Score

Into the gym I go
About ready to play
Opposite of the loud crowd I stand
Up goes the ball as high as it can
Out I reach to grab it
Over my head but I catch it
Upon the players I run
Within the court goes the ball
Into the basket swoosh! I score.
Salina Sarabia, Grade 6
Fox Creek Jr High School, AZ

Know

Knowing that I keep it in
Knowing I need to tell
Knowing if I don't
I will explode no doubt
Knowing they are there for me
And that I can tell them anything
They are my friends
That is all I know.
Destinee Navarro, Grade 6
Fox Creek Jr High School, AZ

A Falling Star

The moon is cartwheeling
Across the sky.
She's very appealing,
Yet very shy.
Shining brightly,
The moon talks and sings.
She moves slightly
With invisible wings.
As I watched,
I heard a sound.
I turned around
And looked down.
I saw a star.
A star I knew
Was from afar
And very blue.
It had fallen
From the sky
In many pieces.
I wonder why!
Honoré Bordelon-Cardin, Grade 4
Big Park Community School, AZ

The Sky Is the Limit

The sky is the limit
With a very weak wall
Don't take it; just give it
And you will not fall
Take my advice
And you will have friends
The sky is the limit
And the sky never ends

If the sky never ends
Then you may go far
Up, up and away
Away you will soar
And while you are soaring
Look down

Looking down on the world
You can see all
Trees, parks, and buildings
And blue waterfalls
So if nothing else, remember this friend
The sky is the limit and the sky never ends

Dustin Middlemist, Grade 5
La Veta Elementary School, CO

It's a Twisting Turning Winding Road

It's a twisting turning winding road.
I'm not sure where it leads or what will happen.
There is a fork in the road and I'm not sure where to go.
This road is full of decisions.
Right or wrong I must continue.
It's a twisting turning winding road.

Emma A. Scherzer, Grade 5
Ainsworth Elementary School, OR

Animal in Me

There is a coyote in me with
Eyes as bright as the moon.
It leaps like a cheetah,
It lives in my soul, and eyes,
And it makes me want to run!
I wish it would show itself or show its feelings.
It makes me want to blend in the night sky,
And it makes me feel active!

Byron Flores, Grade 5
Hafen Elementary School, NV

Rainbows

Red, blue, purple, and green,
Those are your colors that gleam in the light,
You come to cheer us after a sad day of rain,
You always come when we're in deep pain,
You brighten our days and fill us with glee,
And that is why I admire thee

Galen Anthony, Grade 5
Seltice Elementary School, ID

Megan

Encouraging, Christian, athletic
Who wishes to graduate from college in the future.
Who dreams of having straight A's through college.
Who wants to travel around the world.
Who wonders what she wants to be when she grows up.
Who fears death.
Who is afraid of snakes.
Who likes New York.
Who believes in God.
Who loves sports.
Who loves her family and friends.
Who loves chocolate.
Who loves to read mysteries.
Who plans to raise a family when she's older.
Who will always believe in herself.

Megan Brosius, Grade 6
Patton Middle School, OR

Ghost Town

A town in the middle of nowhere
As the town rots to nothing
The memories of the town appear
The sound of horses' hooves ringing through the street
The wail of women crying for their husbands
The singing of drunken men in the saloon
The sound of the shot that tore the town apart
The cry of "gold!"
The sound of falling timber
As the sun sets on these ancient ruins
The past dies
In the ghost town

Matthew O'Leary, Grade 6
Fruitland Middle School, ID

Dark Battlefield

Watch people die as they come by,
shoot the moon in attempt to destroy it as it comes
or you may be in doom because of the moon
especially for you.
For you are blind like a blind mouse
and your enemies have sight of you
don't say I didn't warn you.

Brandon So, Grade 5
Lister Elementary School, WA

Winter

Winter is my favorite season
I like winter for a reason
The cold snowy weather
Floats to the floor like a light feather
The white snow
The wind blows
When snow stands
It makes it look like a winter wonderland

Yaa A. Owusu, Grade 6
South Middle School, CO

Spring's Assets

My brother shouts,
"Come on, it's nice out here"
It's winter to spring,
And my brother has no fear.

I finish my cocoa,
With a grin on my face,
I run to my brother
As if it were a race.

Colorful flowers
Spring up high,
Like cornstalks
Proud and mine.

The rain washes
Bad weather away,
Makes me feel proud
Makes me say "hooray."

People love
The things they see,
In spring
especially.

Tanner Lecumberry, Grade 4
Grass Valley Elementary School, NV

Boomer

My dog was sweet, family,
Parents' first child,
Loving friend,
They all have their time.
He got old, big bones and flesh,
Howling in pain during the night.
Dad not home, just Mom and Sister,
Not enough, alone, alone.
Mom called Dad "Time is up."
We got Boomer Dog Lilly in the car,
Drove him to a vet,
Crying, crying, moaning, moaning,
"Is this the right time?"
I hugged him, said "Bye"
Sister did the same.
Mom stayed with Boomer,
When the needle went in,
Sister and I stood outside, hugging.
Was this the right time?

Isaac Lilly, Grade 5
West Mercer Elementary School, WA

Dragon

My crackling breath
And my bloodshot eyes
Send people in fear

John Ouellette, Grade 6
Peyton Middle School, CO

Smile

Smile…The most important word in a language
A smile is pure and comes from the heart

A smile can be spoken in any language…anytime…
A smile shows peace and love of all things, yet discovered

A smile brightens the day…Lightens the hate…
While walking down the sidewalk, not to see a single soul smiling

Wondering why this world is filled with hate and despair?
Asking yourself…Have I smiled today?

Have you made our world a better place?
Have you just been so caught up in all your problems,
you didn't seem to notice?

So, I'm asking you, when you get ready in the morning,
Look yourself in the mirror…Smile…

After all, it's a powerful way to give a little piece of humanity…to someone
Making an everlasting connection…lasting a lifetime…

Kelsey Freeman, Grade 6
Hermosa Vista Elementary School, AZ

Excited But Sad

I see desks and a humungous amount of people
I hear the click clacking of pencils rushing down to desks and a bell ringing.
I touch the ground and feel the vibration of a stampede of feet rushing out the door.
I smell the wonderful food that the preschool is preparing.
I feel sad but excited because I have been released.
I know I'm at the school I love.

Amy Wray, Grade 5
Eton School, WA

Everything…Just About

I am a mysterious girl who likes just about everything.
I wonder when we won't have gravity anymore.
I hear an earthquake passing by me.
I want to have a pet cockroach.
I am a mysterious girl who likes just about everything.

I pretend to be a flying monkey ninja.
I feel the Hi Ya!! in Hi Ya!!
I touch the moon with my kabillion foot long finger.
I worry when a cricket loses his crick funk.
I cry when I lose a germ off my body.
I am a mysterious girl who likes just about everything.

I understand when a flea on a dog has to go.
I say to hold hands with a monkey.
I dream of me riding a beetle.
I try to keep track of my toenail clippings.
I hope to be a sweet and normal girl. (It's not like I am already.)
I am a mysterious girl who likes just about everything.

Hannah Harris, Grade 6
Cadwallader Middle School, NV

Hiding

Deep, deep down inside of you,
You'll find the soul you know is true.
The one that's kind to others,
That doesn't mind her brothers,
While the outside of you is…
Nasty! And really mean,
That talks so bad your mouth turns green,
The one that's an annoying machine!
So you must come out of hiding.

Katelyn Davis, Grade 5
Colbert Elementary School, WA

Beauty

Beauty is lovely and fair
beauty is without compare.
Like a baby's face when born
Not hard nor ugly like a thorn,
but pleasing to the eye.
Beauty could be anything
beauty could be something
one thing it is not is nothing.
Like the beauty of a rose
or an oyster's pearl.
Everyone has beauty in their own special way.
Real beauty comes from the inside
but natural beauty you cannot hide.
God created you special the way you are
with His tender soul that lies in your heart.

Breanna Gregorio, Grade 6
Green Valley Christian School, NV

Among the Heart

Among the heart
Within the kindful care
Underneath the silky skin is a helpful heart
Opposite of bad is an excellent person
Above the caring person is wonderful
Past the nice tree is an evil one
At the evil tree you don't have any fun
Upon the caring kids are bad kids also
Within who is bad doesn't get their way
To be kind are many ways
Through your brain is your decision

Kayla Walters, Grade 6
Fox Creek Jr High School, AZ

My Life in a Book

So many memories throughout my life
One book that brings all my memories together
One book that speaks out to me
One book that makes me as joyful as a kitten
One book that captures my life
One book I'll keep forever
My life. My memories. My photo album.

Lexi Polmear, Grade 5
Greenwood Elementary School, CO

Pretend

Pretend you are a shiny scooter.
Zoom around the glowing blacktop.
Race with a speedy friend.
Speed crazily by your mother.
Spin circles by your dad.
Fly straight down the gleaming sidewalk.
Cruise speedily like a race car down the other way.
Go Go Go Go Go!
AAhhhhhh. Crash Boom Bang. Owwww!

Justin Clark, Grade 6
Midway Middle School, ID

Ancient Egypt

Ancient Egypt is the place to go,
You will see obelisks and the Nile River flow,
Maybe watch a burial session,
With jewels, gold, and other possessions.
Go inside of a pyramid,
Or see the king.
Learn to speak Egyptian
Watch Anubis start embalming.
To prepare a mummy,
You have to take out its liver and tummy.
Egyptians believe in the afterlife,
They even believe to be buried with a knife.

Kelly Reardon, Grade 6
Pope John XXIII Catholic School Community, AZ

Frosty Day

A frozen day
a layer of snow
glittering and shining
beneath the cloudless blue sky
icicles dripping down gutters
like waterfalls frozen in time
a cardinal sings his winter song
flying in and out of the green green trees
today is perfect like a stream ribboning down mountains
and across valleys
a perfect day for a winter bird

Ali Grossweiner, Grade 5
University Park Elementary School, AK

Spring

Spring is all about the flowers,
And the leaves growing,
Spring is about having fun without coats,
Spring is about wind blowing through your hair,
Spring is a fun time with a little breeze,
Spring is about the grass growing greener,
Spring is about playing all the time,
Spring is about trees, T-shirts, warmth,
And no more cold,
It's almost like summer!

Jacob Montoya, Grade 4
McCormick Elementary School, NM

Boys/Girls
Boys!
Sweet, funny
Jumping, running, swimming
Strong, sporty, pretty, energetic
Smiling, laughing, talking
Lovable, wonderful
Girls!
Nikki Fujiwara, Grade 6
St Cyril Elementary School, AZ

I See You Uncle Peter
I feel your presence all around me
I see your smiling face
Your eyes oh how they sparkle
Can you hear me when I talk to you?
Do you know how much I miss you?
I especially miss your hugs!
Sometimes I wake up crying
Because you were in my dreams
I wake up feeling your hugs
And real are what they seem

I remember when you were here
You were always very near
I remember when you were sick
And I wished I had something to kick
You wouldn't talk to anyone
You opened your eyes for me
And I went to God to plea
Now that you are gone
I continue to stay strong
Because of the memories of you and me
Timothy Decker, Grade 5
St Cyril Elementary School, AZ

Friends
F un
R espectful
I ntelligent
E xample
N ice
D reamer
S weet
Lauren Tofell, Grade 4
Gause Intermediate School, WA

Blue-hoo
Blue is the color of sorrow
The color of the sky tomorrow
It makes you cry
As you sigh
Blue is the color in which goldfish swim
In which waves rush in
The color of a Marlin's fin
Cierra Dootson, Grade 6
Bright Beginnings School, AZ

Mirror
What is that thing I see?
What is that thing in front of me?
What is that thing I see!
What could it be?
What is that thing I know I've seen?
What is that weird old thing!
What? Oh ya! It's me!
Cory Fowers, Grade 5
Thomas Edison Charter School, UT

We Live Free
Today we still live free,
Without fear and slavery.
Sing *The Star Spangled Banner*,
Help our flag fly higher.

The brave soldiers in the army,
Fight for our liberty.
Stand tall is my saying,
For them we keep on praying.

Battle and war,
Make us mourn.
But we still stand tall,
Though we may cry and bawl.
Jonathan Fiscus, Grade 4
Cokeville Elementary School, WY

My Dog
Under a maple tree
The dog lies down,
Lolls his limp leg
Yawns,
Rests his long chin
Between his front paws
Looks up alert
Chomps with heavy jaws
At a small fly
Blinks, rolls
On its side
Sighs closes his eyes
In a deep sleep
All afternoon
In his skin.
Jessica Crim, Grade 5
Gold Canyon Elementary School, AZ

Running
Running through snowy trees
In the pale light I run
I run with the wolves of Alaska
My surroundings are calling me.
I wish I could stay
This happy forever.
Cameron Connally, Grade 4
Scenic Park Elementary School, AK

The Country
Farming with tractors
goats and a pig
bunnies so cute
animals so big
sheep and cows
fields side by side
"Freedom!" "Freedom!"
taking a horseback ride.
Nicole Sitton, Grade 6
Patton Middle School, OR

God
God is great
God is good
God is right
God is true
God is always
There for you
Nadiya Sokolan, Grade 4
Christian Faith School, WA

The Desert
The shy cactus wren
Flies in the Saguaro cactus
Hides from predator.
Cameron Corbridge, Grade 5
Kingman Academy of Learning, AZ

Spring
Spring is wonderful, spring is great.
Spring is beautiful every day.

Flowers bloom nice and tall.
Much better than in the fall.

The grass turns nice and green.
It's hard to keep your clothes clean.

The sun shines and it is warmer.
Summer is just around the corner.

Spring is wonderful, spring is great.
Most kids I know, love spring break.
Samantha Pardue, Grade 6
Meridian Middle School, ID

Stars
Stars
Light, small
Shining, burning, glowing
Gases, pinpoints, pressure, colors
Orbiting, studying, explaining
Big, bright
Planet
Spencer Bond, Grade 4
Olympic Range Carden Academy, WA

Rain

Rain
Beautiful, cold, wet
Falling from the cloudy sky
Falls to the ground, creating pools of water
Rain
Beautiful, cold, wet

Katiana Van Dyke, Grade 5
Kingman Academy of Learning, AZ

Everyone Loves…

Everybody has a love
Deep down in their heart
But here are the things I love the most

Who I love most is the strongest of all
He is the master who started us all
He is my God, my Savior, my Father
That's who I love the most of all

Next I love the people I know best
The people who support me
Wherever I go they're so sweet
So nice and so loving
I couldn't be happy if I didn't have my family

Also, the people who support me
With great pride and glee
The people who help me
With homework and more
As you might have guessed
These people are my friends and teachers

I love a lot more but lastly I love
The ones who run around outside in the free

Jamie Forster, Grade 6
Pope John XXIII Catholic School Community, AZ

Photo

A photo has many values
just because it's supposed to
It brings the joy of memories
It shows a painting from a flash
Click, Click
To start an explosion, of emotion

You look at the photo and you smile with joy
It's a picture of you and your very first toy
Then you frown for your sister flushed it down
Splish, Splash
Your face turns from a pale pink sunset to a red hot pepper

You close your eyes and fall asleep
your day has gone with your camera's painting
But, the next day is still waiting

Ana Villasenor, Grade 6
Spring Creek Elementary School, WY

My Family

Mom, is always there for me.
To make sure that I have good grades.
I could never have a better mom.
I love you mom.

Dad, you are always there for me whenever
I played in a basketball game.
You would always give me money when Mom wouldn't.
I could never have a better dad.

Alyssa, you always came when I was crying.
You taught me how to play basketball.
You always let me cruise with you.
Now I know I could call you sister.

Kailee, you always try to make me smile
whenever I am mad.
You are always there for me.
You are the best little sister I could ever have.

Rikki Horn, Grade 6
Harlem Elementary School, MT

Birds

Sweet singing in the air
I've never heard anything like it anywhere

Parrots talk
While some birds mock

Pika is my bird
His whistle is the best I've ever heard!

Libby Volk, Grade 6
St Patrick's Catholic School, WA

Life

Life is full of twists and turns,
With roads that lead you up and down,
Until you almost collapse because your whole body burns,
And nothing can be seen on your face except a gloomy frown.

Through one twist the road is rough,
And the next it is smooth,
The road is rough when life gets tough,
And smooth in moments of truth.

When life gets bad,
God carries you,
He will get you through times that are sad,
He will help you on your journey through.

Now remember, when life goes downhill,
God will help you up again,
There is no price at all, and no bill,
He is just waiting for you at where you began.

Talia M. Moyer, Grade 6
Albuquerque Christian School, NM

School

Math, writing, homework
Working until recess
Reading until writing time
Working at 4th grade time
Reading a book at recess
Playing at recess time
Doing homework at recess
Being a good friend
Being a great friend.

James Wilson, Grade 4
Gause Intermediate School, WA

Whirlwind

A whirlwind, a twirl wind,
A swirling, twirling wind,
Around, around in circles,
It swirls and twirls forever,
Why does it swirl and twirl,
Like a dog chasing its tail,
It suddenly changes,
A mad, rushing tornado,
Rushing, pushing, tearing up,
Everything is gone,
Torn away, shorn away,
Like hens from a fox,
All hope is lost, gone,
Lost, gone, hopeless.

Molly Iwasaki, Grade 5
Uplands Elementary School, OR

All

All have a purpose.
Not all fulfill it.
All have expectations.
Not all meet them.
All have beliefs.
Not all the same.
All have humor.
Not all good.
All have temptation.
Not all heed it.
All have thoughts.
Not all know.
All have these.
Not all want them.

Matthew Meyer, Grade 5
Aurora Quest Academy, CO

Dragon

Dragon
Fearless, adventurous
Soaring, hoarding, roaring
Its searing flames are very hot.
Creature

Grayson Metzger, Grade 4
St Viator Elementary School, NV

My Place

The waterfall flows through the water like a bird flows through the sky.
As I write this poem I write it from my place.
My place is not my brain but my heart and my soul.
That's my place and my work's domain.

Devan Johnson, Grade 6
Meridian Middle School, ID

No

"No," a word that can do it all
It can crush someone's heart
It can tell the truth
It can tell a lie
It can save someone from doing something
It can make someone do something
It can answer a question
It can be a question
The word "No" can change your life
A simple word like "No" can do it all
"No" has many different meanings, and can be used in many ways.

Sachi Royer, Grade 6
Santa Fe School for the Arts, NM

Shedding Red

Red is the color of stoplights, which signal us to stop
Red is the color of an angry man who is afraid to open up
Red is the color of roses in bloom, which will make a lady smile
Red is the color of blood we shed when life shares its sorrow

Katie St. Peter, Grade 6
Bright Beginnings School, AZ

Hephaestus

Hephaestus, the lame, ugly forge man,
Lived inside the volcano, Mount Etna, on the island of Sicily.
Son to Zeus and Hera,
He was noble, strong, creative and loyal.
Hephaestus married Aphrodite for love but she did not love him.
Aphrodite left him for Aries, the handsome, vain god of war.
The lonely Hephaestus despaired his loss of the lovely Aphrodite
To the cowardly Aries.
So the lame blacksmith threw himself into his work to forget her.
He helped all the gods, goddesses and demigods create their dreams —
He made their armor, weapons, jewelry, and vessels of all kinds —
He even made the woman, Pandora, who would bring all evils upon humankind.
But nothing relieved his pain.
Unless Aphrodite came to her senses and returned to him,
He would be alone forever on his forge
For he knew he was ugly and no one would ever love him again.

Taylor Tebbs, Grade 6
East Valley Academy, AZ

The Color Pink

If I were the color pink, I would be a heart pounding in my grandpa's chest.
I would be a rose given to someone for Valentine's Day.
I would be cotton candy getting eaten by a child.

Dusty VerValen, Grade 4
East Evergreen Elementary School, MT

Fun Is...

…Sports
Hitting a ball down the third base line,
Being chased down the field with a football
Shooting hoops with a swoosh and watching it fall.

…My Sister
Hanging out with my sister,
Annoying her in so many ways,
It's one of my favorite ways to spend my days.

…My dog
Jumping, playing, running,
Throwing a ball as he runs around the bend,
And walks just chilling with my best friend.

…Fishing
Watching the river rippling past my waders,
Casting across smooth waters and reeling in a fish,
And landing a big one, oh yeah, that was just a wish.

Court Nelson, Grade 6
Spencer Butte Middle School, OR

Basketball

Basketball is my favorite sport
I like the way they dribble down the court
Because they always shoot into the hoop
And they make an alleyoop
They go everywhere to play their games
And everyone asks for their names
Then they tell them
They act like stars, they're a gem!!

Denisha Ross, Grade 6
Harlem Elementary School, MT

Hi

That sweet summer day a warm breeze came in,
and a bumblebee danced by
then a tiny thought came into my head
to tell it
    Hi
      Hi
        Hi

Maggie Stanczyk, Grade 6
Eagle Ridge Elementary School, CO

To Be Free

Freedom isn't free.
How can that be?
Our soldiers fight for our rights.
They defend our flag all the days and nights.
They have always won,
The wars that had begun.
I'll give them a hug and a sob,
For their wonderful job.

Justene Moody, Grade 5
Cokeville Elementary School, WY

The Walk

Bob and Joe went on a walk.
When they go around they like to talk.

They walked around a very large park,
When they walked past a dog, it started to bark.

When it started to bark, they both ran away,
Then Bob and Joe went home for the day.

They met again later that night,
But only walked where there were lights.

Poor Bob it seems he tripped and fell,
Right into a deep, dark well.

The firemen came with ladders in hand,
And got Bob out, what a lucky man!

Now Bob and Joe walk only during the day,
That was quite a story wouldn't you say?

Taylor Emerson, Grade 6
St Cyril Elementary School, AZ

My Hands

My hands take me places
Places I have never been before

My hands let me feel soft
Soft is the bird's feathers
My hands let me feel rough
Rough is the bark on a tree
My hands let me feel smooth
Smooth is the mirror upon me

My hands are like the feet of a tap dancer
Dancing on piano keys
My hands are like spiders weaving webs
Creating memories in yarn

My hands are like dogs digging holes
Holes to plant seeds in
My hands are like messy pigs
Messy with cookie batter

My hands are the key to my world!

Breanna Dahlin, Grade 6
Walt Clark Middle School, CO

Autumn

Red, brown, and orange trees
Piles of leaves going crunch when I step in them
Cool gust of wind surrounding me
Snowflake or two
My favorite season

Carson McKelvey, Grade 4
Lincoln Elementary School, AZ

Sharp Shooters

Playing hard is what we do
We support each other
And help each other
That is what makes us the best
We work as a team
One alone is not enough
All of us have special talents
Some can shoot
Others can pass
It doesn't matter
'Cause we work as a team

My coach is the leader from the bench
But on the court
We coach each other
So, when you want to play
The Sharp Shooters
Be ready because
We are the best
Whether we are on the court
or off the court
Yeah

Kaunaloa Kama, Grade 6
Corpus Christi School, CO

Love

Love is a best friend
It's a partner for life
Someone who's special
For the time in life
You will love this person
You will be together forever
Cherish this friendship
'Cause there isn't a lot.

Taylor Butler, Grade 6
Fox Creek Jr High School, AZ

The Veterinarian

There's pain in his eyes,
There's blood on his body,
Tears dripping down his face.

I see many crimes
Most of which I can't believe
Abuse and neglect are against my beliefs.

Many countries abuse them like Mexico.
They don't see them as companions
But as a target to shoot or run over.

But here comes the light
A beautiful dream,
I'm here to make a difference
To help the animals be free.

Mayra Miramontes, Grade 6
South Middle School, CO

Basketball

B ouncing and dribbling
A ssist the ball
S core as quick as you can
K eep up the defense
E couragement to win
T ime to defeat
B asket after basket
A ll is coming to an end
L ast three seconds time is low
L ay-up at the end will win the show

Jaeson A. Herrera, Grade 5
Cuba Elementary School, NM

Emotional Hues

If your world is sad,
It must be too blue,
So add some yellow
To make
a greener hue

If your world is too happy,
It must be yellow,
Add a drop of orange,
To make it
Mellow

If your world is mad,
It must be too red,
So mix in a few stripes
To make it
Plaid

Now you've seen the colors
And what they can do
Just by adding a few
You can feel a different hue

Sophie DeGroot, Grade 6
St Anne School, WA

Earthworm

Deep under the ground
a little earthworm snoozes
in the freezing rain.

Dillon Woodland, Grade 5
Ammon Elementary School, ID

Christmas

Christmas
The lights on my house
The foresty aroma coming from the tree
The bells on Santa's sleigh
The candy in your stocking
All of your presents
Christmas

Drew Weaver, Grade 4
Coal Creek Elementary School, CO

Brothers and Sisters

We fight and scream brothers and sisters
WHY ME!
We fight and yell at night
We fight scream in the morning

We fight at school
We fight at home
Brothers and sisters
WHY ME!
We fight at lunch
Brothers and sisters
WHY ME!
We may fight and scream and yell
But we love each other
SHH!
don't tell

Olivia Byrd, Grade 6
Eagle Point Middle School, OR

Reading

Reading is the subject I do not like
It is not interesting
I hate to read books
And there's too much testing
I'd rather be in a good mood
And eat junk food
I'd want to watch TV
And then go ski
It should be more fun
And we should always play in the sun
And make stuff with clay
And play every day
Teacher, if you make reading interesting
I will finish all my testing.

Anthony Venuti, Grade 4
Rogers Elementary School, NV

Lie

I am a lie.
Have you seen me
Hurting people,
Breaking trusts,
And causing pain?
People find me as an excuse.
I reassure people
Only to have them worried once again.
Do I sound familiar?

Elizabeth Botte, Grade 5
Aurora Quest Academy, CO

Beaches

Waves on the shore
Making me feel joyful
Under the warm sun

Kim Malella, Grade 6
Morgan Middle School, WA

A Very Bad Day

My alarm went off and I jumped out of bed
On the top bunk I did hit my head

I went to the freezer to get some ice
When in my hair I found some lice

When I found the lice I screamed for dad
Which only made him very mad

I already knew what to do
I washed my hair with lice shampoo

The stinging shampoo got in my eye
Which in turn made me cry

With tears in my eyes, I ran out
And into the world I did shout

"I know I might get in trouble deep
But, darn it, I'm going back to sleep."

Luis Yescas, Grade 6
St Cyril Elementary School, AZ

Treats

Candy is sweet, it's always a treat.
Candy is forever, candy is clever.
Candy is good, you know you should,
Eat it, and eat it, and eat it.
Brownies are brown, they turn your frown upside down.
Brownies are yummy, yummy in my tummy.
Brownies are good, you know you should,
Eat them, and eat them, and eat them.
Ice cream is creamy, it's also quite dreamy.
Ice cream is freezing, it's always appeasing.
Ice cream is good, you know you should,
Eat it, and eat it, and eat it.
Treats are good, you know you should,
EAT THEM, AND EAT THEM, AND EAT THEM!!!

Sophie Albanis, Grade 5
Uplands Elementary School, OR

Your Life

When you can't take the pain
you can't take this life
you can't take this world
so why have a life?

When you see it coming
and you don't stop,
then it happens
and you don't drop.

That's when it hurts the most.
So you choose the way you want to live your life.

Michaela Towns, Grade 6
Fox Creek Jr High School, AZ

The White Feather

The floating white feather that sweeps down low,
Has blended in, in the light, puffy snow.
The swift wind has taken a blow,
The feather swoops up, look at it go!

Through the town of Littleville,
The feather lands on little Will.
He takes it home on 7th Street,
He races his brother, he can't be beat.

In through the door, while the snow comes in,
He sees his mother caught in the wind.
He runs back over to close the door,
And helps his mother sweep the floor.

He shows her the feather he has found,
"It was there Mother. It was on the ground."
The mother puts it on the table,
And beneath the feather she wrote a label,

"A pretty feather Will has found,
Just lying there upon the ground."
Will was proud as he beamed,
He smiled at his mother, while he gleamed.

Venessa Bayer, Grade 6
Beulah Middle School, CO

All About Camping

Fireflies fly around fried flies,
Moo — cows munch melted macaroni,
While wildflowers waltz in winter,
Wild wingless horses walk while winking in windblown winter,
My mother mellows out after making me macaroni,
Fair father follows a fallow deer while hunting in fall.

Megan Bowen, Grade 6
Desert Mountain School, AZ

Close Up

When I see things from far away
I take them for granted
I think they're small and have no value
But that's not really true

Close up is the best sight that there is
Because you can see everything
For what it's really worth
And because it's a better sight

Zooming in is not far or close
When you zoom in
You might see some things you didn't notice before
Like if a baby cow were behind its mother
You wouldn't see that from far or close
And that's why zooming in is so important

Nicholas Rahall, Grade 5
Blanco Elementary School, NM

Peak Breezes

The beautiful and exquisite peaks
blow slightly in the soft wind.
The cruise ship strolls
in the calm water.
The tall trees
wave side to side
with the flow.
The sunset water
roams
with the mellow
breezes.

Marcus Coleman, Grade 4
Audubon Elementary School, CO

I Found an Antique

I found an antique,
It's my gum from last week.

I forgot it was here,
behind my ear.

Juicy Fruit,
or is it Mint?

I forgot,
and the flavor's spent.

Kyleigh Downey, Grade 5
Bates Elementary School, CO

Life

Sometimes life is hard.
Hard to see it clearly.
Hard to always be happy.
It is like a river,
Never knowing where it goes,
Where it stops flowing.
It is so filled with wonder.
There's just no answer
To the mysterious world
We live in.
So full of love.

Samantha Miles, Grade 4
Sedona Charter School, AZ

Friends

Friends can be mad
but they can also be sad
I have the nicest friends you can have
some live in California
some live in Washington
some live far away from me
but some live close
sometimes I pray to God
that they will never leave me.

Danielle Villa, Grade 4
Colbert Elementary School, WA

Fire

Fire is a furious thing,
Fire represents evil,
Fire is like somebody playing a fast song,
Fire sounds like someone whispering,
Fire can happen in a surprise.

Sean Parks, Grade 4
Hunters Glen Elementary School, CO

The Sun and Moon

The sun is friends with the moon
They make light together
The moon at night
The sun at day
Together
The sun and moon

Kelsey Philp, Grade 4
Scenic Park Elementary School, AK

Spring's Beauty

Spring is so peaceful
So lovely and beautiful
I can hardly wait.

Addie James, Grade 6
H Guy Child School, UT

It Was All a Dream

When I walk down the street,
I feel like somebody is following me.
When I go down to the beach
And get in the water,
I feel like somebody is there with me.
When I go down to the mall,
And I walk down through the hall,
I feel something that's maybe looking
Through a little hole in the wall.
Also when I talk to my mom,
I think somebody is beside her
Trying to do something to her.
When I'm asleep, I forgot
That this was all a dream.

Eva Moreno, Grade 6
Somerton Middle School, AZ

Softness

Like a tissue in the breeze,
Then you feel the need to sneeze.
Like a puppy or a kitten,
Or a shirt that has been knitten.
Like the hair on your head,
Right after you go to bed.
Like the strap that keeps you in,
May I take you for a spin?
Like a flag in the breeze,
Now I think you need to…gazundheiht.

Kyle Cline, Grade 6
Uplands Elementary School, OR

Summer and Winter

Summer
Hot, dry
Burning, flaming, growing
Brilliant, cloudless, icy, cold
Snowing, raining, hailing
White, cloudy
Winter

Brandon Steinmann, Grade 6
St Cyril Elementary School, AZ

Wolf Bamboo

Wolf bamboo is like a raging storm
fiery as a raging cauldron.
It will bend back
to its full extent
when being attacked by the wind
then snap back at its attacker
then when it has eaten its fill
it howls at the moon.
After that
it will sleep peacefully.

Eamonn Neff, Grade 4
Wilson Elementary School, WA

Camping

I went camping for the first time.
Things kept falling from the big pine.
It was really fun.
We ate hot-dogs on a bun.

We roasted a lot of marshmallows.
We met a harsh fellow.
We went to the ocean.
There was a lot of commotion.

I found sea shells.
I heard lots of laughs and yells.
We slept in tents
The wind sounds like elephants.

Dante Miller, Grade 5
Lewis & Clark Elementary School, OR

My Thoughts

By the water I lay
Deep in my thoughts
Thinking of all the ways not to stay
I think I might drown
Might scream and yell
Things I don't dare tell
It might hurt people's feelings
But yet here I am
Here I lay by the
Water deep in
My thoughts.

Courtney Rodrigues, Grade 6
Glacier Middle School, WA

Love

Love is for all to keep,
Dream of your loved one
As you sleep.

Love is like the spy,
It's endless and never
Says a sad good-bye.

Love is all nice and snug
All together forever in
One big hug.

Love is like a rainbow
In every different way,
So chose wisely for a happier Valentine's Day!

Kylie Urias, Grade 6
Somerton Middle School, AZ

The First Day of School

Kids talking, parents walking
In the distance I can see the bus
It's just too bad that it's covered with rust
Getting on, finding a seat,
Lots of new people to meet
Finally parks at our school
Which by the way is very cool
Go inside, find your desk
Start off school with another test
Do hard work, get good grades
So you can go home and play with the King of Spades
Bell rings, and another day has gone by
At home awaiting me is apple pie
Go to bed and get good rest,
So tomorrow you can do your very best.

Jessie Lesniak, Grade 6
Colbert Elementary School, WA

Bloomability

Ideas are like flowers.
If you don't pay attention to them, they'll fade.
But if you keep watering them with thought,
they get bigger and even more fantastic.

Mattie Adams, Grade 6
Thomas Jefferson Charter School, ID

Baseball

B at the ball
A t 1st base you run to 2nd base
S and in the infield
E xtra inning games
B aseball is fun
A nyone can hit the ball
L osing means you need more practice
L ove the game

Sawyer Newell, Grade 5
Conestoga Elementary School, WY

Dark and Light

black is dark
so you can't see anything
black holes in space, nights we sleep
in the old times they had mines
tar as a black hole when it is dark
and there is a dim light
you make a dark shadow
if there's going to be a storm
look out the window and I bet you will see dark clouds
at night almost always you can see the moon
in the never ending sky
a star and a quasar are almost the same
because they shine brightly in the vast dark blue sky
they are like two atoms
combining together in the Big Bang
energy comes from light
light and bright the same thing.
gold is like the sun in our system
the white clouds we see every day
as like the moon we see every night
dark and light

Hannah Ballman, Grade 4
Khalsa Montessori Elementary School, AZ

Freedom to Be

Freedom to me isn't what it says to be.
You can't do whatever you want,
You have to follow what the rules want.
But then America would go crazy.
But freedom still has its advantages.

When I thought about freedom,
I thought about "lead them,"
When I say freedom,
Good thoughts pop up in my mind,
But that don't happen all the time.

Now I'll tell you how it's free,
You can still practice your own religion,
And give public speeches,
But can't you go and preach it.
But you can see still how freedom has its advantages.

Matt Kelpien, Grade 6
Pope John XXIII Catholic School Community, AZ

My Hamster

My hamster is cute and soft and furry
He runs in his wheel like he's in a hurry
He likes to eat nuts and seeds and stuff
He fills his cheeks 'til he's had more than enough
He stays up at night and naps all the day
When I pick him up he's too sleepy to play
He's not like a cat or a dog I'll admit,
But I really do love him quite a bit!

Danny Neudecker, Grade 4
Eton School, WA

The Poem

A poem is not just a bunch of rhyming words.
It has lots of feelings in it too.
You will always remember a poem by the emotion you felt while reading it.
Whether you like it, you hate it, or you just don't get it.
You read and read more poems each day trying to find a special one but find none.
People write poems for money but others do it for fun.
You can write about anything you want, things that only live in your mind or things that are real!
Just say how you feel.
Anyone can write a poem. You can too.
Give it a chance and try something new.

Jessica Garcia, Grade 6
St Vincent de Paul School, AZ

To Touch the Stars

Blank vastness, pinpricks of lights; the stars. You reach out,
try to touch them, but they're always just beyond your reach.
You go through life, trying to amount to something, to change the world,
to be remembered. How do they know when they've accomplished something?
How do they know when it's time to stop for a moment? When they look into space
and see the stars, when the entire world is quiet with peace, you know doing something
worthwhile. And when people fight for freedom, with courage and honor,
Why do they get up to face the hardships? Why do they
sacrifice themselves to save their country. I'll tell you why.
They go through it so we can walk across the street without looking
over our shoulders, so we can go through our life and are able to
die knowing that they have made the world a better place for everyone that will come.
They do it, so that finally we will be able to touch the stars.

Tanner Garrett, Grade 6
Acme Elementary School, WA

Abraham Lincoln's Assassination

That fateful day was to be happy, that day was to be great,
No one knew Abe's tragic death was coming soon, but then I suppose that that is fate.

That terrible occurrence, the crime committed by John Wilkes Booth,
Was at first going to be a kidnapping, (and that, my friend, is the truth.)

This happened in a theater, a very fine one at that,
(Booth had everything very well planned) that, acquaintance, is a fact.

John Booth showed the guard something in the middle of the play,
We don't know what this trinket was, but the man let John go on his way.

Wilkes Booth ascended the staircase, then shot poor Lincoln in the head,
At the time everyone was laughing, and didn't hear his wife scream "Help! My husband's dead!"

(Now don't be all worried about Booth getting away,
Later he was caught and killed, similar to his victim, but on a different day.)

I do know it's hard to think about, I'm aware that it is sad,
But Abraham Lincoln is in a better place, and for that we can be glad.

(Now here's a little tidbit, a non-so-well-known fact,
On Friday, the thirteenth this all happened, this devious, murderous act.)

Laura Jean Stromback, Grade 6
Eagleridge Enrichment Program, AZ

Kona

Kona bear is his name,
He's five months old,
And he's a real thrill.
He's my bugga boy and my lubby dubby,
We play football, basketball and baseball,
We roughhouse, we sleep, and watch TV.
He's my baby boy,
He's my kitty.

Cassie Ferrall, Grade 6
Hazelwood Elementary School, WA

Ocean

The loud lulling foghorn tears through the
Calm, quiet, steady ocean as it hums,
Yelling, laughing away to the taunting birds.
They quickly dive flowing over the barking tide.
Kids make sand castles, ocean waves wrap
Cold, wet arms around the warm, dry sand,
Hot light shines down.

Rachel Braun, Grade 6
Uplands Elementary School, OR

Thanksgiving

Thanksgiving Day

It tastes so juicy I can hardly wait
The stuffing, turkey, sweet potatoes, and all the drinks.
Yum, Yum, and Yum
I'm starving.
My face mashed up on the glass of the stove.
All the guests are coming,
Bringing more food, more drinks, and more supplies.
I can't wait,
What's next for Christmas dinner?

Brian Holzhauer, Grade 6
Nikolaevsk School, AK

Football

Football is fun,
especially quarterback.
I sometimes
get frustrated,
I sometimes get mad,
but I'll never stop playing football real bad.
Football is my sport,
it's the best sport
that I ever had.
I'll always like football,
glad, glad, glad.
Making touchdowns,
run hard, playing hard,
kicking a field goal,
and more scoring.
What team do you like?

Jordan Carlton, Grade 4
Acacia Elementary School, AZ

Nightly Noises

About to fall asleep
Drift into timeless dreams
It begins
Crickets chirp, owls hoot, cats yowl, coyotes wail.
Had enough!
You want to yell
"Quiet! I'm trying to sleep!"
Close your eyes
Breathe deep
Relax
Owls, crickets, coyotes, cats
Say goodnight
Thank you nightly noises.

Kevin D. Anderson, Grade 5
Home Choice Academy, WA

Ryan

Who is: intelligent, trustworthy, and talkative.
Who wishes to be a musician
Who dreams of world peace
Who wants to live in California
Who wonders if there are aliens
Who fears lawn gnomes
Who is afraid of becoming poor
Who likes rainy weather
Who believes in God
Who loves math class $2+2=4$
Who plans to be rich
   Who enjoys being free

Ryan Davis, Grade 6
Walt Clark Middle School, CO

Soapy Bubbles

Bubbles, bubbles all around
some are shaped and some are round.
Ones you can blow up high
and can catch the breeze and almost fly,
all the way, up into the azure, blue sky.
Detergent bubbles can really be mean.
To get clothes and dishes clean.
They do their jobs to bust your bubbles.
But when their work is done it's time to say
"hello drain," and goodbye bubbles!
Time to meet your fate!
Then, poof! They just EVAPORATE!!!

Emily Maynard, Grade 6
Wallace Elementary School, AZ

World

W aking up to a new adventure
O ceans sparkling before your eyes
R educing terror, hunger and pain
L earning new cultures from around the world
D eciding to help in any way we can

Justin Warren, Grade 4
Conestoga Elementary School, WY

Horses

Horses
beautiful, strong
cantering, galloping, jumping
they're what I adore
Horsies

Alexis Andrus, Grade 4
Gold Canyon Elementary School, AZ

Stars

Bright and beautiful
Shining through the dark night sky
Glowing all night

Alyson Foust, Grade 6
Heath Middle School, CO

Imbecile Man

I'm always there,
But to them I am never there.
They see me in a different way,
One cool jerk,
Unable to stand up to their words,
Sometimes the words they say,
Come out from their mouths,
Without them thinking twice,
How much it could hurt
A person,
Even the littlest word,
Could hurt a person,
So bad,
Sometimes persons don't realize
Those words are much
Much more powerful then punches.
Punches only hurt for a while,
Words sometimes hurt for days,
Or they hurt for a while,
Some don't hurt anymore,
But some get stuck in your mind forever.

Irving DeLaO, Grade 6
Swansea Elementary School, CO

Summer

The cool summer breeze
rushes
through the open window
stinging
my pale blue eyes
whipping
my hair around

The burning sun rays
destroy my face with the heat
giving me sunburns here and there

Summer is so comforting!

Torie Power, Grade 4
Bromwell Elementary School, CO

Mother Moon

Mother moon is sleeping now,
But soon she will awaken.
The stars, they are her only friends.
She always sleeps until day ends.

If you go up close you'll see.
Craters are the golden sea.
That's where stars are born at night.
Every star is different.
Stars are born all the time.
You never see the same.

The stars are multiplying as we speak.
They are getting ready for tonight.
The moon watches us from above.

Destiny Brasher, Grade 5
Sally Mauro Elementary School, UT

Hamster

Hamster
Friendly, pretty
Running, eating, drinking
Food, wheel, bedding, water
Sleeping, hiding, exploring
Beautiful, cuddly
Chandler

Brady Shoemaker, Grade 6
Greybull Middle School, WY

The Booger Man

The Booger Man is watching you,
He's watching you tonight.
You'd better get a Kleenex,
And hold it very tight.

He could be lurking anywhere,
In the basement, in the dark.
You can't hide from him at all,
He's like a bloodthirsty shark.

Sure, he will not find you,
Well, at least not right away.
But once he knows where you are,
Believe me, he's with you to stay.

You might think this is funny now,
But you just wait and see.
He has ways of knowing
When and where you're going to be.

So get your tissues ready,
He'll be here anytime.
He could be right behind you,
As silent as a mime.

Wil Braun, Grade 6
Bradford Intermediate School, CO

Christmas

Christmas
Santa at the mall
Mint from the tree needles
The soft sound of music
The juicy hot ham
The carefully wrapped presents
Christmas

Conor Grieshaber, Grade 4
Coal Creek Elementary School, CO

All About Me

T all as a yellow and black giraffe,
A crobatic hip hop dancer,
Y oung, but almost a teenager!
L oud!
E leven and
R eally crazy!

H omework hater
A thletic as a flexible monkey
R esentful of schoolwork
V ery thoughtful
E ntertaining
Y oungster!

Tayler Harvey, Grade 5
Hafen Elementary School, NV

Field Day

Running
800 yards
Out of breath
Long run

Relay
Hand off
Racing with people

Kenny Levy, Grade 4
Copper Canyon Elementary School, AZ

The Dog

in our house there is a dog
she really isn't a very big hog
so if you see that dog
don't be frightened after all it is a dog
that's not that much of a hog

Wes Beeman, Grade 4
Mills Elementary School, OR

Ocean

Crystal clear water coming right at me
Waves hitting the shore
Surfers trying to catch pipes
Salty seaweed
A soft mist

Garrett Chartier, Grade 4
Lincoln Elementary School, AZ

Guardian Angels

An invisible person
Who guides my way
In my troubles they brighten my day

A friend to me,
God's messenger,
I'm relieved heaven sent
Someone to be
Always watching over me.

Juliana Eichenberg, Grade 6
Pope John XXIII Catholic School Community, AZ

Butterfly Wings

I walk outside, at the middle of the night.
I look around and see colors flashing bright.
One flash is coming close, closer to me.
It is a butterfly I can now see.
And then it all makes sense the flashing lights.
These each were butterfly wings moving through the night.

Taylor Hitchings, Grade 5
McGraw Elementary School, CO

My Creek

The water flows rapidly
Fallen branches snap when I step on them.
Splashing water soothes me
Pine, ferns smell oh so good
I step in
It's ice cold
Pushing against me

Callie Goodell, Grade 5
Carrolls Elementary School, WA

Farming

Farming smells like choking dust.
Farming tastes like black soil of the earth.
Farming feels like a padded steering wheel.
Farming sounds like a noise from a freight train.
Farming looks like fudge stripes on a cookie.

Braxton Todd, Grade 6
Denton Elementary School, MT

Moving from North Carolina to Arizona

Eight family members,
Five days long!
Lots of sights.
Aquariums, museums, cool rocks.
Movies in the car.
Lots of cars.
Sleepy.
Waking up at 6:00 a.m.
North Carolina is humid.
Arizona is dry.
We are here at last.

Lauren King, Grade 4
Acacia Elementary School, AZ

A Dragon's Eye

A dragon's eye so glossy, so sleek
Like the scale of a fish down in the deep
As shiny as a star in the night sky
As beautiful as a butterfly
And in the dark of the night
It glows so bright
That it gives knights in armor a terrible fright
A dragon's eye is never meek.

Derek Eaton, Grade 6
Morgan Middle School, WA

Tears

tears so clear and cold
tears are something that can't be sold
tears crawling down your face
tears are falling off your face
tears are something that you'll have when you're dead cold

Jacob Bennett, Grade 6
Syracuse School, UT

My Best Friend and Me

The thought of that bite,
Oh, what a fright!
Until my friend grabbed my hand,
To pull me back to safe land.
I'll never forget that day out back,
When I thought I'd have a heart attack.

My best friend and me, forever we'll be,
Best friends at heart, never to part.

When I heard that shout,
I ran to find out,
What happened to my friend,
Who had disappeared around the bend,

I saw that cactus sticking out of his foot,
I ran to get help as I hollered and hooted,
His mom got there to save the day,
Now my best friend is okay.

My best friend and me, forever we'll be,
Best friends at heart, never to part.

Zackery Crismon, Grade 5
Gold Canyon Elementary School, AZ

Baby Dino

Baby triceratops said to her mother
I'd like a straw doll and a bottle to go with her
With gold braided hair and button blue eyes
And a little silk dress with cherry red lips
But mama triceratops just simply said
You've got twenty-three dolls already
Or more I think.

Carrie Nelson, Grade 4
Summit Elementary School, UT

Baseball

I love to play baseball.
It is my favorite sport.
I could play it anywhere.
I could even play it at my fort.
Oops, I threw it over there.
Can you get my baseball please?
Throw it back not too hard.
But please don't tease.

Dakota Sammons, Grade 6
Meridian Middle School, ID

Poetry Hides

Poetry
hides in
a blue stone
because it looks like
tears running down my chin
Also because it looks like
fish running through the water

Alexis Prieto, Grade 5
Edgewater Elementary School, CO

My Country

I live in a country
And its flag is red, white and blue.
It is my home
It is where men and women
Would fight for
And give their lives for
It's America
The sweet and beautiful country
Men and women died for you
I live in red, white, and blue country.

Colton Olson, Grade 6
Glacier Middle School, WA

Taekwondo

T horough workout
A wesome
E xciting
K icking
W earing sparring gear
O n stage at Kids Fest
N ever boring
D on't get kicked
O lympic sport

I nteresting
S weating

F orced to the limit
U nbelievable
N on-stop fun
!!!!

Jake TeSelle, Grade 6
Monforton School, MT

Soaring Forest

Bears, deer, mountain lions, squirrels…
This is nature, the beauty of the forest.
Wildlife, rocks, and mountains…
Everything is here.
Sitting silently, I hear a crackle, again.
Suddenly out of the trees, a bear slowly comes out of the forest.
Then a mountain lion creeps out of the trees with three deer slowly behind it.
I look up…squirrels running and playing in the trees, limb to limb.
I turn around to get the camera, look back, nothing…they're gone.

Holden Reecer, Grade 5
Nederland Elementary School, CO

Whisking into a Change

The aromatic fragrance of young cherry blossoms call softly.
The damp perfume of the thawing ground breaks away the murky winter scent.
Sugary apple blossoms swell in order to touch the clouds.
Off we go whisking into the change of spring.

Chiming voices of birds bore the plumpness of the new.
Silence sings a peaceful melody expressing the feeling of Earth.
A whistling whisper may tell you a lovely secret.
Off we go whisking into the change of spring.

Crystalline petals of magnolias call you into being.
Translucent daffodils flutter toward the celestial sun.
Glamorous lilacs sit motionlessly planning their flight.
Off we go into the change of spring.

The fuzziness of new life brushes away the touch of death.
Fragile, fresh tufts of grass poke up their heads shyly.
The arms of weeping trees kiss the steamy ground.
Off we go whisking into the change of spring.

Alkaline innocence reaches the singing clouds.
The mellowness of the air amuses your taste buds.
Tender, earthy seeds get ready to pounce.
Off we go whisking into the change of spring.

Lacey Simonich, Grade 6
Bella Vista Elementary School, UT

Blue

Blue is a color that makes me feel happy inside.
People think it represents sadness and depression.
It's part of the American flag.
Red, white, and blue.
When it's on the flag, it means freedom.
Just about anywhere else it means nothing.
The ocean is blue, the lakes are blue.
It paints the sky, way up high.
Yeah, those are important things, but most people really don't care.
They go about their day, la de da, but once it's gone, it won't come back.
Since now that we have a pollution problem,
One day the sky might be black, the ocean might be green.
Then we won't have that wonderful color, blue, to cheer us up.

Kaitlyn Hill, Grade 6
Walt Clark Middle School, CO

Spring

When spring is near
Easter is almost here
the sun shines bright
what a delight!

In my thoughts I dream
a way that spring will stay
no more rain or cloudy skies
only the reflection of sun in my eyes

The grass is green, the flowers are in bloom
it takes away all our gloom
summer is near the kids have less fear
they know that summer is almost here!

Kaitlynn Finley, Grade 6
Eagle Point Middle School, OR

The Planes That Started the War

Tears falling down your face.
You see the plane
and your heart starts to race.
People dying, others crying.
Fear is all around.
Then with a crash
one tower goes down.
Things are happening too fast.
You hope that that plane was the last.
No
there was more to come.
Your heart is beating like a drum.
Then the second tower goes down.
You saw the fear as it hit the ground.
Over one thousand were dead.
There was nothing else to be said
except for hoping there would be no more
of the planes that stared the war.

Ellie Maurer, Grade 4
Wilson Elementary School, WA

Easter

Easter is a holiday
When lots of people love to play.
For others it is to rejoice
Still some don't want to make that choice.

Easter eggs go out to everyone,
Just to make this holiday fun.
But we know the true reason to celebrate,
Because He got rid of sin and hate.

We Christians celebrate this event
When Jesus Christ made His ascent.
We love Easter for this reason
It's the reason for the season.

Milan Montero, Grade 6
Green Valley Christian School, NV

If I Were

If I were a fairy godmother I'd pick the stars for you.
If I were a big bird I'd fly in the sky with you.
If I were a kitchen I'd make a cake for you.

Vanessa Zabala, Grade 4
Jackpot Combined School, NV

Ten Little Monkeys

Ten little monkeys went swinging on a vine
One swung too far and then there were nine.
Nine little monkeys were looking for a mate
One chose wrong and then there were eight.
Eight little monkeys were watching channel eleven
One got sucked in and then there were seven.
Seven little monkeys started eating Trix
The rabbit got mad and then there were six.
Six little monkeys went out for a drive,
One rolled down the window and then there were five.
Five little monkeys went to core
One made Mrs. Downs mad and then there were four.
Four little monkeys went to pay the monkey fee.
One forgot his money, then there were three.
Three little monkeys went to see a baby kangaroo
One forgot about the mama and then there were two.
Two little monkeys went to the park to have some fun
One saw a dog and then there was one.
One little monkey set out to be a hero
He forgot to wash his socks and then there was zero.

Austin Kelly, Grade 6
Patton Middle School, OR

Magic Box

I will put in my Magic Box…
All of the magic in a pearly white cloud.
All the gorgeous colors of the rainbow.
All the grace of the clouds as they dance in the sky.
The sadness of the rain and the happiness of the sun.

I will put in my Magic Box…
The feeling of the fine sand, dancing between my toes.
A sky-blue wave as it rises off the ground.
The beaming sun warming everything around it.
All of the elegance of a swan as it skims across a lake.

I will put in my Magic Box…
The first leaf that falls to the ground in autumn.
The first flower to bloom in the spring.
The first snowflake to touch the ground in the winter.
The first berry to be picked in the summer.

I will put in my Magic Box…
The crimson sun as it sets behind the snowy mountains.
The pale white moon as it rises into the night sky.
All the stars as they tiptoe past the moon.
The charming smile of a flower that gets watered.

Nika Shafranov, Grade 5
Mesa Elementary School, CO

Inspiration

Inspiration is like an invention
Someone has to find it
And develop it
Until it's ready to use

Inspiration is like an invention
If you don't take advantage
It could slip away
Unnoticed
Maia Raeder, Grade 6
Southern Hills Middle School, CO

The Jungle

A lush green jungle
A fearless jaguar mauling
And a black panther
Blake Waddington, Grade 6
Sequoia Village School, AZ

Iambs

For I am writing in Iambs today
to keep those horrible zeros away
to pass this class would be a pleasure
so give me an A for this great treasure
Christina Hein, Grade 6
Fox Creek Jr High School, AZ

School

Some kids think school is fun
Others would rather play in the sun
Some think school is a bore
Others fall asleep and snore
When gym class comes around
Some smile some frown
Lunch time is almost here
They can't wait it's so near
Recess time hooray!
Time to run, jump, and play
Recess is now done
Spelling time for some is fun
Reading is here hip, hip, hooray
They have waited all day
Teachers laughed and had lots of fun
Now the day is done
Jennifer Ladouceur, Grade 4
Pinnacle Charter School, CO

Trees

Luscious and green
Bud in the spring
Provide oxygen
Summer they begin
the beauty of earth
and perfume of nature
Zipporah Schumaker, Grade 6
Deer Creek Middle School (JHSO), CO

My Flowers Are

My flowers are

blue and purple
butterflies' paradise
children of Mother Nature
unique inspirations
sources of happiness
gifts to people
babies' blossoming smiles
what made Mona Lisa smile
keys to Heaven
two pieces of sunshine
dancing flapper girls
my gifts to God
eyes for the blind
ears for the deaf
the angels tinkling laughter

My flowers are me,
and I am my flowers.
Karis Addo-Quaye, Grade 4
The Meadows School, NV

Blue

What do I see in you?
You know if I am sad
You know when I just don't care
You are there to comfort me
When I need it the most
I see loving tender eyes
Your spirit seems to come alive
Riding you makes me happy
Thank you
For being here just for me
Leighanne Rayome, Grade 6
Walt Clark Middle School, CO

Sadness

Sadness is cloaked in blue
which freezes my body
forming icicles inside.
The refrained taste of salty
tears slide across my taste
buds and down a long dark
tunnel, as if it shall never end.
Soon the coldness envelops me.
The aroma of wet, rotten leaves
gravitates through the air,
while notes of a sad song
drift inside my head like
falling rain.
Snowflakes start to surround
me as though it is a cold,
dark night.
Shayna Brewer, Grade 6
Lolo Elementary School, MT

The Heart of a Flame

If you ever look at a flame
Or some ashes or a spark
You will never be the same
If you delve into its heart

It jumps and it dances
It sizzles and it cracks
It leaps up in quick flashes
It eats all in the black

When you touch it, it feels blistering
Translucent and so silky
It feels so very scorching
The wood just starts a popping

When you see it, it looks blinding
So orange and very bright
It sounds as if it's cackling
At someone in the night

So next time you go camping
And start to cook some hot dogs
Remember to go delving
Into the fire's heart
Dallin Childs, Grade 5
Barratt School, UT

Night and Day

Moons die as suns rise
Night falls as light collapses
Days go on and on.
Sam Zentner, Grade 6
Morgan Middle School, WA

Gray

Gray is the color
Of old folks' hair,
The hide of a rhino
The sweats I wear.

Gray is the color
Of a rainy day,
The color of a bullet
The color of clay.

Gray is the color
Of reflected moon light,
The pencils lead
The armor of a knight.

Gray is the color
Of gravel and rock,
The color of cement
And my old dirty sock.
Troy Lundquist, Grade 6
Kendallvue Elementary School, CO

Winter Is…

Winter is a time for caring and loving
It is a time to relax
A time to spend with your family
A time of joy and happiness

Winter is a time to help others
It's misty and damp
With rosy cheeks and noses
And there's nothing like a sleigh ride in the snow
And hot chocolate of course
What could be better than winter

Cami Tanner, Grade 5
Blanding School, UT

The Brave of America

The peace on Earth is fading fast.
It makes you wonder how long it'll last.
But Justice will stand with sword and shield.
To make sure o'er the country no evil will wield.

His course leads straight to enemy lines,
To widen the loop and pull tight the binds.
Through summer, winter, sun, or hail
He strives to know peace will prevail.

When war is over his job is through.
He looks at his country, so noble and true.
When we need great old Justice again,
They'll fight in the service, both women and men.

Anna Marie Rapp, Grade 5
Clarkmoor Elementary School, WA

Questions Without Answers

The world is an unanswered place.
It has questions without answers.
Why do we have oceans?
Why do we have seas?
Why do these strange creatures keep on looking at me?
Why do we have love?
Why don't we have world peace?
These are the questions that never have an answer.
There are so many questions that never have an answer.
What made the sky?
What made the Earth?
What made life?
Why are all people different?
Why is there land?
Why is there water?
Why are there no answers, to any of these questions?
If there are answers, how do we know they're right?
Why is there death?
Why is there disease?
Why can't we stop these evil, evil things?
Why do we have questions without answers?

Megan Gibson, Grade 6
Bright Beginnings School, AZ

July

Sweat dripping down children's faces
As they run around and play
I stand not alone
But with my friends
One and all
As I blow out the candles and make my wish
And I dream tonight that my wish may come true.

Pam Osborn Popp, Grade 6
Bright Beginnings School, AZ

Sea World

Sea World, Sea World what a place,
Just take a glance at Shamu's face.
She'll swim around and make a splash,
But beware, she'll drench you in a flash!
See the dolphins one, two, three,
They swim around, happy as can be.
They jump so high, they'll touch the sky,
It even looks like they'll start to fly!
Next comes the Sea Lions, lazy as can be,
They lie in the sun completely carefree!
They're trained to act in lots of plays,
They are hysterical, and can go for days!
Have you checked out the rides?
If not just relax and watch the tides.
Last but not least a must see are the sharks,
It's one of the highlights among the parks!
I want to go back, it's been some time,
And now it's time to end this rhyme!

Jeffrey Herbert, Grade 6
Syracuse School, UT

Understand

Our planet, Earth, is a wonderful one,
packed with rich soil and life giving rain.
Blessed with a mystical moon and energetic sun,
adorned with lush plants and a prodigious sky.
All colors can be seen here, the air, pure and clear.
Where geese skim the water like dancers. Enjoy Earth.
Leap over a brook, twirl and run.
Sit with butterflies under the crimson sun.
Tangible, wonderful, like a beautiful dream.
Hum along to the tune of a placid stream.
Forget the poignant troubles in your past.
Feel free, free at last!
Look past the rainbow, into an empty sky.
Nothing moves, no birds fly.
Is this the terrible life that lies ahead?
A road that leads straight to dread?
No, you haven't seen it yet, it all depends how far you get.
If you walk slow, or which way you go.
You could put the world in misery by trying to hold it in
your hand, or you could make it beautiful by seeing
the treasured in the land.

Rebecca Novy, Grade 5
Gate City Elementary School, ID

For Now, I Must Wait

The trees are beautiful.
The forest is wide.
everything's good.
For now, I must wait.

Travelers come in.
They start a bonfire.
I wish for a spark
So I, a fire, can start.

There, I get to explode!
I run up the tall trees!
Then, I get to disappear
And carry on underground.

I get to do my damage.
All's charcoal and burned.
Soon seeds start to sprout.
The life cycle is renewed.

Trevor Gaffney, Grade 6
Beacon Country Day School, CO

Blind

Look down the street at eight A.M.
Smilin' faces lookin' back
That's all you see
For that's all you want to see
No more,
No less,
But smilin' faces
Lookin' back

Molly Gregory, Grade 5
Frontier Valley Elementary School, CO

Freedom

Freedom in this country
Freedom in you and me
Look inside and you will find
The amazing golden key
If you believe
You will achieve
We will get very far
Farther than the moon
Farther than a star
It's more than hope
It's more than love
It's freedom

Katie Metzger, Grade 5
St Cyril Elementary School, AZ

Big Moon

Big moon shining high
Kisses sweet tulips good night
Good night little ones.

Kayla Findley, Grade 6
Hamilton Middle School, MT

Color Is the End

Black is the thing that shrouds, cloaks, veils, and hides things
The darkness and night like mystery
Not only a color, but also a skin type on the canvas, image, and work of art
The roughness is not necessary for segregation, isolation, and separation
The color is not just a color, but so much more.

Grey, the color that mixes, combines, and brings together white and black
A sign of peace and love
The gray is the partial showing of anything that was surrounded in darkness
This color is the one that is calm and cool
It brings peace among all

White is bright, revealing, and illuminating to all things
This is the other half of the prejudice
Although, black is the gas white is the match
The fire burns with each
This color is the end

Dakota Joplin, Grade 6
Blanco Elementary School, NM

Rain

When it rains what is there to do?
You can't laugh for there is nothing to laugh at.
You can't cry because the Earth is already crying.
You can't be happy because there is only rain to be happy about.

What will you do if it rains?
Will you sit at your bedroom window and watch it fall
Or be out and playing in it?
Will you watch television until the rain stops
Or take a nap?
Will you be happy and enjoy the rain as if it was sunshine?

If it was sunshine would you play or be bored?
Would you carry on a conversation or do homework?
When it rains it is all your choice on what to do.
You could stop the rain if you enjoyed it
Because all it wants to do is bring down your spirits.

Caitlin Burke, Grade 6
Green Valley Christian School, NV

Soccer

The nets on the goals waving in the wind.
Rippling as the ball skims it.
Banging off the post and out of the goal.
Bringing happiness as the ball perfectly floats to the top right corner.
Players.
Hearts racing as they sacrifice their bodies for the team.
Trapping the ball and setting up for a shot.
Rushing to win it back.
The ball.
Curling as it is hit powerfully.
Being bumped and caught, headed and trapped, smacked and saved.
Soccer.

Luke Traeger, Grade 6
Sequoia Village School, AZ

Aquamarine

The wonderful blue-green of our endless sea,
Brings mysterious feelings to me,
Sparkles so delicately,
Beautiful dye of thy birthstone of March,
Energetic,
The shade that inspires me,
Blissful or poignant, neither it makes me,
Soft and gentle is aquamarine,
Beauty divine is its scheme,
Gem of a ring for a wife-to-be,
Aquamarine, a color for me.

Teah Smith, Grade 6
Robert Frost Elementary School, OR

The Race of Fear

Anger, fear, frustration, sad
Nightmares, stories, dreams that are bad
It all adds up to one last day
People are happy "yay, yay, yay"
But I am scared I don't say yay
As I walk up into the depth of fear
I notice my dad is near
I calm down, I count to tens
As I see my friends
I am happy, I don't have fright
I start to see the light
As I dive in, I think of God
I wave at my dad and he nods
After the day of fear and badness
There's NO ANGER, NO FEAR, AND NO SADNESS!

Zanetta Uy, Grade 5
Elger Bay Elementary School, WA

Rain

The sky is crying
Water coming from her eyes.
The roots of plants are happy
All the plants turn green.

Now the sky is a musician
Beating hardly on the drums.
Shedding light for all to see
On this cold and stormy night!

Brandon Senior, Grade 6
Pope John XXIII Catholic School Community, AZ

The Beautiful

The amazing rainbow is as beautiful as a fluffy cloud,
If you listen and wait, you will hear the water; it is loud.
It is loud like a thunderstorm.
After the storm, it is as calm as a cat.
Before the storm it is as restless as a bat.
It looks like the sun is peeking.
It also looks like it is seeking.

Christina Auger, Grade 5
Sally Mauro Elementary School, UT

Family

What is a family?
    A group of people who love you unconditionally
    A hardworking, caring, peaceful, and safe gang
    What provides your source of energy
    It is about snuggling in the rocking chair,
    watching a movie and eating popcorn
    It's what helped me construct this poem for you to read.
That is a family!

Bryan Combs, Grade 4
East Evergreen Elementary School, MT

Summer Fun

The last season of school is spring,
When it's the next season that's one happy thing.
Summertime is so much fun,
That is, until it's done.
During summer you can hang with a friend,
I just wish it would never end.
When summer and I begin to part,
I know that school is about to start.
When the learning does start,
I begin to grow smart.
During summer you can eat ice cream,
At school you can only dream.
During summer you can hang in a pool,
You can't do that while you're in school.
In summer you just wish it were over.
Good grades make me feel glad,
I guess school isn't so bad.

Reilly Bangerter, Grade 5
Eton School, WA

Waiting

In the obscure he sits
Waiting for the instance to come
In the still
On the floor he sits
He hears a car
Disrupting his silence
KaBoom! KaBoom!
The car roars down the street
His heart beats as quickly as a hummingbird's wing
The sweat drips from his face
He can hear the man coming
Clunk, clunk, clunk
The soles of his shoes strike the concrete
Nearer and nearer he approaches
Ding! Dong!
The doorbell sounds
He opens the door
He screams! Haaa!
The FedEx Man!
"Do you have my package?"
"Yes," the FedEx man replies

Desmond Harvey, Grade 6
St Anne School, WA

The Storm

The rain is pouring down
The wind is howling
Hail is crashing into the ground
Far off I see lightning dancing
I hear thunder playing music
The rain goes pit-pat-pit-pat
Pitter-patter, crash crash, boom-bang
Loud noises rearing in my brain
And then it all stops

Alyshia Barwin-Bahner, Grade 6
Fox Creek Jr High School, AZ

Skylight

Shining sunny skies
Light filling the peaceful earth
Silent afternoon

Megan Hoffman, Grade 4
Midland Elementary School, CO

The Desert

It is hot in the desert
So dry, nothing to drink
We need water, before we die

It is hot in the desert
The sun, shining on us
I can barely swallow

There is rarely a cloud
In the desert
We need water

Richelle Sexton, Grade 5
Kingman Academy of Learning, AZ

The Man with a Headache

There once was a man named Fred
Who jumped on his triangular bed
He saw quite a sight
While at such a height
But going down he missed the bed

Gabriel Ochoa, Grade 4
St Thomas the Apostle School, AZ

Endless Horizons

Miles and miles,
run, run, run, forever run,
endless horizons.

Sarah Blog, Grade 5
Tara School, NM

Orange Sweatshirt

Ugly orange sweatshirt,
looks better on an orange tree,
but great for hunting!

Jesse Cavalieri, Grade 6
Hamilton Middle School, MT

Ode to Turtles

Turtles are there in
woods in streams
in moist fallen leaves.
They are in your homes
sometimes for pets.
They crawl and climb around the woods.
They're like small living
rocks slowly inching their way
to their destination.
They are a variety of colors
red and brown, blue, green and black.
Giant green sea turtles
come ashore to bask in
the sunlight and lay their eggs.
They do not need to
be fast because their shells protect them.
They live for hundreds of years and
keep on staying alive.

Andrew Boyle, Grade 5
Barratt School, UT

Friends

A wesome
B londe
C ool
D aring
E xciting
F un
G iving
H aving fun
I mportant
J oking
K ind
L aughing
M ighty
N ice
O h my gosh they are awesome
P opular
Q uiet
R espectful
S illy
T hat is how my friends are

Skylar Saathoff, Grade 5
Gold Canyon Elementary School, AZ

Snow

When it's snowing it looks like
Crystals falling from the sky.
Wherever I look,
It looks like crystals on the ground.
I wish they were real crystals.
But they aren't.
And the next day
All the crystals melt away...

Kelton McNair, Grade 5
Fulton Elementary School, CO

My Dog

She needs a bath.
Her breath smells.
It's a girl.
She's good friends with my cat.
Her name's Kira.
She's tame.
Very fat and lazy.
She has black fur.
Smart.
Protects my brother Andrew, who's two.
She's crazy when she has to go outside.
Kira's usually calm.
I love her.

Emily Cardenas, Grade 4
Acacia Elementary School, AZ

Growing Up

Babies
Crying, sweet
Sleepy, playful, wonderful
Working, cooking
Adults

Chandlar Schubel, Grade 5
Sequoia Village School, AZ

The Softest Sound

The softest sound might be
The gentle river flowing
Further and further
Slowly and sometimes fast

Perhaps the softest sound
I could imagine
Is a flower blooming
Quietly opening its petals
Blossoms coming forth

As I lie dreaming
The softest sound I hear
Is the ticking of the clock
Telling me it's time to sleep

Solana Pino, Grade 6
Washington Intermediate School, CO

The Flag

When I see the flag I think
Of the soldiers who fought for us
And made this land free.
When I see the flag
I'm grateful to be free.
When I see the flag I think of
My uncle. When I see the flag
I remember that I am an American.
And that's the truth.

Jordan Curdy, Grade 5
Grantsdale School, MT

Take a Book Trip

Walk Two Moons is a very good book
So come over here and take a look
Some books are great
Some books are grand
Some have fate
Some have bands
Just read a book
Then you'll see
The great places you will be
A book can take you anywhere
Make a wish and then you're there
Just read a book and then you'll find
One of the many great places in time

Danielle Failor, Grade 5
Seltice Elementary School, ID

Spring

When the leaves all come a pok'n out
and crocuses and lilies start to sprout,
that's when children and adults both can shout,
"Hey, spring is here!"

When people act all happy and new,
and smiles travel from happy old me to happy old you,
that's when you're sure spring is coming!

And when you can tell that the earth
is smelling oh, so fresh and sweet,
kids are saying, "Cool! how neat!"
They say spring is here!

So you simply can understand
why spring is such a wonderful thing!
And if you wait for this thing,
you'll see, here comes spring!

Jane Thompson, Grade 4
Cameron Elementary School, CO

Spring Is All Around Us

Spring is here, it's all around us,
Daffodils, daisies, and posies surround us.
No one can ruin such a beautiful day,
Except for one dark cloud in the bright blue highway.
The water is sparkling in the delicate ponds,
This is the time friends really bond.
I sit here in my hammock waiting and waiting,
For the sky to begin its lovely shading.
Of blue, gold, crimson, and pink,
This is the time to sit here and think.
Of a fawn's big, curious eyes,
And of Mother's sweet wildberry pies.
Also of the spring that surrounds us,
And the daffodils, daisies, and posies all around us.

Anna Mae Hoerner, Grade 6
Colbert Elementary School, WA

Enchanted Library Alcove

About the library is a serene feeling
Along the walls are shelves
On the shelves are volumes and tomes
Beyond the shelves is a room
Through the door I go
Inside, I find armchairs to sit in
Under those are trap doors
Beneath them are ladders that I climb
Toward the bottom I fall
Below is a well lit alcove
In it is a collection of my favorite books
Near them are comfortable chintzy chairs
With the Harry Potter series, I sit
From then on, I visited that library every day
Up until then, I never saw that alcove.

Amber Sheldon, Grade 6
Fox Creek Jr High School, AZ

Trumpet Trouble

There once was a young girl from Klumpet
Who strummed a shiny new trumpet.
She couldn't quite do it
So she went to return it
And the clerk said, "Oh, you must BLOW it!"

Whitney Sargent, Grade 5
Ammon Elementary School, ID

True Love

True love is in your heart.
True love is two people loving each other.
True love will keep everyone in your family together.
True love will keep your heart together.
True love stays with you forever.

Tereasa Boring, Grade 6
Discovery Plus Academy, AZ

Blue

The color of the new day's skies
as a soldier says his sad goodbyes

The color of a baby's big happy eyes
as her mother sings her soft lullabies

A little girl cries blue tears
as others sit near unleashing jeers

A happy couple sits under the navy stars
as people ride in their flashy blue cars

A small boy's favorite shade
when his life began to wither and fade

Blue, the color of joy and gladness
but also the color of devastation and sadness

Shannon Galligan, Grade 6
Walt Clark Middle School, CO

Raezheen

Crazy, shy, resourceful
Wishes to be a boy
Dreams of helping people
Wants to cure people
Who wonders what lies within (me)
Who fears being depressed
Who is afraid of darkness
Who believes in herself
Who likes friends
Who loves dogs
Who loves school
Who loves food
Who loves family
Who plans to go to college
Who plans to love others
Who plans to live a good life
Who cares for her family
Pascua

Raezheen Pascua, Grade 6
Patton Middle School, OR

Forests

tall green trees
colorful leaves
the whistling of the wind
as quiet as a stream
tweet tweet of the bird
growl growl of the bear
blue sky above
nobody in sight
brown dirt below

Michael McAniff, Grade 4
Eton School, WA

The Tree

In my front yard
There is a green tree
That is far bigger than me
I know because I bumped my knee

Riley Patterson, Grade 5
Copper Creek Elementary School, AZ

Summer

Under my shady tree,
I watch my friends
Splash in the shimmering sea.

As the sun sets,
Surfers settle down by the shore.
After my sister swims,
She sings while she showers.
I take my last sip of Sprite,
And take seven seashells
Before I go home.

Ariel Haynes, Grade 4
Eton School, WA

Deep in the Grand Canyon

Deep in the Grand Canyon there is a soft stream of water that touches your heart.
You can taste the freshness of the stream.
You can hear the echo of the water and wind.
You can smell the sweetness of the green leaves full of water.
That's deep in the Grand Canyon for you.

Cody Simons, Grade 4
Great Expectations Academy, AZ

Seven More Years

Problems with my parents are tearing me down.
The perfectionism of my mother is impossible to live with.
I can't stand the screams anymore,
I count the days for me to turn 18.
Seven years that seem to be endless,
I can't believe how much I've wished to get out of this house.
The house that once was my sanctuary,
The parents that were once my protectors, my heroes
Are now like leeches sucking out all my strength and love.
That love that most of the time doesn't exist.
There are times that I feel
There is a mutual lack of love and patience in my mother towards me.
Why should I try to change my feelings about her
And my attitude toward her
If nothing I do is ever good enough anyways?
I used to have hope to change,
But now it's all clear to me.
She's not going to change and neither am I.
Until then, I'll keep being the same
Waiting, waiting until I can get out of that prison.
Just seven more years.

Kevin Enriquez, Grade 6
Somerton Middle School, AZ

Colors

If I were all the colors, I would be a child's ruby-red cheeks, crying to his mother.
If orange, I would be one of the colors of the northern lights on a cold night.
If yellow, I would be the hot sun giving light to the Earth.
If green, I would be the grass if front of a white house.
If blue, I would be a gorgeous waterfall.
If indigo, I would be the ocean crashing against the beach.
If violet, I would be a sour grape.

David Mitchell, Grade 4
East Evergreen Elementary School, MT

True Love

True love is like an arrow that struck you.
True love is like an ocean deep and wide.
True love has its bits of dark holes.
True love might be bitter.
True love might suck you in and you'll live your life with sorrow.
True love may be happy.
True love may give you a heart of gold.
True love is something you guard.
True love is defeating all the problems through eternity.

Shayla Hernandez, Grade 6
Discovery Plus Academy, AZ

Dragon

Dragon
Fierce, brave
Flying, devouring, dwelling
Scaly and feared, powerful and dangerous.
Beast

Jared DeJoya, Grade 4
St Viator Elementary School, NV

Sleep

Today is just another day,
The sun comes up in a different way,
I wake up in a tired mood,
Then school will come very soon.
I have to learn, listen, and write to get an education.
I am half happy, half bored, but getting smart is my motivation.
I don't know what else to do,
I'll thank the heavens when I go to sleep.

Yasmin Bethel, Grade 6
West Point Elementary School, AZ

Gymnastics

Gymnastics is fun.
It is expensive for your parents.
The tricks you learn are very hard.
To learn them, you use your strength.
Back flips, front flips, front hand springs.
Although if you do them, you don't get any candy.
You achieve and move up levels.
Gyms make up names like Desert Devils.
Vault,
       bars,
            beam,
                 floor.
Back walkovers, cartwheels.
running fast, weight lifts, kicks, and a lot more.
I'll believe in myself,
and reach for the gold.
but no matter what, I'm never too old
to do all these tricks,
For gymnastics is a sport of fun.

Rebecca Johnson, Grade 4
Acacia Elementary School, AZ

I Remember That Night

I remember that night
when the wind blew out the light
I remember the big crashing sound
when the thunder shook the ground
I remember being upstairs
when grandma was showing me photos of bears
I remember running down
when we heard a new sound
I remember being glad
the storm had gone and the rain came bad!

Kiki McDonald, Grade 5
Elger Bay Elementary School, WA

Strange Guy

I'm sitting in a dark room with my eyes wide open,
aware of everything that is going on.
Then I notice something has changed,
but I don't know what.
Then I realize that the light is on,
and I hear my mom call "Dinner time!"

Luke Kallam, Grade 5
Lister Elementary School, WA

The Sea and Me

Under the sea is where I like to be
Around me are animals I've never seen
Out of the sea jump whales and dolphins
In the sea are fish swimming fast
like race cars zooming down a track
Through the coral reef hide tiny little fish
afraid to come out in case of big fish
Down the seas are huge fish looking for food
Above the sea are boats looking for a place to scuba dive
Over the sea sets the sun
By the dock is me standing there
saying good-bye to the sea
But I will see the sea once more
along with all its wonders

Kaleigh Queen, Grade 6
Fox Creek Jr High School, AZ

When

When it is cold outside he will hold you close,
Because love is as warm as the sun.
When you are sick she will take care of you,
Because love is medicine to the heart.
When it is Valentine's Day and he gives you chocolate,
Because love is as sweet as candy.
When she cooks your favorite meal for you,
Because love is delicious.
When he sings you a song he wrote,
Because love is a beautiful melody.
When a baby is magically brought into this world,
Because love is a miracle.

Anna Cluff, Grade 6
Discovery Plus Academy, AZ

Favorite Teams

The Yankees won 27 World Series
The Seahawks are the best team in the NFL
The Suns are very tall
The Coyotes rock on the ice

Derek Jeter makes the difference
Shaun Alexander, the best running back
Steve Nash, one of the finest guards
Wayne Gretzky coach extraordinaire

Ross Snyder, Grade 4
Copper Canyon Elementary School, AZ

Ball

Across from the tree
Below the door
Over the floor
Past the dog
Past the cat
Under the glass
I see a ball

Christian Brady, Grade 5
Cottonwood Elementary School, CO

Tornado

I am a tornado,
I swirl with time,
Swallowing my troubles,
From off the ground.
I suck up my joy,
And throw my sadness away.

Madison Baker, Grade 4
Hunters Glen Elementary School, CO

White Is...

paper out of my agenda
clouds that spin and swirl in the sky
fresh-fallen snow
plain, unbuttered popcorn
cool whip on top of my pie

Alex Alvira, Grade 5
Wheeler Elementary School, AZ

Winter

Winter nice and cool
But you are not a fool
It might be cold
But never be bold
Birds will go
Far and low
Winter

Biftu Aliye, Grade 5
Phoenix Metro Islamic School, AZ

Chase Winters

C avalier basketball fan
H as athletic ability
A ble to jump
S o energetic
E ats lots of candy

W inter snowboarder
I like Quicksilver
N ikes rule
T V watcher
E ndless energy
R oughhouses with dad
S uch a fun life

Chase Winters, Grade 5
M A Lynch Elementary School, OR

Rainy Night

Don't you hear that rain,
It is pouring down so hard,
It could flood the street.

Austin Mach, Grade 6
Hazelwood Elementary School, WA

Walking with Day

Walking with day.
Sleeping with night.
A scary dream,
Will bring fright.

I close my eyes,
After I pray.
And soon enough,
It is day.

Alarms ring.
Birds sing.
And I begin,
Walking with day,
Sleeping with night.

Kimmy Schloesser, Grade 5
M A Lynch Elementary School, OR

My Teacher

My teacher has been fifty-eight
His class loves to procrastinate
Sometimes he has a celebration
When he has some civilization
His class loves to exaggerate

Tyler Worley, Grade 5
Hafen Elementary School, NV

The Problem Child

I love to ski,
    but I hate the snow.
I love to swim,
    but I hate the water.
I love riding horses,
    but I'm allergic to fur.
I love the beach,
    but I hate the sand.
I love eating candy,
    but I can't have sugar.
I love brushing my hair,
    even though I'm bald.
I love bean burritos,
    but they make me fart.
I love the sun,
    but I hate the heat.
I love milk,
    but I'm afraid of cows.
I'm what you call, a problem child.

Arien Mills, Grade 5
Running Creek Elementary School, CO

Snow Boarding

Snow boarding is fun.
It is wet.
And you sweat.
And it is cold.
It's really steep.
And when you fly
you think you will die.
You won't.
Balance is everything.

Hunter Schneider, Grade 4
Acacia Elementary School, AZ

Me

I am hyper and strange.
I wonder how zippers work.
I hear my annoying dog.
I see movies every night.
I am hyper and strange.

I pretend to be stupid.
I feel happy.
I touch pencils at school.
I worry about cancer.
I cry for my dad.
I am hyper and strange.

I understand how paper is made.
I say the chicken came before the egg.
I dream of random things.
I try to beat video games.
I hope for world peace.
I am hyper and strange.

Austin Schmitt, Grade 4
Silvestri Middle School, NV

Running

Running up
running down
I just keep running all around,
    if I stop I'll go kaplop,
        onto the floor,
    I'll think oh no
I can't run anymore!

Austin G. Giles, Grade 6
Sequoia Village School, AZ

Christmas

Christmas
Snow floating to the ground
Pine needles in the air
The "Ho Ho Ho" of Santa
Red and white candy canes
Wrapping paper that's all over
Christmas

Jessie Chesnut, Grade 4
Coal Creek Elementary School, CO

Seasick

I don't like this ocean.
I wish I brought lotion.
I have a fish.
I wish I had a dish.
I have treasure that's going to give me pleasure.
And that's why I call it seasick.

Brian Romero, Grade 5
Bennett Elementary School, NV

Hannah

My hair is like copper spun silk
My eyes are deep pools of mystery and warmth
My smile is indulging like hot cocoa
My heart holds energy
That is pink and glistening
As glitter lip gloss
I live on the modeling runway
And eat miniskirts and 4 inch stilettos

Hannah Hess, Grade 6
Heath Middle School, CO

Under the Bed

Under the bed,
Beyond the shoes,
Over dirty dishes,
Past the folders,
Across the clothes,
Toward the lost earring,
Before you get to the tackle box,
After you pass the totes,
Between the books,
Against the walls, sits a furry little rodent.

Carolyn Fry, Grade 6
Fox Creek Jr High School, AZ

Bullies

Bullies take your Lunch money, and if
You have a honey
(girlfriend Or boy friend)
He'll tease you and Say 'you have a honey.'
He'll put You in the trash
and he'll give you a rash
And if you say "Leave me alone"
Say, "OK here's a bone."
But most of all they do
is take your money
and tease you if you have a honey!
They put you in the trash
and give you a rash.
But if you say, "Leave me alone"
They'll give you a bone!
And this is all about
BULLIES!!

Shaelynn Espinoza, Grade 5
Sally Mauro Elementary School, UT

Bob's Icy Cold

My name is Bob.
I sell ice cream.
I have flavors of all time.
Most people enjoy them because they're icy cold,
but most of all,
I'd have to say,
flavors are my favorite.
Banana splits,
     yogurt,
          smoothies,
               double ice cream,
and much, much more.
So I hope you stop by at Bob's Icy Cold.

Francine Beck, Grade 4
Acacia Elementary School, AZ

How to Believe

Assemble your challenged mind to grieve
Dive in and believe in yourself
Travel the rocky mountains of life to return to health
Invite your mind to a million thoughts as you sleep
Translate stop to walk as you travel your mind
Awake to the promise to carry the burden of strength
Wipe away the silent tears and awake to a new beginning

Tierra Houston, Grade 6
Edison Elementary School, WA

My Lost Love

Love is about passion, kindness and companionship.
My life is always about sadness; despair and loneliness.

My true love is endlessly lost.
No one there to help me out;
No one there to keep me warm.

My tall dark and handsome will never come.
I need someone to hold me close.

Close to the sun; close to the stars.
Up on a rocket and onto the moon.

That's the kind of love I choose.

Steffani Myers, Grade 6
Discovery Plus Academy, AZ

Snow Is…a Story

An adventure that takes me to a whole new world
Where glistening diamonds cover my house.

A mystery that I am tempted to solve, looking out my window
I wonder why the blanket of snow looks so perfect.

Something humorous like someone falling in the snow.
Something that I read every winter night.

Madison Blount, Grade 4
Hunters Glen Elementary School, CO

Me

My name is a disgrace
I can't hold my weight

I'm down in my debts
I'm too young to bet

I can't go to bed
My head's too dead

My shoes don't fit
I'm too fat to sit

I've come to known
My life is my own

This is my story
Will I find my glory

Travis Turner, Grade 5
Discovery Plus Academy, AZ

What I Love

I
Love to jump
On my trampoline
At night
My brothers aren't there

Amber Schmidt, Grade 5
Gold Canyon Elementary School, AZ

Alone in the World

Alone in the world,
No one's around.
No one to talk to,
Can't hear a sound.

Hear the wind calling,
The ones that I loved.
Listen to the heartbeat,
Of those from above.

Remembering those who cared for me,
Who I cared for as well.
Hoping that they went to Heaven,
Instead of down to Hell.

Wishing that they would've stayed,
Or I could've gone with.
Hoping, praying, that someday,
I might get one more wish.

Missing fam,
Missing friends.
Missing people,
While I'm alone in the world.

Kelsey Pearce, Grade 6
Eagle Point Middle School, OR

The One You Remember*

The one you remember has a friendly face,
She'd never forget a moment, her heart full of grace.
You know she loved life and to show it she smiled,
When you see her, you know that at heart, she's a child.
She laughed, she cried, she cherished each day,
When you looked at her you felt the same way.
She's the kind of person you want to be around,
She's the kind of person to love and surround.
The one you remember had a friendly face,
You have to believe in your heart that she's now in a better place.

Zoe Brain, Grade 6
Spring Creek Elementary School, WY
*In memory of Krystn Rennick

Love

To love is to feel strongly about someone or something.
To love is to feel empty when that person or place is gone.
To love is to wake up to the morning just to see that person or place.
To love is to feel a special feeling.
To love is to be breathless when you see that person or thing.

Sammantha Daniels, Grade 6
Hidden Creek Elementary School, WA

A Dancing Horse

On a beautiful snow day,
I went out to play.

I wanted to feed my horse hay,
I asked my mom and she said ok.

When I got to the barn, you wouldn't believe what I saw,
But when I saw it I was in awe.

My horse let out a big neigh,
I turned around and he was doing ballet!

Not only was he doing ballet,
But he told me he was taking lessons from a blue jay.

I told my mom what I had seen,
She said "of course, that horse has always been a dancing machine."

Kaleigh Kelsey, Grade 4
Elementary School, ID

Fire

Fire is a part of your heart that melts away.
As you watch the fire dance you see the soul of life.
Life becomes stronger and at the same time it becomes weaker.
Slowly you watch. The moon is your guide.
The fire is your soul. The ash is your wisdom.
The moon glows above your head as the fire shoots out sparks like a bullet.
The sparks are not ash and fire, they are people who slowly watch over you.
You watch their light go out, and you watch them glide away to the moon.
When it reaches the moon it shines brighter than ever.

Hannah Trembath, Grade 4
Mitchell Elementary School, CO

My True Love

When I see you, I'm shy.
When I touch you, I seem to fly.

When you stare at me, I feel I slip on sleet,
But I know you will come and sweep me off my feet.

When I'm around you, I know you're not fake.
I dream to be with you when I light my birthday cake.

I know we will meet someday.
I'm sure my heart will show me the way.

Kimberly Delgadillo, Grade 6
Somerton Middle School, AZ

Blindness of Mortality

An empty, black hole
That everyone fears
Behind it — eternity
Hidden by tears

The blindness of mortality
Restricts us only to what we see

Our hearts search for light
In the veil no one's wearing
In the deafness of darkness
Where the truth shows no bearings

O the day when Hell is truly conceived!
The light be revealed, which no tainted sinner's received

Morgan Bierbaum, Grade 6
Walt Clark Middle School, CO

School

School is school
But it's usually so dull
That I fall asleep
And while I sleep
I dream of me
And what I might be when I'm 58
Maybe a grandma, or a mom
Or just a sister that talks on the telephone
Then I wake up from this dream that I had
And I find myself at school
Reading out of a math book.

Emily Dwyer, Grade 6
Green Valley Christian School, NV

Blue

Blue is the color of the sky day and night.
The color of bravery that represents our country.
Blue smells relaxing when I smell Columbines.
A winning color of success.
Blue is the power of spirit.

Bailey Jackson, Grade 4
Hunters Glen Elementary School, CO

Walking By!

Above the green tall trees stood the shining sun.
Along the faraway trail was a snail on a pail.
Against the snail was a rock pushing hard.
Beyond, a kid who was crying in a car.
Upon the trees were birds chirping loud.
Above the birds stood a lonely old cloud.
On the ground were daisies growing wide.
Until I saw the kids going inside.
Behind the kid's house was a park full of toys.
With kids everywhere girls and boys.

Kimberly Hooten, Grade 6
Fox Creek Jr High School, AZ

Centaur Season

Centaur season is here
can't you see or hear?
Where, where are the centaur?
Over here, can you see over there?
That big cloud
that's where they are quickly moving in a flare
as they move from here to there.

Jacob Williams, Grade 4
Wilson Elementary School, WA

Life of a Fifth Grader

All throughout life we have turns in our path,
There are even twists and turns in math,
Like subtraction or addition,
I'm not even sure how to spell coalition,
What about multiplication and division,
They all have a collision,
Now it is all in my head,
I wish I could go to bed,
I can't sleep now,
I'm thinking of a cow,
But I still have to finish my math,
Well I told you about my horrible path,
Now I am going to sleep,
So all the knowledge may you keep.

Maria Teresa Hidalgo, Grade 5
St Cyril Elementary School, AZ

Thing

There once was a thing,
That lived in my brain.
He tells me what to do when I don't want him to.
He grows so I growl, he cries so I cry.
I can't stand this thing he makes me so mad.
When I'm mad he's sad.
When I'm sad he's mad.
I don't know why this thing picks on me,
I wish it was dead
Maybe it's because I'm dumb and it's all in my head.

Brandon McKiernan, Grade 5
M A Lynch Elementary School, OR

Shh…

Shh…
Can you hear the trees?
Whispering and swaying in the wind,
Hear the fish
gently swimming through the stream,
Hear the birds
whistling their sweet tune.

Can you hear the salmon
jumping up the waterfalls?
Hear the robin
flying from perch to perch,
Hear the crickets
getting ready for night to conquer day.

Shh…
Can you hear the silent trees?
Hear the fish
swimming to find shelter for the night,
Hear the birds,
tucking in their young,
Hear all the little woodland creatures
scurrying back to their homes.
Nathanial Wietfeldt, Grade 6
Barbara Bush Elementary School, AZ

The Cat

The cat was strolling,
In the beautiful green grass,
Searching for a mouse.
Baili Lubke, Grade 6
Hamilton Middle School, MT

Football

F eet kick the ball.
O ut on the rough field.
O n the beach is the best.
T he ball always scores.
B est of all it wins the game for you.
A fter the crowd cheers.
L ots of noise they make.
L ast of all the whistle blows.
Christian Brewer, Grade 6
St Cyril Elementary School, AZ

Basketball

We slam dunk the balls.
We bust the rims.
Hitting the backboard.
Swishing the ball.
Making some shots.
Missing some shots.
Who'd win —
Michael Jordan or Shaquille O'Neal?
Xavier Altamirano, Grade 4
Acacia Elementary School, AZ

War

It hurts,
Pain jolts through me,
My back,
My arm,

Everything is going black,
A swirling mist,

Pain,

I try to fight back,
My arm,
Is it gone?

Blood fills my mouth,
I try to spit it out,
I can't,

I'm lifted up by helpful arms,
I'm going to be injured for life.
Bryce R. Delamater, Grade 6
Santa Fe School for the Arts, NM

Can You Walk?

Can you walk?
Can you talk?
Can you see?
See a bee
Do you have an ear?
Can you hear?
Can you blink?
Can you think?
Of course you cannot
You are a tree
Not like me
Soichi Tanabe, Grade 5
Uplands Elementary School, OR

The Thing Under My Bed

The thing under my bed
keeps me awake.
It is scary
and big.
He drools,
and fools
everyone
in town.
Taylor Schuben, Grade 5
Frontier Valley Elementary School, CO

Rain

Sound of the calm rain
Hitting the roof of my home
Soothes the ache in me.
Kara Wetzsteon, Grade 6
Hamilton Middle School, MT

Imagination

In my imagination
I can go to far away places
Even past tomorrow
Into the future

I can go to wonderful places
Deep within my mind
To another planet
Leaving today behind

I can go to outer space
To see the planet Saturn
To the lake of Lochness
To see the Lochness Monster

In my imagination
I can go back to the past
Back to yesterday
I can go anywhere
John Burch, Grade 6
Washington Intermediate School, CO

I Am From

I am from the ragged doll
I sleep with

From the love in my family
That makes me feel safe

I am from my kittens Snowball and Curly
That I hug tight

From the hot summer breeze
That makes me feel warm

I am from the basketball hoop
That I play with in the day

From the family reunions
That help me know my family

I am from the bowling
We do every Sunday

From "Ohio Gazziemas"
We say in the morning
I am from all of those things
Hailee Blunt, Grade 4
Grass Valley Elementary School, NV

Not to Start Again

A school filled with kids
Kids that want the year to end
Never to start again
Marissa Lumpkin, Grade 6
Morgan Middle School, WA

Spring

Spring is a time of year when flowers bloom.
Birds start chirping pretty medleys of songs.
Children buy ice cream,
and play outside all day.
Wind starts blowing,
bees start buzzing around the blooming flowers.
Butterflies start landing on flowers to get pollen,
So, be ready for spring.

Kenosha Medina, Grade 4
McCormick Elementary School, NM

Martial Arts Tournament

I sit with the yellow belts
Waiting for the tournament to start
I feel sick to my stomach
It begins
I lose the sickness
Replace it with competitive excitement
And still some nervousness

Before I compete I find there are nine others in my round
It is my turn
I go up and do my form
I feel I'm the best
Everyone gets a lower score
I do my sparring
I always lose the first round
I win the second

It closes I get my scores
First place form
Second place sparring
I am overrun by pure joy
I carry my artifacts of remembrance two shiny trophies

Austin Sisk, Grade 6
Walker Middle School, OR

Mice

Mice are nice
Even though they may have lice
Some are white some are black
Some are small like a stubby thumbtack.

Mice love cheese
But they never say please
So just give them what they want
Or else they may go out on a jaunt.

When they come back you scold them
But they never understand what you told them
So teach them manners
As your write in your planners
You write, "Mice are nice."

Tara Pillai, Grade 4
Eton School, WA

The Point Is…

The point is,
My name is Joe.
The thing beside the point is,
Joe is a very nice name.
The thing beside the, beside the point is,
My favorite super hero is SUPERMAN.
The thing beside the, beside the, beside the point is,
I like cheese!

Natan Brauner, Grade 5
Ober Elementary School, NV

Morris (Morrie) Turner

On December 11, 1923
A boy was born, free from sadness and woe,
And no one knew what he would be,
Or where the boy would go.

His mother named him Morrie;
He loved to sketch and draw,
Now I'll tell you his story,
How he drew the things he saw.

Morrie created the Wee Pals comic,
That warmed American hearts,
The reactions were atomic,
Its feedback off the charts.

Morrie Turner lives today
And he's doing just the same,
Drawing comic strips like Wee Pals,
That gave him all his fame!

Mari Swinnerton, Grade 6
Rogers Adventist School, WA

My Mom

My mom is an angel
falling from the sky,
with clear white pearls,
so I try to hold her tight.

Amelia Salgado Dominguez, Grade 5
Escuela Bilingüe Pioneer Elementary School, CO

Paint Your World

What if you could paint a world?
A world your own
Paint the skies with blues and violets,
Paint the moon with the face of peace.
The stars as a flame against the cold night sky,
Paint the sun with rays of vibrance,
Paint the hills alive with wonder,
Paint the valleys brilliant with reds
And violets, yellows and greens,
The mountains cold with silence,
Let your imagination guide you…

Allie Hall, Grade 4
Spring Creek Elementary School, WY

Winter

Snowball throwing
Fun and cold
Sipping hot cocoa
Snowballs being rolled
Hanging out with siblings
Dressing up warm
Making snowmen
With a special form.
Austin Coppinger, Grade 6
Glacier Middle School, WA

Bright Light

The light that warms
Around the world,
A set of arms
Falling around us.
Sun rays!

They're silent, peaceful
As calm water.
Changing your shadow
Throughout the day.
Sun rays!

They say good-bye at dusk.
Then return again at dawn,
To bring the day joyfulness,
Until they disappear again.
Sun rays!

They disappear behind the
Clouds, behind the earth,
Playing hide and seek.
It's dark, dim, and dingy without
Them, find them once again.
Sun rays!
Marissa Runolfson, Grade 5
Barratt School, UT

A Horrible Day

I saw a big rat
Being chased by a cat.

The cat looked at me
And then got stung by a bee.

I threw a rock at that cat
And hit a big bat.

I went to tell my mom
And got hit by a bomb.

That was the end of me
As we know it to be.
Matthew Harris, Grade 6
Morgan Middle School, WA

My Life

Every day I wake and I always think I look pretty
But when I go to school the populars look better
I try to compete but I never win, so I give up
The next day comes and I hope that they don't notice me but they do
They come over and say that my outfit looks like trash
And they tell me to never wear it again
So I followed what they said
That outfit is now three years old and I never touched it since
Cheyanne Moore, Grade 6
Hidden Creek Elementary School, WA

Coins

Among all the coins I have like the buffalo nickel and a Chinese coin
during all those days and nights I learn a lot
from morning to dusk I learn so much and sort so many.
By now I am half done
near the end
Outside is a beautiful oak tree
For when I'm done
under that tree I will be sitting
Shawn Druckenmiller, Grade 6
Fox Creek Jr High School, AZ

The Just Right Christmas for Me

The just right Christmas for me would be chock full of snow,
The Christmas tree would be perfect size and shining with a glow.
Everyone would arrive safely and would be happy about being here,
But what gets me jumpin' are the presents!
Presents from Santa,
Presents from friends,
Presents from family again and again!

Small, tall, lean, thin!
I just don't know where to begin!
From teddy bears to cards filled with love,
It's great to give and even better to receive,
I just can't wait till Christmas Eve!

I never want to leave,
That amazing, imaginary, Christmas Eve.
Drew McLaughlin, Grade 5
Firwood Elementary School, OR

What Is Freedom?

Freedom is doing what you want and doing what you please
Buying your own goods and not paying other's fees
Ain't going to work them raw hands, and be kneeling on these busted knees
I'll move to my own house and buy me some moments of peace

Now I can get to learnin', even if I get back, some of those dang darn D's
I got my own crop now, and I can eat a whole bowl of fresh green peas
I couldn't buy freedom at the general store,
But now with my help, and those from other slaves,
I have gotten the chance to live my very own life
Meaghan Mahoney, Grade 6
Pope John XXIII Catholic School Community, AZ

My Little Friend

To a new comer, my little friend
is very shy and cute.
When my little friend
and I are alone she is very sly.
My little friend sometimes
is as stubborn and defiant as a warthog
who is in an atrocious mood.
My little friend can be as
gentle and calming as a sleepy kitten.
Whether my little friend is shy, cute, sly,
stubborn, defiant, gentle
or calming,
…she is my little friend and is just right for me!

Una Harris, Grade 6
St Anne School, WA

Memory of Me

Looking through these pages;
makes me cry a lot.
For I am not a baby but a new me.
I feel like I understand how I acted back then.
Crying, smiling, and even frowning.
Easter, Christmas, and my birthday were lots of fun.
I even traveled to Mexico to lay in the sun.
When I first peeked my eyes out
I was the cutest no doubt.
But now I am older,
And I'm much more bolder.
What a memory of me!

Brittney Rivera, Grade 5
Greenwood Elementary School, CO

Nature

Wind blows the clouds like candles on a cake
River flows and goes along quietly
Sky grasps the earth in a blanket of light and dark
Sun beams its prideful glow
Moon shimmers its nightly glitter

Annalise Pownall, Grade 6
Morgan Middle School, WA

No More School

When summer comes, school is out
All of the kids play and shout
They can yell and scream as they please
They don't have to cover their mouths when they sneeze
They stay up all night
They have a pillow fight
They play with all of their friends
All of the fun never ends
They talk, laugh, and play
They have fun every day
They scream and they shout
"Hooray! School is out!"

Lacey Vater, Grade 4
Shields Valley Elementary School, MT

A Flower's Life

A flower blooming is a marvelous sight.
The gentle petals unfolding,
to the natural, pure air.
To have its scrunched up petals unfold,
is like to see for the first time.
Untouched flowers have not a dent.
Spring air briskly pushes the leaves,
in every direction.
Come winter, snow heavily packs on a flower,
creating a white scene.
The once lovely, luscious, flower,
now sits shriveled up and frozen.
Frozen like an ice cube.
When snow drifts away,
you see a languid dead flower.
One touch and it crumbles away.
Don't worry, come spring,
a flower will bloom, again.

Odyssey Villagomez, Grade 6
Vikan Middle School, CO

Muck

I got out of school last week
Today I think I will visit the creek
Yesterday I saw my sister reading Yuck!
Then I went to the river to see Muck.
My horse that likes to buck
One day he bucked and made the bees swarm
Then we covered ourselves with mud
Boy did we look like fudge
Next Muck and I went fishing in the river
We also washed up but it was cold and we shivered
Now summer is almost over
And I have to start school all over.

Colton Maier, Grade 4
Shields Valley Elementary School, MT

Nothing

I see you but you can't see me.
I drift away to a different kind of life.
If you could take away my pain I could build a paradise.
Is this a dream or my lesson, am I overreacting?
Falling apart and all I'm asking, is this a crime?
All my rhymes are slipping away.
I don't believe I'll be okay.
I don't believe I'll be all right.
I don't believe how you could throw me away.
Give me something to bury him with.
All my tears never change.
Give me something to bury this alive with.
I do believe you didn't try.
I do blame you for every lie.
I look in your eyes and I don't see mine.

Erica McIntyre, Grade 6
Hidden Creek Elementary School, WA

Pike's Peak North Face

The bold blue sky
hangs over
Pikes Peak's north face.
Dark heavy clouds
sail through
the early morning sky.
The bright orange peak
sits above
the misty forest.
Grassy plains
sit below the peak
and shows off colors
like orange,
red,
black,
and green.

Dalton Dickey, Grade 4
Audubon Elementary School, CO

Food Is Good

Food is good,
You can't live without it.
Pizza is good, so is ice cream.
They taste so good.

Pie is sooo sugary,
And fruity
And chocolate…

Leo Liu, Grade 6
Hazelwood Elementary School, WA

That Fateful Summer

The house is empty,
The light is calling me,
It's too strong,
What can go wrong?
The light is fading,
Heaven is waiting,
My soul is lifting,
I feel I'm drifting.
That summer I died.
I left the Earth,
The angels are singing,
My ears aren't ringing,
I feel better,
I'm as light as a feather.
Now I feel peace!

Amanda Dimick, Grade 5
Sally Mauro Elementary School, UT

Chocolate

Chocolate is sweet,
It's the best kind of candy,
Best tasting to eat.

Seth Mason, Grade 6
Hamilton Middle School, MT

Predator

Eagles, cool birds that
Eat little mammals for lunch.
They are really big.

Chris Meadors, Grade 6
Hamilton Middle School, MT

A Good Friend

I want a friend who would
stand by my side.
I want a friend who would
back me up all the time.
I want a friend who will stay
with me 'till the end.
I want a good friend.

Jessica Gallo, Grade 6
Eagle Point Middle School, OR

Never Ending Mountains

Never ending mountains
are miles and miles long
They're as beautiful
as a Colorado river

Calm winds move
through its trees
soft and slowly whispers
The sun stretching
to the other side
Mountains are never ending

Ricky Perez, Grade 5
Edgewater Elementary School, CO

The Goat and Boat in the Moat

There once was a man with a boat,
Who bought it and thought it would float.
It was brought to a moat,
Along with a goat,
And sank in a big gator's throat.

Michelle Huang, Grade 5
Oak Creek Elementary School, OR

Baseball

America's true pastime
Fun to hit home runs
Can I play?

Jake Como, Grade 4
Copper Canyon Elementary School, AZ

American Flag

Stands for our country
Red, white, blue and glorious
Waving in the air
Stars represent fifty states
The stripes go on forever

Jaydon Flori, Grade 4
Copper Canyon Elementary School, AZ

The War

There is a war going on
Do we really know what's going on
Planes dropping bombs
Kids been separated from their moms

There is a war going on
Do we really know what's going on
People keep dying
Children keep crying

There is a war going on
Do we really know what's going on
Toxins being poured
People getting abhorred

There is a war going on
Do we really know what's going on
Families keep crying
'Cause soldiers keep dying

Yael Aguilar, Grade 6
South Middle School, CO

My Love for You

My love for you,
is filled with passion.
My heart is filled with gold.
I hope you love me,
the way I love you.
I hope you call,
or we won't be together.
I know I should have told you,
that this was love at first sight.
We are meant to be together.
If not,
oh well!
I love you,
I cherish you,
you like me,
I love you!
I will be waiting someday,
for a perfect man.
I'll be waiting,
for you to call.
If you call at all!

Ashley Edinger, Grade 6
Franklin Middle School, CO

Make a Difference

Go out there and make a change!
Go out there and make a discovery!
Go out there and be yourself!
Go out to do as you please.
Feel proud of yourself,
Remember, *you* make a difference!

Michelly Martinez, Grade 4
Lewis E. Rowe Elementary School, NV

Chances

My sanctuary was destroyed
All through this time of war.
The harder I try, the lower I score.
Even though I have failed, trudge on.
I can see through despair, hardship, and death
Once dwindling crumb of hope.
I am falling, falling from grace.
It is as if I have died one hundred deaths, just to trip again.
Suddenly my apprehension slows and stops.
I wish to stand but I am to scared to tumble.
A small voice in my head says,
"Life means taking chances."
Now I'm on my feet again.

Taryn Wood, Grade 6
Gate City Elementary School, ID

Lion Tears

He watches from his window,
As a lion watches from his perch.

He stares at the driveway,
As a lion stares at his valley.

He hopes for his mother's return,
As a cub hopes for its mother's coming.

He cries in his seemingly never ending wait,
A lion has no tears, so his sorrow is trapped.

Pablo Moreno, Grade 6
Somerton Middle School, AZ

Greenbacks

Money holds the face of fossils
Starring back like statues
Which by fact
Were Presidents
Of the United States of America
"In God We Trust"
Is a quote it has
Money comes in quite a variety of values
100
50
20
10
5
1
Rarely you will see
A 2 roaming like a camel in the desert
Through wallets and cash registers
Having money is exciting
And it can be easy to become obsessed over
Like monkeys with bananas
Money looks like a piece of seaweed

Cody Thurston, Grade 4
Brush Creek Elementary School, CO

Forest by the Stream

I began walking in the woods
when I came to a stream.
The reflection of the trees
looked like blobs of white, yellow and green
paint on a paint board.
The moss looked like an island on the stream.
The cattail looked like trees at a distance.
I felt like telling the world about this stream,
so I did.

Donovan Hoover, Grade 4
Great Expectations Academy, AZ

If I Were

If I were arms I'd give you a hug.
If I were shoes I'd let you stomp on the Earth.
If I were a pencil I'd write stories for you.
If I were meat I'd let you have a wonderful dinner.

Deise Flores, Grade 4
Jackpot Combined School, NV

The Music of the Night

Late at night,
When the shadows creep out,
Can you hear the heartbeat,
Of the ground?

Can you hear the leaves rustling
Hard and fast?
And the wind howling,
As it goes past?

Can you hear the frogs croaking
Down in the pond?
And the thunder rolling
Far beyond?

But as soon as night
Comes to its end
The music hides away
Waiting for night to come again.

Regina Molina, Grade 6
The Gilkey International Middle School, OR

The Truth

She knows there's something there
Something covered yet so bare.
Her best friends just won't speak about it,
To cover up the truth.
And when she thinks about it,
She doesn't know what to do.
Sometimes she gazes at the moon
Knowing her life is not in tune.
So alone she cries herself to sleep
Listen close to her weep.

Elizabeth Matalomani, Grade 6
Granite Falls Middle School, WA

Ocean

The ocean is blue,
The sand is warm,
Birds are flying high;
It is really hot —
I see a lot of boats,
I feel the breeze blow —
The ocean of home — Philippines.
Jordan Laboca, Grade 4
Juneau SDA School, AK

Lights

Lights in the sky,
Way over my head,
They look so beautiful
Tinted, with red.
Tracy Sierra Lynn Nerpel, Grade 5
Firwood Elementary School, OR

Mom

Mom
is beautiful
is a worthy person
does lots of things for people
is wonderful,
is loving,
does good deeds,
is a pretty lady,
wears glasses,
5,1",
works all day 24/7,
is a mother,
is a loving wife,
cooks the most delicious,
food you could imagine,
even tastes that good,
mom is the name,
I call her
Her real name is Anita,
No matter what we call her,
!We all do love her!
Maranda Addison, Grade 6
Vikan Middle School, CO

Black Hole

I'm stuck, trapped, nowhere to go.
It's dark in a black hole,
will I get out?
Lake Klare, Grade 6
Hamilton Middle School, MT

Rain

Lightly coating the earth,
Rain drops fall to the ground
Rain clouds fill the sky.
Krystil Rotte, Grade 5
Kingman Academy of Learning, AZ

Blowing Wind

Tree leaves floating by
Whistling winds blowing here and there
Calm and peaceful
Fresh and clear air
I touch the invisible breeze.
Peaceful day
Tenzin Ward, Grade 4
Lincoln Elementary School, AZ

Robots

Why can't we feel it?
The human's love, hate, and joy.
I need a real heart.
Maggie Reynolds, Grade 6
Hamilton Middle School, MT

Fourth of July

Fourth of July
Fireworks booming in the air
Barbecuing hot dogs
Bang and boom all through the night
Popcorn hot and nice
Hot ashes coming down
Fourth of July
Kyle Kihn, Grade 4
Coal Creek Elementary School, CO

Veterans' War

Veterans fought with all might
For what they thought was our right
There have been many a war
Each causing their own uproar
When veterans fought, they fought brave
Many lives they did save
They bravely fought a war
And protected a flag that had been torn
And as it still stood
As proudly as it could
Veterans would sit each night
Around the fire
Discussing the day's fight
Before they would retire
Joshua Wheeler, Grade 4
Peck Elementary School, ID

Butterflies

A butterfly,
Mature,
Colorful,
Beautiful,
Graceful,
Gentle,
Flying.
I wish I could fly like a butterfly.
Micah Walburg, Grade 6
Hazelwood Elementary School, WA

River of Time

Long is the river of time
Forever leaving, moving always
Toward the ocean of the past it twists
Cold are the tears of rain
That spill back into the river
Repeating itself, as history does.
Alyssa Gallotte, Grade 6
Southern Hills Middle School, CO

Dear Alison

I'm sorry that
I ate all the cookies

But they were so
fresh and chocolatey

I know it was wrong
but I couldn't resist
they were so sweet

I'm sorry I ate
the cookies
and you didn't get
to have any
I feel bad
but I wish it was
peanut butter
Adam Martin, Grade 5
Edgewater Elementary School, CO

Shadows

If you the shadows have offended
think of this, all are mended.
If you have but slumbered here
while these visions did appear,
all the creatures will disappear,
no more yielding, but a dream.
Dane Dillon, Grade 6
Harlem Elementary School, MT

Time Travel

Wouldn't it be nice to time travel?
Something else to unravel?
Like the Medieval times,
And the military lines,
The gods' evil wines!
Or instead of being 7,
You could be 11.
Instead of having pollute,
You could salute.
Time flies fast,
Lower the mast!
From an ordinary old farmer,
To a knight in shining armor.
Alden Hoag, Grade 5
Windsor Charter Academy, CO

Me

Anthony
Who is cool, caring, funny.
Who is a child of Preston and Susie McEachern.
Who loves books, my family, and dragons.
Who feels outgoing, special, and #1.
Who needs books, more friends, and a pencil.
Who gives smiles, love, and laughs.
Who fears heights, dolls, and loneliness.
Who would like to see a white tiger in the jungle.
Resident of Montrose, CO
McEachern

Anthony McEachern, Grade 5
Cottonwood Elementary School, CO

Candy Shop

If I walked into a candy shop,
I'd tell you what I would buy.
I'd grab the biggest bag they had,
And hold it to the sky.

I would head straight to the lollipops,
And find my favorite flavor.
Then walk to the other aisle
Where I would see lots of Life Savers.

Next I would head towards the jelly beans,
With all of the different sorts.
My mouth would water with delight,
I'd buy about a quart.

Then I would walk toward the check-out counter,
I'd gather my money getting ready to pay.
The clerk would give me my bag,
Then I would walk out, teeth ready to decay.

Madison O'Dell, Grade 6
Bradford Intermediate School, CO

Obesity, Summarized

Way back in the day,
When people liked to play,
Everyone was fit.
Few people ever ate a grease-covered chip.
But one day things changed, just like that,
Everyone went from fit to fat.
They sat on their sofa, their piggy eyes gleaming,
Watching their video game characters screaming.
Sitting for hours,
Crunching on junk, never bothering to even take showers.
School quizzes and tests were never studied for,
'Cause their backpacks lay in a heap behind the door.
This is obesity pure and true,
Don't ever let it get to you.
Things have changed a lot from back in the day,
Now hardly anyone will go out and play.

Kyle Downs, Grade 6
Miller Middle School, CO

Sandoval Makes a Hollywood Movie!

I can see the headlines now "Sandoval Makes It Big,"
With a famous movie.
It will be my great big gig.
    Will my movie be a story,
About true love or worry?
    I can see my name up in lights,
And I'll go and see my movies,
Every Friday night.
    It'll be so cool, it'll be so hot
They'll come and see it,
From grandpas to tots.
    That, oh yes, will be my future,
But right now I'm just a kid,
Listening to my English teacher.

Taylor Sandoval, Grade 6
Corpus Christi School, CO

Life Is Like

Life is like a train
    hurry, hurry
Never stopping, never slowing down
Life is like a running dog
    hurry, hurry
Never running out of energy, never slowing down
Life is like a river
    hurry, hurry
Never running out of water, never slowing down
Where is my pause button?
But there is no pause button
So my life goes on

Keith Miller, Grade 6
Barbara Bush Elementary School, AZ

Three Thousand Hits Made by Yankee James Stiltner

In the beginning it wasn't so easy
Practice and work on the field makes it easy
Batting and catching are the most fun
The best times to play are in the hot sun

When the challenge began it didn't seem easy
No one thought it could be done
I showed how easy
And it was fun

When the crowd cheered and screamed
I felt a strong feeling
The ball would go screaming
Into the fans cheering

I began to run the bases
The fans cheered in their places
I waved to the fans from the bases
I crossed home plate and saw the happy faces

James Stiltner, Grade 6
Corpus Christi School, CO

Deep Green Valley

As I was walking in the deep, green valley, I smelled the aroma of the fresh, white flowers. I heard the birds chirping on the grassy, green hills. I felt the fluffy, green grass under my feet. I tasted the mist of the newly fallen water as it rolls to the beach. The water is like a ghost floating down the stream. I see the puffy, baby blue sky as it hits the ghostly waves. The freshly bloomed flowers are as white as snow. I feel the fresh air running down my spine.

Cecilia Archuleta, Grade 5
Sally Mauro Elementary School, UT

If I Were in Charge of the World

If I were in charge of the world alcohol and cigarettes wouldn't be invented. School would end at 1:30 p.m. All the people would be rich. There would be no snakes. Everybody would be nice. Candy would be free for everyone. Every family would live in a mansion that had 2 pools. You would be able to drive when you were 14. You would be able to get a cell phone when you were 10. Everybody would have their own laptop.

Melisa Gonzalez, Grade 4
Jackpot Combined School, NV

The Sky Bird

Great long wings, longer than an eagle's.
Hawk's beak, long and broad, perfect for biting and nipping and cutting.
Look carefully in your binoculars, look into the sky. There you see her, the sky bird.
Her wings are swift in moving, they look like a big white blanket covering the sky.
The sky bird is different from the others; never wavers in a storm, doesn't even cry out when in great pain.
That is the sky bird for you.

Blake Snelling, Grade 5
West Mercer Elementary School, WA

My Savior Touches My Heart

My Savior touched my heart for He is beyond the brightest light about and has blessed me with a special love
He is my Creator, my beloved brother, my strength, and my Redeemer
He gives me the wings to soar and fly and is close in my grateful heart when I cry
His devotion to others is unthinkable and His passion for people's happiness is unbelievable
His heart is a never-ending chain of kindness and to me He is considered the finest
His cries are precious drops of love and His pureness is as white as a dove
I put my faith and trust in His hands for I know this is His glorious plan
If we follow His plan His spirit will not part for this is why my Savior touches my heart

Hannah Jackson, Grade 6
Hermosa Vista Elementary School, AZ

What I Liked Then and Now

I used to never want to leave the arid, scorching city of Tucson, but now I want to go traveling to the beautiful country of Japan.
I used to be a carefree, playful, and a workless child, but now I am in 5th grade with tons and tons of homework.
I used to read picture books with eight pages, but now I read exciting Japanese manga books.
I used to devour all of the hard, sugary candy I received, but now I only eat creamy, rich chocolate.
I used to despise almost every vegetable there was, but now I love carrots, lettuce, and minuscule peas.
I used to be as short as a garden gnome, but now I'm almost as tall as my caring mom.
I used to love to eat tons of eggs, but now I know that artery-clogging eggs are bad for my cholesterol.
I used to play joyous one-player arcade games, but now I play MMORPGs like Maplestory.
I used to run like I was just learning to walk, but now I run with long strides.
I used to be afraid that I would drown in bottomless pools, but now I always swim in the deep end.
I used to like simple Velcro shoes, but now I like shoes with shoelaces.
I used to adore watching childish sing-along videos, but now I love exciting Japanese anime.
I used to only know simple addition and subtraction, but now I know how to do complex math problems.
I used to collect papery trading cards, but now I know that they are just colorful pieces of paper.
I used to have lifeless action figures and toys, but now I play on the electrical computer.
I used to hate complicated schoolwork, but now all the assignments are a breeze.

William Lee, Grade 5
Wheeler Elementary School, AZ

Montana

Montana is beautiful and wonderful too,
And the sky is also very blue.
Montana is kinda lame,
Most states ain't the same.
The biggest cities are Billings and Butte.
The smallest city is about as big as you.
Montana is beautiful and wonderful too,
Everyone likes it I hope to find you.
There are tourists and guests, I hope everyone's on their best…
Come join the fun like the REST!
Montana is beautiful and wonderful too,
Our state is also very BIG.
But the population is about as small as a twig.
But that' OK, our state is still very GREAT!
Montana is beautiful and wonderful too,
The winter is so cold, you will probably turn blue.
So you better be careful 'cause you might get the flu.
And summers are hot,
so a cool drink will sure hit the SPOT!

Makyla Fetter, Grade 6
Harlem Elementary School, MT

Nightfall

High up in the mountains exotic birds fly.
As the day ends, a glossy orange layer covers the land.
A storm fades away as a glorious rainbow fills the sky
    just before the sun sets.
A cool night air creeps down the mountain as animals find
    shelter and stare up at the breathtaking sky.
Constellations line up and sparkle like the sun hitting water.
A wolf gets a drink from a nearby stream and then lies
    down in the crunchy leaves.
As silence falls, a gentle wind blows rustling the trees,
    making them say "Good Night…Good Night."

Jesse Kephart, Grade 6
Barbara Bush Elementary School, AZ

Sunset

The gentle breeze blows from the west
And birds return to their nest
The golden ball starts going down
lights go out all through town
Many colors fill the sky
The last bird goes flying by
The sun is setting

The darkness is here
But morning is near
A shooting star flies across the dark pool
The morning air is crisp and cool
The glow behind the mountains is growing brighter
And our side of the world is getting lighter
Morning is here

Lindsey Fano, Grade 6
Southern Hills Middle School, CO

Warriors of Darkness

Count Dooku is a master swordsman.
General Grievous is a deadly cyborg.
Darth Maul has a double-bladed lightsaber.
Darth Vader is more machine than man.

He blasts lightning from his hands.
He can fight with four lightsabers at once.
There are small horns on his head.
Most fear in the Dark Lord's presence.

Justin Sand, Grade 4
Copper Canyon Elementary School, AZ

How to Swallow a Smile

A smile is dazzling as it grows upon your face
Shimmer, shine, and glisten
Gobble activities that you adore;
Shopping
Swimming
Spending time out in the sun
Tell a joke
Spend time with friends
Gulp up a pleasurable time
Devour the fireworks on the 4th of July
Bake cookies and watch the sunset
And as the day ends,
Smile and watch your teeth twinkle and gleam.

Stephanie Allen, Grade 5
Kyrene De Las Brisas School, AZ

September Eleventh

September eleventh was a really sad day.
People calling help or save me.
Sirens blaring really loud.
New York echoes with a sad thought.
There were fear and tears within every heart.
Kids, babies, parents in all,
We will always remember this sad day.
All the people sat down to pray
As the planes approached on this sad day.
They crashed the two towers on this sad day,
Every firefighter risking their life.
We could only look up to George W. Bush,
Saying oh Lord help us on this day.
September 11th,
    We'll always remember this day.

Elizabeth Harmon, Grade 4
Roy Moore Elementary School, CO

Sunset

Sunset is so beautiful the light in the sky.
The light over the mountains.
The pink in the sky.
The sunset in the closing of day.
That is so very beautiful.

Katie Fransen, Grade 5
Sangre De Cristo Elementary School, CO

Softball

Step up to the plate,
Stance.
Swoosh, Ping!
Follow through.
Push off the plate.
First,
Second,
Third,
Home!
A cheering crowd
There to greet me.

Abby Elggren, Grade 5
West Mercer Elementary School, WA

This Is Who I Am

I am who I am
Not a girlie girl.
I don't act like a man,
But a normal girl.

My name is Yllen
And I'm in sixth.
I am eleven
And I'm glad I'm past the fifth.

I like to play instruments
But I mostly like only one.
I don't like the drums,
But the guitar is my favorite one.

I've played for five years
And I've gotten better.
I hope I can make more years
And never quit it ever.

Yllen Lopez, Grade 6
Somerton Middle School, AZ

Spring

S ome flowers bloom
P eople have Bar-B-Q's
R ain falls
I ce melts
N ature wakes up
G reen grass starts to grow.

Shirley Roberts, Grade 4
McCormick Elementary School, NM

Stars

On a clear night
In the sky
Across the horizon they twinkle
Above the ground
Among the planets
Beyond all imagination

Megan Yakavonis, Grade 6
Blaine Middle School, WA

Flamingo

Long and slender necks,
feathers pink from eating shrimp,
graceful flamingo.

Natalie Bremer, Grade 6
Hamilton Middle School, MT

Black

Black is the color
Of a fighter's blackened eye,
The batteries in your clock
The haunting midnight sky.

Black is the hat
Of the witch on Halloween night,
Black is the absence
Of color and light.

Black is the color
Of a cow's painted spots,
A tire on your car
And little ink dots.

It's the color of a skunk
A steak that is peppered,
Crows in the sky
And the spots on a leopard.

The outside of an Oreo
The center of my eyes,
A round hockey puck
And burnt apple pies.

Kailey Dye, Grade 6
Kendallvue Elementary School, CO

Moonlit Night

The moon is bright
and full of fun
It hangs in my window
when there is no sun.

I try to catch it
every night,
But it floats away
in misty light.

I wish the moon
would sleep with me
Then things in my room
would be plain to see.

I'd hold it tight
with all my might
So I would always
feel safe at night.

Kylee Ching, Grade 5
Ammon Elementary School, ID

Dog

Big fat active dog,
running playful active dog,
sleepy hungry dog.

Samantha Fraser, Grade 6
Hamilton Middle School, MT

Frog

Swimming in a pond
Leaps out of the water now
Eating many flies

Justin Bavier, Grade 5
St Cyril Elementary School, AZ

Where Food Comes From

Have you ever noticed
The money your parents are makin'?
If you do you will realize
That they bring home the bacon.

Luke Rosenbaum, Grade 6
Mt Olive Lutheran School, NV

The Roze*

There is a Roze,
Standing in a field,
All so lonely,
By itself,
I go study it,
In the wind,
I watch what it does,
How it moves,
I kneel down,
To smell the Roze,
I think,
I whisper,
The Roze is my best friend.

Brittany Gould, Grade 5
Williwaw Elementary School, AK
*Dedicated to
Kleopatra Destiny Roze Riley-Chute

Rebecca

Little Rebecca cute and sweet
Loves to suck on her feet
Eats her Fruit Loops every day
How I love to watch her play

Tiffany Antener, Grade 5
Bates Elementary School, CO

Colts

Colts
Fast, big
Running, passing, catching
Offense does not protest
Team

Tyler Johnston, Grade 4
Copper Canyon Elementary School, AZ

Tiger

T rekking through grass and vines.
I t's hiding, about to catch its prey.
G rowling and roaring as it fights.
E veryone run from the ferocious beast.
R eady to pounce and attack.

Michael Garcia, Grade 6
Morgan Middle School, WA

Katrina

This week a hurricane came named Katrina.
It hit the land and the marina.
The wind blew hard and lots of rain fell.
From the top of my lungs, I wanted to yell.
For these people, I feel sad.
It kills people, it makes me mad.
I will pray for all.
They will survive and stand tall.

Jacob Gandara, Grade 4
Tombaugh Elementary School, NM

Spring

Springtime blossoms bloom in the air.
The beautiful fragrance makes springtime
a wonderful thing to share.
But when spring ends it's summer again,
and then the blossoms are rarely there.
Through the year as seasons change
the pleasure will fall upon you once again.

Savannah Grossman, Grade 4
Cottonwood Montessori School, NM

Stars

Stars shine bright,
they shine at night,
as they give us light,
when the sun comes out they say good night.

Maddison Cole, Grade 5
Cottonwood Elementary School, AZ

Social Studies

Social studies is such a bore
I hate getting the book out
Reading about places makes me snore
And remembering everything makes me pout
I'd rather write exciting stories
Or have fun in physical education
Learn about history in different varieties
Or have math and learn elimination
It would be better if the book was lighter
And we didn't have to read about places
Or visit a historic site
And not read fiction about people with faces in distant places
Teacher, if you don't read about places
I will study a map about outer spaces.

Alan Whalen, Grade 4
Kathy L Batterman Elementary School, NV

Weather

As I watch drifting clouds go by
In the big enormous sky
I sit and get grass stains on my old jeans
I see yellow, orange, and patches of greens
Autumn's leaves are changing their color
And Winter's coldness that make your teeth chatter
Summer is great for sports like tennis
And when it's Spring you look at boats that may say rent us.
But what's most fun of all that you can do in any weather
Is write a poem, a story whenever

Mariah Andreasen, Grade 5
Lake View School, UT

Virus

I want to be a virus,
my arms grabbing onto oncoming blood cells,
making my way unseen and undetected

I sneak around infecting others,
replicating myself until I have a whole army

My eyes are the eyes of all of my duplicates,
guiding them into battle,
telling them where to stop and start

My swift legs are the carriers of my recruits,
dragging them along through narrow passages,
escaping from the enemy's threshold

My mind so smart and cunning,
bringing my replicates through shortcuts,
my objective is to sneak into the body and spy on their plans

With no intention of harming it,
just passing through; finishing the job

Andrew Truswell, Grade 4
Kyrene De Las Brisas School, AZ

Running

Like running on and on
Like wind in face and hair
Like all troubles gone
Like no one is with me
Like flying through limitless sky
Like cheetah hunting its lunch
Like running through the jungle
Like without running I would be a fish out of water
Like running to and fro
Like past and present
Like nothing in my way today
Like running on and on
Like all troubles are gone
Like running away

Skylar Marshall, Grade 6
Walt Clark Middle School, CO

Frogs

Frogs are in the sun
One is on a lily pad
He sees a fly, gulp!

Bradley Hankel, Grade 6
Hamilton Middle School, MT

The World Around Us

The world around us
Reminders in the air
Things we don't notice
Rushing through our hair

The world is our gift
From our God down to us
The world is our treasure
So just don't make a fuss

Things we don't notice
Leave as we speak
We figure out what we've lost
Then try to seek

You have more than others do
You take it for granted
Unlike others who disagree with you

You have so much
It may not seem like a lot
But to others it is
So just know what you've got

Kendall Smith, Grade 5
Copper Mesa Elementary School, CO

My Walk on the Beach

On the damp, sand beach
in the never-ending warmth of the sun,
at high noon
the shells on the beach are glistening,
the seagulls are squawking,
crabs are scuttling on the sand,
fish are swimming in the tide pools,
children are laughing,
surfers are riding the waves,
I take a deep breath
as I watch the sea foam,
peaceful and happy.

Meghan Doyle, Grade 6
Robert Frost Elementary School, OR

Awoo!

Long sorrow howl,
angry at the moon,
all the wolves yowling,
Awooo!

Natalie Emmons, Grade 4
Double Eagle Elementary School, NM

Angels in My Garden

There are people in heaven,
Wearing big white robes and white wings.
They flew into my beautiful garden,
Sat down and had some tea with chocolatey disc of cooked dough.

I said why are you two here,
They said because you have the most beautiful colorful wonderland,
Of course I should have guessed that,
But I didn't,
Then the angels were done and went back to heaven.

Lisa Kelpien, Grade 6
Pope John XXIII Catholic School Community, AZ

Colors

If I were blue, I would be a bright silver river
The overalls that Peter Rabbit wears

If I were pink, I would be a sponge full of water
A shirt with a yellow sun and big flowers

If I were red, I would be a big rubber ball
A medium size bow in a little girl's hair

If I were green, I would be a yard of glistening grass
I would be a tulip sprouting from the ground

If I were purple, I would be a multiplication chart on a white desk
I would be a pair of Easter shoes

If I were white, I would be a rocket taking off into space
A sparkly snowflake falling from the sky

Amanda Bernick, Grade 4
East Evergreen Elementary School, MT

If I Were

If I were an animal, I'd be a zebra exploring the plains of Africa.
If I were a car, I'd be a yellow slugbug convertible.
If I were a city, I'd be Forest Grove, Oregon.
If I were a river, I'd be the Tiber.
If I were a pet, I'd be a dog that loved to go on walks in the forest.
If I were a food, I'd be a juicy, red, ripe strawberry.
If I were a planet I'd be hot, red Mars.
If I were a building, I'd be the Leaning Tower of Pisa.
If I were a famous person I'd be Audrey Hepburn.
If I were a sport, I'd be swimming.
If I were a country I'd be Italy.
If I were the world, I'd try to make world peace.

Olivia Vance, Grade 6
Patton Middle School, OR

Spring Is Here

I smelled strawberries, roses, and fresh made gingerbread houses.
The fresh twirling grass smells like peppermint.
Oh the sweet smells of spring after a cold winter day.

LaTijera Brana, Grade 4
Lewis E. Rowe Elementary School, NV

Mountains

Air cools down
Sun rises
Colored rocks gleam in the sun
Ice cold water running down the mountain spring
Winter is in the air.
Clouds drift through the sky
The pines always stay green.
The pink sun rises always
Never drops
Never until the time has come.
So don't mind.
Don't chop down those trees.
Think about it,
It is my home.

Sierra Bingham, Grade 4
Acacia Elementary School, AZ

Sun

When the sun comes up
it is a beautiful sight.
In the east it comes
in the west it sets.
The clouds are colorful pillows,
a pretty thing to see.
In the morning the sun shines like a big smile
and in the evening it runs away,
behind the mountain it goes.

Gina Orlando, Grade 6
Corpus Christi School, CO

Animal Inside Me

Hated and despised the raccoon plans his demise
sneaky and cunning yet brave and stunning
from the shadows nearest
you will see the eyes that show no fear
But beneath its fearless striped fur
you may see something even greater
a heart that's purer than a pot of gold
and a soul that stands out big and bold
so why must the raccoon be despised
if you have not looked through its eyes

Tommy Kroboth, Grade 6
Walt Clark Middle School, CO

The Voice of the Night

I feel the darkness of the sky.
I hear the rattle of the bushes in the wind.
I smell the danger in the air.
I see a shadow through the water.
I am tired but I stay awake and search through the night.
I do not know what I will find but I hope it is good because
I will not stop until it is found.
    Good night!

Riley Bearce, Grade 4
CLASS Academy, OR

The Singing Tree

The leaves rustle and fall to the ground.
They're red and beautiful all around.
They sway and drift to the soil.
They lie there dying and fading in the sun.

But new ones sprout in the spring.
Giving joy to all living things.
In the winter it is bare.
Snow gathering upon the branches.

The snow falls down all night and day.
Yet the tree still lives in a silent way
Just sleeping now until spring arrives
With sunny days and cool rain showers.

I can hear it singing all year long.
Through snow and rain, singing its song
You hear the wind like a dragon breathes fire
It makes them whistle and hum.

Jessa Wright, Grade 6
Southern Hills Middle School, CO

Faith

F ire in the hole! Do you have faith?
A wesome! Nothing is going to blow.
I n a matter of time this war will be over.
T roops fight for faith and freedom.
H urt, you hurt a troop when you lose faith.

Jesse Barney, Grade 5
Discovery Plus Academy, AZ

Rejected Puzzle Piece

I am the rejected puzzle piece,
    the one that stands alone.
I am the rejected puzzle piece,
    that's all I've ever known.
My edges are all bent, and my ridges are all ripped.
If you try to place me in, I'm surely not to fit.
You don't know where I came from,
    Maybe a dog bite or the rain.
But every time you judge, point, stare, laugh,
    My heart feels a little pain.

"That puzzle isn't for me," I say.
    "It's not where I belong."
You can't squeeze me in there,
    something is so wrong.
So then you throw me out,
    the rebel without a cause.
I am just unique, but everyone has flaws.
Maybe I fit better laying next to the puzzle,
To get away from all the crazy hustle and bustle.
But maybe you don't even know where I should be.
Maybe, just maybe, I'm better fitting in as me.

Grace Levy, Grade 6
St Anne School, WA

What Is It?
Cold as ice,
Hot as fire,
Gentle as a butterfly,
Dangerous as a lion,
Fast as a cheetah,
Slow as a slug,
WHAT IS IT?
Jamie Jiang, Grade 5
West Mercer Elementary School, WA

Full Moon
Full moon color of
an egg, yoke yellow, with a
pinch of milky white
Caressa Barnard, Grade 4
Scenic Park Elementary School, AK

The Fight
Love is a fighter
For freedom between people
So love who you are
Eduardo Jamaica, Grade 5
Bates Elementary School, CO

Arctic Wolves
In the frosty arctic,
The hunters, they all stray.
Silently hovering,
Searching for their prey.

At midnight they glisten,
Like moonlit air.
Swiftly watching,
With their gentle stare.

As they beg the moon,
For a longer night.
But soon that bright circle,
Is out of sight.

These beautiful creatures,
Whose ways are so grand.
They're different dogs,
A howling band.
Nicole Guilott, Grade 5
Barratt School, UT

Poetry in Motion
Wind through my mane.
I feel like I'm flying.
My heart races on.
My hooves pound the earth.
I'm faster than you.
Can't catch me.
Jessa Clay, Grade 5
Aurora Quest Academy, CO

Mia Hamm
Mia Hamm
Playing soccer? Yes, she can!
She kicks the ball down the field,
But her goal she must shield.
Lauren Thompson, Grade 4
Copper Canyon Elementary School, AZ

Cooking Storm!*
Cooking in the kitchen,
With a really hot griddle,
The whole house smells so good,
Flipping pancakes!
Yum, Yum, Yum!
Steaming hot flapjacks,
Making people warm,
Oh, what fun it is to do,
Cooking up a storm!

Oh, cooking's fun!
Cooking's fun!
Cooking all the time.
If only I could stop a moment
To make the last line rhyme!
Yum!
Katia Nalimova, Grade 4
Eton School, WA
Sung to the tune of Jingle Bells

Sisters
Sisters are very wiggly,
You tickle them to make them giggly.
All they do is nap nap nap,
To try and wake them you must slap.
You will get into many fights,
To get out of them you must bite.
They sure can tease,
They sure can wease,
But they sure are cute,
But oh my goodness they can toot.
Markie Marie Meredith, Grade 6
Syracuse School, UT

Mother Is Wonderful
Mother is beautiful.
   Mother is great.
Mother is kind.
   Mother is fine.
Mother is caring.
   Mother is sharing.
Mother is exploring.
   Mother is excellent.
Mother is Godly.
   Mother is worthy.
Mother is…
Madison Schneider, Grade 4
Acacia Elementary School, AZ

Prayer
I bend my knees, I fold my hands
I pray to the Lord again and again
At the end I say amen I love you Lord
And all my family and friends
Jackie Ryan, Grade 4
Christian Faith School, WA

Kite Experiment
Ben Franklin with his kite
Flew it in a storm without a fright.
It flew steadily through the night
And suddenly it was struck by a light,
Whizzing down the string to a house key.

With his knuckle he
Moved it to the key.
He knew this would be
Written in history.

His thought was true,
And now I'm telling you,
So you can tell someone else
Then they can tell a friend
And on and on till the end.
Dixon Cooney, Grade 5
Mary Blair Elementary School, CO

Spring
First day of spring,
flowers start to sprout,
leaves start to grow on trees.
Rain showers start to fall,
the sunny sun shines,
and lots of grass turning green.
Children riding bikes,
playing basketball.
Lots of rose bushes,
going to parks,
and playing baseball.
Philiciano Castiana, Grade 4
McCormick Elementary School, NM

Mystic Tales
The deep blue sea
Is part of me
The mystic blue
Is part of you
The wondrous tales
Of ancient whales
And oh the stories
Those divers wail
But, the deep blue sea
Will never completely
unfold to me
Hayley Watson, Grade 5
Julia Randall Elementary School, AZ

Loneliness

Loneliness is blue
It smells like a flower without a fragrance.
It looks like someone all alone without any hope.
It tastes like cold food that's supposed to be hot.
It sounds like nothing.
Loneliness feels like your friend is moving away.

Megan L. Peterson, Grade 6
Hidden Creek Elementary School, WA

Knowing

'Tis spring again,
I hear the Chinook whispering,
The sap is running fast
People are gathering with buckets.
I know, I've seen through the windows long ago,
What happens to the sap.
But they must hurry,
For I feel the summer sun coming
When the leaves grow.
Then fall will come
When the leaves turn gold and crimson
And fall to the ground.
Winter will come as it's always done
With snow resting on my arms and fingers.
I'll sag with sleepiness and weight.
I know, I've seen it all,
Again and again
For after all,
I'm the MAPLE TREE.

Dani Jordan, Grade 5
Colbert Elementary School, WA

Love

How can you know what you feel inside?
When you feel something deep?
Think think is the feeling real?
It's nothing that I could ever imagine
It's weird but yet amusing
The feeling it's coming to me
I don't know what to do? It's got me hypnotized
I am trying to think but I can't
It's making me go crazy
I can't stop thinking it's so complicated
It feels like nothing it has so many meanings
How can you get it? I'm trying but failing
How can you think? Think think focus focus
Why can't I stop it keeps on going on and on
Is it eternal? Does it have a beginning? How can you know?
I'm thinking deep thoughts my everyday thoughts
It's love you can never live without love
How can you live think eat
Without love there is no life no destiny
Without love you're simply not a person
Simply love is like a spirit trying to find its soul

Marwah Al-Jilani, Grade 5
Islamic School of Educational Trust, OR

Clock Fox

There once was a fluffy white fox who lived in a box
He made many big circular clocks
He would scrub and rub them in the bath tub
While he was singing rub-a-dub
He gave them to a funny fox who wears red socks

Madisen Stanley, Grade 5
Copper Creek Elementary School, AZ

My Grandpa

I think of you everyday since when you left us.
My dad told me stories about you, how you raised 11 kids.
I know grandma had a hard time when you left that day,
The whole family did.
We miss you.

I wish you were still here,
So I could get to know you.
You left too early, so I couldn't see you.
We miss you.

I know you're watching me to keep me safe,
From getting hurt.
If you were still here you would be there for me.
We miss you.

I wish you were still here with us,
But I know you're in a better place.
I know I'll meet you one day.
We miss you.

Skyler Speakthunder, Grade 6
Harlem Elementary School, MT

I Am

I am nice and funny
I wonder why people are so mean
I hear dogs barking
I see a monster in the closet
I want to live in a mansion
I am nice and funny.

I pretend I am a dog
I feel scared around spiders
I touch my grandpa in my dreams
I worry that I might fall on my roller blades
I cry when I think of people dying
I am nice and funny.

I understand that people love me
I say God is my shepherd
I dream that I am in Heaven with people I love
I try to do my best all of the time
I hope I will go to Heaven when I die
I am nice and funny.

Mari Stumpf, Grade 5
Kingman Academy of Learning, AZ

Giants

On day I was walking and
Not really thinking
The stars and the moon
Seemed a blur in the sky.
I saw a small child
Who was smiling and sitting and
Chanting, "Oh, why, why, why…"
I knelt by the child,
Asked her why she was sitting
She looked and then she replied,
"I'm thinking about
The stars and the moon and the
Darkness and all kinds of light
About kindness and clouds
And small cones of ice cream
And the way the wind sounds like a sigh.
The world, my friend stranger
Is full of good people,
But most people just can't see
That while children to you are all puny and small,
You grown-ups are giants to me."

Breanna Bliss, Grade 6
Eton School, WA

Millie Mae

My dog and I are special friends
For me there is no doubt
As we play and laugh all day
I know what love's about

She lifts my spirits, knows my feelings
And when I'm feeling low
She licks my face and cuddles warmly
She always seems to know

My dog and I, we are companions
And in my heart she will stay,
Through all my life, love will be strong
For my little Millie Mae.

Chelsea Guyot, Grade 6
Pope John XXIII Catholic School Community, AZ

Black and White

Black is the crime in the streets
Black is pollution
Black is smoking
Black is the deaths every day
Black is the fire that burns everything

White is the shining light
White is the enforcement that stops the crime
White is pollution free cars
White is the cures that lowers the death rate
White is the water that puts out the fire.

Kyle Burleson, Grade 6
Walt Clark Middle School, CO

Worriness

To be worried is to be frightened
To feel worried is to feel inside a small box like you can't do anything
To feel worried is to feel pain
To be worried is like shrinking and being shut in a book

Paxten Foster, Grade 6
Hidden Creek Elementary School, WA

The Beach

I'm walking on the beach
sand between my toes
I see beach balls flying through the air
I feel the nice cool breeze
some people are playing volley ball
the waves are so much fun to play in
people are tanning, and walking dogs
The beach is so much fun
It's fun to swim, and to find shells
I have found so many shells
There are so many cool things about the beach
You can find star fish or watch birds
Sometimes there might be surfers.
At night you can have a campfire or walk on the beach
Also at low tide you can walk farther than before
You can build sand castles, but don't put it too close to the water
Even sometimes you can bury yourself under the sand.
When you go to the beach don't forget sunglasses
I love the beach so much, I wish I could build a house
Well it's almost time to go home
but, I know I'm coming back tomorrow

Amy Glatt, Grade 6
St John Vianney School, WA

Mother Mountain

She hugged me
In a tight and motherly embrace
She sang to me,
Hymns pouring from her green cloak
She fed me,
Berries and treats hidden in her leafy pockets
She talked to me,
Her voice airy but withering
She clothed me,
Her many skins wrapping around my thin frame.
She listened to me,
Humming in agreement with my every word.
She danced with me
Her slow and heavy movements countering my quick and flitty jumps.
She watered me,
Her crisp endless supply of fresh drink watering my dust ridden throat.
She protected me,
Her hard arms and legs thrust out to fight off attackers.
And so without worry,
I put my head on her shoulder,
And nestled into the sweet, mothering mountain.

Andrea Molina, Grade 6
Southern Hills Middle School, CO

Nature
Fog is like running through the clouds.
Water is a blue 1st place ribbon.
The sun is a huge golden fireball
Falling down on the Earth.
Tree bark is like brown rocks
Falling from mountaintops.
Nature is such a beautiful place.
Amber Corbett, Grade 4
Fulton Elementary School, CO

Stars
Stars shine brightly
in the night's cool air waiting
for their time to go
Maria Bourn, Grade 4
Scenic Park Elementary School, AK

My Grandpa
My grandpa is a friend,
who lived in New Mexico's end.
His family was awful farmy,
So instead he joined the Army.
But I think of him in my head,
because now my grandpa is dead.
Logan Miller, Grade 4
Acacia Elementary School, AZ

Reading
I do not like reading
There's always a test
I wish we could draw
Or take a nap and rest
I want to do poetry
I'd rather do math
I'd rather fly in a plane
Or take a bubble bath
I wish reading was done
I like to draw in the sun
I want reading to be fun
I'd rather be in P.E. and run
Teacher, ban reading please
I am ready to beg on my knees.
Gabriella Esposito, Grade 4
Rogers Elementary School, NV

Christmas Bells
Christmas bells are ringing
Carolers are singing
I sleep under the tree
My soul is filled with glee
Everybody knows
That I like snow
I just love when the Christmas bells ring
And when the carolers sing
Jessica Disotell, Grade 5
St Mary's School, ID

With a Friend
With a friend
I can feel great.

With a friend
I can tell secrets.

With a friend
I can feel important.

With a friend
I feel I can do anything.

With a friend
I can have fun.

With a friend
I can feel good.
Elizabeth Hawley, Grade 5
Washington Traditional School, AZ

Rainbow
It's red, orange and yellow
It's green, purple and blue
It comes after it rains
when on the ground there's dew

I love to watch the colors
All straight and aligned
Some day I may see one up close
and maybe magic I will find

Sun when it shines
Snow when it snows
Hail when it hails
and grass when it grows

All of those are nice
but rainbows are the best
They are brighter
and more colorful than the rest

There may be gold
at the end
I'll climb to the top
Then I'll slide and descend
Kaycee Cronk, Grade 5
Harlem Elementary School, MT

Snow Fort
snow fort
big, white
protects, covers, melts
winter club house
ice fort
Austin Jensen, Grade 5
Ammon Elementary School, ID

Tennis
My racquet is a part of me.
Another arm,
It helps me open doors
To my dreams.
Sends me,
To another world.
Gives me power,
To fight my enemies,
And take control
Of the court.

I take baby steps
To rush to the ball
Just in time.

It doesn't matter,
Win or lose.
As long as I
Put my heart,
Into every
Shot.
Amy Lin, Grade 6
Walker Middle School, OR

Precipitation
Snow
Pretty, white
Falling, landing, melting
Very beautiful
Sleet
Brett Carpenter, Grade 4
Miller Elementary School, WY

Tiger
A tiger
soft and huge
runs and jumps
silently
Cat
Cara Anderson, Grade 6
Fox Creek Jr High School, AZ

Home to the Fairy
I looked in a hollow tree
And saw in the hole
A moss blanket
And a cobweb pillow
And a mushroom with a small cup.

I saw a candle with a bit of fire
(I think the fairy reads in bed)
I got out parchment and wrote
"Please fairy, come out and play.
I would like to meet you."
Samantha Antenucci, Grade 4
St Andrews Episcopal School, NM

Swimming

S lowly drowning in
W ater so cold
I t feels like ice.
M any have failed
M any have succeeded,
I n learning to swim.
N ow I know I was not one,
G one, gone, gone, my life now is.

Andrew Mickelson, Grade 5
Thomas Edison Charter School, UT

If I Were the Teacher…

If I were the teacher,
Everything would be fun!
Kids would be able to
Skip or run.

Tests would be gone,
And homework, too.
We would play games
Like Cranium Cadoo.

Lunch would be good,
Not toxic and yucky.
Children would eat any time,
Isn't that lucky?

If I were the teacher
Everything would be great!
Kids would no longer
Want to be late.

Lexi Hassel, Grade 6
Bradford Intermediate School, CO

Beautiful Things About Spring

Spring rains are
as wet as my
dog getting a
bath
Spring flowers
are as cool as getting
dabbed with colorful
paintbrushes
spring foods sometimes
are as cold as
getting a brain
freeze
spring sun is as
bright as a lightbulb
getting shined in my eyes
In spring
I like
to climb in a countless amount of
trees

Tiffany Abbott, Grade 4
Skyline Elementary School, WA

I Am From

I am from the smell of candy
Baking in the kitchen

From my aunt May's front porch
Looking upon a little town

I am from the smell of melted chocolate
Whispering "follow me"

From a house full of odd love
All around me

I am from candy always on the table
Waiting for me to come home

Samantha Burns, Grade 4
Grass Valley Elementary School, NV

John's Lawn

There once was a lad named John,
Who had a humongous lawn,
He bought a mower,
To make it lower,
And that was the end of John.

Matthew Vaughan, Grade 4
Brush Creek Elementary School, CO

Moon

M eandering all night
O n top of the sky
O ver the clouds
N ever anything but blue

Billy Fraser, Grade 6
Fox Creek Jr High School, AZ

Nature

Nature is good,
Nature is kind,
I always can see,
I always can find.

Wherever I go,
I just look above,
To see the best nature,
All nature's love.

Nature shows good,
Never shows bad,
If nature was evil,
That is just sad.

Nature is good,
Nature is kind,
I always can see,
I always can find.

Samantha Sun, Grade 4
Durham Elementary School, OR

I Am

I'm not who you think I am.
I'm not who I think I am.
I'm not worthless.

I'm taking a stand,
Every step I take
I understand myself more.
You can't tell me who I am.
I am me.

I want to change the world.
I won't hesitate again.
I'm not who you say I am.
I stand here,
Lost, grieving,
But I am strong.

I will shine.
I can make a difference,
I'm not a lot of things.
But I am. I can.
And I will.

Lauren Restivo, Grade 6
East Middle School, CO

Smile

A smile like spring sunshine
Warming
Soft
Gentle

A smile like the sun on a windy day
Mischievous
Tricking
Laughing

A smile like the sun on the snow
Twinkling
Beautiful
Warming in the cold

A smile like the sun on the ocean
Burning
Warming
Blazing

A smile like sunshine

Kate Rosenlof, Grade 6
Southern Hills Middle School, CO

Seashell's Dream

The seashell sits calm
Water hides it in the sand
Still hopes to be found

Kate Darling, Grade 5
St Cyril Elementary School, AZ

Winter

I walk out to the crisp morning
The wind shoots an icy breeze down my spine
Petite snowflakes sail the harsh wind
Landing gently on my nose and eyelashes
I plow my way through the freshly
    Fallen snow,
    And I know
    That winter has arrived.

Morgan Briggs, Grade 6
Southern Hills Middle School, CO

Friendship Is Something Real!!

Friendship isn't something that just comes out of the ordinary.
It's something real
it's something you can feel
deep in your heart.
Don't even start
this is for real.
It's someone who you can laugh with.
Or even call them and do math with.
Friendship is something real!!!

Kiara Smith, Grade 6
Hunt Middle School, WA

The Beach in Alabama

The waves wash up and down the shore.
Your feet tingle as the water sprays on them.
The water pushes on the sand and moves it along.
As the water washes up, seashells are left behind,
The seashells come in different colors, shapes and sizes.
Children run up and down in the water,
They splash and swim.
Families talk and play with each other,
While the rays of the sun reflect down toward them.
Surfing and building sand castles are fun to do.
After swooping and diving around everyone,
Seagulls fly ahead looking for bits of food to eat.
As the waves wash up, the kids play.
Soon, the sun disappears.
It is time to go home.

Maggie Varuska, Grade 6
Walt Clark Middle School, CO

inside this poem

undiscovered
inside a cave
darkness awaits you
never been seen
never been spoken
undisturbed slumber
unawakened stalactites
waiting for mortal eyes to see
hearing us, tasting us in their giant mouths
full of dead water struck paths

Tanner Goldsberry, Grade 6
Walt Clark Middle School, CO

Love and Hate

Love, coarsing to your face.
Love, powerful like God in Heaven.
Love, peaceful and relaxed.
Love, wonderful seeing the planets of the Universe.
Love, cheerful child on their birthday.
Love, runs through our soul.
Love, has no hate.
Hate, has found some of our hearts and torn them.
Hate, sticks like glue but we always release from it.
Hate, is lonely like a star in the night sky.
This dreadful thing came into this world like magic.
Oh, hate whose heart are you going to tear through next?
I wish love could conquer you,
people would never hate again.
Someday, somehow love is going to conquer you.

Alexandrea Anderson-Romero, Grade 4
Khalsa Montessori Elementary School, AZ

New York

The Statue of Liberty stands very high
It looks like it touches the sky.
It is a scene of freedom
For people who come from England.

The Empire State Building has a point at the top
As people drive by they come to a stop.
The building is much taller than any they've seen;
It's gray, tall, and lean; it's fit for a queen.

Times Square is a place where you can see plays,
But you have to wait in line for days
To see actors in the fancy costumes they wear —
Some with long braids in their hair.

There is a place called Central Park;
You don't want to be there when it's dark.
There are scary people everywhere
And all of them have crazy hair.

To get around, now that's a different story,
The subway is fun and not boring.
The smell from the sewer is a fright,
It's always the worst at night.

Joshua Chamberlain, Grade 6
Reid School, UT

The Flip Out

I want to go outside,
my mom won't let me —
because I came home late,
and now she doesn't trust me!
I don't know why she flipped out about nothing
she probably hit her head or something!

Gabrielle Ames, Grade 5
Bennett Elementary School, NV

Landscapes

The clear blue sky
looks like dashing colorful waters.
Three mountains
shine like mirrors
reflecting off the water.
Scattered trees
give us fresh air
with their wonderful
green pine needles.
The amazing water
makes the Garden of the Gods
wonderful
with its sparkling blue
amazement.

Jeffrey Davis, Grade 4
Audubon Elementary School, CO

The Champion of Football

At football
I will be best.
Being good
at wide receiver
makes me important.
Football comes to me
and I come to it more.
To be a champion
at football
feels like
being in love.

Vincent Jester, Grade 4
Acacia Elementary School, AZ

The Other Day

The other day I saw you,
Looking calm and peaceful,
The other day I saw you,
Playing in the meadow,
You were there,
You were everywhere,
We need your help,
Please, please come back?
Everyone needs you,
Our hearts are out to you,
When we saw you the other day,
How could I have let you go?
Most important person in the world,
We look up to you but most of all I do,
How could you leave us?
It was your own home,
Now you live far, far away,
I repeat, please come back,
Again I repeat, please come back,
Where are you?
I weep always.

Mariam Said, Grade 6
Ismet School, OR

Did I Say That?

Rumors say that Reagan had a memory loss.
At a press conference with the boss —
A reporter spoke up who was not a foe.
"President, you said you would resign if your memory started to go."
Reagan laughed and said, "I don't remember saying that Ross!"

Christopher Chin, Grade 4
Eton School, WA

Swift Hermes

Hermes, messenger god,
Living on Mount Olympus
With his father Zeus, his brothers and sisters,
Young Hermes, so swift and happy, protective and intelligent,
Doesn't care much for women but loves communication —
He hears everything.
Proud of the gift he was given,
He doesn't need much but gives health, protection and messages.
He fears nothing, because he can move swiftly enough to escape any harm
And has no time to feel anything anyway.
He is always looking forward to meeting the next person
And giving some sort of message!

Makayla Begay, Grade 6
East Valley Academy, AZ

Mr. Pete

While I was walking down the street I met a dog named Mr. Pete
He had no bones he had no hair he just limped everywhere
He was a very odd dog who smelt like a hog
Mr. Pete had a nose that grew down to his toes
His tongue was so long that when he walked it left a line like a piece of chalk
I followed the line to where he went and found a bag of peppermints
He offered me one but I said no for I saw him touch it with his nose
As I looked at the bag I saw something green it was something I wish I had never seen
As I left him there with his stuff I went home I had seen enough
No one knows who Mr. Pete is but he's the strangest dog there is

Rebekah Jillson, Grade 6
Meridian Middle School, ID

All About Aaron

I used to be a tiny and scared kid but now I'm a big and bold 5th grader.
I used to love chewy candies but now love shockingly sour candies.
I used to like plastic toy figures but now I like to play on my adorable PS2.
I used to hate banging loud instruments but now I play one.
I used to make fun of old creepy people but now I respect them.
I used to play in old boxes but now I like to play hardcore paintball.
I used to like bald eagles but now I love fat pigs.
I used to like little baby sing-along songs but now I like amusing Green Day.
I used to love baby blue but now I love dazzling silver.
I used to want to be a teacher but now I want to be a pro skater.
I used to like small critters but now I think they are better than dogs.
I used to like to pretend but now I like to play mad soccer.
I used to love guns but now I hate them.
I used to love big frosted cakes but now I hate the guts out of them.
I used to like to play in go-carts but now I like to do extreme biking.

Aaron Green, Grade 5
Wheeler Elementary School, AZ

Dogs

Dogs, dogs, I love dogs.
Dogs are fun.
Dogs are sweet.
I went to the park
And guess who I meet?
Lots of dogs all colors and sizes.
They are all in a contest to win lots of prizes.
But the dog I love best is my dog Amanda.
She looks really neat if she's dressed like a panda.
I entered her in the contest
And she won the Best Dressed.
We took her home and gave her a treat.
We really like her.
We think she is cool.
She likes to chase balls,
But never brings them back.
She likes to chase rabbits,
Especially in pipes
She has never ever caught one,
But we know what she likes the best.
Dogs, dogs, I love dogs.

Naomi Thompson, Grade 6
Liberty Ranch Christian School, NM

Great Spirits

Great spirits are with you every day.
They guide you through your troubled times.
Great spirits tell you right or wrong.
Be thankful for your great spirits.
They're a great pleasure to have.
Great spirits is something that is given
by the goodness in you.
Take a good look at the good side in you
for it will show a great deal.
Love and cherish the great spirits in you.
The great spirits in you will love you
forever and eternity.

Idalis Calvert, Grade 4
Evergreen Elementary School, OR

Sleepy Head

My eyes are weary, and my head is heavy,
My feet can barely walk.
My knees are aching, my eyes are red,
And my mouth lets out a yawn.
I climb into bed and pull the covers,
And lay down on my pillow.
I toss and turn, and wiggle and jiggle,
But I just can't fall asleep.
Then a light flicks on and my eyes try to squint,
My head is still dizzy
But then a voice calls out to me,
"It's time to wake up!"

Anisha Datta, Grade 4
Jackson Elementary School, OR

Whispers and Things

I sit at night in this big, big house,
sitting with no light.
I hear a mouse,
at least I think it is a mouse,
and it could have been a louse.
Whatever could it be?
Then I hear a roar,
that could have been a boar.
Oh, the whispers I heard,
the whispers I could not even see.
I was scared, I was hurt,
everything was a blur.
I didn't find my mom,
oh, not even did I find a bomb, but…
…I paused for 22 seconds,
I did not even reason what a shadow I saw,
coming from the swimming pools.
I wonder, did I scare you?
Sorry if I did, it's only April Fools!

Emily Neader, Grade 4
Linderman School, MT

Love

Love gleams with red passion,
Swirls around your tongue like melted chocolate,
Soon, the scent of blue roses sprays me like the water
from the refreshing ocean,
Puckering up their lips a couple kisses on the sunlit lake,
Joy to hearts it's Valentine's Day.

Brittany Rammell, Grade 6
Lolo Elementary School, MT

Tendril Seeds

Spiraling tendrils of rainbow woven into the sky
leading to infinity that's mortality
plummeting waterfall into slowness
leaving behind ruffles grass
sunrise fingers Milky Way's labyrinthine path

In barren eternity's immense stars
sending light, fire through darkening universe
screeching chaos where the brink of existence rests
in delicate flower petals unbeknownst to our world

Push this way, that way
trying to close the curtain of existence
trying to stop stillness, quiet destruction of life's flower
dropping diamond seed picked from the finest nebulas
wispy leaves guarding their fragile flowers
bearing blazing fruit
eternal void pouring with fiery thirst to live

Alone in a murky world, birth begins
diamond seed of life

Rebecca Paxton, Grade 6
Khalsa Montessori Elementary School, AZ

The Sunset

As it goes down
Over the plain of land
The sky darkens
The clouds dark blue

The land turns black
As the pink and orange
Sun goes down to sleep
Some little light fills the air
Yet darkens very quickly

The feeling of calmness in the air
The silence of creatures everywhere
Towns are ready to sleep
When night creatures come out
What a beautiful sunset
Casey Felker, Grade 6
Walt Clark Middle School, CO

Trees

Trees rattling in
frosty breezes blowing from
the mountains up North
Brennen Major, Grade 4
Scenic Park Elementary School, AK

Moon

Stay in the night
so big
so bright
giving us light in the
dark dark
night.
But moon moon,
so so bright in the night
you're out too soon
you're the lightest one
except for sun
letting us see in the
dark dark
night.
Greg Pollard, Grade 4
Scenic Park Elementary School, AK

Christmas

C hrist's birthday
H appy holidays
R udolph leads the sleigh
I t's always fun
S anta comes
T was the night before Christmas…
M erry Christmas is fun to say
A t last it's almost here
S now is always welcome
Tierney Ball, Grade 5
St Mary's School, ID

Champions

Shooting a
bow is
very fun and
uplifting.

When you
pull the bow back
your arms tighten
and it feels
really good.

When you let
the bow string go
the bow gives
a big jerk
and before
you know it
the arrow hits
the target.
James Turner, Grade 4
Acacia Elementary School, AZ

My Soul

I look out the window,
I see the stars brighten,
I think I should run away,
But my soul is at home,
In my bed,
My home is my heart's desire
Cheyenne Bell, Grade 4
New Emerson School, CO

Strange Thing

There's this strange thing,
It does not sing,
It doesn't make a sound,
Yet it's all around,
Here in Alaska,
It sits on rocks,
It gets in my socks,
It falls from the sky,
It gets in my eye,
What is this thing,
I don't know,
Now excuse me while I play in this thing,
Called snow.
Elena Melendrez, Grade 6
Desert Mountain School, AZ

Glooper Blooper

Glooper Blooper is nice and fat
Even bigger than my tabby cat.
He's green and blue with purple spots
And tiny yellow polka dots.
Lyndsi Johnston, Grade 5
Monroe Elementary School, CO

My Cell Phone

Ring ring my cell phone go
It sounds just like a radio
Final two rings I answer the phone
I say, "Hello is this home"
Minutes go by on my phone
I think about that ring ring
It goes ting ting
Turns out my friend calls
He says, "You want to go to the mall"
I ask my aunt says sure
I go to the mall
My girlfriend calls
My final ring ring
Shawn O'Keefe, Grade 6
Walt Clark Middle School, CO

Something New

One bright day,
A smell of good food in the air,
Coming home with fresh cut hair,
Women fill the room,
Gather around something new,
Something fresh and clean
Can you guess what I see?
A newborn baby,
In my arms,
Eyes closed tight,
Pink blanket around her,
My necklace white,
She makes my life better.
Kyle Kelly, Grade 6
Walt Clark Middle School, CO

An Ocean

I am an ocean,
I wave with time.
Rushing my body
Against the shore,
I call out my song
From the bottom
Of the ocean floor.
Trevor Jenkins, Grade 4
Hunters Glen Elementary School, CO

Before and After

lovely lazy waters
long sandy beaches
little grass huts
brown juicy coconuts

black rough waters
hot trash filled parking lots
ugly brick buildings
not a tree in sight
Maddy Hanon, Grade 6
Eagle Point Middle School, OR

Stockelman Takes Gold!!

The Olympics are back in town.
Everyone is jumping up and down!
USA has come to play.
Skis, snowboards, luge, and more
but ice hockey shouldn't bore!
"Do girls play ice hockey?"
Yes they do and boy, they will amaze you!
Kelly Stockelman is the captain, and she'll take gold!
It never gets old.
Today, Stockelman will take gold! Hooray!
　　　At the big game…
　　She skates, she skates, she goes and goes
everyone is on they're toes!
Left and right she curves and curves,
the Olympics have somebody new,
out of the blue, in the spotlight!!
She shoots, she scores!! The crowd goes wild!
The gold goes to Stockelman, what a riot!

Kelly A. Stockelman, Grade 6
Corpus Christi School, CO

Escaping from Winter and Emerging into Spring

Brilliant sun lighting up the earth.
Straight trees bending in the wind.
Fuzzy newborn birds chirping in their nest.
Escaping from winter and emerging into spring.

The swish of fishing lines soaring out to sea.
Everything hushed while I listen to the sweet melody.
Birds twittering in their nest while being fed.
Escaping from winter and emerging into spring.

Sweet fragrance of flowers flying by my nose.
Fishy smell of fish hovering above the lake.
Tempting cherry pie cooling at the window.
Escaping from winter and emerging into spring.

Buttery toast popping in the toaster.
Ripe apples roaring to come out.
Appetizing strawberries leaking out my mouth.
Escaping from winter and emerging into spring.

Leathery petals of new lilies in bloom.
Slippery scales of fish sliding under my fingers.
Sandy beaches with sandcastles and footprints.
Escaping from winter and emerging into spring.

Josh Zufelt, Grade 6
Bella Vista Elementary School, UT

Daniel Crawford

He is a person dear to me
when it comes to football he's no wannabe
tall and blonde
the limit to his love, not the sky it's beyond.

Hanna Wilson, Grade 6
Fox Creek Jr High School, AZ

Flying

Why can't I fly like a butterfly
flapping its wings and drinking nectar from a flower?

Why can't I fly like a bird
soaring through the light blue sky?

William Nussel, Grade 4
Meadow Point Elementary School, CO

I Am an Ordinary Star But Very Unique

I am an ordinary Star but very unique
I wonder if I will become like a hero to people
I hear the crowd roar my name
I see the medals glistening in the sun
I am the one who will wear that symbol
I am an ordinary Star but very unique

I pretend I make the winning catch
I feel the sun heating on my face
I touch the winning medals
I worry about the loss
I cry "YES" when we are the WINNERS
I am an ordinary Star but very unique

I understand a loss is a loss
I say, "We tried, we did our best"
I dream that we will still succeed
I try my hardest to get to my goal
I hope our team will try, like me
I am an ordinary Star but very UNIQUE

Jesse Smout, Grade 6
H Guy Child School, UT

Untitled

I just received the terrible news
about my friend, I did lose.
Because of some unaware driver,
who hit her.
This undeserved deed,
now leaves
me with terrible sadness,
I must confess
I feel hatred building up inside me.
How could this person make her leave?
This world with family and friend.
But eventually, my heart mends.
Because life goes on
without this friend who I've known for so long.
Even though her life has deceased
the memory of her in my heart will never leave.
For this fallen friend,
I will remember to my life's end.
I will never forget
my beloved pet.

Maddie Garner, Grade 6
Colbert Elementary School, WA

Falling in Fog

Walking, Walking,
You stumble, fall
Fall into fog,

Grasp a jacket, dash outside
Peer into fog's sublime depth
Gaze at its beauty
Its rolling clouds of mystery
Wander into it
Inhale what you have desired
Devour fog's nothingness
Seize it, but no
It creeps away from your fingers
Realize that you must admire fog
For it has a mind of its own
Seek it, absorb its serenity
As it glides away
Know that you have just
Fallen into fog,

Walking, Walking,
You glance back
Back to fog.

Sumeet Patwardhan, Grade 5
Kyrene De Las Brisas School, AZ

The Beat of My Heart

My heart beats,
Beats with all my compassions,
Music, animals, shoes
The rhythm of my heart.
I may see someone,
Feel something,
Or do something,
Making my heart skip a beat
My heart can be broken,
By many different things,
People, deaths, or friends
At many different times…
My heart booms with emotions,
Compassion, and love
Only I know the true beat of my heart

Aelix Cunningham, Grade 6
Walker Middle School, OR

Recipe

Page turning and lots of chapters
Suspense and mystery
Staying up late
Sometimes fictional history
Good description
Getting hooked
More advanced
These make a good book.

Joey Mohler, Grade 6
Patton Middle School, OR

Happiness

Happiness is when you lay in the green grass.
With the sun shining and I have a chocolate ice cream cone in my hand.
The scent of fresh brownies in the air.
A river rippling nearby.
The grass swaying in the wind.
I imagine smiley faces in the clouds.

Brady Cather, Grade 6
Lolo Elementary School, MT

Hermana Sol Hermana Luna

Moon oh Moon
how lonely it must be swimming in a sea of darkness
the only friends you have
the twinkling stars
Moon oh Moon
no one can hear your sad melody
drifting through the heavenly skies
no one giving you credit for your great brilliance
yet at night you never leave your companion, Earth
you even let Earth's creation trample your surface
as you linger in the dark
the wolves and I accept your brilliance as day approaches
your brilliance often neglected until the sun drifts into the pitless void of night
are you receded to be neglected
Sun oh Sun
you mock the moon as you dance across the sky
you bring joy as your brilliance shines
God's nimble fingers formed you so beautifully
you bring joy to the land, melting away weeping clouds
you are accepted by all
but the wolves and I can see past your disguise

Marshal Tucker, Grade 6
Khalsa Montessori Elementary School, AZ

The Pathway

When the pathway fades, the hills grow high; the woods are long and unbroken
When the roadway fades, and the world slows down, the lights of the city grow dark
When the railroad fades, the track is lost, but the wildflowers grow high
When the trail fades, hate is gone; all that's left is an unbroken world
When the pathway fades, a life is born; it's better there, when your pathway fades

Adam Woznick, Grade 5
Nederland Elementary School, CO

Sports, Not I!

There once was a girl who really wanted to play a sport.
She played basketball, but found she was too short.
Next, she tried to run track, but found it was speed she did lack.
She cried, "An athlete I'm not! I'll give the choir a shot!"
She said, "I'll sing like a bird!"
But there was only screeching that could be heard.
So she decided to take up ballet,
But she went on the wrong day.
There was no goal she could meet,
So she decided not to be an athlete.

Amy Davis, Grade 5
Terra Linda Elementary School, OR

At the End of the World

At the end of the world are mermaids and flying elephants.
At the end of the world there are giants and dragons.
At the end of the world are giant butterflies and phoenixes.
At the end of the world imaginative things live,
They dance, sing, and play.
At the end of the world you cannot go,
At the end of the world.

Danielle Spring, Grade 5
Uplands Elementary School, OR

My Daddy Is Fun

My daddy looks fun because he is fun.
He laughs because it's fun.
He plays games because it's fun.
He spends time with his family because it's fun.
He loves fun.
My daddy is fun.

Amberlyn Shaver, Grade 4
Christian Faith School, WA

Summer

Summer is special, that I'm thinking,
The same song I hear, that sparrow's singing.

I see a splendor beach, splashing water, and people surfing.
I see colorful parks, sunshine, somersaults and kids swinging.

We play special sports, and I ride in a speedboat.
I taste juicy strawberries, spicy subs, and salmon roast.

I wear sunscreen so I don't get sunburns
And I wear shorts so I'm not hot.

In summer I think sunrise and sunset are worth seeing,
That I wish summer the season is never ending.

Rajas Agashe, Grade 4
Eton School, WA

Math

Math I can't relate
Tests are what I hate
You have to use math books
But, the numbers have strange looks
I'd rather go to lunch
And eat my cracker crunch
I'd rather do social studies
Or at least play with my buddies
Specials I'd rather go
So I can play in the snow
If we watch a video about math
I'll take a bath
Teacher, if we use more calculators
We won't be such math haters.

Jade Munson, Grade 4
Kathy L Batterman Elementary School, NV

Blue

Blue is for the rain
Gently falling from the sky
Like a tear that streams delicately down a face

Blue is for sad memories
Swirling around in your head
Like an unstoppable tornado

But blue is also
A clear and endless sky
Like a big blue quilt to snuggle in on a chilly day

Rachel Lockhart, Grade 5
Maplewood K-8 Co-Op, WA

Now You See Me

When will it be my turn?
I hope it's far from now.
I do not want to be like the other trees;
Most have been knocked out of the ground,
To make room for new houses.
If money is such an object,
Then what am I, art supplies?
If that's not the case, then why send us to our grave?
I wish the humans would stop cutting us down.
If they would only stop to see our beauty,
And look at life through our eyes,
They'd see a cold, dark place.
Before them, life was great!
Seeing the sky,
Being homes for birds,
And creating shade.
Now, all we see is smog.
No bird wants to live in a smoggy area,
When will this nightmare end?

Samantha Vitale, Grade 6
Walt Clark Middle School, CO

I Used to Be But Now I Am

I used to be a cute, stubborn, petite girl.
But now I am in meager trouble more often.
I used to be bad at math.
But now I need help with challenging writing, and reading.
I used to be a skinny bone.
But now I have some petite fat.
I used to be bossy.
But now I just go my own silly way.
I used to be picked on, enwound, bothered.
But now I have a little sister whom I can pick on.
I used to live with my mom.
But now I live with an enormous gang of family members.
I used to be a horrible 4th grader.
But now I am a 5th grader that is smart and has lots of friends.
I used to be quiet and very shy.
But now I am loud as can be, and a strong individual.

Mercedes R. Springer, Grade 5
Wheeler Elementary School, AZ

A Coral Reef

When I swam down by the ocean reef
I was plunged into total disbelief

Before me I saw red, green, blue
What a beautiful ocean view!

Little fish swam around me
In this large, salty sea

Bubbles float up to the surface
The whole world seemed to go amiss

"I will not forget this in my whole life,"
I thought as I watched the wildlife.
Lauren Bazley, Grade 4
Eton School, WA

Summer

Like a volcano exploding
Hot day
Heat wave
Monsoon
A day that will only come once
Garrett Hoffman, Grade 4
Lincoln Elementary School, AZ

Hot Chocolate

I like hot chocolate
smooth, creamy and nice
it tastes much better than
7-up on ice!
Laura Sorensen, Grade 6
Syracuse School, UT

Sights of Christmas

Teddy bears, rocking horses,
Christmas takes its usual courses
Candy canes, Christmas sweets,
Those are real holiday treats.

Christmas trees, winter sleighs,
I look out in a dreamy gaze
Balsam wreaths and Christmas lights
Make up very beautiful sights.

Gingerbread with mugs of eggnog
Eaten with the Christmas Yule Log
Reindeer and chiming bells
I can hear the joyful yells.

White snowmen and a stocking
Christmastime has come a knocking
Sparkling ornaments, a Christmas gift
Gives my spirits quite a lift!
Emily Butcher, Grade 6
Lewis & Clark Elementary School, MT

Music Makes Me Lose Control

The music I like sweetens my soul.
It gives me power to do it all.
The powerful rhythm and perfect beat
Makes me start to move my feet.
I start singing and jumping.
Londyn Lopez, Grade 6
Green Valley Christian School, NV

Differences

In the world there are
Billions of people.
Some are tall, short, or
Average-sized.
Others are small,
Average, skinny, or large.
There are also many different
Shades of skin color.
White, black, pink, brown,
Olive, tan, or yellow.
Some have hair that
Is straight, curly, afros, spiky
Thin, thick, long, short or none at all.
But none of this matters
Because everyone is equal.
And no one is better than another
Just because of the way they look
Or by the color of their skin.
Everyone is equal because we all have
A belly button!
Myles Van Vliet, Grade 6
Barbara Bush Elementary School, AZ

Kiara Mancha — Me!

K ind
I ntelligent
A wesome
R eally cool
A mazing

D elightful
A thletic
N ice
I nspirational
E xciting
L oving
L ucky
E nergetic

M eaningful
A spiration
N osey
C ute
H appy
A ppreciative
Kiara Danielle Mancha, Grade 4
Gold Canyon Elementary School, AZ

Everything Changes

As the water fills the ocean
As I get older
Everything changes
As the days go by
As the year goes through
Everything changes
As the grass grows tall
As the flowers start blooming
Everything changes
As the stars sparkle in the sky
As the sunset fills the sky
Everything changes
As the seasons come and go
As the holidays go by
Everything changes
As houses get built
As seniors go to college
Everything changes
Every minute of every day
Nothing stays the same.
Jessica Galvin, Grade 6
Heath Middle School, CO

Math

Math really isn't fun
I'd rather run and run
There are way too many tests
Can't we sit and rest
When I can't understand
You tell me to expand
And when I do
You say it's not true
If we could draw or play
Math would be the best time of the day
If we could do science or art
I would not want to part
Teacher, if you would let us play
I would not be so gray.
Cheyenne Tolbert, Grade 4
Rogers Elementary School, NV

My Little Old Chair

The chair I sit in every day
Is getting old in every way
I think it's just about to break
That's not a chance I'd like to take
All the screws are falling out
And if I fell I think I'd shout
I'd like to get a new one soon
Maybe I'll get one sometime in June
But one day I just sat right down
And I fell right onto the ground
I think the time has finally come
For me to buy a brand new one
Erica Miller, Grade 5
Spring Creek Country Day School, CO

Now Gone Forever Lost

Darkness is around you,
Nowhere you can go,
You scream, you shout, you yelp for help,
But you are alone,

You see visions of your family and friends,
The ones you held so dear,
But now they are gone,
forever lost,
They will not reappear,

It is all a blur,
the memories,
just lots and lots of noise,
A cloud of fog is in your brain,
Of where they used to lie,

You wish you were with them,
No matter where they were,
But the thing that makes you most sad is,
you never said good-bye.

Stacy Hanson, Grade 6
Sequim Middle School, WA

Shimmering Stars

Shimmering stars shine upon the silent night,
Casting a silvery glow among the City of Lights.
Glittering shields of brightness
Cover the fields of blackness in the sky.

Meagen Twyeffort, Grade 4
Sunset Mesa Schools Inc, NM

Spring

S pring clouds pass me by
P retty rainbows spread across the sky
R ed roses start to bud
I rish shamrocks bloom
N oisy humming birds sipping nectar
G iant winds blow

Susie Hinders, Grade 4
Sunnyslope Elementary School, WA

Life

Life is all about the things you see,
and the things you want to be.

You don't know what it has in store,
take a risk, death could be at the door.

If you enjoy life as much as you can,
you will be better than the average man.

Don't take a wrong turn on this crazy road
don't worry, life takes a long time to decode.

Joey Dolce, Grade 4
Aurora Quest Academy, CO

Redwood Forest

I remember
When I first saw the trees.
They smelled so sweet, as sweet as
Can be. The trees looked as old as an ancient
dinosaur and when I kept looking there were
more and more.
The tree was like a skyscraper while
I was the size of a mouse. The trees were so wide
they couldn't hide how glorious and strong they were.
I love Redwood City, it's where I belong. It's
Where I lived for so long.
I'll always
Remember the beautiful
Trees and
The first
Time I
Smelled
Them
As sweet
As can be

Tyler Taydus, Grade 6
Southern Hills Middle School, CO

Freedom

Freedom is like wild animals
Free to do anything
I wish I had freedom
Free to do anything

I wish I could see more movies
With freedom I could do that
I also with I could drive
then I would be free to do anything

Joe Coleman, Grade 6
Pope John XXIII Catholic School Community, AZ

Tomorrow

You fight today,
You'll cry tomorrow,
You wonder if you'll feel pain,
Or sorrow,
You're born today,
You live tomorrow,
It never comes,
It never will,
Until you live your life your way,
You wait and wait until the day is gone,
Hoping in that it shall come again,
As it did for so long,
You fought and fought
Not knowing the consequence,
And now it shall come again
Now that you have taken your chance.

Antonette Ortiz, Grade 5
Escuela Bilingüe Pioneer Elementary School, CO

Dragons

D estructive
R oaring
A wesome
G ash-leaving
O utstanding
N orwegian Ridgeback
S aphira

Tanner Hobbs, Grade 4
East Evergreen Elementary School, MT

Tomorrow

I lie in my bed thinking
about the sorrow that is ending.
But tomorrow a new day is forming.
As I close my eyes
I think about tomorrow.
Here it comes. A new day.

Becky Goodboe, Grade 6
Eagle Point Middle School, OR

Clarinet

Black, shiny
I take it out of case
It is eager to begin
Bring to lips
Breathe life into it
It sings with delight
When I hurt it
It cries out
I wince, keep playing
Music flows
It sings
With a rich sweet voice
My fingers fly, effortless
It is doing the work

Wearing out
Songs less beautiful
It sighs with exhaustion
I put it back in case
Gleaming after bath
Winks at me as I close lid
Shining, singing, now resting

Natalie Pilgeram, Grade 5
Colbert Elementary School, WA

Chicago

C ubs
H ot dogs
I was born there
C hicago Tribune, the newspaper
A wesome place to visit
G rant Park
O prah lives there

Elizabeth Rogers, Grade 5
St Cyril Elementary School, AZ

Distance of Love

A thing that has a distance and this is a special one,
Which is a secret distance.

A secret distance that can be 1 km far away, or can be 1 mm close.
A secret distance which is a "Distance of Love."

Jennifer Lim, Grade 5
Eton School, WA

School

There are many things you can say about school,
that it is boring, long, annoying, stupid, smelly,
and boring again!

But it can help you get into college, fun, you learn a lot, have friends,
And have more fun!

So it's your decision,
Do you want to get good grades, get into college, get a job! Or do you want to be
a lazy fat man, with no job, all alone with out a girlfriend in an apartment!

So what's it going
To be?

Gabe Lenetsky, Grade 6
Santa Fe School for the Arts, NM

I Am From

I am from the tall swaying woods, from Charmin and Dawn.
I am from the smell of two dogs and a cat.
I am from the broken down fountain and the tall dark woods.
I am from eating together and watching TV.
From Jessica and Carson and Justin.
I am from a working mom, Trina, and a working dad, Larry.
I am from a broken leg and a broken nose.
I am from a brother being mean and carrots and ice cream.
I am from an aunt with a broken leg, and an aunt with a broken nose
and a sister with a broken foot.
I am from family photo albums.
I am from waking up at six o'clock in the morning.
I am from a little annoying cousin.
I am from the best teacher ever Ms. Wiley!
I am from a mom who wakes me up early.
I am from a dog who wakes me up in the night.
I am from being named after my aunt.
I am from the best school ever called Evergreen Elementary!

Shelbie Mason, Grade 4
Evergreen Elementary School, OR

Volcano

Lava seeping from the ground, red and fiery all around.
It bubbles, spits, and sprays in the sky, the lava reminds me of a bird flying high.

It's rumbling and ready now to burst, should I stay to watch it blow.
I better not I must now go

Brynja Jonsson, Grade 6
Meridian Middle School, ID

Sadness Is Blue

sadness is blue like rain falling
and also like teardrops rolling
it beats through my heart
it reminds me of people dying
it makes me feel gloomy and like I am alone
it makes me want to run away from everything
sadness is blue like rain falling

Tatum Williams, Grade 6
Walt Clark Middle School, CO

Forest

The trees proudly dance
the luminous sun starts to sing along
The grass plays music.
Soon the forest starts jumping along
All the houses got sick because of all the noise.
It cries help!

Thessa Corsey, Grade 4
Amesse Elementary School, CO

Rottweilers

I'm tough, mean, and big,
Mess with me, you'll snap like a twig.
I'm strong, protective, and have sharp teeth,
Make me mad you'll feel me grief.

I can be nice but only sometimes,
I don't commit a lot of crimes.
I am one of the biggest dogs,
I'm so big I can squash a hog.
Now you know my favorite dog.

Ciara Nestlen, Grade 6
Uplands Elementary School, OR

Easter Bunny

I am the Easter Bunny
I wonder if anyone loves my Easter eggs
I hear people color their own eggs at Easter
I want people to believe in me
I am the Easter Bunny

I feel I need to change my name
I touch my fluffy, white fur
I worry people might not find the eggs I hide
I cry because not a lot of people like me
I am the Easter Bunny

I understand I do the same routine every year
I say I need to change my travels
I dream that I will find a girl bunny to love
I try my hardest to be on time delivering eggs
I hope my mom stops checking up on me
I am the Easter Bunny

Breanna Saavedra, Grade 6
Wallace Elementary School, AZ

Eskimo Baby

When I was a baby
You called me Eskimo baby
And you cared for me.
Every time I think of you
I recall how you would be proud of me.
Now I break down in thoughts
And a single teardrop falls down my cheek
And another and then
It's like a quiet rainstorm.
The more I think of you I begin
To think about when my soul leaves this world
And we'll meet on the bridge of life and death
Hoping you'll be waiting for me.

Ellana Cain, Grade 6
Scenic Park Elementary School, AK

An Ode to Books

Books are silent friends, telling a story of old.
When I read, I see treasures untold.
But when you neglect and forget them,
Their existence will still be known.
They'll haunt you and away you'll be blown.
Books give you knowledge and clarity when you need it.
Books are like matches, so many imaginations they've lit.
Whether it be mystery, history or fiction,
They will always give you a grand conviction.
You mustn't neglect these literary gifts,
And I say to you this:
Be kind to books and they will be kind to you.

Olivia Poisel, Grade 6
Tucson Country Day School, AZ

Spring

The winter snow melts away
And the cold crust is pushed aside
By the endless fields of flowers
The trees which stood still in winter
Spring to life with the smell of new blossoms
Green is everywhere
Life returns
The first bird chirps
And shatters the barrier holding it all in
The world is new and fresh again

Miranda Theriot, Grade 5
Nederland Elementary School, CO

Darkness

That night my closet was left open
Darkness drenched me as it spilled out into my room
My cool sheets tried to cradle me as fear closed in
Looking for options is much harder
When you can't take your focus off everything around you
I will be okay
Was my last thought as I slipped into a deep sleep

Katelyn Caldwell-Hoggan, Grade 6
Eton School, WA

Up Down Up Down

The Stub Nose Kangaroo
Can do what you do.
Say the word
He'll jump high as a bird.

His feet are like
a speedy bike.
He bounces up and down,
No joke, he's no clown.

It's like he's on a trampoline
I swear it, this dude's keen.
His tail is a jump rope,
Say it again, he's no dope.

He carries around joyful joeys
That jiggle and juggle to their toeys.
Now I'd say I'm done.
Did you have fun?
Samuel Johnston, Grade 5
Barratt School, UT

Field Day

Running
Long jump, relays
Receiving blue ribbons
Very competitive

Jumping
High jump jumping for joy
Tanner Kissee, Grade 4
Copper Canyon Elementary School, AZ

Present and Past

Present
Bright, loud
Watching, playing, chores
Spending, purchasing, driving
Electricity, cars, wagons, lanterns
Churning, farming, milking
Swatting, cleaning, baking
Barns, animals
Past
Katie Belongia, Grade 6
Glacier Middle School, WA

My Best Friend

You are my best friend,
My best friend I will never betray
You are my best friend,
and I'm yours.
You bring joy to the world,
You make me smile when I am sad,
You are a friend like friend should be.
Victoria Sandoval, Grade 4
Clawson School, AZ

Spring

S un shines,
P icture day,
R aining,
I see birds!
N othing wrong.
G oing outside to play!!
Emily Gaffery, Grade 5
M A Lynch Elementary School, OR

Him

Every day and night
I cry because
I miss him
I can't stop thinking of him
I feel like no one likes you
And I can't stand this!!

I love him but he's
Ripping out my
Heart…
Every time I see him
I know we can't be
Together because of our parents
But I'll find a way to escape
Out of here and see him again

I want to see him not
In pictures but in person
I remember when we held
Each other's hands when we first met
Cynthia Duron, Grade 6
South Middle School, CO

Black

Black is the color
of the midnight sky,
a bowling ball,
and my black and blue eye.
Black is the color
of a small ant,
a lump of coal,
and a black dog's pant.
Black is the color
of a buzzing fly,
a small smelly skunk,
and a dark and stormy sky.
Black is the color
of a large flock of crows,
a zebra's stripes,
and a black panther's nose.
Black is the color
of a raven's scream,
a tiger's stripe
and a blank TV screen.
Dannique Duran, Grade 6
Kendallvue Elementary School, CO

Sorrow

Sorrow why can't it pass
Sorrow why does it come
Sorrow why do I feel it so much
Sorrow who can I trust

Sorrow when it comes I cry
Sorrow I can't see but feel
Sorrow I can't let people see
Sorrow I can't let it take over

Sorrow I must let you pass
Sorrow I can't let you come
Sorrow I do not feel
Sorrow I know I can trust
Diana Whetten, Grade 5
Discovery Plus Academy, AZ

The Naughty List

It was the day before Christmas
And I wrote a letter
I put it in the mailbox
And I felt a little better.

I thought I was a bad boy
And I almost had a fit
A lump of coal for me
No way! Not if I could help it.

I went to bed that night
Feeling somewhat sad
But on Christmas morning
I was really glad.

Some candy in my stocking
Along with a brand new toy
I got off the naughty list
And I was filled with joy!
John Dyba, Grade 6
Lewis & Clark Elementary School, MT

Dragons

Scaly
Fire breathing
Huge carnivores
Long tails
Bat-like wings
Sharp shiny teeth
Guarding the treasure
Fighting the knight
Beautiful in flight
Hidden in the cave
A dangerous creature
Flying in the night sky
Dragons
Dustyn T. Belgarde, Grade 4
Scenic Park Elementary School, AK

Crystal

Loving, caring, playful
Wants to make people happy
Wishes to become a good flute player
Dreams of making it to the orchestra
Wants to make people happy
Who wonders about movies
Who likes to be around friends
Who is afraid of famine
Who loves band
Who loves church, especially youth group
Who loves little dogs
Who plans to be a great person
Who wishes for a new flute
Who will go to Linfield College

Crystal Smith, Grade 6
Patton Middle School, OR

Family

The most important things in life aren't things;
just as the most important word in any language
is more than just a word
Family…
Not just a mere word, our inner emotions
The center of life
Family…
A human bond that is everlasting
Family…
Someone who trusts you and helps you through your struggles,
forgives you for your mistakes
Family…
Someone you can look up to, get advice from
to help make choices or solve problems
Life…
Is like a house…It's foundation…
The source of one's well being
Family…
The glue that holds the foundation together…
Never to be broken, only added upon
Family is everything

Nate Tingey, Grade 6
Hermosa Vista Elementary School, AZ

Memory

It stares at you forever flashing in your face.
It will never let you forget, at that time and place.

It bothers you in your sleep, and in your scary mind.
The chills go down through your quivering spine.

You want to erase it, your eyes shut tight.
The goose bumps arrive, concentrating with all your might.

Screaming, you try to breathe, the memory comes back.
The death of a person, is in your memory sack.

Levi Moore, Grade 6
Spring Creek Elementary School, WY

Black and White War

Black is the Vietnam War.
Black is this war left families poor.
Black are the men that all died.
Black are the families who all cried.
Black are the soldiers whose temper was hot.
Black is that this got them all shot.
Black are the traps that were set.
Black is that anyone who was hit with one could never forget.
Does everything have to be *black* and *white?*

White is the bravery each man had.
White is the love for his family each man had.
White are the bonds that were formed.
White were the men who were reformed.
White are the lives that were changed.
White is not being a POW chained.
White is not being in the jungle at the roam.
White is being home.
Does everything have to be *black* and *white?*

Geoffrey Call, Grade 6
Walt Clark Middle School, CO

Dreams

Suddenly you're in another place,
A world unlike your own.
You don't live there, yet you can't leave.
You can go anywhere, and do anything.
In this strange, wonderful, magical world.
But as soon as you get there, you're gone.

Megan Belzner, Grade 6
Santa Fe School for the Arts, NM

The Drought

When people are dying,
and the birds ain't flying
no more, people start crying
because they can't survive
when hope takes a dive,
then the sky gets darker,
like being colored with a big black marker,
and then the rain starts to pour,
there is not a drought anymore,
then people stop dying
and the birds start flying again.

Matthew Fischer, Grade 5
Oak Creek Elementary School, OR

The Go-Kart

There once was a man from Runner,
Who liked to ride his go-kart in the summer,
He had a great crash,
In the middle of the pass,
So he lived there for the rest of the summer.

Gregg Broell, Grade 4
Shields Valley Elementary School, MT

The Thought of Moving
They say it, and say it,
and try to persuade it,
but I just can't entertain it!

They say, it's for the better,
well whatever!

We will be able to do this and that,
well I think it's not a fact!

It's the perfect place to do this,
and the perfect amenities come with!

I ask myself why, and I start to cry,
will life just slowly pass me by?

What about all my friends,
we promised to be together till the end?

I won't, I can't,
the thought is so, cold and damp!
Ashly Peters, Grade 6
Eagle Point Middle School, OR

Books
Books take you on adventures,
To other lands and places,
Into a volcano,
Or even a snowstorm,
Books take you anywhere
You want to go,
They take you to a paradise,
On a roller coaster,
Or to a hurricane disaster,
Books take you everywhere,
You could imagine,
They help your imagination,
To think and read and learn,
Books take you anywhere,
They take you everywhere
So do not set one down,
They make you feel free,
So pick it up again!
Michelle McKay, Grade 6
Bright Beginnings School, AZ

Be Free
Take my hand; I'll guide you.
Take my heart; I'll love you.
Learn from me; I'll believe in you.
Sail the seas; I'll be your crew.
Learn a fact; I'll teach you two more.
Fly high; I'll be your wings.
Be free; I'll be content.
Carly Peterson, Grade 6
Hood River Middle School, OR

Sunlight
Sunlight sparkling through the sky
only a true mortal can see.
Sunlight going behind a mountain
going away until tomorrow.
Kaleb Johnson, Grade 4
New Emerson School, CO

Pouncing Cats
C limb trees
A lways acrobatic
T errifying
S leep a lot
Kyra Kirk, Grade 6
Conestoga Elementary School, WY

Cast
My blue itchy cast
Really didn't last
I wanted to remove it
But the Dr. said I couldn't do it
Finally the time had come
To remove that blue itchy cast
Poor old slum
Raina Ensworth, Grade 4
Gause Intermediate School, WA

Buddy
I once had a hamster named Buddy,
To me on Sundays he acts nutty.
On some days he will play on his wheel,
On other days he will start to squeal.
On some days he starts to feel cruddy.
Katelynn Ruff, Grade 5
Hafen Elementary School, NV

Sam
There was a man named Sam
who had soup in a can.
All of a sudden there was a bam!
The soup exploded in the pan.
Brandon Simoes, Grade 5
Gold Canyon Elementary School, AZ

Stupid
I'm on an island of madness
And surrounded by a sea of sadness
There is nowhere to go
There is nowhere to think
There is only yourself and the water
You think you're stupid
And some other things
Then you think you're stupid
For thinking your stupid
That is what life is like
Victoria Bellistri, Grade 4
Lorna Kesterson Elementary School, NV

Sledding
I sit at the top of the hill
And look on the slope below.
Thinking of what will happen
If I push off.

Slowly at first, then faster and faster
This slick piece of wood
Zooms down the hill.

The snow billows up
Like white fluffy clouds,
And suddenly I see the tree.

The world narrows down
To the one pole of wood that was
The barrier blocking my way.

BAM!
Asa Graf, Grade 6
East Middle School, CO

Neat Girl
B ig and cool
R unner for track
I ce cold
A big artist
N ice girl
N eat girl
A ll that
Brianna Taylor Johnson, Grade 4
Mills Elementary School, OR

Sun and Moon
sun
hot, star
boiling, scorching, blinding
yellow, bright, dark, cold
glowing, shining, cooling
silver, dark
moon
Kalee Obregon, Grade 6
Patton Middle School, OR

Loving Labradors*
L ovable
A dorable
B arking
R unning
A thletic
D epending
O bnoxious
R uff
S weet
Chelsea Donnelly, Grade 5
Lister Elementary School, WA
*Dedicated to my dog Lexi

Chestnut

C hestnut is my cat
H unts for squirrels
E vil to new people
S trikes kids under the age of 9
T ries to have fun
N ever is chasing
U nusually nice to babies
T he cat that picks fights with the other cats and wins!

Erica Shafer, Grade 5
Candalaria Elementary School, OR

The Game

Don't get caught up in the fame and game.
It's an old story and it's all the same.
Big bucks and the fancy cars.
Lost in directions and you don't know who you are.
When the game is over you are dead or in jail.
Either way you're stuck in hell.
Stay away from the fame and game.
It's the same old story that doesn't ever change.

Kurtis Vaughn, Grade 6
Cadwallader Middle School, NV

Whatever

People may say you're too fat, skinny
too tall, or too small.
But I say
WHATEVER.

Sometimes people do something on purpose.
But they say that they did it on accident.
But I say
WHATEVER.

People may say "If you hang out with them
you can't hang out with me because they are uncool."
But I say
WHATEVER.

Sometimes people hurt other people's feelings
and they say I can't help them.
But I say
WHATEVER.

Doris Haynie, Grade 6
Eagle Point Middle School, OR

One Hot Summer Day

One hot summer day
I saw an enormous black bull
That darted out of a humongous black truck
The bull was huffing and puffing
Up and down and running
To all the lady cows!

Morgan Lovejoy, Grade 5
St Patrick's Catholic School, WA

Can I Be Someone Else?

Alone in the dark,
Crying out tears of sorrow
You've lost all your friends
What have you done?
Now think about what you could have been
You can't get an image,
Is the problem worse than you think?
You're yearning to change
But something is holding you back
What is it?
Want to know what it is,
It's you…

Monica Vorachack, Grade 6
Gate City Elementary School, ID

Wind

W histling a lonely tune
I n tune with our feelings of being invisible
N ever-ending loneliness
D emanding compassion and friends

Addie Molisee, Grade 6
Fox Creek Jr High School, AZ

A Good Friend

A good friend cares about you,
He or she laughs at your jokes,
Every day they give you a smile,
A good friend trusts you.
They also give you a second chance.
Friends stand up for you,
And you stand up for them.
A good friend will remember you
No matter what happens.
They know what you are feeling,
When you have bad times,
Or when you are mad at them.
A good friend believes in you.
They don't care what you look like or what you wear.
Good friends don't leave you out and,
They always play with you.
A good friend won't care who you like to hang out with,
What hobbies you're into, or what food you like.
So all I am trying to say is…
A good friend is always a good friend.

Moorea Naeyaert, Grade 5
La Veta Elementary School, CO

Freedom

Freedom is jean blue…
It sounds like a band playing on the 4th of July.
It feels like rain gently hitting your face washing away the stress.
It smells like carne asada on Cinco de Mayo.
It tastes like your first American cheese burger
from being over seas.

Miranda Hales, Grade 6
Cadwallader Middle School, NV

Horses, Me and God

Their hoof beats pound the almost perfect earth beholding imperfect humans. My hands behold the lines of a sinner the lines of an imperfect me. For horses they may not be perfect but for they do not sin and they give to others. When I'm around horses it reminds me of God and the blessings I've received. It makes me think of how they have no greed and only try to please. They are perfect friends always sticking with you just like God and when I think of their hoof beats pounding the almost perfect earth I think of God and I know He is nearby.

Kailee Miller, Grade 6
Rocky Heights Middle School, CO

Black, Gray, and White
Black

Black is darkness, gloom, shade, dimness
Black is sadness, sorrow, grief, pain
Black can be good, fine, superior, first-class
Black is a good color but it causes pain and misery
Black is an unlucky color and I don't think that would be a good color to have in your life

Gray

Gray is a normal color like when you're having a casual day or when you're just mellowed out
If you are just happy and sad at the same time then you're the color gray
Gray is a color of fantasy when there is peace and love in the world
Gray is life

White

White is a good color but it can be evil, harsh, and cruel
And I think that if you act as if you are the color white on the inside or outside
You are not better than anyone else you are just the same
Because every man is made equal

Lucus Griego, Grade 5
Blanco Elementary School, NM

Freedom

Freedom flies through the hearts of all. It can fight and win wars. Freedom's cousins are love and justice. Freedom helps us stand up and do what we want. Freedom is there to lend a hand. Together, we could make a stand. Freedom is trusting to me. It fills my heart with such glee. It makes me proud to know I am free. Freedom has never lied to me.

Megan Fritz, Grade 6
Pope John XXIII Catholic School Community, AZ

I'm Scared

I'm scared
I'm scared, will she be all right
I'm scared, will she able to get out of jail
I'm scared, will she get arrested a lot more
I'm scared, will she win our rights
I'm scared, what if she doesn't win our rights
I'm scared, will the white people give in and let mommy win
I'm scared, what if the KKK kills her
I'm scared, what if the KKK burns down our house
I'm scared, what if someone who does not like mommy shoots her like Lincoln got shot
I'm scared, what if mommy doesn't change the white peoples' hearts
and they're still mean to us just for being a different color
I'm scared

Gioia Berlin, Grade 5
Santa Fe School for the Arts, NM

The Settlers

They went into the mountains looking for gold.
The settlers were tired and very old.
The buffalo were walking across the plains.
The miners were waiting for the trains.
The capital of Colorado is Denver, you know.
The explorers were great even though they were slow.
My homestead is in Evergreen,
I'm sure you have seen.

Tiffani Ciminero, Grade 4
Marshdale Elementary School, CO

Life and Hope

Life to some, is nothing but living,
They are rich, they live in Nirvana,
To others it is a sickness,
They can lose everything,
Life to some could never end,
They have eternal beauty and nothing wrong,
To others life has a sudden stop,
They have disease,
Their loved ones die,
Life to some is their own,
They keep everything to themselves,
They care about no one but themselves,
To others life is to help,
They give and want nothing in return,
They help people live,
Life to some is to not let it live on,
They have a loved one die and may forget,
To others life is to let it live on,
It never dies out, it is never forgotten, and it still has hope.
Hope is the key to live,
Never give up, never forget, never let the flame die out

Danny Wiedman, Grade 6
East Middle School, CO

Silent Friends

Soft and furry gentle and sweet,
kind and caring so quiet to be,
in the saddest of times not a word is said,
yet they warm your heart until you're happy again,
by my side until the very end — my dogs.

Kaylin Lovato, Grade 5
Cuba Elementary School, NM

The Unfortunate Chicken

The Easter Bunny was mad,
all his eggs were plaid.
The chicken dyed the eggs,
so the Bunny snapped his legs.
Off to the hospital he went,
the chicken's legs were bent.
The doctor cut off his legs,
so he couldn't dye anymore eggs.

Sabrina West, Grade 4
Edmonds Homeschool Resource Center, WA

A Brief History of Colorado

The first settlers, Ancestral Puebloans,
Lived on the plateau.
Then disappeared
From head to toe.

Next in the mountains
I think came the Utes.
I don't know much about them,
But I think they played flutes.

Trappers came after that
And gave beavers a fright.
Then they would skin the hopeless animals,
And have rendezvous at night.

Finally miners came
Looking for silver and gold.
Some were really nice and
Some were strict and bold.

Riley Mack, Grade 4
Marshdale Elementary School, CO

NASCAR

I like to work on cars,
They have many different shapes of roll bars.
They like to race,
At a very fast pace.
When you crash you see stars.

Tristan Corpron, Grade 4
East Evergreen Elementary School, MT

All Alone

All alone, there is no one here but me.
All along, I pray on my knees.
All alone, praying for my pain to go away.
All alone, I lay.
All alone, I cry.
All alone, watching my life go slowly by.
All alone, I only feel hurt and I feel it a lot.
There are many battles I have fought.
But this is the hardest one yet.
I feel like an animal caught in a net.
I have no freedom, no place to go.
I'm all alone.
I feel a new feeling like my life is new.
What is happening I have no clue.
My depression is almost done and through.
I lay here but my legs need to run.
I need to run away from this pain.
I feel happy once again.
No more sorrow no more pain.
All alone, there is no such thing.
All alone, are two words I don't use anymore.

Bridgette Chelsey Shields, Grade 5
Harlem Elementary School, MT

A Moonlit Walk

A moonlit walk,
An enchanted night,
No need to talk,
Thy soul is high!

Thy dress trails behind,
Crown of leaves on thy head,
The country is lined,
With a flowery bed.

The trees bend and sway,
As if singing a song.
The moon lights the way,
It won't last too long!

I flow up the dune,
Mums in my hands,
Oh, look at the moon!
What beautiful lands!

I look out to the sea,
As I drink up the air,
Is it just me?
Or is this scene rare?
Elle Quist, Grade 6
East Middle School, CO

Smog

Toxic waste hovering
over busy cities
waves of endless
coughing,
surrounding the
infected victims,
of the helpless
city
Spurs of
cloudy smoke
blend in
perfectly,
with thick layers
of fog,
making a
detrimental
body of
smog.
Irene Lee, Grade 6
Uplands Elementary School, OR

Sunsets

Colorful soft
Makes the sky look tropical
Makes me feel happy
Fire in the sky
Nicole Buecker, Grade 4
Eton School, WA

Teddy Bear

So full of life and imagination,
someone to encourage creation.

A happy face to egg you on,
to help you sing your favorite song.

Loving you with all their might,
holding you throughout the night.

A single light to banish fears,
a gentle touch to dry your tears.

With such love and care,
and never unfair.

I will always need,
my teddy bear.
Waverley Kronewitter, Grade 5
CLASS Academy, OR

War

War
Bloody battles
Fighting, shooting, dying
Sad and terrible ordeal
Armies
Stephen Bergauer, Grade 6
Bright Beginnings School, AZ

You Can

I see what's in you
Maybe you don't
I say you can
You say I won't
The little train said I can't
Then I can and he made it up the hill
And so, you can

You try and try harder still
But you say I can't, I won't
Soon you will
Life is a mountain, not a small hill
With thorns and rocks, along the way
But don't worry you'll be okay

You can't give up
You can't stop trying
You've got to keep going
Never stopping

No one can stop you
Only you can
You are going to make it
All because of you
Alison Beecher, Grade 6
Barbara Bush Elementary School, AZ

Frogs

frogs are leaping far
to and fro through water they go
swimming to lily-pads.
Nick Hudson, Grade 6
Hamilton Middle School, MT

Frosted Ground

I go outside early
To see the sun rise
I step barefoot
Into the tall sprinkled grass
I pick up a piece
To see the tiny diamonds
Of droplets
But as I do
They melt away
Between my warm fingers
And as I move on
'Til the sun hits my face
I look back
And see a trail of footprints
In the frosted ground
Victoria Krasovskiy, Grade 6
Walker Middle School, OR

Chocolate

C runchy,
H ot cocoa,
O h chocolate,
C hewy,
O h chocolate,
L uxurious sweet chocolate,
A perfect treat,
T oo good to resist,
E nchanting chocolate!
Halley Jalbert, Grade 5
St Mary's School, ID

Life

No one realizes the racism passed down
By generations
Kids watching kids following
Abuse in the family young ones follow
Attitudes towards people
Not meant for young eyes to see
Family habits passed down
Intelligent minds destroyed
Pressure wrecking lives of others
Anger arises to tear apart people
A memory kids shouldn't have
Losing it all for an addiction
Losing it all over anger
Do it for the ones you love
It's life deal with it
Robert Monson, Grade 6
South Middle School, CO

Spring and Fall

Spring brings life to our planet
and makes the flowers bloom

Spring helps make the world beautiful
with many vivid colors

The children are happy
when spring is here

Fall makes the leaves fall
off the trees and down to the ground

Fall makes the flowers
wilt and die

The spring comes
and everything comes to life again

The sun comes out
and the leaves start to grow on the trees
and the flowers start to bloom

Maya Shaw, Grade 4
Khalsa Montessori Elementary School, AZ

Colors

Green is the color of grass in the morning
Blue is the color of rain when it's pouring
Gray is the color of the storm
White is the color of a snowflake form
Yellow is the color of the sun in the spring
Red is the color of a cardinal's wing
Orange is the color of a fruit I eat
Purple is the color of grapes that are sweet
Bronze is the color of a coin worth one cent
Silver is the color of a dime that I spent
Gold is the color of a rare metal ore
Tan is the color of the carpet on the floor

Bryce Stradling, Grade 6
Bright Beginnings School, AZ

My Little Sister

My sister is adorable.
Her full name is Lyssa Marie Roethle.
She acts like the boss of everyone, like me!

I also have two other sisters in my family.
She has a pet guinea pig.
Stuffed animals are her favorite.

I have to share my room with her.
Lyssa and I make a big mess!
She's really smart.
Lyssa!

Kelsey Roethle, Grade 5
Gold Canyon Elementary School, AZ

Halloween Night

Halloween is the time at last
Where witches, goblins, and ghosts come with a blast
They come with brooms and magic mushrooms
They come in our closet and into our rooms
They're under the bed
And in the hall
Watch your step
Or they'll eat us ALL
Hide under your blankets
And under your sheets
The vampires are coming
And they're wearing cleats
So don't go outside
And don't leave your room
The witches are coming
And they'll bring us all doom

Kelci Joy Bryan, Grade 6
Wallace Elementary School, AZ

The Feeling of Skating

The feeling of skating,
Is like the feeling of flight.
With the tension of competition,
Along with the pride of a landed jump,
You never know what emotion will come next.
It might be the thought that you are flying like a eagle.
The beginning of a program is the most exciting of all!
With adrenaline pumping through your body,
You take your starting pose.
You will always get that same emotion
that keeps building and building
Until you may have won the Olympics.

Asher Smith, Grade 6
Monforton School, MT

I Can't Rhyme

Eeeeeek!!
Shriek!
I just can't rhyme!
This poem is going to stink,
It isn't worth the time!
Please don't make me write this poem,
I'd rather be in bed at home.
This poem isn't going to be worth a dime,
Oh, drat, oh drat, I just can't rhyme!!!

Hayley Kearns, Grade 5
Lister Elementary School, WA

Blue

If I were the color blue,
I would be the roaring waves of the ocean,
The rain pounding to the ground,
The glistening lake in the sunshine,
A beautiful sapphire in a cold dark mine

Ian Wheeler, Grade 4
East Evergreen Elementary School, MT

Take Me Away

Sandy beaches,
As I walk,
Each step I take,
Waves crash over me,

A taste of salt water,
In my mouth,
As I keep on walking,
I spot a special reunion,
Of families gathered together,

Wind blowing through my hair,
Sounds of a cricket,
Whispering its beautiful song,
In my ear,

A storm has appeared,
A sight so fearful,
The storm has ended,
Take me away.

Mary Joy Quijance, Grade 5
Williwaw Elementary School, AK

Cows

You see, they don't talk,
just an occasional "moo,"
I can't resist cows!

Laura Foster, Grade 6
Hamilton Middle School, MT

Dribble

Dribble
On the court
Wildly and rapidly
Swoosh! Goes the basketball
The crowd roars
Buzzer counts down
We won!

Jordan Baginski, Grade 5
Bates Elementary School, CO

The Dogs Down the Street

There is a HUGE
house d the street
    o
    w
    n

inside of the house are
a lot of small yap yap yapping dogs

   so
you just have to toss a biscuit
in there and they'll be quiet

Victoria Komashko, Grade 5
Gold Canyon Elementary School, AZ

Heaven

The sun shines above, the flowers are in bloom
Where nobody will ever meet their doom.
Satan will be conquered, we'll live forevermore,
The battle will be ended and the sun will meet its core.
The rocks above will come down and the angels will sing in praise,
The pearly white gates will be opened, and we won't only be able to gaze.
Our loved ones will be risen, we'll shout of praise to God,
Our bodies will be strengthened and all people won't just nod.
We'll sing alleluiah alleluiah alleluiah praise to God!

Zackary Brenes, Grade 5
Rogers Adventist School, WA

Myself

Spencer
Smart, artistic, kind, and truthful
Lover of cheetahs, kittens, and video games
Who feels excitement when rollerblading, playing with cats, and playing game cube
Who needs a good challenge, a notepad, and cats
Who gives help to people, love to cats, and love to family
Who fears getting shots, losing a friend, and snakes
Who would like a DS player, a cheetah, and longer weekends
Who dreams of a driver's license, having cheetahs, and meeting my "dead" cat again
Holdaway

Spencer Holdaway, Grade 6
H Guy Child School, UT

Beautiful Mother

Hi there remember me you little honey bee
I didn't know you much but I still love you a bunch
You mad me feel loved I know you won't go above
I know you won't leave but if you ever feel lonely
I'll be there for you definitely if you turn blue
Because I love you when I first met you I was scared
Because I thought you wouldn't care but you loved to share
You found room in your heart for one more I don't care if you're poor
You're the best thing in the world I just thought I let you know that I love you so
Especially when the wind blows mom you're as pretty as a rose
So have a wonderful day down at the bay

Alexandra Mackintosh, Grade 6
E C Best Elementary School, NV

Baseball

Standing on the mound,
hurling the baseball hard
striking people out,
having ease pitching hard.
My skills are demanding work as the inning ends.
Coming up to bat, hitting a grand slam,
scoring the team 4 runs. I am very happy as I go up to pitch again.
I end up getting a perfect game.
It is very fun to watch the people run
as I and my teammates jump for joy happily.
When I went home that day
I was watching the videotape of that wonderful day.

Troy Stolarczuk, Grade 4
Eton School, WA

Jealousy

Jealousy is a knife
Who stabs you at times
When you are happy, it makes you dreary
Why this is so, nobody knows
How this is caused, only jealousy knows.

Jealousy is like a river
Which washes through minds
Just when they settle, another swishes by
It spreads like the waves, which carry the fish
How this is caused, only jealousy knows.

Nick Olson, Grade 6
Barbara Bush Elementary School, AZ

Life!

Life is cruel to you!
You duel to make someone love you,
somewhere your baby's cryin'.
This man in front of me is dyin'.
But we're tryin' to get through.
Someone's out to get you.
That little kid down the street is lyin' for you.
You threw your life away
to get some so-called friends to like you.
You must feel like a stray.
How can you live or be treated this way?
For over a day you lay and pray.
Or just say no way.
You know, life's not sweet
because you get beat.

Lara Parsons, Grade 5
Klickitat Elementary School, WA

Things About Me

I am a weird guy who likes to exercise.
I wonder if we will make allies with Iraq.
I hear sounds in my head.
I see that other kids are teased, so I help.
I want to be in the military.
I am a weird guy who likes to exercise.

I pretend that I can fly.
I feel the sadness of those who are in pain.
I touch the earth and am happy.
I worry about those who are hurt.
I cry for those who give their life to save me.
I am a weird guy who likes to exercise.

I understand when someone is upset.
I say things I mean and some I don't.
I dream of traveling to Mars.
I try to help people.
I hope to make more friends in jr. high.
I am a weird guy who likes to exercise.

Robert Thompson, Grade 6
H Guy Child School, UT

Aaah Refreshing

While at the pool the other day
I saw a funny but most awkward girl
She would hop up on the diving board
and glare down about 8 feet towards the pool

She launched herself off the edge of that diving board
and stuck her legs straight out
The very next thing that you heard was "SPLAT"
that came thundering out from the water

To come was the most hilarious part
when she swam towards the ladder
'Cause she shook of the water in a proper way
and would say…"Aaah refreshing"

And then she'd keep refreshing again and again

When finally I had to go home
but came back the very next day
to see that very same girl
doing her daily routine…"Aaah refreshing"

Meg Lieb, Grade 6
Miller Middle School, CO

Lunchtime

I see the long line of kids, waiting to get their food.
I hear the sound of children talking loudly with friends.
I taste the crisp and sweet taste of a delicious green apple.
I touch the gooey peanut butter and jelly sandwich.
I smell the delicious smell of food galore.
I feel hungry, and get full when I finish eating.
I know I'm in the school lunchroom.

Lindsey Perino, Grade 5
Eton School, WA

Pollution

Pollution, Pollution, it's everywhere,
On the ground and in the air.
It's in the asphalt, on the street
Even in the lands that are most discreet.

Pollution, Pollution, it's in the weirdest places,
And even in your dad's cigar cases.
But wait, the poem's not at the end!
We're 'bout to go 'round a drastic bend!

Why do we pollute?
When people in the white house just stand and salute
They let polluters go
And their frustration doesn't show.

Especially when it's really bad,
The polluting really makes me mad!

Tom Van Gulick, Grade 5
Mount Carbon Elementary School, CO

Spring Fruits

Cherries and berries are yummy.
They fill your tummy.
They are delicious,
But not vicious.
They are sweet,
And also a treat.
Spring is so fruity,
And filled with beauty.
Peaches and grapes
Come in different sizes and shapes.

AhLam Ghannam, Grade 4
Phoenix Metro Islamic School, AZ

Christmas

Christmas
Brightly lighted tree
Freshly baked delicious cookies
Quiet Christmas music
Tasty cookies and eggnog
Christmas

Andrew Rodriguez, Grade 4
Coal Creek Elementary School, CO

Cats

Meow!
Meow!
Cats! sleep all day, awake all night.
Nocturnal eyes see stuff like it is day.
Catch mice like a mouse trap.
Sharp teeth and claws.
They make nice pets.

Colin Cherry, Grade 4
Acacia Elementary School, AZ

Uncle José We Miss You

My uncle was my life
He was like
a second dad to me
He is gone
but his spirit stays alive

My Uncle José was a
BIG
part of my heart

The only thing
I have left from him
is a card
and a stuffed animal duck

Uncle José
we know you are gone
but you are going
to always be in our hearts

Carmen Velazquez, Grade 5
Edgewater Elementary School, CO

Cats

Cats are soft and fluffy
Just like my cat Fuzzy
Some will eat chocolate or fudge
Just like my cat Smudge

Jessica Wakefield, Grade 5
Monroe Elementary School, CO

My Cocoon

My cocoon, so white as the moon.
It was so bright, just like the cloud.
But one day my cocoon broke.
I was in wonder!
A butterfly came out so bright.

Vanessa Gallardo-Perez, Grade 4
Lewis E. Rowe Elementary School, NV

Gum

No gum at school
Don't spit it in the pool.
Use the garbage can as a tool.
I told you, no gum at school fool!

Daniel Rueckert, Grade 6
Syracuse School, UT

San Francisco

One cold rainy day,
the restaurant smelled like creme brulée
waiting for my breakfast burrito,
I saw a crazy man walk by in a Speedo.
my tummy full from the food,
I was feeling good and in the mood.
the boats moving all about,
to be heard I had to shout
my excitement building for Alcatraz,
I was really acting like a spaz.
the day was fun,
the trip was done,
hoping tomorrow there will be sun.

Justin Sampson, Grade 6
Walt Clark Middle School, CO

My Dream

When I have a chance
To be a writer
Then
Stories will open like a rainbow
From my pencil
Like a stream of words
Dreams and fantasy will spill
From a splashing waterfall
Of imagination
And when I wake from my dream…
My dream of being a writer is
Already fulfilled

Pamela Yang, Grade 6
Walker Middle School, OR

Leaves

October leaves swirl
dancing lightly on swift winds
painting the fall sky

Mia N. Phelps, Grade 4
Adams Elementary School, CO

Spring Sensations

Spring rains
are clear little droplets
beating upon my head.
Spring sun is as bright
and warm as an oven
set to 360 degrees.
Spring flowers are as colorful
and bright
as the sun when
you're 2 inches away
from it.
Spring dews are clear
droplets on webs
in my barn door.
Spring trees swallow
me with their
dark, cool, shade.
In spring I daydream about
vacations in the
summer like
going to Hawaii.

McKenna Welker, Grade 4
Skyline Elementary School, WA

Life on the Tip of a Pin

Life on the tip of a pin,
Is a world of your imagination
A palace or a castle,
Full of your creation

It is your very own place,
That you have discovered or
Read about in books
A place where you can be
A prince or princess with
Your own professional cooks

You can be anything you have
Dreamed about in your imagination
Of clouds
A doctor, a banker, whatever fills
Your heart with sounds

Life on the tip of a pin,
Will always be a part of you
A world that's in your heart,
It's all the feelings within you

Alexa Schneider, Grade 6
Hermosa Vista Elementary School, AZ

Warm Sunshine

Once the sun rose gracefully.
The sunshine walked slowly up the street,
its warm gentle fingers feeling all it shone upon,
listening to every breath I take.
It looks upon me sweetly from the east,
breathing upon me a gentle breeze, still looking.
Always looking till the last warm fingers,
slip away from me waiting for the next day.

Hjalte Durocher, Grade 5
Governor's Ranch Elementary School, CO

World in Pain

So hurt
As if you are in a car crash
In the hospital
Full of thunder sadness

The world is polluted
Just as a big junkyard and animals
Running in your house

It is crazy —
People running around just as it is a jungle around
You

It is full of sadness
Just as if people are sacrificing
Between life and death

Jared Manibusan, Grade 6
South Middle School, CO

Flowers

Flowers can be bright
And some can be **dark**

        p
Flowers can grow u
And some fall d
       o
       w
       n

They can be BIG
Or small
They sway in the cool breeze
They smell lovely and citrusy
Flowers have a lot of special petals and leaves

Plant flowers
       w
       o
       r
And watch the sun g

Skylar Van Nimwegen, Grade 4
Gold Canyon Elementary School, AZ

Forever Loved

One who is loved is loved forever
He could think only of her.
Every time he thinks harder, more of her comes to his mind.
So he ran away as far and silent as the wind.
He realized wherever he goes,
She's in his mind.

Cody Litts, Grade 6
Orient Elementary School, WA

My Anger Is…

Mass destruction and mayhem falling from the sky.
The fire from my head escaping to my enemy.
A waterfall of madness slowly approaching land.
A roaring ocean of pain and misery.
A red temper that runs from my head to my toes.
An unsolved problem of chaos.

Jimmy Farley Hussein, Grade 5
Coyote Springs Elementary School, AZ

The Shining Spirit

Light is liquid sunshine being poured into a bottle.
Light is a warming wind being cut off from the sun.
Light is always welcoming you into its arms.
It has but two enemies.
Its enemies are Darkness and Shadow, a mischievous pair.
All they bring is cold and despair.
Shadow is a great coward, always to hide.
Darkness is power whose domain is the night.
There's an ongoing war between night and day.
The winner's a secret for some, but not me.
I hope others shall seek it.
In liquid Light it shall be.

Ryan Smith, Grade 6
Spring Creek Elementary School, WY

Thinking

When you think, you stare into space,
Go far away, to an unknown place.
Think about pirates on a ship,
Think about a monkey doing a flip.
Think about living in the water,
Think about floating in the air,
Think about lying on the beach,
Sand flying through your hair.
Think about war,
Think about politics,
Think about a pyramid made of toothpicks.
Think about hello,
Think about goodbye,
Think about flying in the sky.
Think about walking around your school,
Think about going deep in a pool.
You know you think, you do it every day,
Think something new, today.

Tessa McEvoy, Grade 6
St Anne School, WA

Nessie

Boats are rippling across the water,
when something comes a spotter.
Then the waters come alive,
moving at every five!
The monster eats 'til satisfied,
leaving nothing but a hide.
Then it slinks way back down,
seeming like it has the crown.

Taylor Pierce, Grade 6
Sequoia Village School, AZ

Red

Fast is red like fire
Also like the sun
It burns through my soul
It reminds me of the sun
It makes me feel angry
It makes me want to be mean

Regan Musilek, Grade 6
Walt Clark Middle School, CO

The Gymnast

There once was a girl from Kentuck
Who practiced doing a back tuck
The first time she tried
She just about died!
But then she had better luck.

Paige Kohler, Grade 5
Ammon Elementary School, ID

Summer

When summer arrives
it shows a big surprise,
for many different reasons.
When young are born
and they step on a thorn,
they realize that they have feelings.
When one cares for another
and when one is hurt,
they feel compassion for that one.
They know that they care for them.

Brianna Mendez, Grade 5
Orient Elementary School, WA

Football

Getting hit hard
Fumbling the ball
Amazing intercepts
Calling flags
Running for the touchdown
Tackling the quarterback
Making the field goal
Getting penalties
Football!

Jacob Reed, Grade 4
Acacia Elementary School, AZ

The Lake

Sitting on the balcony, looking at the lake.
Seeing the glistening blue water.
Seeing a cluster of trees surround a lot of white houses.
A green boat rushes by the house.
An eagle swoops and soars through the weightless clouds.
A mountain peaks over the treetops into the water.
The blue sky is reflected into the water blending with the horizon.
A woodpecker pecks curiously at a tree.
The waves roll until dawn.

Lucas Weisman, Grade 4
Eton School, WA

The Fairies

Faintly glowing lights dance under the pale moon.
Mistaken for fireflies,
The fairies float about in the crisp, spring air.
No worries at all,
For this is the time to be joyous,
A time for celebration.
The harvest has come.
Finally.
The fairies twirl among the white lilies and yellow buttercups until dawn.
Then they will sleep.
They will rest in the old cherry tree,
Until the next sundown.
For the harvest has come,
And this is the time to be happy.

Ryan Haney, Grade 6
Corpus Christi School, CO

Dawn

Everything is dark and gloomy
Tall, looming figures stand tall like the shadows of strangers
The only noise is crunching leaves underneath your feet
A smell of early morning dew enters your nose
You can taste the dawn air
You feel unwanted as you see your surroundings of uncomfortable shadows
Suddenly, you stop walking
High above the hills, in the distance, rises a floating yellow ball
All your uncomfortable thoughts shatter out of your head
A soft chirp signals birds to start their merry cries
Everything around you is alive with sound and color
As dawn arrives on your morning walk

Caroline Friend, Grade 6
The Colorado Springs School, CO

Butterflies

Oh butterflies, swirling in the air!
How beautiful the colors are!
I love the purple and orange butterflies because they look like my blanket.
Inside my imagination they whisper in my ear!
They say lovely things to me always make me smile.
In the summer, in the mornings I get up and see the b-e-a-utiful butterflies.

Adriana Morán, Grade 6
Meridian Middle School, ID

Hot Pink

Hot pink is a flamingo and a balloon and a shirt.
Hot pink is the taste of bubble gum.
Strawberry and cherry smell hot pink.
Happiness makes me feel hot pink.
Hot pink is the sound of birds chirping and kids playing.
Hot pink is girls' bedrooms, the mall, and a spa.
Putting makeup on is hot pink.
Dancing is also hot pink.
Hot pink is coloring.

Misty Severance, Grade 6
Patton Middle School, OR

The Ocean

The ocean is very calm
There are little crabs that fit in your palm
They run and they scurry
To get to their homes, hurry, hurry, hurry.

Shauna Garrison, Grade 6
Fox Creek Jr High School, AZ

I Think I Have an Evil Twin

"I think I have an evil twin,"
I told my dad one day.
"He does bad stuff and then blames me,"
"That's what I have to say."

I went outside to catch him,
and when I finally did,
I told my dad, he said "All right,"
"You're such a lovely kid."

But when he saw the broken window,
he said with a shout:
"Your twin is gone, but trouble's still here!"
and he put me in time-out.

Isaac Wang, Grade 5
Home Education Exchange, WA

Why Can't We Fly?

Why can't we fly?
Everyone needs to push off,
into the fresh air,
to cool off from Earth.
Why? I mean,
everyone who knows everything,
has been everywhere,
still needs to get home another way.
What if it's a the-world-is-pounding-on-me kind of day?
Don't you just want to have that
cool, refreshing breeze?
Or, to juxtapose all your problems?
To finally straighten out your bookcase?
Tell me again —
why can't we fly?

Caley Johnson, Grade 4
Frontier Valley Elementary School, CO

Pretend

Pretend you're a tiny tiger.
Roaring against the cold wind.
Jumping over big grassy hills.
Swimming in the nearby lake.
Teasing your enemy for fresh food.
Chasing a wildebeest across the fields.
Sharpening your claws against a tall tree.
Spying on your grazing prey.
Playing in the long dry grass.
Pounding on the dirt mounds like a falling bomb.
Clawing the ground underneath you.
Swishing your tail rapidly behind you.

Kimberly McCauley, Grade 6
Midway Middle School, ID

I Say This to God, I Pray

When you go to heaven you're high in the sky,
you're never sad, you never cry.
Babies playing, cherubs singing,
people laughing and bells ringing.
I will be with you someday, I say this to God I pray.

My awesome God, you love us all,
you always catch us when we fall.
I love you and that's why I say,
I say this to God, I pray.

Molly Guardino, Grade 6
St Paul Catholic School, OR

My Best Friend

His chalk white fluff caught my eye,
He is so cute I just can't deny,
His cherry red collar, makes me not want to hide,
His snow white fur just passes me by,
his small black eyes hide inside,
trying to find a way to get by,
he is so cute I just cannot deny

Courteney Saeman, Grade 5
Greenwood Elementary School, CO

Soccer

Something I enjoy to do is soccer
Sometimes I'm forced to yell "block her"
It's extremely fun
Our team is #1
All the time we're running
People agree our team's stunning
We always hope it's a sunny day
That's our favorite time to play
Whenever we're close to the goal we shoot
Count on us to give it a good boot
During games we get covered in grime
But we just get out there and have a good time

Sierra Dodd, Grade 4
Colbert Elementary School, WA

Scary

A windy night
I am scared
I got out of bed
I see my brother and sister asleep
I go check on my parents
They aren't there
I look at the clock
It's 12:00 over and over again
There's lightning I wake up
I look at the clock
It's 7:10
Ah! I have to get ready for school!

Cameron Beeson, Grade 6
Fox Creek Jr High School, AZ

We Still Live Free

Freedom means a lot to me.
I have 2 military brothers,
One is in the U.S. Army,
The other is at the Air Force Academy.

They're helping us live free.
We are so proud of them.
Each day we pray with faith,
That they will get home safe.

Shaundra Lyn Warner, Grade 4
Cokeville Elementary School, WY

A Place

This summer I'm going to a place
This place is my own space
I'll go there every day,
Just to run and play,
But this place I can't retrace.

Eden Micka, Grade 4
Shields Valley Elementary School, MT

The Sea Lion

Prancing penguins she sights;
Thrashing her jaws, she fights
And like a drought, she bites.
She then shows off her food
Suddenly, as if cued,
The penguin ends the feud.

Kelsey Easton, Grade 5
Liberty Common School, CO

Sunshine

One day I looked up,
and saw the sun smile.
The golden rays shone down,
and over the days,
I could not believe,
I saw the sun smile!

Madie Allen, Grade 4
Wilson Elementary School, WA

Friendship

Friendship can be sunny
And oh, so very funny

Friendship can be sad
Which makes you feel bad

Friendship can be glum
It could bring fights of some

But when it comes to a friend
There really is no end

Jennifer Anderson, Grade 6
Bradford Intermediate School, CO

Mountains

Mountains in the sky,
the hot sun sets behind them
painting them bright pink.

Tayne Tingle, Grade 6
Hamilton Middle School, MT

The Brave Veterans

There once was a war
That took place in 1864.

The veterans that are males
Tell long lost war tales.

The veterans that are strong
Will never do wrong.

Asahel Jenkins, Grade 5
Peck Elementary School, ID

Birds and Sharks

Birds
Happy, playful
Flying, chirping, singing
Multicolor, smooth, dangerous, scaly
Swimming, eating, preying
Multi-shape, quick
Sharks

Jacob Lucas, Grade 5
St Cyril Elementary School, AZ

Why

I wonder why the human soul can't fly,
High in the sky,
And why Jesus didn't want to kill,
But was crucified up on a hill,
And why we only feed,
On this thing called greed,
And why hate,
Uses you as bait.
Just tell me why.

Tyler Gallegos, Grade 4
Aurora Quest Academy, CO

Moon

The moon is a beautiful sight
It is very very bright
It always comes out to see
Me sleeping o' so quietly
And all the other people too
And all the animals in the zoo
All the silent lonely trees
And all the tired sleeping bees
And all the nature that lives outdoors
And all the soft carpeted floors
And everything is all asleep
While homeless children softly weep
Then in the morning it sadly goes
And the sun comes out to warm my toes

Claire Gaskins, Grade 5
Eton School, WA

The Chill

The chill is cold
the chill is breezing,
I think I'm frozen
it's always freezing.
the whisper is coming
the ghost is here,
you could tell
when the chill is near.
It creeps and crashes
squeaks on the floor,
if you don't want to get injured
better lock the door.

Codie Morgan, Grade 4
Mills Elementary School, OR

Joey

J oyful
O vercoming
E nthusiastic
Y ard man

W arrior
I ntelligent
E quipped
G enius
A wesome
N ever boring
D rum beater

Joey Wiegand, Grade 6
St Cyril Elementary School, AZ

I Want a Kitten

I want a kitten of black
With cotton slippers
And a cream belly
With a tail dipped in milk.

Natalie Applegate, Grade 5
Fulton Elementary School, CO

Enemies and Heroes

Halt! Look! There is the army
Oh! No! It's the Babylonians
Boom! Crash! There goes the temple

Halt! Look! Another army
Oh! No! It is the Romans
Boom! Crash! There goes the temple again

Look! There! It is the Maccabees
Look! There! It is the Zalots
Hurray! Hurray! We're almost free again

Look! There! It is Jesus
Look! There! He's teaching Judaism
Look! There! He starts Christianity Hurray!

Melia Ochsner, Grade 6
Pope John XXIII Catholic School Community, AZ

I Am From...

I am from pellet gun and dirt bike.
I am from Seattle and Oregon.
I am from German and Japanese.
I am from Christmas and 4th of July.
I am from *Duke* and *Snow White*.

I am from dirt bike riding and quad riding.
I am from football and hockey.
I am from scabbed arm and shark bite.
I am from *Punk'd* and Monster Garage.
I am from spaghetti and meat balls.

I am Leonard Randall Ballard.

Leonard Randall Ballard, Grade 5
Evergreen Elementary School, OR

Math Class

Math class is fun...math class is great
Math class is funny...when I'm not awake

Who needs all that junk when you can just sleep
No one knows I'm sleeping 'cause I don't make a peep

I dream of dancing teddy bears and kitty cats galore
And as soon as I awaken I fall back asleep for more

I can have all the candy in the world all in just one dream
It all taste so yummy and sweet or so as it may seem

I never bother with math I never even care
Because of all the smart talk it's just hard for me to bear

Too bad I hate it so much because I really am a whiz
Sorry teach' I just don't do that biz'

Crystal Marney, Grade 6
Miller Middle School, CO

Candy

Andy loves Candy
Candy hates Andy
If you're thinking about Candy
Candy is not candy
Candy is a girl's name
Andy doesn't love candy
Andy loves sweet Candy
And if you're thinking about really sweet candy
It's not, it's Candy the girl
Candy hates Andy
And if you're thinking about candy it's not
Candy is sweet candy with sugar
So everybody hates and loves candy.

Memo De La Torre, Grade 5
M A Lynch Elementary School, OR

I Will Miss You

I know that as the years pass by,
I'll miss you more and more,
But I have to stand here,
Watching you walk out the door,
Your tassel has turned,
You passed all of your tests,
The lessons you've learned,
I've only known you for one short year,
But I've learned to love you with all my heart,
And now I'll shed tears,
As many years go by,
I miss you more and more,
And I will never forget you,
You will always be in my heart.

Monica Gonzalez, Grade 6
Robert Frost Elementary School, OR

Green

If I were green, I would be a turtle standing on its hind-legs
A pencil writing on a white sheet of paper
A snake slithering in a forest
A sleek frog catching a fly

Derek Disney, Grade 4
East Evergreen Elementary School, MT

Stupid Steak

One day I was out with my rake
and I saw a steak
I picked it up and brought it inside
It came alive
It went outside and grabbed a saw
I tried to flee
but it hit my jaw
I took the saw and sawed that steak in half
I went inside, sat back and relaxed
I ate that steak in
less than a minute and a half.

Ben Federspiel, Grade 5
Frontier Valley Elementary School, CO

A Friend

A friend is a soul that can fix anything.
A friend is a friendship that would last forever.
A friend will always be in the good
And bad things that happen to you.
A friend should be like your secret treasure
That keeps all of your secrets personal.
A friend puts your secrets in a little box
And keeps all promises.
You did more than a friend
That almost liked your life
That you are living in your own imagination.
You are my friend.

Karen Flores, Grade 6
Somerton Middle School, AZ

Water

Listen to the falling water,
Coming from the roaring waterfall.

Heat its loud boom like thunder,
On a dreaded rainy night.

With the water splashing down,
On the ocean right below.

The light of the full moon,
Gives it a shimmery silver glow.

The frozen raindrops falling,
Crunching under my feet.

So beautiful and free,
Falling wherever it pleases.

The icicles hanging on the windowsill,
Tasting like popsicles.

The sound of the water soothes my heart,
And eases my soul.

Alex Robredo, Grade 5
Foothills Elementary School, CO

A Night to Remember

Being with someone in the night,
do not worry, no need to fright

Love is to be remembered,
and you can give it with a present in December

But on that night a moon full of love,
then comes a letter from a turtle dove

She shall read it and here comes this,
this is known as the one true kiss

Steven Quick, Grade 5
Lister Elementary School, WA

The Sounds of Baseball

C'mon give it to him, let's go pitcher, strike out that snitch!
These are the sounds of baseball before the pitch.
Crack! Woo hoo, yay! Watch out he's throwing a meatball.
The sounds of the crowd when a player hits a ball.
Sweet, nice hit! That was awesome! What a gun.
That's the sound of a home run.
Oh no, I can't believe this. Now the game is never to be won.
That's the sound of the other team's fans of the team who hit the home run.
C'mon let's go, you can do it! Hit the ball already, dear Lord!
That's the sound of the crowd when they're bored.
That was a good game, that game was exciting, I had a lot of fun.
This is the sound after the game has been won.
I can't believe this, it's all right, wait how much did that ticket cost?
This is the sound after the game has been lost.
Those are the sounds of baseball.

Evan Wrons, Grade 6
Grant Middle School, NM

Race Day

As I stand in the starting gate
I feel the rush
The butterflies are there in my stomach
But covering them is a feeling
A feeling of fight, a feeling of going fast!
"3, 2, 1, Go," the starter shouts!

With a pull, I leave the gate
I hear the yells from my friends, cheering me on
And I go, go, go!
The gates start coming at me fast
But now the butterflies have left, I'm just going
In training, it's "pole plant," "get close to the gates," this and that
Now it's programmed into me
I take the tight line and relish the speed

I cross the finish line
There is cheering from the people watching
But I barely notice; the rush is still there
I get my skis off and run to the scoreboard
I check out my time
Then I let out a squeal
I won! I won, I say! I won!

Ali Noel Gunesch, Grade 6
Welches Middle School, OR

Horses

Horses are the prettiest animals I have ever seen,
when their mane and tail flutters in the wind,
they run as graceful as the river flows,
when you stand beside them you think they are trying to speak to you,
when they ride the wind it is like us riding waves,
so gentle so relaxing and full of spirit,
horses can beat any beauty of any animal,
when you count your blessings you should count your horse twice.

Majestic Shaw, Grade 6
Vikan Middle School, CO

Get Through It
Everyone goes through hard times
Because if it weren't for hard time
There would be no crimes
We all wish the world was perfect
We wish there wasn't ever war
Is it really worth fighting for?
We wish there wasn't such a thing as cancer
But always remember no matter how hard it gets
There will always be an answer
So strive and thrive to survive because you
Know in the end everything comes out right
Even though things might give you a fright
Sometimes you need to say good-bye
But if that happens please don't cry
Because God is still watching over you and I
You need to breathe
You need to fly
Even when you feel the need to cry
So when you're gloomy and depressed
Always remember you are truly blessed

Megan Lamb, Grade 6
St Anne School, WA

Hypochondriac
My nose is runny.
I have butterflies in my tummy.
My arms feel like jelly.
Something is gurgling in my belly.

I think I might need surgery.
It may be something in my circulatory.
I think my body will fall apart.
My heart may not even start.

So I'm sick no matter what you say.
I will stay home all day.
I'll sleep and sleep.
Without making a peep.

You say I'm faking.
But look I'm shaking.
You make me go to school anyway.
But I know I'm sick no matter what you say.

Maresa Larranaga, Grade 6
Albuquerque Christian School, NM

My Eyes
My eyes see everything around me
They see the stars late at night
They love to shine when I am right
My eyes help me see my friends when I am sad
They try to fight the tears when I don't want to cry
They look mean whenever I wake up
My eyes.

Diana Yazzie, Grade 6
Walt Clark Middle School, CO

Roller Coasters
The first thing they ask is, "Why,"
Staring at the structure in the blue sky.
But many cannot resist the temptation
Of riding the first one built in their nation.
It races by the treetops,
And over the hills.
Then upside-down for a few extra thrills.
Up and up it goes,
Slowing down.
But then it zooms back down to the ground.
A loop,
A twist,
A giant, mega dive.
And by the time it's over, the riders all know,
Without a doubt,
That roller coasters are the thing
That will be talked about.

Jeremiah Peña, Grade 5
Thomas Edison Charter School, UT

Big Brown Eyes
One of my best friends looked up to me,
He told me how life's supposed to be,
Telling me that we were doing things wrong
He almost sang it in a song
You've got to know when to bark,
Have time to play in the park,
You've got to know when to stand your ground,
When you don't get the biggest bone, you don't frown.
Though in your life, you may run into some cats,
You still need to love, you still need to act,
When life locks you up in a kennel,
This is not a time to think minimal,
Bad breath is just a fault,
It doesn't mean life isn't a ball,
When someone turns to give you a slobbery kiss,
They're your friends, giving you bliss,
My best friend looked up to me,
Telling me how life's supposed to be,
But what really filled my mind,
Is his beautiful big brown eyes.

Andrea Brush, Grade 6
Walt Clark Middle School, CO

Popeye and Bluto's Bilge River Raft Barge Ride
Fun, exciting, entertaining,
a wet cool ride,
splashing in rapids and falls,
getting soaked by being shot by water,
helping Popeye save Olive Oyl from Bluto,
Bluto shooting you with water,
Popeye defeating Bluto,
extremely fun ride!

Ian Reho, Grade 5
Lewis & Clark Elementary School, OR

Snowflakes

Snowflakes dazzling soft
Cold pearls gently tumbling down
Grounds glitter with flair
Hogan Auyeung, Grade 4
Midland Elementary School, CO

My Flowers Are

My flowers are

    sunflowers and roses
    very beautiful
    blankets that give me warmth
    blossoms in the sun
    yellow-like smiley faces
    Santa Claus' face on Christmas
    like the stars

These are my flowers.
Michael Grigoriev, Grade 4
The Meadows School, NV

Graveyard

Moonlight slices across the graves
Leaving encrypted messages alight
1940-2000 RIP
1942-1996 RIP
A couple
A sister
A grandparent
All buried there
Waiting to rise up into the life beyond
I walk along a path
So as not to disturb
Those who sleep here
Listening
To the soft wind blow
Like those who rest
Have done for a hundred years
At the Trinity Graveyard
Emily Stephens, Grade 5
Colbert Elementary School, WA

Have You Seen?

Have you seen
My brother's
Room
Messy as a pig
I tell yah
Candy wrappers
And toys
All
Over
The floor
Have you seen?
Trenton Haley, Grade 5
Edgewater Elementary School, CO

My Heart

My heart is energized and fun.
But part of my heart is out at sea.
It is with a man keeping us free.
He is out at sea with his team.
He calls every so often,
but not often enough.
I like to write him like this,
online of course.
That part of my heart,
out at sea being so brave,
is the part of my heart,
my dad keeps away.
So out at sea helping with war
is that part of my heart.
Meghan Miller, Grade 6
Walt Clark Middle School, CO

Christmas

Christmas
Lots of decorations
Warm, steamy cookies
Ho, Ho, Ho-ing of Santa Claus
Golden baking ham
Prickly, piney trees
Christmas
Olivia Coleman, Grade 4
Coal Creek Elementary School, CO

Halloween

Halloween
Wicked costumes
Moldy pumpkins
Screaming
Skittles galore
White doorbells
Halloween
Kyle Billingsley, Grade 4
Coal Creek Elementary School, CO

Crimson Red Tears

You never saw me,
And never will.
I am surrounded by people,
But I am lonely.
I am confused,
Yet aware.
I am lost,
In a world I've always lived in.
You know me by who I used to be,
Not by who I am now.
You say you care,
But you're never there.
You just sit there and watch,
As I cry my crimson red tears.
Brianna N. Maldonado, Grade 5
Aurora Quest Academy, CO

Teacher

Funny, nice, serious,
Homework.
Like them,
Cherish them,
Hold them 'til there's nothing left.
Read, spell, write,
That's what you do
Don't let it pass you by.
Pencils, paper, ruler
It's what you need.
Well teachers like
Apples!
Gabrielle Patrick, Grade 5
Lewis & Clark Elementary School, OR

Destiny

The space so large
with millions of stars.
A place so small
with millions of people.
The Earth is one
and the stars are many
but together they make
one beautiful destiny.
Elizabeth Henney, Grade 6
Eagle Point Middle School, OR

Night

Night
Dark scary
Darkening cooling blackening
Dimness twilight scorching daytime
Lightning heating brightening
Bright sunny
Day
Josh Schumaker, Grade 6
Fox Creek Jr High School, AZ

Red

Red is blood,
and red is my heart.
Red is a cherry.
Licorice is red.
Stop signs are red.
Red is a blushing person.
Red is fire.
Love is red.

Playing basketball and soccer
and listening to music is red.
Eating strawberries and cherries
reminds me of red.

Red is love.

Evan Morales, Grade 6
Patton Middle School, OR

Reading Champion

I'm a reading champion
When I read, I'm set aside from my mind.
If I start to read,
there is like a television in my mind.
I set a goal for reading.
Most of the time I succeed.
Once I start,
there's no stopping.
If I read at night,
sometimes I read the same thing over and over.
I read the same thing over and over.
I read the same thing over and over.
I read the same thing over and over.

Hali Wetzel, Grade 4
Acacia Elementary School, AZ

Camping

I keep hiking the last few yards to the campsite,
Finally I think, this is it
I flop down and close my eyes,
Waiting, waiting for the morning to come, then I will hike
the rest of the trail to Diamond Lake.

Larissa Hunt, Grade 4
Mesa Elementary School, CO

Save Me!

A child no more than 10 just walking along
I cry to him but he does not hear
"Save me, oh please save me," I cry
But he just stands there
Watching me die
And as the lumberjack cut me down
Tears of sap come streaming down
And I whisper my last words
"Please, oh please, won't someone save me?"
With a large boom
I fall

Marjorie Howard, Grade 6
Blaine Middle School, WA

Families

Who are they?
People that love you
Stand beside you
Nurse you when you're sick
Hold you when you feel helpless
Give you a friend when you're lonely
Who are they?
People who see you when you're not seen
Make you beautiful when you feel ugly.
They are the people that forever will be a part of you.
This is who they are.
Who are they to you?

Katherine Collins, Grade 6
Pope John XXIII Catholic School Community, AZ

The "Ping"

Old lady in a black bonnet holding a pot
I flung in half a dollar just to hear it go "ping."
Remembered then. Felt shivers. Heart just stopped.
I had thrown away money I had saved for shopping.
Though my mother wasn't mad but smiling.
I call that "ping" the greatest gift I have ever given.

Valerie Parrish, Grade 6
Home Choice Academy, WA

I Live for Music

I live for music.
It whispers in my ear.
It keeps my heart thumping.
It tells me everything I want to hear.
Singing the highest note.
Staying in perfect tune.
Playing chords on the piano.
Performances in late noon.
It replaces my anger,
And fills me up with joy.
It's like having an indestructible,
Everlasting toy.
It's like wind that blows through my soul.
But it all starts with passion and faith,
So every song
Has voice and strength.
I love music,
It gives most pleasure.
It also brings happiness,
That is not able to measure.

Manon Ward, Grade 6
Spring Creek Elementary School, WY

Spring

Can you hear the sound of a river flowing?
Can you smell the sweetness of spring?
Can you see the lovely colors of flowers?
Can you feel the misty dew on your skin?
I can!
Butterflies, ladybugs, and cute caterpillars,
Cubs, pups, chicks, and foals,
All so young, all so new.
All are signs of spring.
The sun is dancing through the trees.
The grass is growing green.
All so pretty, all so nice.
All are signs of spring.
Lovely flowers, so bright, so beautiful.
The sky so blue with clouds so fluffy.
All so beautiful, all so different.
All are signs of spring.
All the smiles and happiness fill the air.
And love is flowing through pair to pair.
Because spring is finally here.

Kristin Palmer, Grade 5
La Veta Elementary School, CO

Smoking Is Bad for You

When you try it
The smoke burns
You will start to enjoy the nasty pit
The chemicals churn
You will start to throw fits

You start to become someone new
Someone nobody likes
but you don't know the few
From doing the same bad things you do
So take a hike
and never come back 'til you are the same
like everyone knew

Courtney Matera, Grade 6
Green Valley Christian School, NV

Patches

My friendly lovable friend
She loves hay, cubes, and grain
She also loves to eat weeds outside her pen
But that is the only thing she thinks about

Her name is Patches
The little cute miniature pony
The beautiful tan and white spots she has
She is my cute lovable friend

When the weather gets bad
She runs wild in her pen
She bucks, kicks, and runs
And has a fun time

She has hard times sometimes
But with her friends me and Bommer
She gets through the day
My friendly lovable friend

Cayley McComas, Grade 6
Walt Clark Middle School, CO

Albuquerque

The land I once called home in the Rockies
I traveled over roads of rock
In caves I dared to brave
We traveled an area of sixty-one miles
To see Area Fifty-one, the White Sands
One of the only natural wonders still to stand

At last when I was three
We moved to the land of the trees
I missed home so much I wanted to flee
But how could that be
If I was three
So I leave behind Albuquerque.

Corbin Post, Grade 6
Uplands Elementary School, OR

Lava Lamp

Laying in my nice comfy bed, feeling safe and warm,
I'm watching shapes melt, and then again reform.

First I see a clown, juggling happily in the air.
Next I see a lion tamer and a great big grizzly bear.

All of a sudden the bear is gone, the lion tamer too.
But in its place quickly appears a small lime cockatoo.

Bye goes the cockatoo, up comes a doll.
Rising next come shopping bags from the Denver mall.

I see many interesting shapes, all of different size and form.
But the ones that really catch my eye, are a tornado and a hailstorm.

These things kind of scare me, but I know it will be all right.
For all I've done is watch my green lava lamp tonight.

Teal Jenkins, Grade 6
Spring Creek Elementary School, WY

From My Window

The moon reflected across lazily drifting clouds,
Turning them to wonderful white blues, and brilliant blue whites.
Uranus's belt lit the sky, twinkling up so very high.
Flowers closed sending out their last perfume.
The birds twittered their last lullaby to me.
The church steeple glowed nearby up on high.
The trees wavered in a breeze.
The moon, a pure white shining pearl,
Set a shine on the yard of mine.
The grass glittered with late evening dew.
Clouds sleepily drifting to bed in the morning they'll start a new.
Streetlights glimmered in the distance
I had seen a day close with pride!

Erica Henderson, Grade 5
Discovery Elementary School, ID

Recipe for a Wishing Star

Mix 1 star,
A pinch of happiness,
A cup of wishes,
Two flashlights,
A pinch of salt and a cup of beliefs.
Put happiness and wishes in a yellow bowl.
Mix with the flashlights until it's glowing as yellow as the sun.
Pour in beliefs to make your wish come true.
Bake in a 20 X 20 pan at 975° F until glowing at sight that is so bright.
Take it out and add the star immediately.
Sprinkle on the salt to make it pop.
Close your eyes.
Think of your wish.
The star will be gone but your wish will be there.

Richard Martinez, Grade 5
Desert View Academy, AZ

I Can Feel Spring Getting Closer
I take in the damp aroma of spring in the air.
The sweet tempting odor of flowers in the air.
The scent of blossoms blooming is very unique.
I can feel spring getting closer.

I can lick the bitter taste of rain.
The overripe fruit is good on my throat.
The mellow grass is bad for you to eat.
I can feel spring getting closer.

I feel the damp grass on the breezy night.
Wet feel of flowers feels good on my hands.
Warmness rushes through my body out in the sun.
I can feel spring getting closer.

Tiny flowers bloom in the spring season.
Irregular scene of animals awakening from hibernation.
The cloudy sky drops rain in the spring.
I can feel spring getting closer.

The beat of ducks quacking fills my ears.
Clamor as the raindrops fall in the spring.
Thumping of peeping birds up in their tree.
I can feel spring getting closer.
Zach Green, Grade 6
Bella Vista Elementary School, UT

My Flowers Are
My flowers are

different
unique
really interesting
very tall
each a different source of happiness
a pollen paradise
so beautiful they make the robins stare
able to bring sunshine to Pluto
the highlight of my day

But my flowers still cannot be perfect.
Henry Halkyard, Grade 4
The Meadows School, NV

Monkeys
M any different tricks
O h, they also play with sticks
N ow you know they eat bananas
K eep listening, they wear bandanas
E ast, west, north, south — they can't tell
Y ou'll see they don't listen well
S o, do you like monkeys? (I sure do)

…swell, 'cause they like you, too
Courtney Miller, Grade 4
Hidden Hills Elementary School, AZ

Another Dimension of School
I'm in another dimension
Where it is easy to pay attention

I know I can read and write
Study every day and night

Spelling, grammar, reading and math
All leads me down a path

The days go as fast as a flash of light
That beams to the stars in the dark of night

But here in fifth grade
I will be here for the end of the day.
Carlos Vega, Grade 5
St Patrick's Catholic School, WA

I Am
I am a talented guy who likes pirates.
I wonder how many pirates can fill a pirate ship.
I hear 25 pirates singing, "Yo ho yo ho a pirate's life for me!"
I see Captain Jack Sparrow sailing the "Black Pearl."
I want to be a real pirate sailing on the "Black Pearl."
I am a talented guy who likes pirates.
I pretend to be one of Captain Jack's shipmates.
I feel the ships deck underneath my feet.
I touch my weapons as we get ready to battle.
I worry if our ship becomes taken over by the other one.
I cry at the sight of a sword blade to my throat.
I am a talented guy who likes pirates.
I understand being a pirate means putting your life on the line.
I say, "God will guide me to my destination."
I dream of being a pirate all day long.
I hope one day I can become a real pirate.
I am a talented guy who likes pirates.
Andrew Collins, Grade 6
Cadwallader Middle School, NV

My Dream Place
My dream place is big and gigantic,
It has forests and houses and big arcades,
It has animals of all kinds,
They're all big and small,
I have a tower where I can see,
All with candy and soda,
I can play games,
It is a paradise,
But when I wake up from a daydream,
Or get up from bed it is all gone,
Till I go back to bed,
Or daydream again,
Where I start all over,
Again on a new adventure.
Nicolas Crespin, Grade 5
Cuba Elementary School, NM

Jellyfish Job

I've got a job for a jellyfish,
Here is what you do,
You take this unfortunate jellyfish,
And squeeze out all the goo.
Jonathan Davidson, Grade 5
CLASS Academy, OR

It

Oh, I'm alone in the dark,
Always hearing a bark.
I have no one to hold,
So I am told.
Some people don't understand
My fears in the dark.
All alone in the dark.
What's coming out?
My parents are gone
And I can't give a shout.
Here it comes closer, and closer, as so.
Don't give up! Go, go, go.
Don't ever give up without a fight.
It's coming closer in the night.
Ryan Hoag, Grade 4
Fulton Elementary School, CO

Basketball

Basketball
Fun, hard
Running, shooting, passing
Go for the shot!
Sport
Elida Mendez, Grade 4
Jackpot Combined School, NV

Do You Love Me?

You see me, I see you
You look so very, very blue
I wish you wouldn't look this way
I don't want you to go away

Let's talk about the way you feel
Let's make sure our love is real
I love you lots, do you love me?
I need to know, tell me I plea
Steven Van Cott, Grade 5
Colbert Elementary School, WA

Heaven

H armonious living
E ntering lives
A ngels worshipping
V alues concrete
E verlasting joy
N ations united
Tim Pittman, Grade 6
Spring Creek Elementary School, WY

Grass

The shiny green grass
Waves warmly in the garden
Like waves in the sea.
Tanner Rhineheart, Grade 5
Sequoia Village School, AZ

The Secret Window

Behind the window lies a secret,
The story was never shared.
Nobody noticed, except for me,
I was the only one to care!
No one will ever dare to touch it.
No one will dare, to peek.
The truth lies beneath the window
For it will never be seen.
Porsha Grimmett, Grade 5
Sally Mauro Elementary School, UT

Snowboarding

As soon as you
Get off the lift
It seems as if
You're surfing on snow,
Gaining some speed
It's like you're going
500 miles per hour,
Hitting a ramp
You are gliding
Through the air,
And when you fall
You land in a puffy cloud,
Snowboarding in the woods
Is like flying
In a magical place.
Taylor Willan, Grade 6
Monforton School, MT

Magic

Magic is delightful,
which brings me luck.
I wish I was a fairy,
that would take every wish,
the light that brings,
can be a drag.
But it has brightness.
I make a simple wish,
that would come true.
The fairy comes by,
and grants the wish I make.
I wished the whole world…
would be a good, lucky, world.
The fairy grants the wish.
Then, good bye to the evil people,
and to the magical fairy.
Paige Talks Different, Grade 5
Harlem Elementary School, MT

The Snowy Night

One snowy night it was
snowing and I was awake.
I went outside twirl and swirl,
round and round I went.
It was a miracle it was snowing!
Abigail Nieblas, Grade 4
Clawson School, AZ

Rain

Out of the clouds
Through the sky
Among the leaves
Beyond the mountains
Between the branches of a bush
During the rainfall
Under the covered porch I sit and listen
Marissa Nielsen, Grade 6
Blaine Middle School, WA

Shadows of the Night

Shadows, shadows
Everywhere
Haunting, taunting
Laughing their wicked laughs
Creepy, enchanting
Eerie, amazing
Lying there,
Waiting for
Light.
Ellie Stelter, Grade 4
West Woodland School, WA

Springs Gymnastics

Springs Gymnastics rocks!
There are sweet and sassy gymnasts.
Kind coaches and nice people.
You can't eat too much fat or sugar.
Hiphop,
Dance,
And Jazz is what we're good at.
Can make a loop
with their body
because we're so flexible.
We're unbeatable.
We're so strong.
We will rock you out of this world.
That's why I like Springs Gymnastics.
Amanda Widen, Grade 4
Acacia Elementary School, AZ

Marbles

Where are my marbles?
I now only have a few.
Oh, where have they gone?
Charlie Olson, Grade 5
Gold Canyon Elementary School, AZ

The Frozen Wilderness

The furnished frost stuck
With famished fear,
Bristling moonlight was
Wounded like a devil.
An unusually timid brute,
Snapping frost was worn out fire,
A frozen leaf snapped at
The eager dog.
The fire sprang from the wood with an
Unusually timid demon frozen to a pine tree,
The fire at last sprang to a leaf with a frozen goodbye.

Evan Baylis, Grade 6
Liberty Middle School, CO

Writing = Boring

I just don't like writing (well duh! look at the title)
It makes my brain start to melt
But I have to write this story
And it's reeeeeally start'n to bore me!
I'd rather play
And talk all day
Hang out with my friends
And, of course, go home!
I don't want to write
I just want to think
It takes all night
When I have to write
Teacher, if you hire guys to write it for me
The faster I will be.

Joshua Guski, Grade 4
Kathy L Batterman Elementary School, NV

Gardner Takes Gold

Laurel was excellent at volleyball
She didn't waste her time at the mall
One day she tried for the Olympic team
She made it and sported a big beam
She went all over town
Never letting anyone get her down
Laurel was determined
She knew that she could win

Laurel didn't know if she could make it
Although she did have incredible wit
She did her best
To be known all over the west
She could not believe what she had been told
She had won the Olympic Gold

She is remembered to this day
She is cool in so many ways
And she will make you smile
All the while

Laurel Gardner, Grade 6
Corpus Christi School, CO

Flaming Sunset

Like a rock on fire
Beautiful reds, yellows, and oranges,
Behind the low mountains I live upon.
Crickets beginning to chirp as daylight fades
Bats flying about looking for their meals
Fresh dew upon the grass
All alone relaxing to the fire in the sky,
Thinking about the sun in my imagination,
I touch the stars as they begin to come out
And the crystal clear moon as its light floods my eyes.
Thinking about tomorrow's sunset takes over my mind,
At home having everything be the same as yesterday.

Emma Littrell, Grade 4
Lincoln Elementary School, AZ

Sun Rays

When summer begins the sky turns a soft blue,
the grasses turn a shocking green,
the leaves are now full on the trees,
flowers of many kinds blossom,
and color the meadows, valleys, yards,
and fill the air with sweet scents.
Children play about the tall grasses,
and bumble bees buzz everywhere.
Lakes, ponds, rivers, and streams,
are full of fresh, cool, and sparkling water.
But most of all the sun rays,
are the most beautiful of all nature's magical world!!!

Meagan Wagner, Grade 5
University Park Elementary School, AK

Me All Alone in My Room

Me all alone in my room.
I sleep when I am tired.
I read when I have a good book from the library.
I color when I feel like coloring
I jump on the bed
When I feel like jumping on my bed.
I listen to slow music
When I am in the mood for slow music.
I listen to hard music
When I am in the mood to have some fun.
That is what I do most of the time
When I am all alone in my room.

Jessica Gilmore, Grade 5
Sangre De Cristo Elementary School, CO

The Moon

The moon is bright;
The moon is brightly shining out of my window on a cold night.
The reflection of the moon gave me a fright.
I looked out my window on that cold night.
The moon was brighter than ever.
Then morning came to sight.

Riley Manahan, Grade 4
Christian Faith School, WA

I Wish I Had a Star

I wish I had a star in the night,
as my light
so I won't feel alone.
All the time when it's dark
I wish I had a star.

Gabriel Martinez, Grade 4
Lewis E. Rowe Elementary School, NV

Brown

Brown is the color
Of an apple seed,
Peanut butter
And a millipede.

Brown is the color
Of a nice warm beach,
A cup of dirt
And the stem of a peach.

Brown is the color
Of a can of rootbeer,
Hot carmel apples
And the fur of a deer.

Brown is the color
Of bark on a tree.
The meat that I eat
And sometimes a husky.

Brown is the color
Of logs on the ground,
A pile of mud
And the floor of a pound.

Brook Erhart, Grade 6
Kendallvue Elementary School, CO

Pogo

I have a pogo stick.
I jump all day and night.
I can do a fancy trick.
All I do is hold on tight.

It is made of steel.
The colors are blue and red.
It takes a lot of skill
Or I'll end up in bed.

My mom tells me to stop.
My dad tells me to rest.
When I am just about to drop
I know I have done my best.

My pogo stick is great.
I'll jump tomorrow — I can't wait!

Jayde Adam, Grade 4
Reid School, UT

Peace and Chaos

A pack of dogs quarreling over a long-lost morsel
Far away in a realm of peace, a star sits on the edge of the Milky Way
The moon's reflection twinkling in a puddle — a foot
The reflection shivers, then gone
Gliding in the sky a spirited dove emerges from behind the clouds
Below the endless battle between man and the impossible
A speeding bullet slices the air
An unsuspecting target frozen in Time
Flickering, the single flame of a candle
A gust of wind engulfs the warmth, smoke spiraling in the air
The outstretched arm of a galaxy beckoning vibrant colors into its trance,
A black hole giving no mercy to it victims
The peaceful trickle of a mountain stream
The mess of a cluster of stars in the center of an ever-growing galaxy
A crowded Tokyo crosswalk
The far away serene setting of a mountain summit
Waves licking the sandy shore beneath the surface,
The chaos cloud of ink announcing an octopus's exit
Tranquility of blank nothingness, only pure silence
The piercing shriek of a hurricane wind
Swirling thoughts, the peace of simple life

Heath Hilliard, Grade 6
Khalsa Montessori Elementary School, AZ

Santa Paws

I don't know if there's Santa Claus,
But at my house there's Santa Paws,
They have beards, eat cookies, give gifts and a kiss.
Although Santa Claus says "Ho, Ho, Ho,"
Santa Paws says "Go, Go, Go."
Even though you don't see Santa Claus with your eyes in any way,
I see Santa Paws eating pies every day!
Merry Christmas

Callen Falash, Grade 5
St Mary's School, ID

Colors

If I were blue, I would be a gentle river flowing to the ocean.
If green, I would be a lochness monster lurking in the depths.
If I were silver, I would be the rocks laying on a stream bed.
If I were white, I would be a mouse sleeping in the hay bales.
If brown, I would be the bark of a tree that was part of a beaver dam.
These are the colors that I'd be.

Boone Tullett, Grade 4
East Evergreen Elementary School, MT

Football

I see the quarterback getting ready for the play on the fourth down.
I hear my team cheering me on.
I taste the cold water as I pour it on my head and drink it during a timeout.
I touch the rough ball as I catch an interception.
I smell the immense amount of sweat that is all over my body
I feel happy because I just made an interception and ran 25 yards for a touchdown
I know that I'm playing football.

Varun Bahl, Grade 5
Eton School, WA

I Know

I know of a place
Where anything is possible.
I can do what I want,
And the world around me changes.

The stars shine like silver
The sun glows like gold
The sunset is as radiant as ruby
And the clouds are as dazzling as diamond.
I know of a place
Where anything is possible;
Where I can escape.

I go there
When my eyelids grow heavy,
And darkness takes me.
I travel to a parallel world,
Where impossible things happen.
I know of a place
Where anything is possible
And I can find peace.

Paul Zukowski, Grade 6
Walker Middle School, OR

I Don't Like It!

I don't like spaghetti
I don't like zucchini
I don't like the noodles that hang from fettuccine.

I don't like ugly sunburns
I don't like when your stomach churns
Because if you eat too much you might get heartburn!

I don't like people who are rude
Or even people who are all over tattooed
I don't like studying about latitude and longitude.

I don't like that noisy truck
I don't like when you run out of luck
Because if your car breaks down, then you are really stuck!

But now it's time to say good bye
I know I'm sad, I will not lie,
So hurry, go before I start to cry.

Adriana Valentin, Grade 5
First Baptist Christian Academy, AZ

The Scary Day

I hear a noise in my house,
I'm so scared that I don't want to go downstairs.
I take a peek, and no one is there.
I go outside.
It's only the leaves rustling in the air.
Whew!

Guadalupe Lujan, Grade 4
Lewis E. Rowe Elementary School, NV

Magic Box

I will put in my magic box,
The sounds of a train thundering down the track,
The sound of planes jet crying like a little baby,
The sound of a car engine booming as loud as can be.

I will put in my box,
The sound of a train's whistle like a cry for help,
The sound of a plane roaring down the runway,
The purr of a car racing along the concrete road.

I will put in my box,
The loving family so warm and fuzzy,
The baby always saying "bla-bla,"
The sounds of a family.

Brett Matissen, Grade 5
Mesa Elementary School, CO

Love

If love was a color it would be pink
If love was a candy it would be sweet
If love was a food it would be delicious
If love was a blanket it would be warm and fuzzy
If love was an animal it would be soft and cuddly
If love was a flower it would be a rose

Love isn't a color, or a candy, or a food,
Or a blanket, or an animal, or a flower.
Love is an emotion that I love!

Vanity Hoopes, Grade 5
Discovery Plus Academy, AZ

Death

Death, it comes and goes,
Sometimes without a warning,
And takes us away,
Sometimes in our sleep,
And sometimes,
In the midst of our family,
Then we begin,
A new life,
And sometimes,
Even a never ending journey,
A journey,
That will take our souls,
And then our body,
Lay back down,
On Earth, where it will always be,
Then our spirit grows, grows into one last shape,
Then that journey will start again,
One last time,
Once that spirit dies,
We will finally,
Go to a peaceful place, a sleeping state.

Jennifer Abbott, Grade 6
Barbara Bush Elementary School, AZ

A Rainy Day

A rainy day, just looking to play.
Sitting inside, nothing to do.
Then I see something,
it just peeks over the mountain,
the sun.
I ask Mom if I can go outside,
but she says it's too wet.
So here I am
looking out the window,
but would you look at that,
a rainbow.

Ashley Stephens, Grade 4
Acme Elementary School, WA

Ladybugs

Cute polka dot bugs
fly in the air with small wings
I'd like one for me

Catrina Quigley, Grade 4
St Thomas the Apostle School, AZ

The Door

Behind the cabin door
Within two mountaintops
Among the river valley
Between the grassy field
Along the bushy path
Toward the bright star
At the rocky hill
Down the river pole
Up the colorful fence
Behind the cabin door.

Miguel Hernandez, Grade 6
Fox Creek Jr High School, AZ

Dream On…

Go ahead
my little child
dream on,
go ahead and dream on
for a while.
Dream on…
go ahead and dream on
about your little dolly
coming alive,
or dream about
good…
lollipops,
ice cream,
a frog,
or even about
getting a dog.
Just go ahead and dream on
my child.

Kiana Ziola, Grade 4
New Emerson School, CO

I Am From

I am from guns with noise
Blasting from the barrels

From the warm fire place
With light flashing

I am from the corncob fields
That rise with green
With rabbits hopping with delight

From the French bread
So hot in the oven

I am from hunting with Dad
That makes me proud

Garrett Arndt, Grade 4
Grass Valley Elementary School, NV

Black

Black is the color
Of a bowling ball,
A gorilla's fur
And the old lady's shawl.

The glare
Of Zorro's midnight act,
Also the color
Of a bat and a cat.

Stripes on a zebra
A panda bear,
Eyeliner, mascara
And very dark hair.

A Raiders jersey
A hockey puck,
Dark chocolate, licorice
And very bad luck.

The midnight sky
A raven's dark eye,
A spider, a beetle
And black berry pie.

Sierra Barela, Grade 6
Kendallvue Elementary School, CO

My Feet

My feet running everywhere
Telling me where to go
Turning this way and that
Making me go places I want to go
Or don't want to go
My feet big and strong
Just the way I like them

Allison McIntire, Grade 6
Walt Clark Middle School, CO

If I Had a Dime

If I had a dime
For every time you made me cry,
I swear
That I would be a millionaire.
I'd swim in cash
Instead of tears
And dream of hopes
Instead of fears.
If I had a dime
I'd buy myself some time
That I could feel alive.

Cheyenne Meadows, Grade 6
Desert Mountain School, AZ

Low Rider

Hydraulics, classic cars,
Two doors, batteries,
They jump high.
To buy you've got to do lots of chores.
Four wheels pop up
Then break down
The car gets lighter
"So cool, so cool!"
This makes a low rider.

Freddy Rosales, Grade 6
Patton Middle School, OR

Armies

Armies
courageous, strong
protecting our country
gratefulness is upon armies
Heroes

Amanda Matheson, Grade 4
Trails West Elementary School, CO

Ivory Snow

Trees around ivory balanced
Snow cluttered,
Gloomy snow falls
Through hands along icy roads
Sharp and shaggy

Sierra Leslie Cain, Grade 5
Hafen Elementary School, NV

Oliver

Oliver, how do I love thee?
Let me count the ways,
You're fat and fluffy,
You eat and sleep
Then eat some more,
You go to stretch out on the floor,
You lay on the bed and I pet your head,
That's why I love you Oliver.

Pete Akerele-Ale, Grade 5
St Cyril Elementary School, AZ

Ben Franklin

There once was a boy; he flew his kite
In the mid-blue-sky light
While clipping his toenails,
Not lifting a finger
Zooming across the river.
"Who," you ask, "Who is this crazy boy?"

This boy is Ben Franklin,
A citizen, an inventor, don't forget kind man.
He invented the Franklin stove,
Did you know?
Oh, Ben was an awesome citizen
Ben organized the first volunteer fire department.
A boy, a man, a philosopher
Ben Franklin
Ben Franklin
A man that saved our lives.

Michelle N. Petrie, Grade 5
Mary Blair Elementary School, CO

Spring Is Here

Spring is here,
when the wind is blowing.
The sun shines over my head,
while I ride my bike.
The best part I like is playing baseball all day.
I pay for ice cream that cools my body.
Be sure to be ready for spring,
because, it is here.

Pablo Garay, Grade 4
McCormick Elementary School, NM

Sightless

A tragic accident kept him from seeing,
And now problems are popping up from nowhere,
We were out at the horse pen
When his life was twisted towards utter darkness,
We have to be careful with him now,
Since he has gone blind.

Kathryn A. New, Grade 5
Sangre De Cristo Elementary School, CO

Navy Blue

Navy blue is war like Navy men dying
and also like war ships getting blown up.
It fights through my heart.
It reminds me of death all over the world.
It makes me feel angry and sad.
It makes me want to help.
When I grow up I will learn all there is about war.
I will fight among my fellow men
and defend my country
even if I don't survive.

Tylin Hartman, Grade 6
Walt Clark Middle School, CO

The Wind Master

The wind blows,
carrying a mystical wolf known as
The Wind Master.
His eyes are black,
yet you rarely see him.
His fur seems to camouflage,
making him virtually invisible.
When this wolf is angry,
he scampers around the clouds in fury,
causing a storm to occur.
If The Wind Master is pleased,
he lets out soothing breezes across the land.
As the night arrives and clouds part from the moon,
the wolf opens his mouth and he lets out a long, peaceful howl.
Slowly, The Wind Master begins to age.
His eyes become dull, yet full of hope.
He releases his final breath and the winds die down.
The Wind Master is gone.

Anika Faruk, Grade 4
Kyrene De Las Brisas School, AZ

All About Sarah Dail

I used to be a little girl,
But now I am a young lady,
I used to be scared of monsters under my bed,
But now I have a mess under it,
I used to be a little one year old,
But now I am an 11 year old kid,
I used to go to Esperanza,
But now I go to wonderful Wheeler,
I used to be in kindergarten,
But now I am in fifth grade,
I used to ride a bike with training wheels,
But now I am riding a huge bike,
I used to drink from a bottle,
But now I drink from a cup,
I used to live in a mobile home,
But now I live in a real house.

Sarah Dail, Grade 5
Wheeler Elementary School, AZ

Ode to the Snow

I love you snow, so very much.
How you glimmer and shine in the sun,
Some days so fluffy and light,
While others bitter cold.
Sledding down hills,
Gliding on your fluffy powder
Is always fun.
So are snowball fights and making snowmen,
Building igloos and tunnels.
But when it comes to an end,
There is less and less of you; we are very sad,
But we know you'll come again!!

Ashlyn R. Wong, Grade 5
Mary Blair Elementary School, CO

Weeds

Dandelions grow in your soil
They sit there day and night.
It's like a mark on someone's skin
When the owner sees it, he has a fright.

They don't have much color
They wait as the days go by.
They've watched history
While they slowly die.

They drink the deadly poison
And we are the poison itself.
It's not beautiful
It's not so smooth.

You can make a wish
The seeds are a flying ghost.
And yet we're killing life itself
And the thing we desire most.

Marina Johnson, Grade 5
Barratt School, UT

A Storm

Eyes blaze like an open fire,
Awaiting an attack,
The trees dance excitedly,
Stars dive deep,
Hiding from a devil,
Ancient life returns,
Haunting a young soul,
Blood cries throughout a silent forest,
Moonlight brightens everything,
Glistening, jealousy strikes,
A storm of anger erupts,
Lightning falls, thunder screams,
A slow failure departed,
To his despairing doom,
Leaving a triumphant winner,
Standing upon glory,
Watching over his obedient followers,
The forest tastes fresh,
Trees weave through the air wickedly,
The forest rejoices,
Then becomes ghastly calm.

Meagan Bak, Grade 6
Liberty Middle School, CO

The Hairy Berry

There once was a man named Larry
He didn't want to get married
He saw a girl
It made his head twirl
But her face looked like a hairy berry.

Abdella Ismail, Grade 6
South Middle School, CO

My Cat

My cat is yellow;
  Mostly he's mellow.
    His heart is of gold,
      His attitude bold.
He's a hunter of mice.

My cat is daring,
  Cuddly and caring.
    Soft is his fur,
      And deep is his purr.
He thought I was nice.

My cat is a prize,
  Soft are his eyes.
    Adventurous and fun,
      I know he's the one:
The one cat for me.

My cat is so great,
  But came home very late.
    He sat on the lawn;
      The next day he was gone.
No more will I see the one cat for me

My cat *was* yellow…

Seth Rickard, Grade 6
Walt Clark Middle School, CO

Basketball

Jumping, running, fouling
Scoring, dribbling, shooting.
  I like to have a hard game
But I like to win those games.
  Good teamwork and trust
Wins championships for your team.
  Basketball is my favorite sport,
I like the way you run around the court.
  I love basketball!!!

Marco Rodriguez, Grade 5
St Mary's School, ID

My Rabbit

My rabbit is soft,
  So cuddly,
    And cute.
Gray is her color
  With brown
    Adorable eyes.
What color will she be
  When she's an adult?
    It's a mystery,
And that's her name…
  Mystery.

James Robinson, Grade 4
Brush Creek Elementary School, CO

Blue

Blue is mellow.
It's fresh and flowing.
It cools you on a warm summer day.

Blue thrives in everything,
Rides on clouds,
Drips into faucets,
and covers the world.

Blue is round
and soft.

Blue is inspiring.

Justin Sherburne, Grade 6
Patton Middle School, OR

That Special Time of the Year

The sound of the stream
minnows dance from rock to rock
what a peaceful sight

Alyssa Knauer, Grade 4
St Thomas the Apostle School, AZ

Springtime

Beautiful spring smell
lilies growing up and down
like a quilt of life

Amy Toman, Grade 4
St Thomas the Apostle School, AZ

What Love Brings

Love comes with its faith
Knowing the sun will rise
Lighting every coming day
As faithful as a friend
As trustworthy as a family member

Love comes with its pain
Like the bellows of the sea
Banging across the ocean side
As painful as the grief of life
As painful as a strike of a sword

Love comes with its depression
Like the cry of the rain
As dreadful as a howl of a wolf
As fearful as the dark

Love comes with its hope
Like a seed of a rose
Hoping for the showers of rain
As hoping it will soon grow
As hopeful as the shine of the sun

Kyra Hatch, Grade 6
Discovery Plus Academy, AZ

Dear Eagle

High up in the sky, watch the beautiful eagle fly,
the land was his till he met a gun,
the eagle died so he left his son,
the poison killed one by one,
but the little eagle wants to die he was free,
until they let him be,
one day the little eagle met a man's son,
so he left his only one.

Casandra Jones, Grade 5
Klickitat Elementary & High School, WA

Fire

Fire all things devours
birds, bees, trees and flowers.
It burns all in its path,
inflicting pain on the innocent.
Fire, oh Fire what will you burn next?
I desire to rule fire, but not kill or hurt.
I will use it for good or my name isn't Ruger.

Ruger Tyron Goodwin Bradley, Grade 4
Roy Moore Elementary School, CO

Run Away

Run away to the things that are fun
Run away from the clouds that block the sun

Run away to celebrate the race that you won
Run away from those who didn't cheer you on

Run away from gossip and schemes
Run away to your wildest dreams

Run away because your friends want you to go
Run away from the feelings that hurt you so

Run away to your secret hiding place
Run away so you can hide your face

Run away from the ones who bug you
Run away to the people who love you

Janie Higgins, Grade 6
St Anne School, WA

Sleepers

Haven't you heard of the people that creak in the night
but sleep in the day.
You haven't heard of the people that sleep under
your bed and steal half your head?
So tell your teacher about the people
that creak in the night.
So that's what you tell your teacher when you doze off
in class,
that you lost half your
head…

Kaela M. Piehler, Grade 6
Acme Elementary School, WA

Things in Life

Life is fair
Not fair
Or maybe just right
You may cry
You may laugh
Or you may be fearful
Friends may come
Or friends will go
People may die
But don't cry
Other people are on their way
People come
Put your smile on
To receive them right
Parents yell at you
It's only for your safety
The world is unsafe
But may have a safe place somewhere
Everybody that loves you will help you forever
And love you forever.

Yareth Corral, Grade 5
La Veta Elementary School, CO

I Love Summer

One of the seasons I love is summer
Because of the wonderful scents you smell outside
Summer is the season I can wear
Fun, fashionable, and funky flip-flops
Without freezing my tiny toes like I would
In winter
Summer is the season where you can have
"Fun in the Sun"
And sip your ice-cold lemonade outside
The season where you go shopping for a new
Bikini for swimming and tanning
Summer is the time of year where all the
Astonishing flowers bloom once again
I Love Summer!

Alanda Barash, Grade 6
Desert Mountain School, AZ

Morning Sunrise

The morning sun, rises up
Behind the mountain peaks
With streaks of radiant light.

The sun's warmth as it rises into the sky
Awakens those who slumber.
Birds tweet to greet the new day.

I notice the beginning of a peaceful day.
I imagine being able to touch the horizon
As I enjoy the beautiful sunrise.

Victoria Garnica, Grade 4
Lincoln Elementary School, AZ

All About Amanda Modica

I used to be a giggly first grader, but now I am a responsible 5th grader.

I used to have short thick hair, but now I have long thin brown hair.

I used to put my hair up in colorful ponytails, but now I use colorful poky teeth hair clips.

I used to live with my dad and my mom, but now I live with my mom.

I used to be a lazy 9 year old, but now I am a very active 11 year old in track.

I used to live in a house with my grandma, but now I live in a big apartment with a pool.

I used to be clean and frilly neat, but now I don't mind getting dirty and muddy.

I used to not read boring books, but now I love to read and explore great books.

I used to write very badly, but now I write neatly in cursive.

I used to have fish, but now I have calico cats, and a weird hamster.

Amanda Modica, Grade 5
Wheeler Elementary School, AZ

Daddy

When I was little, and couldn't read, Daddy read to me before I went to sleep.

Now that I'm older, Daddy tells me to have the best dreams ever, so through the night I could have good thoughts to keep.

He'll always tell me I'm the best little kid no matter how old I get, no matter what I do.

I know that any problems I face, Daddy will help me through.

He always checks on me no matter what, to make sure I'm safe and sound.

It makes me feel better when I know that Daddy is around.

He would do anything it took to make sure our family is okay.

I know that because he tells us every single day.

I know that Daddy truly loves me, and my family too.

So Daddy, this is my way of saying thank you for all the things you do.

Megan Armstrong, Grade 6
Colbert Elementary School, WA

Homework Frustrations

I lay on my bed, hands in my head, wondering why my English paper wasn't being proofread.

On top of that I've got a report on the Mayas that's at least five pages, even though I've known about it for ages.

If that isn't enough I've also got a P.E. paper about how to stay physically fit and buff.

By now you think this couldn't be real, well you don't know the whole deal.

I've also got math, reading and writing, not to mention my science project, two lab rats, are constantly fighting.

By now I'm thinking my grades are rat food, and I'm really not in the mood.

Unfortunately this is my entire fault, I've slown down, put progress to a halt.

The lesson to be learned and do not scoff, is to work progressively and not put things off.

Ashlen Funke, Grade 6
Heatherwood Middle School, WA

Sunset

As I wait for my taxi in the busy streets of New York, a vivid light overlaps the city

As I look up, the explicit details of the evening sunset hit me like never before

The blazing colors of red and orange shined and sparkled as though it had been given a good wash job

The vivid colors of the sun had now backfired to the sky itself

I watched the sun as it slowly departed back to its snug home for the early arrival the next day

And as I got in the taxi, I caught a last glimpse of the wonderful sunset, and had the fleeting impression that it winked at me

Isaiah Self, Grade 4
Gold Canyon Elementary School, AZ

The Sun

The sun is a passionate flower, blooming day after day, in the sky. It has a unique glow that no light-bulb can match. It sends brightness and purpose to the sky like a postcard, being sent to every mailbox in the world. It outlines every peaceful meadow and sets the world on fire, with colors of orange, pink and yellow. When you see that sweet sunset, love comes to mind. Sun dries up the rain and sorrow, placing a beautiful rainbow in the sky, so high.

Katie Riggs, Grade 6
Glacier Middle School, WA

In My Room

In my strange messy room,
Under the nasty disgusting bed,
Up off the dirty grimy floor,
Beside the pretty colorful dresser,
Down towards the black green-eyed cat,
Up to the plain white door,
Around my contaminated unclean desk,
By the enormous gigantic book shelf,
Upon the dark dusty closet,
Near my beautiful golden cross,
You will find my T-shirt I was looking for.

Brooke Koster, Grade 6
Robert Frost Elementary School, OR

How to Make Music with a Rainbow

First you take the red in the rainbow,
And let it chirp loudly, like a red cardinal,
Singing its flute-like voice in the morning.
Grab the orange and listen carefully,
You'll find its tones as sweet as fresh oranges,
Picked ripe, just right, from the orange grove.
Coax the yellow, it needs encouraging,
To sing the notes of sugary lemonade.
Get the green and blue as the solos of the choir,
Oh-so-calm green makes the same,
Beautiful rustle of the leaves brushed by a breeze,
But only if you blow the rhythm of the wind for it.
The blue will, of course, shine with a song of sad blues,
With the same beat as waves of the ocean, slapping the shore.
Indigo keeps the steady beat: boom, boom, boom, boom!
Its pitch low, like the value of its color is dark.
Last is purple, wonderful purple. Gently arouse it,
Until it is in the mood for waving the baton, and conducting,
The amazing, wonderful Rainbow Orchestra!

Serena Suwarno, Grade 5
Kyrene De Las Brisas School, AZ

Brother

You did not know the people you'd hurt
You did not know the hearts you'd break
When you did the thing you thought was cool
But it was really very lame
Now that you know
And now that it's too late
To change what you did
If you could go back, would you do it?
For the people you hurt
But mostly for you
You changed your life in so many ways
Things you can't go back on and fix
But things you have to live with
For the rest of your life
And try to make better.

Jessica Kildow, Grade 6
Fruitland Middle School, ID

Lacrosse Ode

Players head to their positions,
Stare each other in the eye.
     Sweat rolling down
In the hot sun
Under the pads and helmet.
Heart beating loudly
The ref gets ready.
     "Tweet."
The game begins.
Charging, passing, shooting,
Sprinting, checking, blocking.
The quarter ends — refreshed players come back on.
Trying to make a good name for their team.
Here's a shot, great save.
Coaches yell and penalty flags are thrown.
One quarter left in the game.
The shooting, checking, sprinting harder than ever.
The crowd is cheering. The game is over.
A win goes up for our team.

Evan Batten, Grade 6
Pine Grove Elementary School, CO

Spring

Spring is the time of the year when birds sing,
the bees and bugs come out,
the grass turns green,
flowers begin to bloom,
the wind blows hard,
the sun feels warm on my head,
and bears wake up.

Nicholas Tenski, Grade 4
McCormick Elementary School, NM

A Weird and Strange Guy

I am a weird and strange guy
I wonder if I'll still be alive in 2099
I hear the squealing sound of a T-rex
I see a gun pointing at my face
I want a million dollars
I am a weird and strange guy

I pretend that I am the strongest guy in the world
I feel that I could lift a billion pounds
I touch the tallest building in the world by jumping
I worry about being fat, really fat
I cry when I see people being looked at weirdly
I am a weird and strange guy

I understand that I annoy a lot of people
I say that we are all cool
I dream of becoming a Hall of Famer
I try to do excellent in school
I hope that we will have fewer wars
I am a weird and strange guy

Braxton Buckway, Grade 6
H Guy Child School, UT

Garden

Every Saturday morning,
I hear the sunlight calling,
The robins singing brightly,
To wake the morning slightly.
Chelsea Evans, Grade 4
Colbert Elementary School, WA

Red

I am red because I like you.
I am red paint and I can't stop pouring.
I am a picture
That you like.
I am red.
Kellen Lamb, Grade 4
Wilson Elementary School, WA

I Like

Work is fun.
Work is hard.
You can do work.
Teachers are fun.
Teachers are cool.
I don't like teachers.
Fun is fun.
Fun is good.
Fun is happy.
I like to have fun.
Cats are fun.
Cats are happy.
I love to play with cats.
Rock is hard.
Rock is big.
I don't like rock.
Ember Morgan, Grade 5
Cuba Elementary School, NM

Moonlight

The moon's high
In the night sky
The moon's round
Like a yellow bouncy ball
Sometimes shining
Between the clouds
Making shadows
Off the trees
Moonlight
Ben Clark, Grade 4
Scenic Park Elementary School, AK

Roses

White, red and thorny,
Beautiful in the morning.
They are everywhere.
Andrea Rose Miner, Grade 4
Cokeville Elementary School, WY

School

School's a place to learn,
Math, reading, spelling, and art,
Sometimes homework stinks!
Kym Peterson, Grade 6
H Guy Child School, UT

Junior High, Oh My

Junior High, oh my
Seven classes some days eight
Lots of teachers too
Recess gone forever more
What's a kid supposed to do?
Taylor Bybee, Grade 6
H Guy Child School, UT

My Friend

Her hair is as black as the
Night sky
Her eyes are as brown as
Chocolate
She cares for everyone
And everything
Her kindness is as warm as
The sun
Her heart holds love for
Her family and friends
My best friend
Lorena Rodriguez
She lives with two sisters
And four brothers
She eats around her family table
And eats a family dinner
Taylor Chilton, Grade 6
Fruitland Middle School, ID

Origami

Paper folding art,
Left, right, up, down, inside out,
Folds must be precise.
Doug Myers, Grade 5
Bates Elementary School, CO

The Wind

Whispering, whimpering
in the blue sky
hitting the birds
as they fly
blowing your hair back
I wonder why
wind blows every time of the year
even in July
against a tree
makes a lullaby.
Nate Broughton, Grade 5
Lister Elementary School, WA

Daydreaming

Among the clouds
Beneath the flying birds
Along the wooden fence
Under the oak tree
During the summer
Through the meadows
Past the sunflowers
Beside the farm
Beyond the windmill
Within the cattle herd.
Shelby Garoutte, Grade 6
Fox Creek Jr High School, AZ

Tears

Tears come down from
Red and puffy cheeks

Tears drop down to
Hard and thick floor

Splash! Splash! Drip! Drip!
The tears won't stop

Cold and wet tears
Cascade and slip

Sad and lonely tears,
Why won't you stop?
Katie Cho, Grade 5
Eton School, WA

Jehublie Fungus

Splish, splosh, splish splosh.
The water goes glish glosh.
He lives in green grimy water
and he looks for people to slaughter.
Green, yellow, and pink.
His face is as dark as ink.
He is smaller than a pine tree,
bigger than a green pea.
He is a big ball of fungus,
and we don't want him among us.
Splish sposh, splish sposh,
the green grimy water goes glish glosh.
Ally Lund, Grade 6
Midway Middle School, ID

Gymnastics

Gymnastics
Hard, exciting
Tumbling, twisting, flipping
Happy, wonderful, working
Fun
Shannon Cottrell, Grade 5
Copper Creek Elementary School, AZ

Bliss

I loved the way we used to kiss,
It was such a beautiful bliss,
If what I knew now, I knew then,
Maybe right now we would be together again,
As the days pass with sorrow,
I wonder how I will feel tomorrow,
As the phone rings…I take it to ear,
I hear the lovely voice I hold near and dear,
We meet at the corner of love and again,
We hold hands, and then…

We Kiss!
Such a beautiful bliss!

Jenna Richardson, Grade 6
Eagle Point Middle School, OR

Hurricane

Furious beyond mind this catastrophe winds
Like a babe screeching in the night.
Swaying trees dying to survive this horrific event
After the terror was consumed by sunlight,
Devastation filled every heart
The only living joy left be the light
Trying its best to reach out to the desperate.
People everywhere repairing
Awaiting 'til this terror returned.

Jared Roberts, Grade 5
McKinley Elementary School, CO

What If?

What if we are really close?
What if we are far apart?
What if we get along?
What if we can't stand each other?
What if we agree on everything?
What if we can't agree on anything?
What if we get along with each other's new friends?
What if we hate each other's new friends?
I wonder what the future holds.
I wonder what is coming.
What if it works out?
What if it doesn't?

Nicole Ciriello, Grade 6
Pope John XXIII Catholic School Community, AZ

Midnight Stars

Bright stars high above my head
Calm and quiet sound all through the night
Midnight twinkles shining in the sky
A brand new day right in front of me
Soon is yet to come.
Sitting there looking at the sky
I take one last look and picture myself
Touching the brightest light above.

Angie Coronado, Grade 4
Lincoln Elementary School, AZ

Make Me Believe You Love Me!

Is it true I am the one for you?
Could I hang around and call you my boo?

Could you make me believe you love me with a tear?
Would it be true and sincere?

Make Me Believe You Love Me!

I know there is another her!
Is this so called love a blur?

Could it be you are not the one for me?
Is it that hard to see?

Make Me Believe You Love Me!

I really do love you I just don't know what to do!
The question is do you love me too?

Am I really worth hiding and denying?
Oh man it would be easier just crying!

Cassandra McCabe, Grade 6
St Vincent de Paul School, AZ

Parents

My mom is great,
My dad is glad,
My mom is always late,
My dad is rad,
My mom eats dates,
My dad doesn't get mad,
Most of all they both love me.

My step mom is forgiving,
My step dad is kind,
My step mom likes living,
My step dad makes me mind,
My step mom loves to cook for Thanksgiving,
My step dad sometimes falls behind,
Most of all they both love me.

Kalyn Kovacs, Grade 6
Faith Lutheran School, AZ

St. Patrick's Day

St. Patrick's Day is unbelievably fun,
With the shining, bright yellow sun.
The smooth clovers are beautifully green,
While the others are unexpectedly clean.

Everybody wears a tall, green hat.
None too skinny and none too fat.
St. Patrick's Day is unbelievably fun,
With the shining, bright yellow sun.

Hanaka Koffron, Grade 4
Eton School, WA

Colorado

Like snowy peaks touching the sky
Touching the heavens above
Seeming they will never end.
Like plains of excruciating heat
Filled with days of everlasting work
The open sky is everywhere you look.
Like busy cities filled with people
Buildings towering up
Cars trying to get out of rush hour —
Colorado is everywhere I look

Tori Briggs, Grade 6
Walt Clark Middle School, CO

Snow

Snow is falling down,
Icicles hang from the roof
My nose is so red!

Abigail Meeks, Grade 6
Hamilton Middle School, MT

Spring

Spring is when
The warm feeling of the sun
Comes out
The birds sing
The candy tasting songs
Spring is when
The sweet fresh smell of flowers spreads
The white as snow clouds shape

Diana Gomez, Grade 4
Grass Valley Elementary School, NV

The Sun

The sun is awfully bright
Burning us with scorching light
Every summer day.

Edgar Nash, Grade 6
Morgan Middle School, WA

Night Dragon

I see a dragon upon the night sky.
O where, o where does it fly?
I see a cave in the night
where I saw the dragon take flight.

Cory Davis, Grade 6
Sequoia Village School, AZ

Happy

Happy
Always smiling
Laughing, funny, great time
I am always it, it is great
Smile

Katie Baker, Grade 6
H Guy Child School, UT

Him

He loves me for me,
Completes my life.
He doesn't fill my heart…
With sorrow and strife.
He doesn't judge you,
Of how you look.
But now I know him,
Just like a book.
He doesn't hurt me, but I know he will,
'Cause I gave him my heart…
For I wasn't all that smart.

Ashley Poole, Grade 6
Colbert Elementary School, WA

The Turtle Named Murtle

A turtle named Murtle
had a very big shell.
And inside her shell
it rang like a bell.
So when the cock would crow
Murtle didn't know.
Because inside her shell
it rang like a bell.

Ryan Cheney, Grade 4
Windsor School, UT

Clutch

A freezing football field,
Covered in snow,
Cold, wet, chilly,
Your hands are freezing,
You have to snap the ball.
You hear "hut,"
You snap,
It goes over his head.
Your self-esteem is crushed.
You're called on again.
You snap a touchdown.
Now that's CLUTCH!

Adam Ausmus, Grade 5
Frontier Valley Elementary School, CO

Celestial Family

As she nestles us with her
kindness and abundant nature,
the stars brightly shine in the sky.
The Earth protecting the stars,
like a mother with her young.

The stars like children in the
sky, act so much like we do.
Sparkling, twinkling, shooting
about, as Mother Earth looks on.

Siobhan Scantlebury, Grade 6
Pinnacle Charter School, CO

Listen and See

Listen to the sounds
Birds singing,
Crickets chirping
See the trees, flowers,
See the mountains
See the sky and sun
Listen and see nature
And tell me
What you see.

Vanessa Head, Grade 4
Scenic Park Elementary School, AK

The Sun Dissolves

The sun dissolves,
And one by one people
Begin to bare the sun's light.
They each hold their own.
And once the sun dissolves
The people will thrust
The light upon the ground.
It will break, then shine.
Just like the people
Will shine
When the perfect time
Of darkness comes
To let them open up
And to begin
Living as they were meant
To live.

Shelby Perkins, Grade 6
Badger Road Elementary School, AK

Maliyah

Ahh!
How cute.
Small work of God,
and so joyful,
cuddly!
So soft.
A big surprise!
My baby sister.

Tianna Billingsley, Grade 4
Acacia Elementary School, AZ

Hedgehog

My first hedgehog
Named him Odie
He's very prickly
Couldn't find a name
Want more hedgehogs
He's been alive five years
My shrimp eating
Prickly hedgehog Odie.

Sam Aull, Grade 4
Orient Elementary School, WA

Love

Love is just a stronger word for like
Love is used every day
It is said by men, women, kid, etc.
Love means a strong affection

The dog loves the little boy
Fish love water
People love people
And finally, God loves you

Lily Yost, Grade 6
Pope John XXIII Catholic School Community, AZ

The Waterfall Keeps Flowing

The waterfall keeps flowing,
the star keeps glowing.

Sit and think for a while,
think of something that makes you smile.

See anger will never go away,
so you have to let it stay.

Just live life to its fullest.

Just keep the love flowing like a waterfall,
and keep shining like a star.

You don't have to talk to make yourself look good,
it's just how humble you really are.

Daniel Morgan, Grade 6
Eagle Point Middle School, OR

A Pretty and Athletic Girl

I am pretty and athletic
I wonder what I'll look like when I'm 16
I hear the soft sounds of whispers
I see a magical kingdom
I want to get along with my brother
I am pretty and athletic

I pretend I'm a pop star
I feel fairy dust lightly being sprinkled over my head
I touch heaven
I worry about not having friends in Morgan
I cry when I think about moving
I am pretty and athletic

I understand that life isn't always fair
I say there should be no animal abuse
I dream about the future
I try to be a better person
I hope that animals can be treated equally to humans
I am pretty and athletic

Kelli Pringle, Grade 6
H Guy Child School, UT

Sea Star

Sea star, please star,
Tell what you see in the sea, star
I see coral of bright pinks and blues
And fish all around of magnificent hues

Sea star, please star,
Tell what you hear in the sea, star
I hear songs from the whales, moanings and squeals
And the slippery bark of every seal

Sea star, please star,
Tell what you know in the sea, star
I know of the waves, moving the sea
And each little seashell whispering to me

Mariah Farris, Grade 6
Morgan Middle School, WA

Dream Scream

I wish I had a dream
That would make me scream
And in that dream I get captured by a ghost
And I was hungry, so he made me some toast
I like a dream
That makes me scream
When I wake up I say "darn"
No wonder, I'm sleeping in the barn

Aaron Aldrich, Grade 4
Brush Creek Elementary School, CO

Why?

Why can't my family stop being a bad influence?
Why did Dr. King leave the Earth for making something better?
Why does my family make my mom suffer?
Why does my family not try?
Why do people smoke and be a bad influence?
Why can't my family follow the good?
Why can't people thank God for what He gave up?
Why can't the world be a better place?

Claudia Lerma, Grade 5
Edgewater Elementary School, CO

A Journey You Will Take

A path that leads us to our dream
So far ahead, as it may seem
It could be somewhere close or near
Or even here
The journeys you'll take to get there will be
A whole new wonder, as high as a tree
Your dreams are what you want
Let me take you on this hunt
At last you find your dream was with you
The whole way through
So off to sleep you'll drift away
"Into a whole new dream," you'll say

Emily Cox, Grade 6
Eton School, WA

Sports

Playing sports is not lame,
I love the intensity of the game.

Playing soccer is what I do,
I kick the ball with my shoe.

The sport basketball is so cool,
If you don't think so, you're a fool.

I like rollerblading, it keeps me fit,
I wear pads so I don't get hit.

Playing football is so fun,
I like to play it under the sun.

When I grow up I will have fame,
I don't know if it will be the same.
Alan Caraveo, Grade 4
Brush Creek Elementary School, CO

Rain

Rain
Clear, wet
Falling, cooled, sparkling
Cold, wet, not fun, freezing
Covering, shining, blinding
Raining, frightening
Lightning
Branton Feiring, Grade 5
Candalaria Elementary School, OR

Tupac Shakur

He was born on June 16, 1971
A black man
He lived in poverty
Out on the streets
But he grew to be
A very smart man
He spoke the truth
Was kind and intelligent
His music was inspiring
And he had a good heart
It was a tragedy
When he was shot to death
On September 13, 1996
Many people cried
And felt sorrow
But there was nothing
That anyone could do
To prevent him from dying
He was a great leader
And a hero
He will always be remembered
Selena Ortiz, Grade 6
Fruitland Middle School, ID

Colors

Red is a failed homework paper
Yellow is a bathroom draper

Grey is Grandma's funeral
Black is an army general

Green is spring coming 'round
Orange is a flame on the ground

White is a new wedding dress
Blue is a wave with a cress

Pink is a little child's cheeks
Brown is a river when it peaks
Levi Seay, Grade 6
Walt Clark Middle School, CO

Kiss

The magical kiss of breath
Bearing long evenings
The moon reflected through water
Colton Friar, Grade 6
Walt Clark Middle School, CO

You're as Lovely As…

You're as lovely as a flower,
You're as bright as a star,
And no other little girl
Is loved the way you are!
Annie Rodgers, Grade 5
Monroe Elementary School, CO

Spring Happiness

Spring rains are like clear
sparkling crystals with
joys of spring.
Spring birds sing in
the skies, their
singing is like the
sweetest thing
on earth. When
I wake up in
my bed I see the spring
sun shining.
He is like Angels
watching over me
forever. Spring
holidays are joyful, magical,
with wonder, and the joys of spring
holidays. Spring joys build
inside me, I just want
to shout
it all out!
Meghan Rutledge, Grade 4
Skyline Elementary School, WA

Twinkling Stars

Stars twinkling in the sky
I see you every night
You make the sky even more beautiful
People love seeing you
In the night sky
So please twinkling stars
Don't go away
Kiana Mitchell, Grade 4
Scenic Park Elementary School, AK

Jacob

Jacob is my friend.
Known him since we were younger.
Best friends forever.
Sarah Cooper, Grade 5
Bates Elementary School, CO

Zip Line

Around the trees I go,
Over the rushing river,
Within reach of the tall tree,
Past the great big bushes,
Toward a wide and tall fence,
As I'm stopped, I hop off the zip line.
Bryce Kukulan, Grade 5
Cottonwood Elementary School, CO

Sunset Beach

Sun setting
Gentle waves
Sand between my toes
Ocean's mist
Soft wet earth
The beach is a wonderful place to be!
Taleea Headley, Grade 4
Lincoln Elementary School, AZ

Gray Clouds

Gray clouds above us
Droplets of rain fall from clouds
Cover the day sky
Jake Munguia, Grade 6
Morgan Middle School, WA

Basketball

Behind this door
Is a court to explore.
I like it when it's just the basket and me
Just to make one that's worth three.
There are four periods in a game
If you lose that's a shame.
This is my favorite sport to play
I could play it all day.
Erik Hrach, Grade 4
Larkspur Elementary School, CO

Almost Won

Shooting, dribbling, passing did all they were worth,
For CSCS could not spot their dreaded girth.
Neck and neck the whole game through,
All because the points were true.
We ran, we ran, we spat, we spat,
But we could not get past their fat.

We'd tie it all up, but then they'd score by luck,
I might as well have kissed a duck.
We all shook hands the game was over,
We needed the luck of a four leaf clover.
I don't know how they won that game,
Two shots ahead won them their championship fame.

Johnathan Johnson, Grade 6
Corpus Christi School, CO

If It Was the End of the World

If it was the end of the end of the world,
And the world was being engulfed by darkness,
What would you do?
Would you panic?
Would you stay calm?
If it was the end of the world,
And the Earth was falling apart,
What would you do?
Would you be alone?
Or would you be together?
If it was the end of the world,
And the sun was burning out,
What would you do?
Would you fight?
Or would you forgive?
If it was the end of the world,
And the states began to sink
What would you do?
Would you steal?
Or would you pray?
If it was the end of the world…

Jacqueline A. Manriquez, Grade 5
Aurora Quest Academy, CO

The Meaning

Everlasting…everywhere you go…never broken…
Who is it, what is it?

It sails on a dove's wings.

It can never be broken,
For the peace is like an everlasting bubble
Surrounding it.

It speaks its own language,
That only few can understand.
Love.

Kelly Franklin, Grade 4
Aurora Quest Academy, CO

What Will You Find in the Center of a War?

Guilt?
Desperation?
Anger?
Or will you find the cruel darkness of hatred?
The bullets of a gun?
Blood of a warrior?
Fear?
Pitch black darkness?
Cries of,
Pain?
Anger?
Hatred?
Cruelty?
Despair?
Or will you finally find PEACE and HARMONY?

John Michael Smith, Grade 6
Spring Creek Elementary School, WY

Death

I walk in,
Not moving, sprawled in the middle of the room,
The sun is setting,
Going, going, gone.

Others enter,
Silence spreads,
Everyone stares at the person in front of us,
Going, going, gone.

Motionless body on the floor,
No one moving in the crowd,
A feeling of sadness fills me up,
Going, going, gone.

He will always be remembered,
As the coffin is buried under soft dirt,
His charming smile will be a happy memory forever,
Going, going, gone.

Now the gravestone,
With red roses,
Will I be here tomorrow?
Going, going, gone.

Bailey Hilty, Grade 6
East Middle School, CO

Brace Face

B eyond wild
R emover of crookedness
A chy and painful when tightened
C olorful colors
E mbarrassing when stuff's in your teeth
S mile improver

Ashley Pesek, Grade 5
M A Lynch Elementary School, OR

The Spirit of Christmas
Christmas is the season of giving.
The spirit of Jesus surrounds us.
Snowflakes, warm mittens,
fresh baked cookies, and a glowing fireplace.
Memories of past and present.
Stories for young and old.
Family and friends are the reason for the season.
Taylor Kralovec, Grade 5
St Mary's School, ID

Big Clouds
Huge, different shapes of clouds
Wind blowing the leaves on the tree
The feel of soft grass around me
Tender clouds up high in the light blue sky
Smell all the flowers surrounding me
Hard rough bark on the tree trunks
On a summer Sunday morning
Michaela Payne, Grade 4
Lincoln Elementary School, AZ

School Rocks
School rocks!
Math is cool.
And reading rules.
Type the keys
in technology.
P.E. is fun
if you can run.
Learn Colorado history
in Social Studies
with your buddies.
Art is in my
thankful heart.
That is why
School rocks!
Katie Martins, Grade 4
Academy International Elementary School, CO

Bird Flu
Everybody is worried about the bird flu
Stay away from that cockatoo
Everybody is scared about an epidemic
Ever consider this might be a dirty trick

Scientists say it's very near
Before it makes its premier
Quick we need to make a vaccine
Or quarantine ourselves in a submarine

Oh dear, oh dear what are we going to do
I have no clue
People may be overreacting
Or maybe we should start packing
Landon Davis, Grade 6
Albuquerque Christian School, NM

Disney World 9/11
I feel small in thousands of people
Confusion, fear, and curiosity overwhelm me
"What is going on?" I ask
Grandma and Mommy talking in low voices
I hear others talking,
Something about terror, New York, and a crash
Doubt and fear fill me
Later at the pool by our hotel
I forget my fear in the midst of fun
All the adults had false smiles on their faces
Confused, doubtful, scared and small I felt on that horrible, horrible day
Erin Hayes, Grade 6
Eagle Ridge Elementary School, CO

Like That Maui
Like the hot and humid summer days
Like the goopy sand running through your toes
Like the refreshing salt water at just the right temperature
Like the time you get to spend with the people you love
Like the tsunami waves just waiting for you to surf them
Like the itchy towels after they are wet with sand
Like the luau with the fresh roasted pork and the coconut juice
Like the tropical birds chirping on that beautiful Sunday morning
Brooke Olivas, Grade 6
Walt Clark Middle School, CO

Wind Through the Trees
Are we winds just going through the trees?
Are we invisible?
Do people just ignore us because we look different?
Maybe God made us look different because underneath we are the same.
What difference does it make if you can run and if you can sing?
We are all one body, one wind through the trees.
Danielle Chamberlain, Grade 6
Queen of Angels School, WA

Black Cats and Cave Bats
I'm walking in crunching leaves; there are spider webs on my shirt sleeve.
Bats are flying everywhere; black cats are simply everywhere!
Eeeeeeeeeeek!
Hearing sounds of moaning ghosts; hee hee hee, and ho ho ho!
Witches on their broomsticks, do a round of can-can kicks.
Walking by the town's haunted house, past me scurries a little mouse.
No one knows who really lives there; you'd have to be crazy to really care!
Finally, my time to trick-or-treat; this is going to be really neat!
Children knocking at the door, one's munching on an apple core.
Soon floats by me a little ghost; in candy matters, it has the most!
Vampires, with their fangs, are acting like orangutans!
Goblins are running amok, hoping they will have good luck.
Jack-o'-lanterns' glowing eyes illuminate the dark night sky.
When I'm home and the moon starts to fade,
I make a candy barricade!
Adrienne N. Carter, Grade 6
Castle Dale School, UT

Secrets

The vast sunset
cast a red glow
across the land.
Bland rocks
set a dark shadow
looking like an old witch.
Thick water
defined by foggy, bleak air
captures the area
the misty shore
holds dark
and mysterious
secrets.

Mike Watson, Grade 4
Audubon Elementary School, CO

My Garden

You're red, you're white
You're black, you're pink.

My hands they're dirty,
My garden, it's pretty.

My dog, he lays,
My dog, he digs.

My hands, they're clean,
My garden, it's ruined.

Bad dog! Bad dog!
My garden, it's ruined.

I plant, I'm dirty
My garden, it's pretty.

You're red, you're white,
You're pink, you're black.

My garden, it's pretty,
My dog's house bound.

Alora Nelson, Grade 6
Orient Elementary School, WA

Flower

Here is my advice said the old flower.
Bloom naturally,
Be your own person,
Don't bloom to be another flower,
Weave through the wind,
Stand still, hide in a meadow,
Stand out,
Be noticeable,
Reach for the stars,
Touch the ground.

Elizabeth Suriani, Grade 6
Walt Clark Middle School, CO

Stubby and Poozer

Stubby and Poozer
Running around
Licking my face
Jumping up and down
Weaving in and out
Of little pine trees.
Run Stubby!
Run Poozer!
Run you little dogs!

Steven Leachman, Grade 4
Colbert Elementary School, WA

Beauty

Beauty is looks of someone's face.
Beauty is as soft as the night's air.
Beauty is like a rose.
Beauty is love.
Beauty is as lovely as
the fluttering wings of a butterfly.
Beauty has everyone's heart.
Beauty is someone you love.
Beauty is life.
Beauty is how I like it.

Trevor Tallman, Grade 6
Orient Elementary School, WA

Oh, a Summer Rain

They cascade down
Like large tear drops
Falling from the sky.
I reach out my hand,
It's wet, and cold as ice.
The peacefulness in the air,
Suddenly stops with a SPLASH!
It has nowhere to go
It flows down the street,
Like a small running steam.
And in my garden
It's like medicine,
For my flowers.

Oh, a Summer Rain!

Michelle Rohbock, Grade 5
Barratt School, UT

River

In the river
I swim in the cold water
The river is moving hastily
It's hard to swim up the river
It's easy to swim down it
I jump onto the dock
I run and jump off it
It's time to go home.

Adam Schindler, Grade 6
Fox Creek Jr High School, AZ

Trouble

Trouble, trouble.
Oh great, now double trouble!
All because of a piece of paper
And, well, a stapler.
I made a staple shooter
Got in trouble.
Made a paper airplane
Got in trouble.
So here is my warning:
Make sure no one is looking
Before you do something!

Daniel Schlomer, Grade 6
Desert Mountain School, AZ

Sweet Vacation

Aloha from Hawaii,
The wonderful beauties,
Caught my eye,
The colorful parrot,
Touched my hands,
And enjoying being on new lands,
Feeling my heart,
Beat fast,
Hoping the moment will forever last.

Brooke Sibley, Grade 6
Walt Clark Middle School, CO

Snow Melting

White blankets melting
creating rivers so blue
spring is almost here

Sarah Sponcil, Grade 4
St Thomas the Apostle School, AZ

The Skiing Champion

Jumping high
soaring like a bird
fast as a cheetah I can't stop.
The snow is so white
like crystal you fall down.
It's okay get back up try again.
I can't feel the cold
too much fun skiing
down the biggest hill ever
going up I'm in heaven
higher lower down
faster then ever I made it. Yay!

Megan Lomax, Grade 4
Acacia Elementary School, AZ

Nature

Water glistening
Sand twirling around in air,
Butterflies soaring.

Natasha Aragon, Grade 5
Sequoia Village School, AZ

Perfect Day

When the sun shines bright
When the world is light
When your friends smile
And you know they'll be there for awhile
You take in the air
Let the wind blow your hair
When friendships are strong
And they last long
You can have good times
Acting as mimes
Laughing and singing
Loving what life is bringing
It's a good day
A happy day...
A PERFECT DAY

Casey Harlow, Grade 6
Miller Middle School, CO

My Little Furball

I love my little furball,
She is a friend to me,
When I wake up from my sleep,
She fills my heart with glee.

My furball's name is Lucie,
Her fur is brown and white,
She plays with me when I come home,
Every morning and every night.

I feed her grapes and apples,
She surely loves her hay,
She stands up on her little feet,
And begs for snacks each day.

Lucie has a pink igloo house,
She likes to run and dig,
She makes a mess, but I don't care,
She is my guinea pig.

Sidney Haymart, Grade 5
Gold Canyon Elementary School, AZ

What Are My Flowers?

What are my flowers?

Roses and sunflowers
Pretty and unique
Symbols of nature
Set darkness to sleep
Give angels their beauty
Give life to death
Give happiness to grief

My flowers.

Max Sass, Grade 4
The Meadows School, NV

Thanksgiving

Thanksgiving
Steam rising from the oven
Golden brown turkey
Yelling at the football game
Stolen food from the table
My brother
Thanksgiving

Josh Behrens, Grade 4
Coal Creek Elementary School, CO

Does Life Pay Off

Life and Death...
Black and white
hope and dreams...
Does it really seem
Does life pay off?
Are our deeds rewarded
Or are they washed away...
in the tides of every day?

Patty Bowen, Grade 6
Thomas Jefferson Charter School, ID

Outside My Window

Outside my window
Stands a majestic mountain
Crowned with snow
A beautiful daffodil dressed in yellow
All aglow
And little sparrows smoothly
Gliding to and fro

As I look through my window
I wonder — what do children do,
Where it doesn't snow
Where sparrows don't fly
And daffodils don't grow

Then I look up to the sky and see
The sun shining brightly over me
And, I thank God for allowing me
To live, where others only long to be

Bradley Vigil, Grade 6
Washington Intermediate School, CO

Gymnastics

Is about strength
and very good skill,
great sportsmanship and
making friends,
having a good time and flexibility.
It is about some tough times
and when you're older
it all pays off.

Olivia Coons, Grade 4
Acacia Elementary School, AZ

Green Is...

huge maple trees
stalks of broccoli
a branch of poison ivy
ripe sour grapes
moldy wheat bread

Kaytlyn Christensen, Grade 5
Wheeler Elementary School, AZ

Catch

catch a flying football
on a great field,
fetch the throw of the day
how do you do this?
first you get open
then you wait for it,
listen really hard for the
whistle of the ball and
the crowd screaming
catch it! catch it!
as you feel the ball
hit your hands
grasp it will all your might
and get ready to plow
through the rival player
with all the strength you have
and fly for the touchdown.

Jacob Preston, Grade 6
Monforton School, MT

Wolves

The wolves cry at night.
Oh, they cry!
As they lie underneath the moonlight.

Oh, the wolves get the mood to run
To chase after their food.

The rabbits run
Oh, also hide,
But the wolves still run
In the silver moonlight.

As the goat and sheep
baa and maa
The wolves are in the field
As they kill a newborn calf.

Colt Wetterman, Grade 5
Liberty Ranch Christian School, NM

Life Is Wonderful

In a tree birds play.
In the sky planes soar around me.
Life is wonderful.

Preston Murdoch, Grade 6
Greybull Middle School, WY

Tonto Creek Dam

One day I went to the forest.
I saw a beautiful river.
When I saw it, it looked like a stairway you could climb.
I heard an echo of a river of water rustling through the rocks.
I saw the sun's reflection on the rocks.

Karina Valencia, Grade 4
Great Expectations Academy, AZ

Losers

Some people do not consider to lose,
Some people do not think it is a path to choose,
Because deep down inside me, I feel like a loser,
But what makes me feel better, is that I'm a chooser,
A pathway many people are unkind to,
A place where they make fun, and bully too,
But somewhere inside me is that glow of winning,
I feel that glow strengthening when I stop sinning,
And yet, I do not win in fun and games,
And yet, I am still called names,
But I am still not a loser, in my own mind.

Isaac Rounseville, Grade 4
Acacia Elementary School, AZ

A Seal, a Bond, a Love, and a Smile

I'm glad it's over
The fight has stopped
Together we stand strong
There is a seal between us that can never be broken
There is a bond between us that can stay forever
A love between us that can last a lifetime
And a smile we all can share for eternity

Jessie Lam, Grade 6
Peruvian Park Elementary School, UT

Kaylynn

Tall
Trustworthy
Sweet
Wishes to be loved
Dreams of boys
Wants to have lots of friends
Who wonders "Does he like me?"
Who fears emotion
Who is afraid of sorrow
Who likes boys that are dark-skinned
Who likes boys that are nice
Who likes to hang out with friends
Who believes I am beautiful no matter what people say
Who loves music
Who loves hip-hop
Who loves TV
Who plans to go to college
Who plans to have Jay as a friend forever
Whose final destination when 20 is as an FBI agent.

Kaylynn Meechan, Grade 6
Patton Middle School, OR

States

Rose are red
Violets are blue
We love Nevada
Yes we do
Some do, some don't
Some love other states
We might, we might not
We love Nevada
Yes, yes we do!
We like Idaho
Yes, yes we do
For the delicious potatoes,
The corn, the deer, cows, and pigs too,
For the beautiful mountains, for camping, hiking
Other fun stuff too!
We like all the states, oh, yes we do
Like famous places and other places too!

Austin Whitefeather, Grade 4
Jackpot Combined School, NV

Dad

Dad	Dad
I love him a lot	
	He's there when I'm caught
I think he's fab	
	Yet sometimes he's drab
Dad	Dad
He's so, so fun	
	He's bright like the sun
He's my friend	
	On him I can depend
Dad	Dad
He gives me huge hugs	
	And awful big tugs
He watches TV	
	He really loves me
When I'm sad	
	Or when I'm mad
I can always count on	I can always count on
DAD!	DAD!

Erin McCain, Grade 5
Mesa Elementary School, CO

Purple

If I were purple, I would be a twig of fresh grapes
I might be a plum being picked from a tree
A tulip sprouting from the stiff ground
A gem in a gold ring on Mrs. Mitchell's hand
I would be my mom's favorite color
Mrs. Murray's pen for correcting papers
Warm juice in a baby's hand
Purple is a wonderful color

Arista Barron, Grade 4
East Evergreen Elementary School, MT

I Am From

I am from my mom.
I am from my dad.
I am from getting sick.
I am from the snow park in Rogue River.
I am from Medford, Oregon.
I am from preschool.
I am from my first birthday.
I am from my grandpa passing away.
I am from my grandma.
I am from swimming the first time.
I am from my first cousin.
I am from my grandma passing away.
I am from my first camping trip, and the smell of pine needles.
I am from catching a dog and falling in the toilet.

Kimberly Crow, Grade 4
Evergreen Elementary School, OR

Games

I am having fun playing games on the T.V.
While my sisters are stuck washing the dishes,
cleaning the bathroom, and dusting out the rooms.

Mariela Cortes, Grade 4
Jackpot Combined School, NV

Heaven

What will it be like?
How will we look?
Where will our senses go?
What will we eat?
What will we do?
Will we enjoy it?
Where will our pets go?
Where will we get everything?
Will there be stores and supermarkets?
Will we be in one place or spread out?
Why do we have to wait?
Does it even exist?

Nic Orlando, Grade 6
Pope John XXIII Catholic School Community, AZ

The Months

January there is snow,
In February it goes,
In March there is gloom,
In April the flowers bloom,
In May there is sun,
In June we have fun,
In July the kids play,
In August people lay around all day,
In September people go to school,
In October people think their Halloween costumes are cool,
In November people praise Thanksgiving day,
In December people go in the snow to play,
Then the months start over again and here's what you say.

Christian Katlaps, Grade 5
Oak Creek Elementary School, OR

Reading a Book

A book takes you to many places,
A prairie, a castle, and great wide spaces.

When you open a book, many places you go,
Just keep on reading, and you will have the flow.

Riding through the prairie on a horse,
Looking on a map to see the course.

Keep on reading, you will see,
Just how happy you can be.

Annie Gibson, Grade 5
Seltice Elementary School, ID

Middle School Chaos

Ring! Ring! the lunch bell
Hundreds of kids rush to get first to lunch
Everybody sits down to eat vigorously
To get outside and play
SMACK! the fifth and sixth graders fall
Playing tackle football
The boys are playing sports
The girls are gossiping about boys and other girls
Ring! Ring!
The kids "AWWW" as they go inside.

Nick Zylka, Grade 6
Fruitland Middle School, ID

I Am From

I am from learning to walk when I was eight months old.
I am from my family's home cooking.
I am from my dog taking my food when I was little.
I am from lots of pets.
I am from lots of babies.
I am from swimming a lot in the summer.
I am from family picnics.
I am from family gatherings.
I am from camping in the summertime.
I am from two dads.
I am from six names.
I am from a big bushy brown madrone tree in my front yard.
I am from waking up whenever.
I am from a mom who likes elephants.
I am from two hamsters.

Mariah Nolan, Grade 4
Evergreen Elementary School, OR

Clear Creek Canyon

Water trickles down into a creek as clear as ice,
The moist rocks look like small smooth mountains.
Behind the falling water is luscious brush as green as jade,
Fish swim in silence through the clear creek
like a creeping cat at night.

Layne Willson, Grade 4
Great Expectations Academy, AZ

The Journey of a Mermaid

I slip down through the diluted deeps
and sit atop the captain's keep.
This ship fell to Moby Dick
and now the grandfather clock won't tick.
I swim down through a broken porthole
and glide amongst a colourful shoal.
As I float under an arched doorway
I meet upon a fractured stairway.
I paddle on down and what do I see…
a big old shark staring at me!
I fly up the stairs and through the cracked door,
I skim through the porthole and don't ask for more!
I splash through the water and start to calm down,
I start to fluke gently, I take a look around.
I find myself lost in a beautiful sight;
I'm near the surface so I can tell it's night.
A thousand stars are twinkling down,
and the moon is shimmering profound.
I am now calm and the water is sparkly,
So I'll stick around and think about sharks darkly.

Kirra Paulus, Grade 6
Hood River Middle School, OR

Farm

Like the cool wind on a sunny day.
Like the open fields of a farm.
Like the tickling on the wheat grass.
Like the chirping of the cricket in the yard.

Like the smelly stench in the pigs' pen.
Like the strange taste in the well water.
Like the jumping noise of the banging thunder.

Chris Sievers, Grade 6
Walt Clark Middle School, CO

My Cousins

All of my cousins are special to me
They are all great people is what you will see

I know sometimes we don't get along
But we still know all of us are wrong

All of us together make a great team
The best in the world is what it seems

I hope they are with me throughout my life
Even through all the anger and strife

Love is the thing I hope never fades away
But I know it will not stray

There is one thing that I don't doubt
And that's the love that travels about

Stephanie Shanks, Grade 6
Eagleridge Enrichment Program, AZ

Sunset

After a long hot day, the waves die down
the seagulls hush,
the seaweed and dead fish smell disappears.
All the hot turns to cool
just for the shimmering beautiful sunset.
The clouds start to change colors
from white to pink to purple
all while the sun changes to orange
then vanishes
into a sea of darkness.

Collin Kingsbury, Grade 5
Carrolls Elementary School, WA

Monsters

Monsters, monsters, scary, crawling monsters
Lives underneath the ground
Comes out at night.
Chooses who to be with…
Sleep with or even leave with…
Voices, voices all around
Coming from rooms or underground
Ghosts will not leave.
They stay forever.
That's just the way it is!

Emily Ericksen, Grade 5
Lewis & Clark Elementary School, OR

Friends*

We were only together for a week
But we already have a special bond
We learned and laughed together
And of all our times I am fond

We were all shy and scared
When we first arrived that night
We became fast friends and got through hard times
And tried our best with all our might

That last night on the bus
Where we all shed a tear
I know in my heart
We all had the same fear

We knew we might not see each other again
And of this thought we were afraid
Because of our close friendship
That we have quickly made

I will miss you my dear friends
As life goes by and we get along
I hope we will remember this poem
As it runs through our hearts like a song

Erica Zaborac, Grade 6
First Baptist Christian Academy, AZ
*Dedicated to my friends from the
People to People Leadership Forum

Reading

Everyone likes reading
and if they don't they should.
There are books for old
and books for young.
There are also books just to have fun.
So if you're bored and tired,
try a book.
It might just be in your reading nook.
Benjamin Nogawa, Grade 4
West Woodland School, WA

Tall Hat

T all hat
A braham, Abe
L incoln, 16th president
L oved to wear one

H igh he was
A nd the hat made him
T aller, way taller
Eleanor Cummins, Grade 5
St Patrick's Catholic School, WA

School

Math is so last year,
It's a big pain in the rear!
The lunch is really sick,
what else is there to pick?
Spelling stinks like a sock,
what else is there to mock?
Writing is really hard,
I never got too far.
Science flips me over,
good thing the day is over!
Jorge Vazquez, Grade 4
Roy Moore Elementary School, CO

Spring's Things

Spring skies blaze as hot
as boiling deserts
Spring flowers smell as great
as fresh plucked berries
Spring rain gently floats
down as little pieces of wetness
Spring colors shine brightly
all around me
Spring water glitters
in the big bright
and beautiful sun
Spring always has mysterious,
fabulous, and surprising wonders
In spring, I swim like
a newborn fish
Bailey Phillips, Grade 4
Skyline Elementary School, WA

Ode to Laughter

Laughter makes you happy,
Whenever you are down.

It makes your heart healthy,
It makes a wonderful sound.

Laughter is a beauty.
It makes you want to smile.
Even if you smile,
All the while.

The world would be so boring,
Without the laughter soaring.

Laughter is the most,
Wonderful thing on Earth.
Three hundred tons of gold,
Is what laughter is worth.
Julia Bunting, Grade 5
Barratt School, UT

Dreaming

Dreaming
Free, distant
Thinking, flying, believing
Taking you anywhere
Wishing.
Matt Dillon, Grade 6
Greybull Middle School, WY

I Am From

I am from the family rose
That keeps us together
From the big plants
Covering my nice warm house

I am from the homemade bread
That makes me think about my mother
From the ocean seas
That fills me with love

I am from the games played
In my yard
From the cars that go by
Every morning

I am from the cats and dogs
That chase each other
From drinking eggnog
At Christmas

I am from a family
I love
Kevin Fisher, Grade 4
Grass Valley Elementary School, NV

White

White is the color
Of golf balls and tees,
White petaled roses
And callalilies.

Silk on the gown
The letters on the boat,
Milk from the cow
That goes down my throat.

White is the color
Of the icing on the cake,
The white chocolate fudge
The flour that we bake.

White is the light
That cuts through doom,
The stars in the sky
The big full moon.

The ice in the pond
The fresh fallen snow,
And in my hot cocoa
Floats a white marshmallow.
Cory Cranford, Grade 6
Kendallvue Elementary School, CO

Benjamin Franklin

An inventor
A scientist
A great great man
He thought of others
He thought of you
He flew a kite
Into a cloud
A business man
A philosopher
A statesman
A revolutionary
Huh
Why of course
Ben Franklin is who
I speak of.
Katelynn Elizabeth Brown, Grade 5
Mary Blair Elementary School, CO

My Black Cat

Glossy, shiny, smooth
My black cat.
Fast, tiny, wandering
My black cat.
Sleepy, tired, cuddly
My black cat.
Kim Rudeen, Grade 5
St Mary's School, ID

Sports

Throwing a football to each other at practice
Hitting a golf ball in the air 200 yards
Pedaling a mountain bike on Thumb Butte
Batting at a baseball that makes the home run
Shooting a basketball at a basketball game
Sports are great fun.

Morgan Myrick, Grade 4
Lincoln Elementary School, AZ

Darkness

The slinky, slimy, smelliest thing darkness.
When you're in your room going to bed,
darkness springs upon you with its fox eyes.
You cannot hide from it, darkness is everywhere,
whether in the corner of the room, or in the attic.
It crawled from the core of the earth and out of the sewers.
Try to hide, it is no use, it'll just hunt you down,
and cover you with its invisible blanket.
So be afraid.

Kelsey Andros, Grade 5
Nederland Elementary School, CO

Lauren

Loving, loyal, trustworthy
Who wishes to go to Cuba.
Who dreams of meeting Usher or Chris Brown.
Who wants to go to college.
Who wonders what is going to happen in life.
Who fears war.
Who is afraid of dying,
Who likes boys that are cute and nice.
Who believes in friends.
Who loves Mexican food.
Who loves to dance.
Who loves music.
Who loves my friends.
Who plans to be a dancer.
Who plans on having a family.
Who plans on living a good life.
Who wants the good life mostly.

Lauren De Las Heras, Grade 6
Patton Middle School, OR

Ode to Tulips

They wait underground for many nights,
And in the spring they pop up to see the world.
They bring fresh new colors to the season,
And everyone stops and stares at them.
They feel special in their red, yellow, orange and pink dresses.
They sway with the wind,
And stand strong in the snow,
But deep down in that snow they feel warm.
They know they will come up next spring,
But until then they laugh and dance in their colorful dresses.

Brittany Smith, Grade 5
Barratt School, UT

Donuts

Saturday morning breakfast
Sunday midday snack
On Monday in the cupboard
All that is left is the pack

Brother says they're on the counter
I do not agree
For I did not see them there
Oh! Where could they be?

Then my dog came along
As he licked his mouth
So I realized where the donuts were
And I put my dog out

My dog ate all the donuts
He is a bad boy
And this was his punishment
I took away his toy

Kate Mailliard, Grade 6
Pope John XXIII Catholic School Community, AZ

Earth

The voice of the wind tells me everything.
The mouth of the cave is dark.
The heart of the Earth is warm.
The eyes of the trees are still.
The head of a mountain is cold.
The leaves of a tree are like hands.
The tongue of the ocean is big.
The sound of the river is soft.
The Earth is great.

Nick Bonnema, Grade 5
CLASS Academy, OR

Winner

I watch the zamboni slip across the ice.
The zamboni slowly drives off the ice.
I take off my skate protectors and glide on to the ice.
The crowd cheers.
The music starts.
I pose.
Adrenaline rush flows into my blood.
I start skating.
Double toe loop.
Stick the landing.
Glide. Slip. Flip into a trick.
The music stops. I take a bow.
Silence,
THE CROWD CHEERS!
I step off the ice.
10.0 9.6 8.9 10.0
First Place. Winner!

Nicole Collingwood, Grade 5
West Mercer Elementary School, WA

Chores

Every weekend I do my chores,
It's way too hard and quite a bore,
First I have to clean the tub,
Scrub, scrub, scrub.
Then I have to make my bed,
It's only a place where you rest your head!
After I have to clean my room,
I'd rather dust a mummy's tomb.
I have to do the dishes,
that yucky, disgusting chore.
I hate to have to do those chores.

Jessica Stewart, Grade 5
Monroe Elementary School, CO

Nature

The glaciers mist with the ocean breeze
The water falls due to gravity

The baby deer tramples the leaves
While the baby turtle sets out for the sea

The grass sways in the winter gale
And will soon pad the summer trails

The bright orange leaves do not know
That they will soon be covered with snow

The baby giraffes are out to play
While the great big lion sleeps away the day

All the trees are covered in bark
And the branches are home to the meadowlark

The vibrant flower seems to droop
And the algae is like split pea soup

The Spanish moss always grows
Nature is not our foe

Claire Smith, Grade 5
CLASS Academy, OR

Dolphin

An animal inside of me, locked inside my heart
Has a key and is trying to come out
Swims and dances across the sea
While still holding the key it waits for me
Intelligent, sweet, and kind
The dolphin in me has its own mind
I swim and love just like a dolphin
Jumping, whistling, just how they do
With the graceful color of being BLUE
I'm a dolphin inside of me
If you knew me you'd agree
I'm a Dolphin

Morgan Rohrbouck, Grade 6
Walt Clark Middle School, CO

My Treasure Box

In my treasure box you will find
Hot summer days, sailing knots, and the many mysteries of the mind
All of the past is what my memories are made of
The family experiences that I have had
Both happy and sad
The old dog George, the hot Cape Cod days,
And all the friends for which I am glad

The present is filled with wonderful things too
The great days when no one is ever blue
If you are asking me what I do when I am not writing a rhyme
I will play soccer any time
As the present turns to past we looked for the future

My hopes for the future will soon come to be
If you want to know what they are just wait and see
With a new year comes a new school
Along with many visits to the pool
The family members for which I always yearn
And the many mysteries of the future yet to be learned

Thomas Frost Cunningham, Grade 6
Eton School, WA

The Animal in Me

There is an owl in me.
An owl's large eyes burn through the darkness,
Finding my secrets.

Like a wise owl, I am learning all there is to know,
And all that isn't known yet.

Owls are talented, with heads turning around to see behind them,
And so am I, but in different ways.

When I am in a game of tag, I am quick,
Like an owl,
Diving down on his prey as fast
As lightning in a summer thunderstorm.

The owl is perched in my head, telling me what to do
When it's time to be like him.

Camilla Stark, Grade 6
Eagleview Middle School, CO

Meaning of Life

In my life there are 5 purposes.
Purpose 1: I will worship God with all my heart.
Purpose 2: God's family is a great family, they are my family.
Purpose 3: I hope to become like Jesus, but I don't know if I'm ready.
Purpose 4: I will help other people when God sees I'm ready.
Purpose 5: Here's how to meet God and Jesus.
Do you want to know about God?
Do you know about Jesus?
These are my 5 purposes.

Tyler Haeger, Grade 6
Woodland Christian School, WA

The One I Love

You may smell like cedar and pee
But I love you as much as love can be

You may bite for no reason at all
But I still love you enough to get your food at the mall

You may squeak and leak (if you know what I mean)
But you're still the cutest mouse I've ever seen

You make your wheel squeak and keep me up all night
But I still laugh at the sight
Of you spinning around
And I'm so thankful that it's you I found

Irene Anderson, Grade 5
University Park Elementary School, AK

Baseball

"Hey batter, hey batter, hey batter"
The shortstop screams "Swing!"
The umpire quickly yells "Strike 1!"
This time I'm going to hit it, concentrate
Swing…
"Strike 2"
My spirits are down
I just have to hit it
Bat's up, feet down, eye on the ball…Swing!
It's followed by an echoing "Crack!"
Sprinting past 1st, 2nd, 3rd
Go to home?
Yes!
But I get out by the catcher
I hang my head in shame as I slump to the dugout
I hear a single clap, just 1
I turn my head to see
The pitcher is clapping for me.

Keven Carlson, Grade 5
Barratt School, UT

What Freedom Means to Me

Everyone wants freedom
Sometimes it means war
Sometimes it means that we want to be free
Sometimes we just want to drive!

Everyone wants to be free
Like Martin Luther King Jr.
Who wanted black people to be free
And got black people to be free

But I believe that freedom is to be free
I want to be free and drive
Not just have my parents always drive me around
But I have to wait to be 16

Cameron Cerny, Grade 6
Pope John XXIII Catholic School Community, AZ

Up and About

Buzz buzz beep beep
Time to get up and start some beats
Click clack time to pack
Time to get ready don't look back
Slam thud on and off on and off
That big yellow bus
Clack whack there goes my lunch
Time to go home to my family bunch
Bah whoosh time for bed my favorite part of my day
Now I can finally rest my head

Edisa Newcomb, Grade 6
Pope John XXIII Catholic School Community, AZ

Panther

Deep in the inkiness of the black night,
Through the darkness there hovered two lights.

These luminous lights came from two eyes.
These eyes were a panther's; in the darkness he hides.

Black as a pupil the panther sinks down,
His legs like a spring, snap off the ground.

Resembling a razor knife
Filled with cunning, active life.

Hurtling into the dumbfounded deer,
Gone is the struggle, gone is the fear.

Kai Swenson, Grade 5
Hidden Hills Elementary School, AZ

Ooga Bazuga

Ooga bazuga blew his bazuga
in a land far — far away.
He blew his bazuga to wake all the people
in a land far — far away.

Zach Watson, Grade 6
Syracuse School, UT

Gleaming Cave

The cave was gleaming
As if made of ice
It was seeming
Very nice.

I truly love this cave
It fills me with wonder
It's my fav' of favs'
It lies beyond a horizon's yonder.

Now my poem's nearing end
So now's the time to stop reading the poem
Sorry I've got to go and tend
So close the book and go home.

Cody D. Esquiro, Grade 6
Blaine Middle School, WA

When You Left

When you left
It hurt so bad
I pretend to be happy
Inside I'm so sad

You and I were so happy
When you were here
When I saw you go
I was filled with fear

You were my best friend
You left too soon,
For our friendship to end
I'll miss you forever

Myranda Trujillo, Grade 6
Washington Intermediate School, CO

Country

Country
Open, quiet
Relaxing, playing, resting
Farms, pastures, shops, people
Shopping, driving, living
Busy, loud
Town

Lyndsi Podtburg, Grade 6
Heath Middle School, CO

Just a Minute

There once was a girl at a game,
who was planning on winning that game,
She dozed off a minute,
but never set a limit
to find out that she lost her game

Rene Baker, Grade 6
Green Valley Christian School, NV

Nature

Birds are chirping
Early in the morning
It reminds me of
Adventurous hiking
In the woods

The waves at the beach
Calming and relaxing
Seagulls flying
Talkatively

On a scary stormy Sunday
Cold and dark
Loud with rain and
Fast wind blowing

Yurika Asai, Grade 6
Uplands Elementary School, OR

Green Is…

my grandma's eyes
soft grass under my bare feet
marbles in my mouth when I eat peas
the foam on the sea
the woods on Mount Lemmon

Jordan Schroeder, Grade 5
Wheeler Elementary School, AZ

Falling

My friend shouted "biff"
As I was near a cliff.
I was falling through the sky
I thought I was going to die.
My life flashed before me,
I couldn't bare to see.
I looked down and saw a slope,
And knew I had no hope.
As I was about to hit my head
When suddenly I woke up in my bed.

Matthew Kubit, Grade 6
Bradford Intermediate School, CO

You

When you are cold,
I hold you,
When I look into your eyes,
They are shinier than gold.
When I try to look
For a girl like you,
They are all sold.

Eric Cervantes, Grade 6
Somerton Middle School, AZ

Tapping

tap tap tap
   tap tap tap
tapping the beat
the sound
thus the tapping makes the beat
   tap tap
   tap tap tap
this tapping
thus this tapping
it is up there
the rain
   tap tap
the tapping of hammer to wood
the tapping of this pencil,
it writes
   tap tap
   tap
thus tapping
this tapping

Roxy Johnson, Grade 5
Scholls Heights Elementary School, OR

Nice September Day

Why did the planes fly in.
Why on that beautiful September day.
Why did those people die.
Why on that beautiful September day.
Now they never stand again.

Jacob Nye, Grade 5
Thomas Edison Charter School, UT

Trees

Trees blow in soft winds
Light brown leaves drift gently down
Twilight's sunset scene

Vincent Valdez, Grade 4
Adams Elementary School, CO

The Wild Party!

On a fresh day,
At night,
People yell and scream,
People shout "Hurray!"
Everybody dancing crazy,
People singing karaoke,
I talk to people and laugh,
I chit chat and tell jokes,
On a night of a holiday,
I will be proud.

Jasmine Muñoz, Grade 6
Fox Creek Jr High School, AZ

Into the Forest

Through the pine-scented forest I go
Between the tall glorious pine trees
Past all the gigantic boulders
Along the mossy trail
Near all of the hiding forest creatures
Over the grassy hills
Toward the thin creek
Around all of the colorful flowers
Onto the rocky cliff
During a bright afternoon.

Amanda Hunsucker, Grade 6
Fox Creek Jr High School, AZ

Winter

Snow thrashes
down.
Rivers twirl and
swirl
in the dancing
moonlight.
The moon is as
bright
as a glacier.

Savanna Pothier, Grade 4
Skyline Elementary School, WA

When I Grow Up

I have been playing all my life
Running and kicking with all my might
Passing, trapping, and shooting with skill
Parents driving and paying the bill.

The ball we play with is black and white
Hands are not allowed any time day or night
The field is long, green and wide
Teammates become friends on the Pride.

The game gets faster as I grow
My feet get nimble toe to toe
Club, high school and college I go
I want to be a soccer pro.

Mckenzie Prantl, Grade 6
Corpus Christi School, CO

Reflect

When you look into the water, what do you see?
You see water, a fish, or maybe a tree?

No, you see nothing, nothing but you.
Water shows your troubles, your feelings so true.

Water is a mirror, reflecting your want.
You could be a solver, chasing ghosts that haunt.

You could be an angel, flying high in the sky.
You could be a genius, following pi.

You could be a mermaid, swimming deep in the sea.
You could be a bug, the size of a flea.

You could be on broken wings that once flew,
No, you are nothing, nothing but you.

Braeden Fallet, Grade 6
Crown Pointe Academy, CO

At the Beach

At the beach is the place for me
It is so great.
I like to go around, explore and see.

Having the family there makes it a whole lot more fun
I love having them there
Just playing around under the big bright sun.

It is so hot,
Sweat coming down,
It's like a boiling pot!

There's nothing like spending time with family.
It really is beautiful to be together
We sure live very happily.

Daisy Pompa, Grade 6
Somerton Middle School, AZ

Lava and Rock

Lava
Bubbling acid.
Having no boundaries.
Scorching anything in its path,
Burning the ground beneath is beauty.
Reaching water, the bottomless blue.
Vapor clouds, out of the water.
A liquid fire.
A pitch black solid.
Blazing sun.
Dark space.
Smile
Child's face
Spurting ashes,
Fiery fingers, reaching for the child.
Gobbles up the child
A blood curdling scream
Rattles the horizon
Hard rock, covering the small town.
Lava.
Rock.

Chris Wilson, Grade 5
Khalsa Montessori Elementary School, AZ

Old Stinky Bill

There once was a house on the hill
The home's owner's name was Stinky Bill
The neighbors all cried
And some ran to hide
But all Bill needs is a shower still

Christopher Mardian, Grade 4
St Thomas the Apostle School, AZ

Poetry

Sometimes as I read a book,
Filled with beloved poems,
Something that always crosses my path,
Is the simple, or complex question
What is poetry?
It is a way to express feelings?
A way to calm oneself?
Or to overcome your fear?
But as I ask myself these and more,
My mind is overcome by more.
Questions, questions, questions
That is all I hear.
Is poetry a method for weak men to be listened to?
Or for strong men to argue a point?
I fear that I may contradict myself,
But once more I'm back to the question
That it all began.
Maybe the answer is easy,
That poetry should not be answered.

Brandon Binggeli, Grade 6
East Middle School, CO

Ode to Spring

Spring is here hip-hip hooray!
The flowers are blooming
With their sweet smelling perfume.
The scenery is filling.
The tulips and daisies are beautiful.
Strawberries and blueberries are in season,
They are the colors of red and blue.
We pick them and eat them without any reason.
Snow no more, a new beginning.
Red and pink are the colors of the flowers,
I could stare at them forever,
For hours and hours.

Melissa Kallander, Grade 5
Aurora Quest Academy, CO

My Life Being an Indian

My spirit dances with the sun and the moon,
I will never know if I should die soon,
Being an Indian is great,
There's another thing to appreciate,
My skin, hair, and eyes are brown;
I don't need money, jewelry, or a crown,
To show I'm special,
My spirit goes with me everywhere,
And I happen to care,
Just knowing I have nothing to fear,
Or no scary noises to hear,
I'm an Indian and now I know,
It's in my blood and in my soul,
I don't have fortune and fame,
And there's no one to blame,
The heritage I have is mine,
And my life being an Indian will shine.

Mataja M. Ascencio, Grade 6
Sky City Community School, NM

Baseball Dream

I see the pitcher glare at the catcher's mitt
The sweat drips down his face
He stares at the plate
BANG I crack the ball
   Going
      Going
         Going
            Gone
I run the bases
The clinch in the pitcher's throat
The ball soars over and out of the stands
I wake
It was all a dream
But I believed its truth
In my room snuggled in blankets
Cuddled in bed
I drift back to dream again

Matt Godwin, Grade 6
Walker Middle School, OR

Heart Broken

Your heart starts to break and you don't know why,
Is it because it hurts or is it just because he said, "Good-bye."
Now you sit with no one to dance with,
You sit with tears in your eyes and wonder what went wrong.
He left without warning he left without a tear in his eye.
You now wish your best friend was there he could cheer you up,
You wish you had never went to the dance you wish you could just disappear.
You're hurt now and you can't do anything about it,
So you start to cry you cry a river as big as the Mississippi river,
So you tell yourself it is the end but now the beginning.

Kristen Martinez, Grade 6
Vikan Middle School, CO

Grapefruit

Great for eating on a picnic day
Remnants of taste remain in your mouth
Ambidextrous people like them too
Pink fruit inside is luscious and delicious
Elegant decorations for all sorts of events
Freshness with every bit of taste
Refreshing taste every time you take a bite
Underneath the orange peel is something that will make you squeal
Immediate taste is a treat that is very good to eat
Telling stories while eating grapefruit is delightful

Derina de Landro, Grade 5
Firwood Elementary School, OR

Emerging from My Sleep

The sweet sample of fresh air, feeling of trying the food again.
I bite my favorite fruit and savor it.
My friends want me to taste a new nectarine.
Emerging from my sleep.

The smooth squishy feel of the mud on my feet.
The tough caress of pine cones on my toes.
The fuzzy encounter of my hand to the pussywillows.
I even hold the last bit of snow off the ground.
Emerging from my sleep.

Candy-like aroma of flowers blooming. My cold has finally gone away.
I can now really breathe the fresh air.
Mr. Bybee can inhale the scent of the flowers in his garden.
Emerging from my sleep.

All the little girls screaming at bugs and boys,
The boys laughing a lot at the girls.
My mother asking me to help her with meals,
My father helping me fix things in my room.
Emerging from my sleep.

The sweet sample of fresh air, feeling of trying the food again.
I bite my favorite fruit and savor it. Emerging from my sleep.

Jodilynne Ellis, Grade 6
Bella Vista Elementary School, UT

I Wonder

What would you find in the eye of a hurricane?
A dreadful silence?
A cloud of questions?
Or a peaceful song?
What would you find in the center of a black hole?
A lump of coal?
An endless night?
Or a ray of sunlight?
What would you find in the center of the earth?
The fire of a dragon?
The blood of a giant?
Or a twinkling star?
What would you find in the bottom of a well?
A hundred hungry rats?
A cave of bats?
Or a thousand glittering jewels?
I wonder…

Collin Ballard, Grade 6
Spring Creek Elementary School, WY

Baseball

Baseball is a spectacular sport.
It does not take place on a court.

Baseball is America's pastime
The sport is not sour like a lime.

The ball is small and eye piercing white.
When the pitcher throws the ball you hit it with all your might.

To play baseball you have to be fit and strong.
The professional games are fun but long.

People cheer and holler for their favorite teams.
During the season they work hard to fulfill their dreams.

Everyone should play baseball.
It is so fun it will make you feel ten feet tall.

Merideth Byl, Grade 6
St Cyril Elementary School, AZ

Life

Life is mean to me.
It makes me do things I don't want to do.
It makes me learn things I don't want to
Or things I already knew.
I hate it but I just can't say it
Because there's good times I got to choose
But maybe I just took a snooze.
It gave me memories I never want to lose.
Other memories it won't let me lose.
Without life I would not have these memories so maybe I should
let it be and live my life as me the way it should be.

Joshua Gonzales, Grade 6
Morgan Middle School, WA

Trail

Ollie and I we ride the trail,
And trying hard we never fail.

Over logs we pass through,
Opening a mailbox, too.
Walking over a bridge without water,
Ollie's step will never falter.

Side passing over a fallen log,
Onward and forward we will jog.
In the box we turn around,
And then we hear a cheering sound.

You may be thinking, "What trail is this?"
It's a competition I'll never miss.
This is a man-made trail in the ring,
When our names called for the blue, my heart sings.

Lannie Sullivan, Grade 6
First Baptist Christian Academy, AZ

Wish

I wish I hated you
I wish I didn't want you with me
When you're next to me I never want to move
Then I look into your eyes and want to die
Don't love me and I'll try not to love you
If you walk away I'll try to stay.

Channing Hinkle, Grade 6
Eagle Point Middle School, OR

I Can't Keep My Desk in Order

I cannot keep my desk in order.
My book and binders slide along with my recorder.

Spell checkers don't bounce well and my water bottle spills.
My teacher he gets angry and I think he needs to chill

I try to calm him down by sitting in my desk.
I know he doesn't care but it's a different request.

Tiana Barrows, Grade 4
Mills Elementary School, OR

I'm the Champion of Animal Watching

I see lots of animals,
very deep inside.
I'm a bobcat or a hawk.
Every animal I see.
I feel like I'm that animal.
Lots of animals come into
my yard before my very eyes I
see a human in the animals.
I see the animal take place
of one of the Olympic people
and watch it win.

Austin Eggers, Grade 4
Acacia Elementary School, AZ

Dads

Dads
nice, calm
taking care of you
always wanting to be with you
fathers
Christina Miller, Grade 5
Gold Canyon Elementary School, AZ

Parents

parents
peaceful, playful
annoying, loving, hoping
every day I love them even more
parents
Megan Nicola, Grade 5
St Mary's School, ID

Brain

I had a piece of brain,
It was one third of a grain.
I did have a full one,
But it fried in the sun.
This is so very insane!
Dilyn Vargas, Grade 5
Hafen Elementary School, NV

Shine On

The shining sun beams.
In the morning sky so bright.
Can't get out of bed.
Candice Dunagan, Grade 6
Hamilton Middle School, MT

The Lost Girl

I can't see a thing
It's dark and black
I hear people talking
But I can't see a thing
I hear people calling my name
Saying you can heal the pain
Only you have the power to
Heal that pain
Your family needs you they say
Be a role model
Be a hero
But don't be ashamed
Hold your head up high
You got your life going good
Don't let someone go and ruin it
I been down a road like this I thought
I was going to die
Be a survivor
Hold your head up high
Cassandra Elias, Grade 6
South Middle School, CO

Hunting

Feels like cold winter.
Smells like wet leaves.
Looks like elk tracks.
Tastes like cold spring water.
Sounds like the blast of a gunshot.
Jarryd Lahr, Grade 6
Denton Elementary School, MT

Blue

Blue is the color
Of faded blue jeans,
It's depressing at times
And the best friend of green.

Blue is the color
Of the vast night sky,
A first place ribbon
And my favorite tie dye.

Blue is the color
Of the blue jays that sing,
Grey's big brother
And a sapphire ring.

Blue is the color
Of the icee I drink,
The deep, dark ocean
In which ships sink.

Blue is the color
Of a dolphin's back,
A big blue whale
And a Wal-Mart sack.
Natalie Juteau, Grade 6
Kendallvue Elementary School, CO

How to Swing with the Sea

Walk along its sandy beaches,
Look at the waves tumble and play.
Listen to its lilting laughter,
Look among the washing waves.
Pick up shells,
And build sand castles,
Run among the waves and play.
Cover people in piles of sand,
Watch the sea gulls dip and dive.
Hear the cries of sea birds swooping.
Sip up soft drinks,
Swim and surf,
Smell the sea spray in the air,
Walk along the long, long boardwalk,
Visit a shop along the way,
Follow the sun sinking down.
Sonia Fan, Grade 5
Kyrene De Las Brisas School, AZ

Spring's Here

When the weather's warm,
And the sun is bright,
And the windows are,
Reflecting light.
There's only one thing,
That's happening
The seasons are changing
From winter to spring.
The leaves grow back,
And the flowers sprout
And the earth is happy,
All about.
Madeline Burke, Grade 4
West Woodland School, WA

Bunnies

Cute, soft, friendly
Hopping, running
Fast and slow
Bunnies are fun
Black and white
Brown and gray
Won't you come and play!
Kaitlin Marron, Grade 5
St Mary's School, ID

Kristen

K icking a goal
R unning like the wind
I ndulger of sports
S ilently spying
T aco Bell lover
E ating all the way
N ever eating asparagus
Kristen Denham, Grade 6
Heath Middle School, CO

My Wonderland

Little elves swinging around
Playing and jumping.
They never stop.
Four legged animals
Walk on two legs
Foxes, five times smaller
And tigers ten,
Bears five times bigger
Butterflies ten
Nothing is better
Than a reflection you see
On water.
It moves like a wiggly worm
All is in my wonderland
You see.
Isis Salazar, Grade 4
Fulton Elementary School, CO

The Labyrinth

My heart is a labyrinth with an unknown end
so choose now if you will enter.
For if you do you will be lost in the intricate hallways
confused by the many secret passageways.
You'll hear only your thoughts, breathing, and footsteps
all you will see is darkness.
You will feel cold, very cold
sad, alone, unwanted, scared;
like so many before you.
Wandering on the twisting, turning paths.
Only one has made it far and was destroyed by the unknown.
I'm still waiting for one to be conqueror
one brave and strong enough to destroy the darkness.
One to win my heart, mind and soul.
While others wander endlessly
or don't dare to enter.
So come try to defeat my labyrinth.
But…it will be a waste of your time,
your life — unless you're the one.

Andraea Shelley, Grade 6
Fairview Elementary School, UT

Five Senses Cheer

We got five senses! Hip hooray!
We use our senses every day!
See! Taste! Touch! Smell! Hear!
This is our five senses cheer!

Vanessa Martinez, Grade 5
Escuela Bilingüe Pioneer Elementary School, CO

Dancing Feet

Little Susie loved to dance.
    She'd sing some songs and prance, prance, prance.

Her mother and father didn't know why.
    If forced to dance they'd rather die!

Then during one day while Susie was singing a song,
    Something went awfully, horribly wrong.

She tried to stop and catch some wind,
    To find her feet were dancing in!

She yelled and screamed, and tried to move away,
    But all in vain, her feet would not stay!

A doctor, a nurse and seven kids,
    Couldn't stop the dancing kid!

Little Susie hollered "Yah!"
    I get to dance all day and day!

So year after year and day after day,
    Susie kept on dancing 'til her dying day.

Sage Hahn, Grade 5
Uplands Elementary School, OR

Candle

C is for the calm sensation of a soothing scent.
A is for the admirable look of peace of mind.
N is for the naked beauty of the enchanting glow.
D is for the dominant red fire that burns within.
L is for the leisurely time it takes to disappear.
E is for the ecstasy a candle brings you.

Elaina Straus, Grade 6
Glacier Middle School, WA

I Am From…

I am from Baby and Shady.
I am from Jeep and whistle.
I am from macaroni and cheese and chicken.
I am from riding and driving.
I am from soccer and basketball.

I am from bit finger and cut back.
I am from Spongebob and *Trick My Truck*.
I am from England and California.
I am from Truck Driver and Florist.
I am from Thanksgiving and Christmas.

I am Justin Levi Parsons

Justin Levi Parsons, Grade 5
Evergreen Elementary School, OR

Born to Be a Star

September 28th, was when I was born,
and when I came into this world I came out a star.
I love to sing, I love to dance,
the voice of an angel is what I have.
So hey world watch out for me
cause one day I'll be on that big screen TV.
And as my mom and day always say
God bless the day September 28th.
One day I'll own a studio and a big fancy car
cause I know I was born to be a star.

Katie Riley, Grade 4
Christian Faith School, WA

A Rainbow of Colors

Pink is the color of flowers in bloom,
Red is the color of a birthday balloon.
Yellow is the color of the sun so bright,
Grey is the color of a feather so light.
Purple is the color of nice, fresh grapes,
Brown is the color of big, fat apes.
Blue is the color of a cry baby's tear,
Green is the color of monsters you fear.
White is the color of a star in the sky,
Orange is the color of a small butterfly.
A rainbow of colors is pretty, indeed,
Without them, we would be in great need.

Megan Nicole Swenson, Grade 6
Bright Beginnings School, AZ

Codie
His fur is like silk
His eyes are like stars
His toys are unlimited
His passion is playing ball
His heart holds love for his family
That is as yellow as the sun
He lives in a doghouse
And eats dog food.
Amanda Cope, Grade 6
Heath Middle School, CO

Madi and Brittan
Madi
Playful, outgoing
Learning, missing, singing
People, cousins, sister, friend
Talking, drawing, painting
Pretty, trusted
Brittan
Madison Meyer, Grade 4
Copper Canyon Elementary School, AZ

Sea
Once the sun comes up
The waves are shaking,
As a Hula girl dances in the sun.
Once the sun goes down
The sea is rough like the fire
From the fire dancers at night.
Victoria Ramirez-Solis, Grade 4
Fulton Elementary School, CO

Books
Hard back covers.
Soft back covers.
They're interesting,
devastating,
impressive,
exciting,
surprising,
they help us learn,
big,
small,
thick,
skinny,
words,
pages,
pictures sometimes,
summary of book on back sometimes,
chapters,
short stories.
Soft back cover.
Hard back cover.
Benjamin Kreutzer, Grade 6
Vikan Middle School, CO

Seasons
Bitter chill water
in cool season spring
wailed the willows

Lonely silver moon
in the hot season summer
whispered the wind

Quiet bare willows
in the cold season fall
dreamed the moon
Jeremy White, Grade 6
Walt Clark Middle School, CO

Martin's Words
I have a dream,
Were Martin's words,
But some people,
They never heard.

Racism is wrong.
Is it for us to judge?
Black skin isn't evil
So why hold a grudge?

Martin had a dream.
Did it ever come true?
He wanted us to know,
That Jesus loves you.

If Jesus loves you,
Then Jesus loves me.
No matter what race,
We're all God's family.
Karlee Williams, Grade 6
Albuquerque Christian School, NM

Christmas
Christmas,
Blue pots, polka dots
Juicy ham, cooked to perfection,
Jolly music all around
Cooked gingerbread, hot to the core,
Presents, big and small,
Christmas…
Chad Brown, Grade 4
Coal Creek Elementary School, CO

Love
L eaves you all tingly inside.
O ut of your control.
V ery odd.
E asy to fall into.
Breanna Torres, Grade 5
M A Lynch Elementary School, OR

Guinea Pigs
G entle creatures
U nbelievably funny
I ncredibly fast
N ice
E ntertaining
A dorable

P recious
I ncorrigible
G oofy
S mall

To me these creatures
are nothing more than small animals
that were put on this earth
to make people happy!
Carissa Janitell, Grade 5
Creekside Elementary School, CO

Ghost!
Have you seen
The ghost
Walking through the
Hallway
His light gentle
Steps
With a pale face of
Sadness
Have you seen?
Joe Ruiz, Grade 5
Edgewater Elementary School, CO

Fire
Fire
Toasty, warm
Cooking, roasting, burning
Taking all that crosses it
Burning, scorching, heating
Red, hot
Flames
Mckenzie Elstad, Grade 6
Robert Frost Elementary School, OR

River Rafting
While rafting down in Idaho
In the river flow
Don't get stuck on the rock
And be blocked
Reaching the bridge
While standing on the ridge
Don't look down
For there is no ground
Just water!
Jack Gularte, Grade 4
Colbert Elementary School, WA

I Am From...

I am from reading and drawing.
I am from *Pink Panther* and *Modern Marvels*.
I am from Oregon and California.
I am from chicken and potatoes.
I am from "What in the name of the light" and "Don't slurp."

I am from German and Indian.
I am from construction and graphic artist.
I am from Angel and Rain.
I am from fractured finger and bonked head.
I am from Christmas and Thanksgiving.

I am Krysten Anne Marie Siver

Krysten Anne Marie Siver, Grade 5
Evergreen Elementary School, OR

Mr. Mailman

Every day, Mr. Mailman would go to work
At 7:00 o'clock and say "hi" to the clerk
At the local post office, zip 38794,
North Willamette Street, Corvallis OR.
He would go to the mailroom and pick up the mail
If there was a lot he would not even flail.
He would check each one and make sure they were legal
If one wasn't he'd report it as fast as an eagle.
Mr. Mailman liked his job, and he knew that he'd lose it,
If anyone thought that he tried to abuse it.
After all this was done, he'd take the mail to a truck
He would put it all in, even if it got stuck.
Then he would get a key and would drive
Around town and deliver the mail until 5.
Mr. Mailman would trudge through sleet, snow, and hail
Just to deliver and pick up the mail.

Skyler Galardi, Grade 6
Corvallis Waldorf School, OR

Confused

Did you really leave?
Because the image of you is still left in my mind.
Did you really say what you said?
Because your voice is what I'm still trying to find.
Did you really know how I felt?
Or did you guess what was going on in my head?
Did I really know how you felt?
I thought I knew by what was said.
Are you glad I'm gone?
I hope you still hold on to some of me.
But did I really know you?
Or were you something else that was harder to see.
Do you still feel the way I know you felt?
Or when you left, did I leave your mind too?
I think I still feel you, standing here with me.
And throwing away your image is just something I can't do.

Rachael Wimmer, Grade 6
Bright Beginnings School, AZ

Dangerously Peaceful

Without it you can't survive,
With just enough,
We will thrive.

Too much of it causes a flood,
With nothing around
But destruction and mud.

Too little of it and things get dry,
If none comes
Things start to die.

Sometimes it's peaceful and sometimes it's mad,
Sometimes it's good,
And sometimes it's bad.

It forms oceans, it forms the sea
It's a big part of you
And a big part of me.

We read about floods and drought,
Why can't the water just sort itself out?

Conor Henricks, Grade 5
Foothills Elementary School, CO

My Magic Box

I will put in my magic box
All the stunning golden treasures in the world
All the deep beryl shinning seas
The wonderful dog faces

I will put in my magic box
All my glimmering special dreams
The golden raindrops that hit the ground
The dark green grass by the lake

I will put in my magic box
The rush, rush of the horse going by
The power, power of the white winter snow
The fierce lions in the backyard

I will put in my magic box
The hot moist from the sun
The rockets fire from the sky
The wind flying into the air

Alex Vlasity, Grade 5
Mesa Elementary School, CO

A Special Something

Cute, cuddly, soft and furry, with little eyes and a big heart.
Every day you must part.
In the evening you're together again.
The cute little guy is your friend forever.
This little guy is just beginning to be man's best friend.

Tananda Nail, Grade 5
Desert View Academy, AZ

My Pink Blankey

When I was a child, a very young child, I depended on only one thing. And that thing's my blankey, my pink baby blankey, and it depended on me. When I would cry, it would dry my tears, and make monsters run away, wherever I went, wherever I'd play, my blankey would be there, all of the day. My mother would say, "Let's clean it today, it smells like it came from the dump!" So I'd say, "Just as long as we can play, for the rest of the day."

Harley Gibson, Grade 6
Lolo Elementary School, MT

Island of Lost Dreams

Every day there is no hope for us who live on the island of lost dreams
All of our hope is swallowed by the tide
All of our dreams are nightmares,
So every time we sleep we toss and turn

There is no love here, on the island of lost dreams
There is nothing to turn to but the whistle of the wind

When anyone comes here they just watch the sunset every evening and gaze upon the stars
They go to sleep in a world of fear and wake up in a reality of their own
Because of one simple reason, they live on the island of lost dreams

Tashi Serena Swierkosz, Grade 5
Santa Fe School for the Arts, NM

Cherry of Life

Our life is just like a cherry.
There's that tiny, thin stem that helps us grow.
And the sometimes sweet, sometimes sour, plump evening in our life.
But the most forgotten pit is our love, friendship, and joy in that sour 'n' sweet sensation of our life.

Our life is just like a cherry.
The tiny, thin stem of our growth
That wonderful fruit of events,
And our pit of love, friendship, and joy.

Nicole Janitell, Grade 5
Creekside Elementary School, CO

Black, Gray, and White

Black to me can be the color of bad and guilt
It can also be the color of good
It can be the color of bad and guilt to me because when I see the color black I feel the guilt of all the bad things I have done
To me it can also be the color of good because some of the good things that happen in life are because of the color black

Gray is the mixture of black and white
Gray can be the color of something that is sometimes good and sometimes bad.
Gray can be the good side of something that was once dark and black
It can also be the bad side of something that was once good and white
That is what I think about the color gray

White to me is the color of pure good
It can also be the color of bad
I think that white can and will always conquer black
To me God is in the color white
There are a lot of bad things in life that are white.

Black, gray, white have unlikely ways that make them all individual and different.

Bryan Jaquez, Grade 6
Blanco Elementary School, NM

Grandfather

Grandfather shows you how to hunt
He shows you how to respect your elders
Grandfather shows you how to make pottery and jewelry
Grandfather takes you on nature walks
and shows you beautiful places he's gone to as a kid.

Terrance Garcia, Grade 6
Sky City Community School, NM

My Horses

Manes and tails flying,
Galloping through grassy meadows,
Trees billowing in the wind,
Trotting over windswept hills,
My horses are great
Walking up snowy mountains,
Crunch, slip, swish, fast furious,
Dark forests, Watch out, Duck!
Icy streams slow and smooth
My horses are great
Beautiful colors,
Dun, bay buckskin, white, dappled, black, gray,
Chestnut, paint, pinto, appaloosa, palomino, roan
Jumping over logs,
Hoofs beating on the ground like war drums,
And at the end of the day,
The stars shining,
The moon rising,
My horses are great
But all of this is just a wish because
These horses are on my wall.

Xanthe Denning, Grade 5
West Mercer Elementary School, WA

I Am Deric

I am a goofy and friendly guy.
I wonder if I will ever be able to play pro football.
I hear that people say I look like a tower.
I see people that I might be fiends with in the future.
I what to be wealthy in the future.
I am a goofy and friendly guy.

I pretend that I am weird.
I feel that I have a lot of friends.
I touch my families' hearts.
I worry about my grades.
I cry when I am sad.
I am a goofy and friendly guy.

I understand that some people aren't that athletic.
I say a lot of funny things.
I dream that I will be a pro football player.
I try to do my best.
I hope I don't get bad grades.
I am a goofy and friendly guy.

Deric Sorenson, Grade 6
H Guy Child School, UT

Secret

A secret is promise
Something that someone trusts you with
A secret is just not something that people tell you for no reason
It is important to them
It is an oath
A swear
A vow
Something so hard to keep sometimes
If spread like a virus
It becomes dangerous to whoever spread it
Eventually people will not trust you with your word
If a secret is broken it creates
Hatred
Disappointment
Disgust
Anger
But if a secret is kept
People will tell you more secrets
Soon you may even make a friend
That will be forever
Friendship

Kayla Day, Grade 5
La Veta Elementary School, CO

Friends

Friends, they run and play,
with nice things to say.

Stay up all night,
and tell spooky stories by candlelight.

If you're stuck on a problem your Dad is too,
call up your friends, they'll help you.

When you think you're at the end,
they'll help you through thick and thin.

If they don't like you for who you are,
they aren't your friend at all!

Sarah Ingebo, Grade 5
Klickitat Elementary & High School, WA

The Place of Beauty

The place of beauty smells so sweet
The life of wind is calling my name
Wild flowers bloom in the hot spring air
I look around to see the rainbows one by one
the trees are hollow inside with snow
Mother Nature sings a song
The flowers smile one last time
Now it's winter and the flowers say bye, bye
And the place of beauty will come again
That's how it ends and there isn't any more

Megan Anderson, Grade 4
Gause Intermediate School, WA

Lava and Water

Lava is so hot
and water is clear and cool
if you put them together
they make an island
and lava brings new land also.

Sergio Serrano, Grade 5
Edgewater Elementary School, CO

Ballet

Warming up at the bar
I see myself in the mirror
peaceful, graceful
The dancers behind me
quiet as butterflies
The music feels
soothing, calming
My teacher whispering
position one, position two
as she moves on,
I feel free as a bird.

Daniela Lagunes, Grade 5
Carrolls Elementary School, WA

The Mean Dog

There is a dog,
that lives in my neighbor's house,
it barks all day,
right by my house,
I walk outside,
it growls,
and bares its teeth,
so I run,
run so fast,
the dog starts barking,
my neighbors come running,
they quiet the dog,
then they knock on my door,
and yell at me for,
coming outside,
so I say,
"I will come
outside if I want,"
everyone then,
goes home.

Benjamin Sylvia, Grade 6
Vikan Middle School, CO

The Cowardly Hunter

There once was a fool from Tubant
Who stalked a huge el-e-phant
the fellow took aim
at the giant beast's brain
And then suddenly shouted "I can't!"

Cameron Hillam, Grade 5
Ammon Elementary School, ID

Zoom In!

Zoom in.
From afar, it looks plain.
Zoom in.
From afar, you can't see it's beauty.
But then,

Zoom in.
A burst of beauty.
A simple weed.
Then, a gorgeous flower.
Death, then, somehow, life.

You can see its beauty now.
So close, you can see so much.
So many splendors.
Yet, you can see hardly anything.
Zoom in!

Casey McKim, Grade 5
Blanco Elementary School, NM

Darkness

Wearing a dress of all black with
stars upon it. Her eyes the same
and, her skin as pale as the moon.
She covers the daylight with her dress
bringing darkness up on the Earth.
She blows slightly bending the plants
and tree branches. She touches
the water scattering the lily pads.
She smiles as the owls and bats
start flying around to catch their food.
She watches over the sleeping people
and animals as they sleep. She herself
starts falling asleep, letting her brother,
Daylight, take over 'til it's her turn again.

Diana Jimenez, Grade 6
Meridian Middle School, ID

Spring

Spring is the best.
It is just beginning.
But I can't wait for the rest.
I am going to drink lemonade.
On a nice, sunny day.
And ride Rosco.
Then feed him hay.

Pascal Slick III, Grade 5
Whiteriver Elementary School, AZ

Tall Grass

See the tall, fresh grass,
Waving in the fanning wind
Saying 'Hi' to me.

Savanna Cox, Grade 6
Hamilton Middle School, MT

My Shadow

I woke up on a morning
I got up out of bed
I looked out my window
and this is what I said,
"I can probably see my shadow,
I can feel it in my bones."
I went into my parent's room
and they let out lazy groans.
They were two lazy lions
sleeping in a den
or like a lazy dog
whining in his pen.
I went over to my dad
and shouted in his ear
He said to tone it down a bit
He said "I cannot hear."

Benjamin Dunn, Grade 4
Roy Moore Elementary School, CO

The Columbia

The Columbia is so strong,
it's as if she does no wrong,
but her patience comes and goes,
most of the time her waters pose,
up and down the swells are going,
almost as if they are knowing,
soon they will crash on the rocks,
her voice is clear as if she talks;
"No! No! I will not go!"
Down, down, CRASH!

Grace McPhail, Grade 5
Ocean Park Elementary School, WA

Fairies

Fairies sing,
in the sparkling night.
You can hear the ding,
from the bells in the night.

As the moon glistens,
you can hear them twinkle.
And if you listen,
you can hear them winking.

As their fairy dust falls
onto the ground.
When it goes summer to fall,
you can see the fairies flying around.

But when it becomes winter,
the fairies shall leave.
They'll give a slight hint,
when you see them depart.

Taylor Arthur, Grade 6
St Joseph School, WA

Inside-Outside*

My inside self and outside self are different as can be,

My inside self is beautiful,
Clothes pretty as you see,
No grouchiness,
Pure happiness,
It all works out this way,
My outside self is opposite,
But I guess she's here to stay.

My outside self is grouchy,
Not getting enough sleep,
I guess I'll have to stay that way,
For tiredness, I'll have to keep.

Amanda Warren, Grade 6
Walt Clark Middle School, CO
*Patterned after "My Inside Self" by Rachel Field

Silver

Silver is wind chimes and music.
Silver is slippery like a slide.
Silver is the taste of air.
Rain and air smell silver.
Silver is Niagara Falls,
Silver is like playing outside, and being in Alaska.
Singing and crying is silver.
The clouds and snow are silver.
Silver is soft like silk.

Jesi Villasenor, Grade 6
Patton Middle School, OR

Say No to Drugs

Do not take drugs — no exception!
No cocaine, no marijuana, no tobacco!
It's not worth getting addicted or getting high —
DON'T TAKE THE RISK.
If you do, you go to jail. Turn yourself in,
do not hurt and kill because of what you choose.
If you have some tobacco, you will most likely get addicted.
Don't take the chance.
You can kill yourself and others if you smoke.
I don't want to get second hand smoke with your choice.
Taking cocaine will get you high.
You will lose the ability to have good judgment.
It's the same with marijuana —
it alters your brain and body.
Once addicted, it's hard to quit.
Talk with your mom and dad or whoever you live with.
Do the right thing, save lives for the people.
Inhale all the good things, not the bad things.
Inhale God, become a Christian.
Choose the right things in life,
God loves you no matter what — remember that!

Sam Wilburn, Grade 5
Faith Lutheran School, AZ

My World War II Army Helmet

The memories,
The memories,
I have from overseas,
I will tell you some of these.
The head I protect is moving,
But only wants to get out of this wreck.
I smell the gunpowder,
As wounded men ponder.
I taste the sweat from the head I protect,
Comrade helmets fall,
I want to protect them all,
But the rest of the platoon pushes me on.
I touch the ground as a man throws me down,
And all I can hear is the pounding of a heart — boom, boom.
With comrades lying about.
We are taken to the hospital in pain.
The air is filled with moans and groans.
All we want is home.
The memories,
The memories.

Seth Sanguins, Grade 6
Denton Elementary School, MT

All About Dominic Badalamenti

I used to be an immature silly five year old.
But now I am a mature, serious fifth grader.
I used to have nothing but wet, squishy gums.
But now I have sharp, white teeth.

I used to take little baby steps.
But now I take gigantic steps.
I used to be shy and bashful.
But now I'm obnoxious and loud.

I used to watch *Blue's Clues.*
But now I watch MTV.
I used to listen to baby music.
But now I listen to rock-and-roll.

I used to go everywhere with my parents.
But now I go to my friend's house.
I used to like the color of scarlet red.
But now I like grassy green.

I used to be the youngest kid.
But now I have a little brother and two baby cousins.

Dominic Badalamenti, Grade 5
Wheeler Elementary School, AZ

Cats

Cats are cuddly, caring, and cute.
They are curious when they find new places.
They can be scary when they attack.
They can be carnivores, though they are soft.

Bryan Samuelsen, Grade 4
Acacia Elementary School, AZ

Fossil Creek Dam

I see water rushing
quickly down the rough rocks.
Trees hanging down
from the water stream.
Tasting the leaves,
they taste like mint.
I feel mist blowing
through my face.
Seeing yellow monkey flowers
planted in the ground.
Trees covering the water stream
like a sunshade in the spring.

Gabriella Ayala, Grade 4
Great Expectations Academy, AZ

Polly Sue

Once there was a dino Polly Sue,
She always likes to play with you,
If you are feeling sad or down,
She'll turn your frown upside down.

Abby Veibell, Grade 4
Summit Elementary School, UT

School

I went to school this morning,
I saw a lot of desks,
I heard pencils on the paper,
It smells so good,
The food is so good,
The desks are so smooth.

Jessica Halstenberg, Grade 5
Bennett Elementary School, NV

Not That Strong

I'm burning inside out
I'm going to shout
No more stress
I'm becoming a mess
What's with all this hate?
You're too late
I'm falling silent can you see?
That you're destroying me
I'm surprised I've lasted this long
'Cause I'm not that strong
This wasn't supposed to be like this
Need I make a list?
Of everything that went wrong
I could write a song
Of all the suffering I endure
And are you sure
That you'll be able to sleep
'Cause of you I've fallen too deep
I can't last that long
'Cause I'm not that strong

Jaimie Welbourn, Grade 6
Miller Middle School, CO

Two Lights

It makes the sky bright.
It makes people happy.
The many different colors will make people change.
Happy, sad, good, or bad with every color's change.

People say that when you die the light is the wrong way to go.
How could it be as bad as they say if you leave the world behind?
No more war or really bad grades, the light may be the right way.
Why does no one think of that?
And of the peace it brings.

How could two poems of the same title be so different?
Think.

Sarah Richardson, Grade 5
Uplands Elementary School, OR

Wiggins

Every day I wake up the same way
I come down stairs guess who is there
Staring and jumping at me
My dog Wiggins

He is a Cairn Terrier
He always comes over and jumps on me
He is so little that sometimes I almost trip over him
He is black and gray also known as brindle with black tips

When I eat breakfast guess who is right there
When I brush my teeth or comb my hair
Guess who is standing there
My wonderful dog Wiggins

He loves to play with everyone he is loving and very nice
Be careful though he can be trouble when it's dinner time at night
He jumps up and down and all around the most wonderful dog
Wiggins Wiggins!!!

Kaitlin Coffman, Grade 4
Cottonwood Elementary School, AZ

Honesty

Honesty is to tell the truth, even if you will get grounded for a month.
And not to be mad if your friends tell on you, maybe.
When you lie you are only fooling yourself.

Jacob Debernardi, Grade 6
Hidden Creek Elementary School, WA

Death

Death is a thing that no one likes.
Death is a thing that you try to avoid.
So let's be healthy so we can stay.
So we can have fun every day.
Because people stay healthy they can stay for a little longer than they would have.
So let's be like them.
So we can stay and play for a little longer than we would have.

Kyle Tippetts, Grade 5
Thomas Edison Charter School, UT

Where the Waves Meet

The waves meet at a quiet place
where the salt water splashes onto my face
and nearby a dolphin glides
in the sea not in the sky
I smell the salt air and feel your grace
the sand is warm and the grass is green
and in my heart an angel sings
the trees wear a breeze and all is happening
in a quiet place that sheds your grace

Samantha Barakatt, Grade 6
Walt Clark Middle School, CO

Purple Polka Dotted Pig

I am a purple polka dotted pig
I wonder why I don't look like everyone else
I hear people talking about me
I want to be a different color
I am a purple polka dotted pig

I pretend to be red
I feel like I have purple chicken pox
I touch the mud that is in my pen
I worry about being eaten
I cry when there is no mud
I am a purple polka dotted pig

I understand that you can't just change colors
I say we shouldn't be eaten
I dream to be a normal pig
I try to escape to a different land
I hope I will live forever
I am a purple polka dotted pig

Nick Phillips, Grade 6
Wallace Elementary School, AZ

School

School
Children sitting, whiteboards, desks, decorated classrooms,
Markers squeaking on the whiteboard, lockers slamming,
Boring, easy, learning, homework,
Fun, friends are everywhere.

Matthew Grovenstein, Grade 6
Greybull Middle School, WY

Heroes

Heroes are important because
they give you someone to look up to.
They'll give you a friend to play with,
they'll make you smile
it will be worth your while.
Heroes can be a mom, or dad,
a brother or even another.
So keep in your mind for a very long time,
who is your hero.

Augie Provencio, Grade 5
Sequoia Village School, AZ

Brown

Brown is the color of all peanut butter,
A cup of brown sugar and dirty water.

Brown is the color of leaves in fall,
A lion's mane and a leather football.

Brown is the color of chocolate chips,
Dirt and mud and caramel bits.

Brown is the color of cola and rootbeer,
The bark on a tree an elk or a deer.

Brown is the color of robins and beavers,
Maplewood and dark anteaters.

Brown is the color of a grizzly bear,
Mean and rough unlike a hare.

Brown is the color of candy bars,
Chocolate milk and dirt on cars.

Marlena Romero, Grade 6
Kendallvue Elementary School, CO

Mothers' Love

A mother's loving heart is usually the size of the sun,
She spends this love on her most precious treasure:
Her daughter.

Madison Roodman, Grade 5
West Mercer Elementary School, WA

A Fright in the Night

As the fire burns in the night
I think nothing can cure my fright
I watch the flames lick up the walls
The fire burns and our house it mauls
Says the fireman, "All will be all right."
To think this thought takes all my might
When I awake sacred and aware
That it had only been a malicious nightmare!

Charles Petitpas, Grade 6
Eton School, WA

Why You…

I do not understand
Why you shoot a basketball
Why you kick a soccer ball
Why you hit a baseball
But most of all I don't understand
Why you throw a football
Because can't you just shoot, kick, or hit it?
What I understand most
Is sports make you strong
Because I play them

Meaghan Coffield, Grade 5
Copper Creek Elementary School, AZ

The Wrath of a Wildfire

In a lush green forest
filled with peace and serenity
a leaf ignited
with an orange glowing fire.
The flame grew
and grew and grew
until the entire forest
was flourished with flames and smoke.
Trees lit up like torches
and collapsed in piles of ash.
The air was clogged with smog
and the animals were left
to drown in the fire's toxic gas
or to be eaten by the burning wrath
of the red, deadly, crackling wildfire.
What has come to this forest,
that was once peaceful and calm?
Now chaos, destruction,
and insanity roams through it.

Robin Campos, Grade 6
Grant Middle School, NM

Night Time

Shadows dancing across the snow
Pitch blackness swallowing me up
Nothing in sight
Except the blinking light of the leader
The light went out!
Surrounded in darkness
Nothing but the dim glow of my lamp
Pshchsh, pshchsh,
What was that?
A moose!
Let's go boys
Onward home we go
Onward home we go away from danger
Into the light out of darkness
Into safety away from danger
Onward home we go.

Shameka Nelson, Grade 6
Nikolaevsk School, AK

Behind This Door

Behind this door you will seek
a world not blue not bleak
a world of magic and wonder
a place where money shall blunder
a place where puppets come alive
a place where leprechauns thrive
a place where floors do not creek
a place where the pipes don't leak
everyone will want to play
in this land, far, far away.

Nathanael P. Watson, Grade 4
Larkspur Elementary School, CO

The Bungle

There is a big green jungle
Animals there do the mungle
It was their dance
Then it spread to France
Now this dance is called the bungle!

Molly Moroney, Grade 4
St Thomas the Apostle School, AZ

I'm a Bird

I'm a bird
Flying all around
In the sky of blue
Clouds everywhere
Crazy crazy air
Blasting in my face
A wonderful feeling
Just flying
Nothing else
People down below
But they don't matter now
Because now I am flying
Above the clouds
My feathers glowing

Claudia Taber, Grade 5
CLASS Academy, OR

Muffins

Do you like muffins
Raspberry or blueberry?
I like chocolate.

Aaron Mead, Grade 6
Hamilton Middle School, MT

Snost

The snowflakes have a glitter
They're falling one after another
The grass is sprinkled with sugar
On this lovely beautiful day

My nose is lit up with red
Me and Rudolph will now be twins
I came to sit on a bench
But now it is glazed with snow

The bells on the church are singing
This must have a meaning
I do not know but will soon find out
What this lovely meaning is

The sidewalk is slick
You step on it, you slip
The only way to walk
Is to walk at your own risk

Hanah Leonhardt, Grade 6
Spring Creek Elementary School, WY

Mouse

There is a mouse in me
With claws like ash
And eyes like the rain
It creeps like water
It lives in my heart
And makes me feel quiet
I wish it would never go away
Or it will not hide
It makes me want to be quieter
And quieter

Tarina Bachli, Grade 5
Hafen Elementary School, NV

Football Players

They're cruel
they're rich
and they're strong.
They're a t
           e
         a
        m
sport, too.
They work together
They never give in, no matter what.
They get hurt but they don't care.
They get up and do it again.

Ryan Jarkowski, Grade 4
Acacia Elementary School, AZ

Surprise

Ow!
I feel as if my stomach
is going to burst!
We rush my mom
to the hospital.
Me and my sister
in the waiting room.
We wait for hours.
Doctors ran out the door
and told us,
"She had a boy!"
I couldn't believe
what had just happened.
But I was so surprised.

Zackery Dunkelberger, Grade 4
Acacia Elementary School, AZ

The Sky

The sky I see today,
is nice and blue
the clouds are making it gray.
I'm mystified and confused
the snow was falling yesterday.

Amy Aguayo, Grade 4
Mills Elementary School, OR

My Dragon

Flying across the world
To China
Little girls teaching me origami
The origami turning into a fierce dragon
Flying me away to an unforgettable faraway land
The round table in front of me
Battle!
Charging against bad.
My dragon protecting me from danger
Shielding me from arrows shooting towards me
We won!
Me and dragon
I flew home the next day,
On him.

Haley Robinson, Grade 5
West Mercer Elementary School, WA

My Wishes

My wishes always come true
That happened ever since I grew
I always wanted a good thing
One of them was to start to sing
I became older and things have changed so much
Now my dreams are very important to me that they touch
Now I listen to what my heart says to me
And that is how it will always be

Ferah Hassan, Grade 6
Phoenix Metro Islamic School, AZ

Hate

Hate, it's a powerful word
It surrounds us like air, you can't escape it

It's entwined in life like everyday things
Whether it's in school, or somewhere cool

People say it with anger and rage
They act like they have a mic on a stage

They blare their hatred for all to hear
Even though, no one's near

Kids whisper it behind friend's backs
They keep on going, like never ending life tracks

It gives you guilt, it makes you sad
And sometimes it makes you very mad

Before you can stop, everything's out
And pretty soon, regretful ideas sprout

Then you know, what you said was whack
But unfortunately, you can't take it back

Jessie-Anne Penkoff, Grade 6
Barbara Bush Elementary School, AZ

What Is This War Really About?

They say this war's about freedom
The ones who know that's true
Are fighting against the USA
Not for me, and not for you.

Mom says this war's about money —
Oil and gasoline.
But the gas prices are just going up —
We should have listened to Howard Dean!

I think, "What's this war really about?"
It could possibly be
That people just won't get along
And live in harmony.

Sarah Covert-Bowlds, Grade 6
North Bellingham Elementary School, WA

The Dog That Ran Out of Gas

There once was a dog very fast
If you ever raced him you wouldn't last
He jumps like a cat
He always wears a hat
But then he just stopped because he ran out of gas.

Dylan Moos, Grade 6
Fox Creek Jr High School, AZ

Spring Breeze

Spring, a peaceful thing, where the birds sing,
and the right time to do just about anything.
The best part is the breeze,
it feels like a sunset, above the waves.

The breeze can take you to many a place,
but the fastest place is a daydream.
Ice cream and butterflies,
sunshine and rain,
none can compare to the pain,
the spring breeze, is gone.

Samuel Robbins, Grade 6
St Joseph School, WA

Pesky Devils

My brother and sister scratch at me
It hurts when I fall off a horse and land in a tree
Homework, studying, and tests
They really are puny pests
Forgetting my watch, I don't know the time
Now I will pay a fine
A frigid ice cube as cold as snow
Down my back it will go
If I did great on CSAP's, I do not know.
Getting a bad grade, I hope not
Getting yelled at is a lot
You pesky devils

Lindsay Davis, Grade 5
Greenwood Elementary School, CO

Fireworks

Fireworks are red, green, yellow, blue,
bright and clear, just like jewels
pyrotechnics in the sky
green, orange, and gold
stuff like this is never old.

Amos Boegli, Grade 6
Monforton School, MT

Football

Running the ball
as fast as you can.
Don't stop
until you are in the end zone.
Throwing the ball
as far as you can.
Injury on the field:
help the guy up.
Disappointment
comes your way.
don't be mad:
it's the game of football.

Hunter Tassone, Grade 4
Acacia Elementary School, AZ

Sunset

S parkling colors
U p in the crystal blue
N etting across the sky
S tarting a new day
E very morning it greets us
T elling us to awake

Cassy Jolley, Grade 6
Greybull Middle School, WY

Alaska's Gifts

The North Star is bright
In the winter's light
It shines upon the mountains
So high yet so white
We have the best winters
In the world
Even though they're so cold
Our snow shines like silver
and our Northern Lights like gold
The history of this state
The Last Frontier
Has adventures waiting
throughout the year
You will not forget
The treasures
held deep within your heart
As you see Alaska's Gifts
Starting in the dark
Alaska's Gifts

Koralyn Sereyko, Grade 4
Scenic Park Elementary School, AK

McKade Hancock

McKade
Good friend, food in school, smart, good speller
Lover of the Utah Jazz, happy people, and good grades
Who feels good playing sports, snow skiing, and with no homework
Who needs pizza, snow, and my bike
Who gives attention in school, gifts to friends, and respect to the environment
Who fears cliff jumping, drowning, and evil animals
Who would like to have pizza for dinner, more money, and a big house
Who dreams of being a millionaire, a race car driver, and a pizza shop owner
Hancock

McKade Hancock, Grade 6
H Guy Child School, UT

Sweet Is...

Sweet is...giving your mom and dad a hug and kiss goodnight.
Sweet is...gushing honey on toast then eating the sweet treat.
Sweet is...telling friends and family you care.
Sweet is...sharing candy and chocolate with others.
Sweet is...laughing when your friend tells a joke and it is not funny.
Sweet is...sweet is...sweet is...

Kindra Theodore, Grade 4
Frontier Valley Elementary School, CO

I Am From

I am from my mom's home cooking, doing laundry, and listening to old music.
I am from the smell of Lysol and the smell of Umqua ice cream.
I am from my mom doing Tae-Bo and playing a game on New Year's.
I am from Augustine, Anna, George, Robert, Victoria, Chris, and Chris.
I am from my mom saying, "Load them up cowboys" and "Up and adam."
I am from being told to take out the garbage and clean my room.
I am from Grants Pass, Oregon.
I am from tacos and roast beef.
I am from eating a moth for six dollars and sticking my head in the toilet
and licking peanut butter off my toes.
I am from baby pictures.

Gregorio Duarte, Grade 5
Evergreen Elementary School, OR

I Am From...

I am from remote control monster trucks and toy trucks.
I am from enchiladas and chicken (fried).
I am from dogs and birds.
I am from "Get out of my room!" and "Be quiet!"
I am from basketball and quad riding.

I am from football and basketball.
I am from *Spongebob Squarepants* and *Fairly Odd Parents*.
I am from stitches and burnt legs.
I am from Christmas and Easter.
I am from Native American Cherokee and Caucasian.

I am Natane' Christina Stewart.

Natane' Christina Stewart, Grade 5
Evergreen Elementary School, OR

Anger!

Anger is a balloon,
As if I'm lightheaded, I might explode!
Anger is a road block, I'm stuck in and can't get through!
Anger is a fire, I'm burning
Words are my fuel!
Anger is a roller coaster, I'm twisting and turning

Martin Bishop, Grade 6
Spencer Butte Middle School, OR

My Friends

My friends
Loyal, friendly
Keep secrets, very fun
You should cherish friends your whole life
Sisters.

Selena Quiroz, Grade 5
Gold Canyon Elementary School, AZ

Spring

Spring grass is like needles
shaking in the sunshine,
Spring water is as clear
as a piece of glass,
Spring trees are ready
to grow their hair,
Spring birds sing as loud
as a marching band,
Spring deer are ready to prance through the wind,
Spring sunshine is so bright
it would blind you,
Spring winkys are so
weird their heads explode,
In spring I play
basketball to have fun

Madeline Shorey, Grade 4
Skyline Elementary School, WA

The Fairy House

Through the gate, across the path
Where pixies enjoy meeting,
The lilac trees and violets call a cheerful greeting.
There beneath the lilac tree,
I construct a house
For fairies which is very small
Not much larger than a mouse.
With sturdy walls of stone
And a roof of fallen sticks,
A bed of moss
And pebble stool,
The house is firm as bricks.
And maybe tomorrow I will find
A fairy gift for me,
Perhaps a seed or pretty vine,
For my hospitality.

Shalee Moore, Grade 5
Edmonds Homeschool Resource Center, WA

Friends

Friends are important to me…
They play soccer with me
Go to movies with me
Ride bikes with me
But most of all…
They joke and laugh with me

Trevor Moulton, Grade 6
Edmonds Homeschool Resource Center, WA

Rain

Clear night sky with a beautiful full moon.
Clouds gathering and blocking out the star's silver light.
My nose is overloaded with the perfume of coming rain.
They sky is now darker than ebony.
Thunder roars and lightning flashes.
The whistling wind dwindles.
The rain becomes a soft pitter-patter.
A golden sun rises over a clear blue sky.

Henry Brown, Grade 6
Eton School, WA

School

School the place you learn
The place you have fun
And the place to make friends
School where you read
Where you write
And where you eat
At school you get to do fun activities
You play music
And you do work
School it lasts eight hours
It starts at eight a.m.
And ends at four p.m.
School it is fun
It is boring
It is often really uncomfortable
At school you work
You work hard
And sometimes you are lazy and don't do so well
Some schools are little
And some schools are huge
But I love school at least sometimes.

Hannah Everett, Grade 5
La Veta Elementary School, CO

Assignment

I wanted to rip this assignment to bits
I wanted to do it with all of my wits
I wanted to do it and throw it away
But then teacher caught me and let out a "hey!"
I was stuck in detention with nothing to do
So next time I do that I'll try to blame you

Bryce Frederickson, Grade 4
Windsor School, UT

Race Cars
C atching up,
A round the corner.
R acing around the track,
S peeding to the finish line.
Tyler Brown, Grade 6
Conestoga Elementary School, WY

Horrible and Sweet
He was mean like a bully.
He was ugly as a boring day.
He was loud as a roaring lion.
He was odorous as a smelly shoe.
He was hard as a rock.

She was sweet as a candy bar.
She was smart as an expert.
She was quiet as a sleeping mouse.
She was pretty as a flower.
She was soft as a pillow.
HyeNa Oh, Grade 6
Uplands Elementary School, OR

The Best of Red
It is dark and it is light,
It allows your body to live,
For red gives us a lot of food,
Red can lie, and red can be truthful,
Red is like a bird singing its song,
Red is gallant,
Red is strong,
Red is like the blazing sun,
Red is passionate,
For red is good and red is evil.
Josiah Muhr, Grade 6
Robert Frost Elementary School, OR

Palmer Park
Palmer park joins
the beauty of
nature.
The old park combines
nature and society
together.
The greatness of
Palmer Park connects
people and animals
because the animals
get their food
off the trees
and we get picnics.
The wonderful park
shows how beautiful
our world can look.
Zach Diaz, Grade 4
Audubon Elementary School, CO

Math/Bath
I was at school
Doing very hard math
I saw the teacher looking at me
So I started to read a book
I went home and took a bath
Laura Bedolla, Grade 6
H Guy Child School, UT

Softball
"Number five you are on deck"
Coach said simply with a peck
Right into my nerve system
Down into the depths
The batter hits the ball
She zips to first, zooms to second
Heads to third and straight home
It's a home run!
High-fives all around
"Ah oh" it's my turn
I tell myself "don't get out"
All eyes are on me
My nerve system is going berserk
I might choke with everyone watching
My bat just swung
The ball is in the air
I am heading to first, to second, to third
Will I make it?
And I am heading to home plate
"Bad idea" I tell myself
"Oh Shoot" I am out.
Michelle Lipowicz, Grade 6
Desert Mountain School, AZ

If I Were a Pug
If I were a pug
I could sleep in all day
I would be cute and lovable
And food would be my pay

I would be loved
I would be spoiled
There would be people to pet me
My tail would be coiled

I could pick the food I wanted
I would be the best pug
I would sleep a lot
I would be a big lug

A fat black pug is what I am
I would love to sit and cuddle
I would be plump and fluffy
And my nickname would be Puddle.
Cameron Morgenweck, Grade 6
Bradford Intermediate School, CO

Summer
Hot, hot day
Freezing cold swim
Icy drink of lemonade
Awesome water slide
Fan in your face
A blazing summer day
Alonso Law, Grade 4
Lincoln Elementary School, AZ

The Prairie
The buffalo grazes silently.
As the strong Wyoming winds
blow the grass and ripple the water.
This is the home of the buffalo
The Prairie.
Max Wasser, Grade 4
Spring Creek Elementary School, WY

Computer Mouse
Waltzing across the mouse pad
Spinning and clicking
Slipping from thy sweaty hand
Young, compared to its companion
The Keyboard.
My hand is on.
My hand is off.
Click.
Swerve.
Steer.
Pull.
Scroll.
Smell of sweat.
No taste to me.
Nothing like its idol, a real mouse.
Feels plastic.
Wil Vickroy, Grade 6
East Middle School, CO

Black
Black is the color of nasty stuff
Black is the color of dirty fluff
Black is also peace and hope
Love and hate, but not the pope
We go to a funeral wearing black
Hoping God will give them back
Black is a pupil, black is a crow
Black is the color of all woe
Black can be strong
Black can be wrong
Black can be weak
Black can be meek
Black can be happiness, too
Black can be anything to you
Caitlin Powley, Grade 6
Walt Clark Middle School, CO

Is Everything Black or White

Black as a man who goes crazy with power
Black as people that destroy the flowers
Black as a kid who starts to lie
Black as a relative when they die
Black as a ship that takes a wreck
Black as a person that breaks his neck
Does everything have to be black or white?

White as a baby that learns to walk
White as kids that don't start to mock
White as animals that jump and play
White as children that play in hay
White as God being trustful and kind
White as kids being smart in the mind
Does everything have to be black and white?

Collin Cross, Grade 6
Walt Clark Middle School, CO

A Locked Door

Every door is different
They each have a different way of opening
You may try all your life to get through
Though you never found the key
Keys are tricky too
They come in all forms
To fit every lock, the old and the new
You face a problem
You can't get out
You look for a key in and out
You try all your life to get through one single door,
Though you never knew the way out
You can never get out
Or at least that's what you say
Though there's always a way
Just you come and see
You'll find it one day
These doors are like a maze
Out one, but shut out of another
These doors are never ending
But remember to never allow defeat

Tayler Soefje, Grade 6
Bright Beginnings School, AZ

Mrs. Bender

Mrs. Bender is nice Mrs. Bender is sweet,
Don probably likes to rub her feet.
She wears a pretty necklace that she forgot today
But she looks lonesome in her own way.

Mrs. Bender is my teacher,
She is nice as a preacher.
She is the nicest one I know,
But now, goodbye, I have to go!

Carrie Craft, Grade 5
Bennett Elementary School, NV

Unwritten

A small flower,
so real
so delicate
so elegant.
An unread book,
an undiscovered time,
brilliant and lively,
a warm breeze,
sweeping the land,
Colors.
embracing the eyes at first sight,
Smiles.
slowly unwriting themselves across your face,
Spirit.
in vast oceans of happiness,
Life.
to stay forever in some form,
a small flower,
so real,
so delicate,
so elegant.

Charlotte Molla, Grade 4
Khalsa Montessori Elementary School, AZ

Angels

Big fluffy wings and silky white dresses
With homes in the clouds
They give special kisses
They can lift evil shrouds
They were once kind people
When they come 'round there's no need to flee
"I love them, I love them,"
Because angels are good to me.

Rashelle Ptacek, Grade 6
Patton Middle School, OR

Summer

Summer air smells like fresh new flowers blooming.
Summer feels hot and sticky in Ohio.
Summer sounds like kids playing in the park having fun.
Summer looks like lots of fun.
One playing outside.

Margaux Mohler, Grade 5
CLASS Academy, OR

My Pet Basketball

My pet is very unusual!
When it opens its mouth,
Out comes a bounce,
And it goes right into the hoop.
Unfortunately someone might steal him from me,
When we are playing a game.
Although my friends may laugh at me,
I love my pet basketball!

Kristin Berry, Grade 5
North Star Elementary School, WA

War

War is filled with pain and strife,
The strife of war may end your life.
War should not be seen as good,
There should be peace and brotherhood.
People are killed, homes are destroyed,
War is one thing we have to avoid.

Carlos Calderon, Grade 4
Aurora Quest Academy, CO

My Cat

My cat is not lazy,
He plays outside when it is hazy.
It is my cat,
Because he wears a hat,
He is not tall,
He is not small,
But he is perfect to hug,
The only thing is he looks like a bug.
He hunts birds but never succeeds,
I don't know how he ever feeds,
He hunts mice but they always get away,
But he tries again the very next day.

George W. Deeter, Grade 5
Sally Mauro Elementary School, UT

I Am From…

I am from motorcycle and quad.
I am from taco and pizza.
I am from Hank and Buba.
I am from football and wrestling.
I am from sliced head and scarred arm.
I am from football and MTV.
I am from Idaho and Texas.
I am from construction and mechanic.
I am from Native Americans.
I am from church and school.

I am Jason Paul Meichtry.

Jason Paul Meichtry, Grade 5
Evergreen Elementary School, OR

Animals

Animals, animals, what do they do?
Animals, animals, some live in the zoo.
Animals are fun to have.
Animals will make you glad.
Animals, animals, they have lots to say.
Animals, animals, please don't go away.
Animals love to play.
Animals are sad when you're away.
Animals, animals, some are small.
Animals, animals some are tall.
Animals, animals, some live in the zoo.
Animals, animals I love you!

Sara McCaffrey, Grade 5
Clarkmoor Elementary School, WA

Mother Earth*

Mother Earth a gift from God
A place of true beauty.
But now things are not so beautiful.
If you look around at all of what we have done to Mother Earth,
You can see her dying a slow cruel death.

We have burnt her by burning down her forests.
We have choked her with our pollution
We have scarred her from our wars.
See now life is not a toy to be fooled with or to be mistreated.
God asked the help of Mother Earth to help along mankind.
And she gracefully agreed.
But look at what we have done to her.
Is this another way of repaying her?
Tell me because I don't know.
After all of this torture she is fragile.
She is a bomb waiting for the slightest disturbance to go off.
Please think about this, not one person will help not two it will take everyone
And I think Mother Earth needs all of the help she can get!!!!!

Kayla Stacey, Grade 4
Meadow Point Elementary School, CO
*Inspired by Andrew Stacey

A Peaceful World

A peaceful world is a place where you feel safe.
A peaceful world is where there's no gate, keeping you from your dreams.
A peaceful world is where everyone has fame.
A peaceful world is where places are filled with joy and happiness.
A peaceful world is where everyone can be themselves.
A peaceful world is where everyone can be considered one family, one figure.
A peaceful world is where no one cares what you wear, or where you live.
A peaceful world is where we don't have wars and just love each other as a family.
A peaceful world is where there's no crying, fighting, or stealing.
A peaceful world is what we can make as long as we work together.

Brandy Fox, Grade 6
Fox Creek Jr High School, AZ

Violinist

I'm the greatest violinist this world has ever seen.
Even though I've had no lessons, and I'm as horrible as can be.
I performed at my school talent show, it really was quite grand.
Though halfway through the performance, the audience threw sand.
The sand got in my eyes, I ran right off the stage.
When my teacher caught me, she was on a rage.
We walked into the office, she was really mad you see.
I decided it would be best to go unnoticed for me.
So I recited for my cat, he was playing dead.
But when I went to pick him up, it was real instead.
I played at my cat's funeral, that's when the people cried most.
Then they plugged their ears and left, even went the host.
My parents hid my violin, and then they said to go.
I can't figure out why, because you and I both know.
I'm the greatest violinist this world has ever seen.
Even though I've had no lessons, and I'm as horrible as can be.

Tess Ward, Grade 6
Spring Creek Elementary School, WY

Future

I am a crazy guy who likes guns.
I wonder what the new life with Christ will be like.
I hear my parents talking.
I see my life as a grown adult.
I want to be with my family for all eternity.
I am a crazy guy who likes guns.

I pretend that I am the greatest football player in the world.
I feel the hope of my little siblings hanging on me.
I touch footballs all around me.
I worry about losing the big game for my team.
I cry about bad things that happen to my friends.
I am a crazy guy who likes guns.

I understand some girls.
I say some girls are cute.
I dream of a state championship.
I try to do the best I can.
I hope someday I will go to USC.
I am a crazy guy who likes guns.

Austin Kendell, Grade 6
H Guy Child School, UT

Skiing Wonder

I'm fast
Then I crash!
I get to the bottom finally.
Then I go on the lift wildly.
I go in the lodge.
I had lunch.
I go down the stair in a bunch.
I get my skis and go outside.
I go to my lesson down the hill with a crash.

Mykala Killian, Grade 4
B A Winans School, MT

A Stick

One end anger, the other healing.
No matter what you do it's never gone,
piece by piece it is still there. Anger is falling
into a million pieces, never gone, always there.

Julianne Tanis, Grade 6
Acme Elementary School, WA

My Muck Boots

Lined up like soldiers waiting for him to come
Doesn't he know there are miles and miles to explore
Hey, I think, he's coming to slip us on
— me and my partner

Off we go through the snow in the middle of the night
With no light
We keep walking up high and low
Crunch, crunch, crunch through the snow we go

Julius Frehse, Grade 6
Denton Elementary School, MT

Christmas

Christmas
Plump Santa Claus at the mall
Fresh cut Christmas trees
The click-clack of reindeer hoofs on the roof
Sweet sugar cookies
Crunchy wrapping paper
Christmas

Linden Loutzenhiser, Grade 4
Coal Creek Elementary School, CO

Skin Deep

They look at you and judge by the way you look to them.
You're never going to be,
Their Valedictorian.
They say that beauty is not skin deep and that it's from inside,
But who are they to judge you when they have no self pride?
You'll never be enough for them,
and that's just how you feel.
But never doubt your inner self,
Or you will never heal.
Look past their flawless manicures,
Look past their flawless skin.
And you will find that deep inside,
They have no soul within.
Look past your chipped stubby finger nails,
Look past your bumpy skin,
And you will find that deep inside,
There is a heart within.

Sophie Stack, Grade 5
Greenwood Elementary School, CO

Lady Freedom

Locked in a cage made of rules.
Being poked and prodded by authority.
Shackled to the ground,
A lady named Freedom is trapped.

Freedom must fly and by wild.
She can't be contained.
Many have worked to save her.
Some have succeeded,
Others have failed.

Freedom fights for equal rights.
So others can be heard.
I thank the men and women
Fighting by her side.

Sacrifices made to save her
'cause freedom don't come free
the slaves know that
the soldiers know that
but do you know that?
That is what freedom means to me.

Taylor Archer, Grade 6
Pope John XXIII Catholic School Community, AZ

Beautiful Blue
Blue, the color of our dream
Slipping silently through the night
Our soul, it screams
Our imaginations take flight.

Blue, the color of the sky
Where clouds flit here and there
Like love's eternal tie
Together without a care.

Blue, the color of our sadness
Our hearts weep in pain
Our minds scream with madness
And our tears fall like rain.

Blue, the color of our pleasure
Like an open door
It comes with no measure
And sadness is no more.
Victoria Self, Grade 6
Walt Clark Middle School, CO

Gingerbread
There once was a gingerbread man.
All he did was sit on his fat can.
He would lay there and wait,
On his gingerbread plate.
And that night was eaten by a man.
Steven South, Grade 6
Midway Middle School, ID

Snuggler
Someone soft
Your cuddler 'til life ends
Guarder of your secrets,
Never will they leak
Bravely they worship you,
Like gold given to the poor
Loves your toys more than you,
To chew
Rolls through the grass with you,
Springing with dew
Tongue rolls out at the sight of sun,
Nor can they bear the heat
Circus tricks they can do,
Acrobatics in the air
Wagging, wagging in the air,
Like a flag in the wind
Someone furry, soft and cuddly,
Who can it be?
Not me,
A puppy,
Hee, hee!

Gailen Baber, Grade 5
West Mercer Elementary School, WA

There Was a Princess Named Meg
There once was a princess named Meg,
She tripped and broke her left leg.
She slipped on the ice
Not once but twice
Take no pity on her I beg.
Andrew Dunn, Grade 5
St Cyril Elementary School, AZ

The Meadow
The dazzling daisies
Danced in harmony
With the wind.

The whispering weeping willows
Swayed in woe
For the lost unknown.

The blabbering blue jays
Gossiped gaily
About things to come.

The creek
Bubbled and laughed with delight.

And the sun's rays
Tickled the tulips with joy.

The meadow was full
Of life and emotion.
Katie Kinsella, Grade 6
Southern Hills Middle School, CO

Flowers
Flowers smell so sweet.
Red, yellow, blue, green.
Flowers grow so slow
but when they bloom
they are beautiful.
Daisies, roses
Sunflowers
Tulips.
Michaela Annette Fossat, Grade 5
Sally Mauro Elementary School, UT

Heaven
Heaven is a wonderful place
That we have not seen or touched.
It is filled with glory,
Passion, and love from God.
Heaven will be an unbelievable sight
And we cannot even imagine it.
It seems like a dream but
It is not a dream at all.
Christopher Beazer, Grade 4
Aurora Quest Academy, CO

Light, Light and Dark, Dark
The excruciating light
shines so brightly
through the gorgeous trees.
Delightful trees
darken
and become light
as the clouds continue
to cover the sun
and uncover the sun,
as the light shines
through,
then goes away.
Harsh looking shade
grows darker
as the lovely trees
blow in the misty wind
and dark clouds
hover overhead.
Caitlin Salas, Grade 4
Audubon Elementary School, CO

The Followers
He follows me
He follows you
You walk I run
Yours walks mine runs

He follows me
He follows you
You jump and skip
He jumps and skips

He follows me
He follows you
Except on a cold rainy day.
George Logan, Grade 6
Eagle Point Middle School, OR

Lugi the Lion
Lugi the lion
lives in lofty ladders
in the last launch pad in London.
He eats large lettuces,
Latin lamb chop,
lobster, lice, and llama liver.
Lugi likes long leapfrog,
learning in the library,
laughing at Larry the leopard,
and licking lemon lollipops.
He's a little loud,
loyal to life, and
he's likely lazy.
He also littered on my lawn.
Mac Myers, Grade 6
Patton Middle School, OR

Try

If you try
you can get by all hard things.
You will feel happiness
and happiness brings joy.
When you feel joy
because you passed that math test
you will try
on your English test too.

Marissa B. Moreno, Grade 5
Sangre De Cristo Elementary School, CO

Timeout Time

Timeout time I do not like;
I'd rather play with my best friend Mike.
That dreadful place, so dark and scary;
The monster within is so very hairy.
I do not like that haunted place;
The teacher there has a frightening face.
How many times I have been there, I do not know;
I guess I'll see you at timeout time tomorrow!

Victoria Kong, Grade 5
Oak Creek Elementary School, OR

Fall

Fall is a cool time,
But it's also a beautiful time
To look at the colorful leaves
And all of nature's wonders.
I love this season,
So when you say you hate it
Because you have to rake the leaves
Just think of this and it will teach you a lot!

David Vallejo, Grade 6
Presentation of Our Lady School, CO

Pets

They're about friendship,
trust, and caring.
Dogs: are fun to walk and fun to play with.
Cats: they're lovable and playful.
Birds: very colorful, really loud,
and sometimes give you headaches.
Horses: very tall, fun to ride,
and fun to take care of.
Fish: fun to watch and sometimes very pretty.
Pets.

Corey Craig, Grade 4
Acacia Elementary School, AZ

The Dog Made Off with My Homework

The puppy made off with my homework
and covered it quickly with dirt.
And now all the trees that I grow,
have leaves that are made of homework.

Mackenzie Hudson, Grade 4
Frontier Valley Elementary School, CO

A Frosty Night

Moon in the sky twinkling bright
Winking at the Earth all covered in white
Looking the most beautiful at the hour of midnight
What if I had missed this all snuggled up tight?

Through panes in the window I see the bright glow
Taking delight in nature's magnificent show
I throw open the door to leap into the snow
Snow dumps on me from hat to toe.

It was a good idea but now something's the matter
Cold creeps under my skin, warmth starts to scatter
Shivering and shaking teeth and bones begin to chatter
Standing in a frosty night I just couldn't be madder!

McCalle Feller, Grade 6
Lewis & Clark Elementary School, MT

Black and White

Black
Black is darkness and dimness,
Shadows and a time during night,
And during sundown, and a time during evening
And denied of light, and is beauty.

Gray
Gray is a beauty to some people,
It shows that you are older
And you deserve respect from younger people
And that you are a great person.

White
White is the color of light and happiness
It is colorless
Yet it is beautiful and peaceful
It is life and it is good.

Kyle Martin, Grade 5
Blanco Elementary School, NM

The Nature of Love

The nature of love is:
Like a precious tendril on a delicate flower,
Or the sweet aroma of the sea.

The nature of love is:
A cat's soft purr,
Or the cooling breeze.

The nature of love is:
Simple, yet sophisticated
Irresistible, and powerful.

The nature of love is:
The true natural healer,
Inside everyone's heart.

Kathryn Kingsley, Grade 6
Grant Middle School, NM

Football
Tackle, bam
Throw, catch
Block, smash
Quarterback
Running back
Wide receiver
DT, LB, MLB
They're all Blitzing you.
CB, SS, FS
They're all blocking
Your WR.
Sean Draper, Grade 5
Sally Mauro Elementary School, UT

Moon Images
Looking at the moon
Gives me images in my head.
So many different shapes
When I'm bored.
I look at the moon for hours
And when it goes away,
I pout.
Nathan Yelmene, Grade 4
Scenic Park Elementary School, AK

The City
Beyond the city
Above the crystal lights
Along the rocky roads
Below the trashy ground
Through the large buildings
Within the colorful stoplights
Down the bumpy streets
Along the large cars
In the long alleys
Within the gorgeous houses
Along my comfy bed
Brenda Reyes, Grade 6
Fox Creek Jr High School, AZ

My Mind
My mind is a complicated place,
In there I go at my own pace.
I know how to use its techniques,
I give it all it wants to seek.
I go there to hide,
And also go there for pride.
It's full of emotions,
It makes my motions.
It is my battlefield,
It is my shield.
This is my mind,
And it is fine.
No one will take it from me.
Haley Romarine, Grade 6
Walt Clark Middle School, CO

It's Just Life
Trees are green,
Flowers are pretty,
The sky is blue,
Babies are born, little kids cry, while dads are outside
The moon goes over the night sky and little frogs come out to play.
Mountains are high,
Valleys are low,
The ground is brown,
How wonderful it is to be here, as mothers watch their children play outside,
Summer air is hot,
Birds can fly,
Frogs can hop,
The Earth is beautiful,
The Earth can be a wonderful place to be,
But no more wars and no more fighting
Mother Earth is crying.
Felecia Estevan, Grade 6
Sky City Community School, NM

Surfing Ride Fun
As I paddle I enter a wet, blue, wave
And the cold, clear, water splashes everywhere.
It seems like I'm in a watery cave.
Then, like magic I get out, it's like the wave had a tear.

I get on a wave and stand tall and high,
And up on the surfboard I blink.
The shiny, yellow, ball that is in the sky,
Is way too bright for me!

All too soon the ride is done,
And my surfboard is dirty with sand as it is washed up swiftly with the tide.
I then decide, "That wave was just too fun!
I'm going for another ride!"
Marcella Cartledge, Grade 6
Pope John XXIII Catholic School Community, AZ

I Am From
I am from old Domino and I am from Tide bleach and Sun soap.
I am from a creaking house.
I am from poor man's coffee and the walnut trees.
I am from going to the beach and being the official turkey cutter.
I am from Nancy and Paul and Trinidy.
I am from the burping of my older sister and my mom's home cooking.
I am from winning my champion basketball game and making a basket.
I am from "Don't do drugs," "Do your homework."
I am from Grants Pass, Oregon and sweet and sour chicken with white rice.
I am from a great, great, great grandpa who found oil when looking for gold.
I am from the family plate that hangs in our living room.
I am from building small houses and making faces out of candles.
I am from inventing military weapons and riding my bike.
I am from farming corn with my mom.
Devan LaRue, Grade 5
Evergreen Elementary School, OR

Spring Is Here!

March 20th, I love the best,
When flowers are blooming out in the sun.
What does all this mean?
Spring is coming,
Spring is here,
get ready, be prepared.
Spring is coming, don't be scared.
Blowing wind messes up your hair,
Kids are laughing,
having fun,
I know what this means,
SPRING!

Dymond Davis, Grade 4
McCormick Elementary School, NM

Cherries

If I had a bowl of cherries
I'd make a cherry pie
It would be tasty and delicious
Even better than the ones you buy

If I had a bowl of cherries
On top of a cone it would sit
I would eat them with ice cream
And finish every little bit

If I had a bowl of cherries
I'd de-pit every single one
Then I would rinse them in the sink
Now the cleaning job is done

If I had a bowl of cherries
I would make a fruit salad that's oh-so-sweet
Then I'd stick a giant spoon in it
And then begin to eat

If later I had an empty bowl
I'd wait for spring to come
Little cherries will soon grow
And I'll use every single one

Meilyn Weege, Grade 6
Bradford Intermediate School, CO

Hyperactivity

Hyperactivity is a rainbow of bright colors,
flashing before my eyes.
a sensation of Mountain Dew rushes to my mouth.
The sweet smell of bubble gum descends upon my nostrils.
Booming music clicks on in my head,
making my heart beat faster and faster.
Jumping on a trampoline, trying to go as high as you can.
Almost as if you are flying until you fall back down again.
Then all of a sudden, the sight of multicolored polka dots
dancing in your head appears.

Alisa Barker, Grade 6
Lolo Elementary School, MT

Dance

Dancing is like feeling nothing,
Except for the beat of the music
Pounding at the ground with your feet
Wishing that you could keep on dancing
Forever
Never stopping
Dancing is when you can do any move you want
And it's even better with someone else
Being with you
Dancing just like you
Wishing the same thing as you
You two are like synchronized swimmers
Having fun together
Being immune to everything
Except the other person
And the music
That you're dancing to.

Rachel Waite, Grade 6
Bright Beginnings School, AZ

Summer

My sister was outside,
and the bees were buzzing,
buzz, buzz,
the planes flying,
zoom, zoom,
and I was in the house,
hearing the clock tick away,
tick tock, tick tock,
not to mention the faucet,
plop, plop,

And it was summer,
and yet I was still hearing the front door shutting,
slam, bam,
and I want to go outside and play,
but I can't,
I'm sick,
cough, cough.

Sage Allen, Grade 6
Pope John XXIII Catholic School Community, AZ

Summer

When summer comes and there is no school
I like to go to the swimming pool
The water's cool when the sun is hot
And I can wear that new swimming suit I bought
I dive and splash, swim, and play
All through the long summer day
As I go home as the sun goes down
There is no reason to wear a frown
'Cause when I wake up the very next day
I will be able to swim, run, laugh, and play

Hannah Broome, Grade 6
Corpus Christi School, CO

Moon to Sun

When the moon glitters
And stars shower the sky
With brilliant light,
Wolves will howl
And owls will hoot
The words of question.
When the sun rises
To shed light on the earth,
Birds will break the silence of our
Dew spangled world,
Waking up a new life for us
So we may live on happily
No matter who we are.

Emily Rayl, Grade 6
Cam Jr/Sr High School, WA

Camping

The river explodes
As we all jump in.
Like a volcano
Bursting from excitement.
Water splashes in the air
Like a whale
Squirts from his blowhole.
My mom calls us up for breakfast.
Hash. A dish wish assorted foods.
As I exit the water
I think how lucky I am.
I look behind me.
The river glistens
As ripples run through it
Like a race that never ends.
The sun peeks between the trees
Playing hide and seek with nature.
The ripples are like a machine,
Slowing down
And then suddenly quits
As I head up to my campsite.

Jessica Howard, Grade 6
Walker Middle School, OR

Friends

Permit me to tell you of laughter,
Ha-has, giggles,
When you feel happiness
Soaring through your bloodstream,
Or the funnies prickling your skin,
Like tiny needles that feel wonderful.
Permit me to tell you that
The laughter that stands out in my mind,
Is the laughter I remember most,
The laughter that I laughed
When I met my friends.

Chloe Costello, Grade 6
Parrish Middle School, OR

Weather

W ind whips dark clouds
E vaporates water
A reas are disasters
T ornados cause cars to fly
H urling houses
E rupting Earth's surface
R ain washes it away

J.D. Muma, Grade 5
Hafen Elementary School, NV

Roadrunner

Roadrunner
Fast, feathered
Running, hopping, gliding
Desert, friend, family, group
Flying, running, hopping
Small, gray
Quail

Scott Swope, Grade 5
Kingman Academy of Learning, AZ

Love Is

Love is a rainbow
Like Skittles in my mouth
Nice and chewy
Crunchy, delicious

Love is playing football
On a cool autumn day
Coming to school every day
To be with friends and my teacher

Love is my grandparents
Who take good care of me
Hugs from my sister
Playing with my puppy

Michael Maldonado, Grade 6
Washington Intermediate School, CO

Behind Her Eyes

Look behind her eyes
All the tears she cries
Everything she hides
Trying to hold on
But she is only so strong
Trying to keep her hold
Trying not to let go
She's starting to fall down
And there's nobody around
Nothing makes sense to her
Everything's a blur
Nobody's ever there
Does anyone really care?

Nikki Santiago, Grade 6
Molasky Middle School, NV

Seashore

Now close your eyes.
Hear the sea hit the rocks
Like a drum being played.
Listen to the seagulls
Flying over your head,
Hear a boat
Gently gliding
Over the water.
Feel the wind
Through your hair
Like a flowing river or stream.
Feel the different shapes
Of the organic rocks.
Now put your hand in the water
Feel it flow
Through your fingers
Like a rock in it's way
Watch the waves slowly die
As it reaches the shore
Now close your eyes
You're at the seashore

Morgan Kueter, Grade 6
Scenic Park Elementary School, AK

Baskets of Flowers

Baskets of flowers
a big bundle of beauty
all in one basket

Robyn Szczerba, Grade 4
St Thomas the Apostle School, AZ

An Older Brother

An older brother
is someone to look up to

An older brother
is a friend

An older brother
will always be there for me

Through thick and thin

My older brother
has always been there for me

He is a friend
he knows I look up to him

It doesn't matter
how many mistakes he makes

He's my older brother

Brittney Debler, Grade 6
Eagle Point Middle School, OR

A Pet for My Pet

Should I buy a pet for my pet?
My pet can't be dumb, oh you bet.
Should I, or what should I do?
I don't know, but it's not up to you.
My pet isn't careless as I say so myself,
Could it be, or could it not be the size of an elf.
My pet is responsible, but not all the way,
My pet may be lonely, but what can I say?
My pet even has a camera its size,
And with ITS mouth, it cannot tell lies.
A pet for my pet, oh what can it be?
Just read the rest and then you will see.
A pet for my pet, what's the big surprise?
You will see if you open up your eyes.
My pet is a dog, but its pet is,
A brand new HORSE that is all his.

Dayaun Kim, Grade 5
Chancellor Charter School at West Gilbert, AZ

Scorpion in Me

There is a scorpion in me
With claws like huge, dark, black widows
And eyes like beads
It creeps like a lion
It lives in my muscles
And makes me feel like tearing down buildings
I wish it would show its face to the world
It helps me to be strong
It makes me feel like I'm stronger than I am!

D.J. Garrison, Grade 5
Hafen Elementary School, NV

The Daisy Field

I love the feeling
When I am running wild, like a stallion
In the middle of a daisy field
I pick a couple, and smell the aroma
It spreads with the breeze
My hair is flying back, the wind is hitting my face
Then I sit down in the middle
Even my head is covered by the tall flora
I catch a ladybug
And let it rest on my daisy
After a while it spreads its wings
"One…two…"
I count its glossy black dots
Before it soars away
"Seven…eight!"
Then like a graceful swan
It glides through the air
I pick up myself and think
I love this feeling

Olivia Huish, Grade 6
Barbara Bush Elementary School, AZ

Evan

Funny, kind, loyal
Who wishes I could hold my breath forever.
Who dreams I could fly.
Who wants to go in war.
Who wonders what it is like in Heaven.
Who fears drowning.
Who likes nice girls.
Who believes in God.
Who likes hunting.
Who likes fishing.
Who likes snow boarding.
Who likes skateboarding.
Who likes sports.
Who likes living in Oregon.
Who likes going to church.
Martin

Evan Martin, Grade 6
Patton Middle School, OR

How to Slurp Summer

Grasp your swimming suit and dive in
Catch a movie at 12:00 a.m.
Chomp on some popcorn and soda too
And watch the clouds cover up the blue
Go out to eat every night
And in the breeze fly a kite
Hike a mountain and see the city
Rest on the beach with your little kitty
Sit on the porch with a cup of orange juice
And set off with your dad to hunt a moose
Play football with your friends at the park
Watch the stars as they glow in the dark
Make a tree house in a strong oak tree
Tell hilarious jokes as you laugh with glee
Play video games and eat candy
Rinse off your goggles if they're sandy
All these events are so much fun
So get them finished
Before summer is done.

Beau Sitton, Grade 5
Kyrene De Las Brisas School, AZ

Sheep Paradise

The clouds are like cotton balls.
The oak trees are as thick as pea soup.
The sheep are as fat as a stump.
The mountains are as high as the sky.
The pine trees are as big as a tower.
The sheep are like lawnmowers grazing in the meadow.
The sun is like fire scorching down.
The mountains are as blue as the ocean.
The meadow is as green as a crayon.
The sheep are like humans resting in the shade.
The shade is dancing to the baaing of the sheep.

John Erickson, Grade 5
Sally Mauro Elementary School, UT

Route 66

All the cities you pass by
Bikers zooming around
Wind blowing in your face
Fast food in the air
Tire streaks everywhere
The best trip in the world

Tanner Barton, Grade 4
Lincoln Elementary School, AZ

The Wrong Answer

Today in class
My teacher asked
A simple little question.
She called on me
I answered wrong,
Then she sent me to detention!
Today after lunch
I was punished a bunch
Because I answered wrong.
She made me wear the dunce cap
And sing the "Bad Boy Song."
She made me wash the windows.
She made me scrub the floor.
All these chores I had to do,
Were oh, just such a bore!
Even though these punishments
Were cruel and very mean,
It doesn't matter anymore
Because now I get to leave.

Kelsey Frank, Grade 5
Colbert Elementary School, WA

Weather

If weather was a kid,
Then sun would be his happy face.
Then rain would be the cry of his.
Then storm would be the anger of his.
Then cloudy day would be the fear.
If only weather was a kid,
Then he or she would play with me.

Erica Li, Grade 5
Uplands Elementary School, OR

Spring

Spring is my favorite season
I like because of a reason
The birds will sing their beautiful song
But they will not sing all day long
The new animals will be born
Winter will be torn
The family will be happy
The students will be snappy
The flowers will bloom every day
Maybe spring is today!

Nuraina Azhar, Grade 5
Phoenix Metro Islamic School, AZ

Grandma

Your smile is like a soft petal on a beautiful rose on a bad day.
Your voice is a cheerful call to me at my soccer game.
The moments we share are adventurous golden treasures.
My heart is filled with warmth when you take me to magical places,
like when we eat chocolate ice cream at Dairy Queen.
You being there for me tells me that you care.

Taylor Molliconi, Grade 4
Hunters Glen Elementary School, CO

Castle

The grass is as green as a turtle.
The mountains are as high as the sky.
Did you know that the lake is as blue as the sky up high?
The castle is as high as the Twin Towers. Amazing, huh?
The tree's leaves are as green as seaweed.
This sounds amazing, but the chimneys are as wide as a shark, can you imagine!

Keven Mastin, Grade 5
Sally Mauro Elementary School, UT

Broken Arm

I was playing with a hula-hoop that sunny day,
Having a wondrous time.
It slipped off my foot, and I went to go get it,
But I fell under the tree of pine.

Not long after, I was at the doctors',
Waiting for a reply.
My arm was hurting even more now,
And I wanted to know why.

Later on, they had to move my arm around,
And I did not want to feel that.
So, they gave me a choice: I could have a shot or a mask.
I chose by the drop of a hat.

Of course I did not want a shot,
I wanted the cherry-smelling mask.
The mask would make me go to sleep,
And the doctors had a task.

I had to wear three casts, one for each month,
One white, one hot pink, and one dark purple that was waterproof!
All this really happened to me,
And I am speaking the truth.

Cassandra Stauffer, Grade 6
Mt Olive Lutheran School, NV

The Colorado River's Creation

Brown, muddy river flowing at the bottom of a colorful landmark
Wind blowing in my face as I walk on this unpaved trail
Safe beside my father as we hike in the canyon with our family,
I search the sky for California Condors.
I touch my mother's arm to let her know it is okay.
The river will always be running through the Grand Canyon.

Tori McDowell, Grade 4
Lincoln Elementary School, AZ

You're My Dog

Sitting there on a rainy day…looking at my dog.
He's looking back with a humongous smile, so big that
you can swim in it.
He rubs against my leg.
He nibbles at my toes.
I look down at him.
Then he starts twitching his nose.
So I get down on my hands and knees and I give him a big
hug.
And I say to him you're my dog.

Olivia Oshiro, Grade 5
Acme Elementary School, WA

Food

Food is good.
Food is tasty.
Food puts me in a good mood.
I like food.

Food comes in all different sizes, shapes,
temperatures, tastes and packages.
Candy, caramels, chocolate, lemon and strawberry!
All so good I feel sorry for people with braces!

People have fast paces when they're going to get food.
It puts them in a better mood!
Just don't intrude on people when they're eating food
or it will put them out of their good mood.

Food is good.
Food is tasty.
Food puts me in a good mood.
I like food.

Samuel Miller, Grade 5
West Mercer Elementary School, WA

Springtime

Springtime is so beautiful,
as the snow melts,
from white to clear,
creating waterfalls in rivers,
rushing at high speeds.

As the snow melts,
flowers are exposed,
in vivid colors of purple and yellow,
blooming so brightly,
lighting up our lives.

Spring is so cheerful,
it brings people joy,
as the snow covered items show themselves,
water and flowers are created,
it is peaceful as the winter has passed again.

Martina Gilmore, Grade 6
Connect Charter School, CO

Journey to the Ocean

S
P
L
A
S
H
!
Down
Comes
the
water.
Skipping,
Jumping,
Flopping
Though the rocks and blocks.
Little fish swims,
Tiny pebbles roll,
The water sings,
Dancing its soul.
The rider rides, like a champion, to get to a door,
The door that is named the ocean floor.

Benjamin Hsieh, Grade 5
West Mercer Elementary School, WA

Bull Snakes

Bull
non-poisonous, non-cuddly, no rattle, cool
lover of grass, rats, mice
Who feels annoyed when people
catch them, happy when people
leave them alone, hungry when
they haven't eaten in five months.
Who fears almost nothing,
revenge of the mice, hawks.
Who would like to see summer
when it's winter, its hole when it's lost,
a mouse when it's hungry
resident of the Sonoran Desert
snake(s).

Mishelle Vanover, Grade 4
Acacia Elementary School, AZ

Freedom of Slaves

When I see a slave
I put myself in his body
I know I must behave
Because it would be so scary

When I see a slave
I get kind of mad
I want to burst
Because he looks so sad

Michael Bonacci, Grade 6
Pope John XXIII Catholic School Community, AZ

Cry

You cry and I don't know why,
All because he said good-bye
Overseas
Fighting for our country
He told you that
He loved you
Can't
You
See?

You get a call
Then you fall
Like a tree
Knowing your man is
NEVER coming back.

You cry
And now I know why.
Samantha Brown, Grade 6
Cedaredge Middle School, CO

Me

I will be a normal guy
I want to be a rock star
I used to be a non-believer
I let go of my short body
I have forgotten all my dreams
I remember I am me
Sam Hall, Grade 6
Spencer Butte Middle School, OR

The Sappy Love Letter

He gave it to her at the end of class,
She threw it away, clever lass.
Now, I'm stuck up a tree
Because he was bugging me!
I get on the ground,
He chased me around,
I ran to the girls' room
To stay away from doom,
He passed the door,
Will he run anymore?
I sneak out to class
To hide in the mass,
He desperately looked,
Looking like he's cooked.
He looked sad,
Then he was mad.
He yelled my name,
What a pain!
Now at year's finish,
He's my best friend.
That is the end.
Astrud Benson, Grade 6
Mt Olive Lutheran School, NV

Scarce

Going through the maze
there in the corn creatures lurk
s.o.s help me!
Kimberly Lamar, Grade 6
Hamilton Middle School, MT

Beach

I sit on my beach chair,
I hope the fabric doesn't tear.

Sand between my toes,
Watch the sea as it comes and goes.

I surf through a tunnel,
It reminds me of a funnel.

I get in my new suit,
It has pictures of fruit.

I love the beach,
You don't know what it will teach.
Christina Culbertson, Grade 6
Eagle Ridge Elementary School, CO

Spring

The flowers grow,
The leaves grow on trees,
Baby calves are born,
Fresh air everywhere,
Rain showers come,
Butterflies are flying,
Days are longer,
Animals are out of hibernation,
Spring clothes come out for sale,
Kids are outside playing baseball,
It is the season to play.
Jose Montelongo, Grade 4
McCormick Elementary School, NM

People

Walking, talking,
working, cleaning,
sitting, eating,
learning, winning,
fighting, screaming,
smiling, frowning,
running, falling,
to the ground.
Seems that
everything we do
has to
end with
i-n-g.
Matthew Willett, Grade 6
Barbara Bush Elementary School, AZ

Snowflakes

White flakes falling down
Silence, nothing
Cold and frozen
Snowman towering over me
Latest snowfall of the year
Victoria Hanneman, Grade 4
Lincoln Elementary School, AZ

Why?

I do not understand
Why people sing
Why fish don't fly
Why the world goes 'round
But most of all I do not understand
Why boys are so weird
Because they run around playing football
What I do understand most
Is my mom loves me
Because I love her
Kary Olson, Grade 5
Copper Creek Elementary School, AZ

My Mother, Theresa No Ngo

Theresa No Ngo is my mother's name,
She should be in the hall of fame.
I think she really is number one,
Theresa I think is really fun.
I think my mother is the best,
Theresa is better than the rest.
She works full time, and goes to school,
I think my mom is very cool!
Tiffany Ta, Grade 6
Hazelwood Elementary School, WA

Tears

T hey stop when you forgive
E veryone has them
A nyone can make them
R ound in shape
S ending a message from God

Tears

Shalise Barnes, Grade 4
Rowland Hall-St Mark's School, UT

Ground and Sky

Ground
Flat, rocky
Rolling, staying, laying
Dirty, dusty, mighty, infinite
Flying, flowing, moving
Blue, majestic
Sky
Sean Logan, Grade 6
St Cyril Elementary School, AZ

Flying

Flying
The joy of the day
Fluttering aimlessly through
The darkness of space
Light shining brightly
Like your soul
Soaring past the millions
Of stars
Spilling through the depths
Of the universe
Discovering many stars of
Glamorous light being consumed
By the night
And in our dazzling universe
Darkness and light roam everywhere

Adam Karsten, Grade 4
Khalsa Montessori Elementary School, AZ

Ode to Grandma

She's seen it all before;
She's suffered beyond explanation.
She's the reason you exist.
She'll always have an answer to every question.
She always has a new way to say hello.

That's true; she is old.
She almost always has a treat for you.
She's never mean to you.
She weeps when you leave, if you live far away.
She once dressed in such a fashion you'd be shocked.

She may have passed away, but you still love her.
That's why I give my ode to Grandma.

Marissa Anne Grafel, Grade 5
Mary Blair Elementary School, CO

Survivor

The taste was bad in my mouth
Sounds around me were flowing into my head
The sight was unimaginable
I was frightened for myself and my friends
I ran across the field with my life on the line
My hands were dirty
My eyes were raw
My legs hurt so bad I almost fell
Down into a darkness of hell
My arms ached
My mind was shaken
For I'm an old man
Who stormed the beaches of Normandy
Outlasted the Nazis
And helped protect America's freedom

Shane O'Connell, Grade 6
Heath Middle School, CO

A Recipe for a Teacher

Take a cup of knowledge and a cup of friendship
Add a cup of pencils, markers, white boards, rulers and kids.
In a classroom they will go.
Mix some clothes, hair until it is smooth.
Throw in a half cup of color.
Fry it in a fire; it will do at 482° F.
Until it stands still.
You can tell it's done when it looks like a teacher.
Let it stand still for an hour.
Add a half cup of jewelry.
Slice it, and serve it in a classroom.

Matthew Emge, Grade 5
Desert View Academy, AZ

Turquoise

Turquoise is a blend of green and blue,
It's the color of the ocean, too.
The sound of waves breaking on the shore,
A twilight shadow on the floor.
Turtles and dolphins, maybe some fish,
It's also the color of a summertime wish.
Turquoise is the smell of a salty breeze,
A tickle on your nose that makes you sneeze.
It's the taste of something chewy and sweet,
Or warm, fuzzy socks you put on your feet.
You might see turquoise in early spring,
Or a turquoise stone, set in a ring.

Hannah Hatchell, Grade 6
Enterprise Middle School, WA

Night Sky

The comet dances 'tween the stars
Tail stretching endlessly on,
A bridge between worlds.
Gracefully glowing
Soft skirts flowing like a river,
The comet dances 'tween the stars.

Lady moon sedately steps across the sky.
Her marvelous dress silver,
Glowing with inherent light.
White wave — horses run lightly,
Prancing in the heavens.
Beautiful stars curtsy as she passes,
A lovely vision of perfection.

A raging sea boils beneath the calm sky.
Scylla scintillates,
Swirling silkily and smoothly.
Waves lap at the rocks,
Sea horses running in the water.
Blackness dominates the sea,
Absorbing light like a void of life.
The raging sea boils beneath the calm sky.

Emily Randall, Grade 6
Southern Hills Middle School, CO

Eleven Minutes 'Til the Bus*

Eleven minutes 'til the bus
Scads of time what's the fuss

2 to dress
  1 to brush
    1 to flush
      2 to eat

That leaves five to catch the bus
Scads of time what's the fuss.
           Averie Rist, Grade 4
Meadow Point Elementary School, CO
      Inspired by David L. Harrison

I Am

I am smart and funny
I wonder about politics
I hear screaming
I see myself in the future
I want to be famous
I am smart and funny.

I pretend to be a star
I feel comforted by family and friends
I touch people's hearts
I worry about death
I cry about a good memory
I am smart and funny.

I understand sadness
I say things that are true
I dream about war
I try to do my best
I hope to be loved
I am smart and funny.
         Matt Jennings, Grade 5
Kingman Academy of Learning, AZ

Spring

Through the broken snow
Tiny buds begin to show.

Mountain ice-caps melt
Cool March winds are felt.

Birds begin to sing
Nature has a fling.

Mud sticks to my shoe
Wintry weather's through.

Spring is here to stay
Each and every day.
       Andrew Barlow, Grade 5
          Reid School, UT

Spring Fling

Spring rains are
little pebbles pummeling
you.
Spring grasses are
like little asparaguses.
Spring water is
as clear as a
little piece of
plastic.
Spring break is
every kid's
dream.
In spring, I see
all of these wonders
everywhere I am.
        Kyle Baker, Grade 4
Skyline Elementary School, WA

Nature

There was a rushing
waterfall surrounded by
beautiful trees
and rustling leaves.
The water was as speedy
as a roadrunner,
the trees were like
pieces of broccoli
if you use your imagination
you just might see.
     Ruben Beltran, Grade 4
Great Expectations Academy, AZ

Tears

I can't hold back tears,
  I lack the capacity.
I'm too big to be small,
  but too small to be big.

I can't hold back tears,
  it's not on my resume.
  On stage I will smile,
    but off, I'm ordinary.

I can't hold back tears,
  I don't have the ability.
  I'm talented but not,
  I'm wise, but untaught.

How'd I end up rhyming?
  I don't know how or when.
  But one thing I know,
  is to let the tears go,
and hope I'll find peace in the end.
    Shannon Ludeman, Grade 6
    Arbor Elementary School, WA

Cloudy Day

Gray and blue.
  Some yellow too
Mountains you can barely see.
A big gray blanket
  Covers the blue sky
The sun is sleeping in the blanket
When suddenly gray rips apart and
Sun tries it's hardest to
  Come out
    And wake up.
       Brooke Davis, Grade 4
Scenic Park Elementary School, AK

Fall

In
  Fall my
  Brother and I
Rake up all the leaves in the yard
Then we jump in the pile of leaves
Then we look up in the sky and try to
  Find a cloud that looks
    Like a walnut
    Halloween
      Is
      H
       e
        r
         e
    Skyler Coppenrath, Grade 4
Olympic Range Carden Academy, WA

Light

light.

so gentle, so soft
but intimidating.

how it covers objects,
and consumes shadows.

but with one flick
of a finger,

gone.
     Devon Funderburk, Grade 6
    Eagle Point Middle School, OR

Milk

Milk
Healthy, good
Drinking, dunking, stirring
Milk is healthy
Milk is YUUUMMMYYY.
  Candace Greene-Ruiz, Grade 4
Jackpot Combined School, NV

The Pop of Spring

Ahhh, sweet spring at last, sweet, tangy ripe fruits.
Peeps of a bird sitting on a branch of a birch tree.
Fun and laughter of kids playing with their dogs.
Ahhh, sweet spring at last.

Chirp of a bird, bark of a dog, hum of a bee.
Fuzzy sweet fruits, smoother fragrant fruits.
Hot sunny day, roaring ice cold water.
Ahh, sweet spring at last.

Big piney pine trees with a variety of birds.
Swooping seagulls flying all over a salty lake.
Fishy sweet fish swimming around in their pond.
Ahhh, sweet spring at last.

Roaring of a crowd at the beginning of a sport.
Smack of a ball slamming into a bat.
Fresh scent of a nice juicy ball park hot dog.
Ahh, sweet spring at last.

Spring is coming let everyone know.
Get everything ready, plan a vacation and go.
Jump in a pool with a big splash, fast.
Ahhh, sweet spring at last.

Cameron Stowell, Grade 6
Bella Vista Elementary School, UT

Friends

Friends are there
When you need them most.
Friends are there to help you.
They should be there to keep you company.
I have a friend that is truer than true.
I hope you have a friend like mine,
Or one in mind.

Amanda Carbajal, Grade 6
Somerton Middle School, AZ

Leaves

Leaves fall
Droplets of sparkling snow drift to the ground
Wrinkles bright golden leaves pound the cold
Hard cement

Snowflakes flutter down on them
The space like darkness retreats

The sunlight arises
Pink and white blossoms sprout
Taking the place of the lifeless fallen leaves
Like white dwarfs taking the place of a fallen star

Winter is past
Spring has come

Emmet Miller, Grade 6
Khalsa Montessori Elementary School, AZ

Morning in the Desert

I wake up and sun beams on my face,
But I am used to this desert place.
I get dressed and go outside,
To saddle up my horse for a long long ride.

We head down the desert trail,
Listening to my horse whip his tail.
Weaving through the desert plants,
Getting cactus caught in my pants.

We realize how lucky we are,
To be able to ride so far.

Amanda Lund, Grade 5
Cottonwood Elementary School, AZ

The Student

There once was a girl who had straight A's
In 3rd, 4th, and 5th,
But once she entered middle school
Her grades began to slip.

She started to forget about her homework
Just so her friends wouldn't think she was some dork.
But then she found out her parents were disappointed
So she focuses on her grades for just a moment.

But then again they dropped so low
So her mother grounded her for a month or so.
She couldn't even watch her fav show,
Two and a Half Men.
So she decided to focus on her grades again.

Karolina Mendoza, Grade 6
Corpus Christi School, CO

Zooming In

Big does not show detail
Big is just plain, simple, basic
Big shows a lot of your surroundings
Everything that is big seems far away
Detail matters for expression, appearance, phrase

Closer up everything is beautiful
Colorful, multicolored, vivid, bright, rich
Details show every stem, petal, leaf
A flower has many little details not noticed like seeds
Little petals growing, budding, emerging, rising, developing

Everything is beautiful close
Natural, usual, normal, ordinary
But so beautiful so rich and pure colors
Extravagant, excessive, profligate
Little leaves growing, breathing, living, surviving

Evelyn Gutierrez, Grade 6
Blanco Elementary School, NM

Mi Regalo Del Rio

Mi regalo is pretty big. When I opened it, it was just a small regalo for a pretty big box. I thought it was going to be a big regalo. Actually, it was just a small medal. I was pretty disappointed but then when I read it and it said, "For my baby girl, love Mommy." That's what it said all right. After I read that I was very happy. Now, I always wore it. After I opened my regalo we went to the rio. At the rio I saw beautiful birds. I also saw the beautiful rio just floating away. At the rio we toasted marshmallows and fished. The next day we went back and left to our new mansion.

Yanitza Ybarra, Grade 4
Clawson School, AZ

My Heaven

I lay there as still as a piece of stale bread, waiting for my time. I pretend to look at other things trying to keep my mind off the haunting black lumps that have consumed the fragile skin of my body. I wish to cry over the pain I am receiving, for it is greater than anything I have ever experienced; but my body cannot let any more tears out. I feel so hopeless and lost, for I can only need and not give. Then what is my life, here anymore if I have nothing to offer. I will die anyway. This disease is just a shortcut to the Promised Land. Soon I will be there for eternal life; there I will begin the birth of flawless perfection. Hopes and dreams will be at my side. "Yes," that's when I would be there, the place in my dreams. That's when I will have found my heaven.

Maddy Etre, Grade 6
Santa Fe School for the Arts, NM

The Snow Field

White all around, nothing but pale curves, slopes and small footprints of a squirrel's passing.
An icy breeze chills my face and rustles the trees above.
More snow begins to fall, it comes slowly like tiny parachutes, the mountains turn from gray to white.
The higher I go the colder it gets. The snow now stings my eyes. It seems it will go on forever.
Finally the top appears. The slopes below turn from white to green a wonderful sight.

Ben Peterson, Grade 5
West Mercer Elementary School, WA

Spring

Sweet, sweet spring the season after winter and before summer. Four months of great, wonderful weather. All the sunny, wet weather for all plants to develop their beautiful flowers and sweet-smelling scents. The flowery aroma that fills the house is like a soft, soft flower petal floating through the cool breeze. The warmth of the sun beams on your skin feels like the clothes that have barely come out of the dryer. Everyone likes to leap in the air outside and land on the green, green grass. As you drink your lemonade by the lemonade stand you put your quarter in the little box, thank you, thank you for coming.

Chelsea Brenes, Grade 5
Dorothy Eisenberg Elementary School, NV

A Certain Love

I can describe many things, I can describe wind and rings:
Rings, a promise of eternal love
Wind, air that blows gracefully like a dove.
I can describe a dog and a cat:
Cat, a furball that sits and gets fat
Dog, an animal that runs and can bark.
I can describe a room and a lark:
Lark, a bird who sings in a tree
Room, a place you get into with a key.
All of these things I can see or touch, but there is one thing I cannot clutch.
It is hard to describe for these reasons, for it doesn't come in any seasons.
This thing that I can't touch, describe, or see, is my Mother's eternal love for me.
My Mother's love goes to an endless length, but my love for her is stronger than Arnold Schwarzenegger's strength.
My love for her goes on forever, this love won't stop, nope, never.
I could care less if I were a peasant, knowing she loves me is the best present.
I hope she now knows how much I love her, and that she is the best Mother!

Kailyn Johnston, Grade 6
The Colorado Springs School, CO

Awakening into the Best Spring Ever

Was just in winter, now in spring
Walking outside, is one of the best things
Perfumed flowers right outside of my door
Going back to bed and awakening in the best spring ever

Going outside and picking ripe fruit
Winter is over, I don't need my boots
Listening to the birds and watching them be clever
Going back to bed and awakening in the best spring ever

Winter has ended and it's warm outside
What a nice day, I think I'll go for a bike ride
Next time I see a snow man, it seems like never
Going back to bed and awakening in the best spring ever

It's a bright clean day and outside it's sunny
Since winter is over, my nose isn't runny
Having it sunny outside, I'll love it forever
Going back to bed and awakening in the best spring ever

Listening to the birds chirp and sing
I am so glad now that we are in spring
Spring is the sign of the start of warm weather
Going back to bed and awakening in the best spring ever

Brandon Lerry, Grade 6
Bella Vista Elementary School, UT

The Longest Day Ever

If twenty-four hours was the limit,
I would do as much as I could,
While putting the most fun in it,
And making it last longer than it should.

I would start the day at school,
Then travel to Quincy town,
Off to Hawaii, would be so cool,
Play in the ocean and try not to drown.

Next would be Paris, the city of lights,
And to Italy to see the Leaning Tower.
To see such famous sights,
Would give me so much knowledge and power.

It's time to go home,
And be with all my friends,
Stop all of my travel
And see how my day finally ends.

It's to bed that I go,
And wait to see what I do.
Because another day will flow,
And I need to get a clue.

Paige Amburn, Grade 6
Albuquerque Christian School, NM

I Wonder

I wonder how you are going to feel
when you find out I wrote this instead of you.
I am writing in my room
with the sun beating down upon me
making me look like I am from heaven,
with my stuffed animals beside me
helping with my problems,
with my Beta swimming
waiting to be fed into my poem,
with my brother
waiting to use the computer,
with my dogs barking
waiting to played with,
and waiting to be played into my poem,
with my mother waiting for me to come to dinner
so I can be rejuvenated to write more.

Eastlyn Fell, Grade 6
Badger Road Elementary School, AK

I Am…

I am kind and humorous.
I wonder if the night sky will listen to my thoughts.
I hear the whinny of heavenly horses.
I see the world in all my ways.
I want a horse to ride and run free.
I am kind and humorous.

I pretend to drift off into my own world.
I feel the softness of the horses mane.
I touch my horses so small and soft.
I worry about what's coming into my life next.
I cry when I'm hurt in my heart.

I understand I need to follow directions.
I say I can be who I want to be.
I dream of being a famous jockey.
I try to succeed in things I want to do.
I hope to have all my dreams come true.
I am kind and humorous.

Maddie Kramer, Grade 5
Elger Bay Elementary School, WA

Faith

Why do you not pray?
Why can't you stand up and say
God is holding my hand today!
Why don't you go to church?
Are you scared of them to see you
I can't answer this
I can't be you
Why do you not stand up and sing?
Get up and praise to the king
SING, SING, let it RING
Why do you despise every one of these things?

Ashley Zafaranlou, Grade 6
Pope John XXIII Catholic School Community, AZ

The Ocean

The ocean is
blue as the sky
sandy beaches
time flies by
colored coral reefs
sea animals
bright sun
surfing
fun has begun
night time
white moon
laying on the beach
under the stars.

Marisa Sweetland, Grade 6
Green Valley Christian School, NV

A Hawk

High in the night sky
a hawk sights and tracks his prey
on the moonlit night.

Jesse Ritter, Grade 5
Ammon Elementary School, ID

Shoes

My favorite type of shoe is the boot
They are so pretty
But they cost a lot of loot
They are cute as a kitty.

My second favorite is the high heel
But you can't wear them to school
They look good when going to a meal
High heels totally rule.

My third favorite is the flip flop
They are awesome
To get them we must shop
They are not made out of possum.

Shoes are great.
Shoe shopping? I'll never be late!

Brielle Poulter, Grade 4
Reid School, UT

The Night

The night is so quiet,
as if time had stopped.
When the sun goes to bed,
street lights wake up.
The dark streets and alleys,
become illuminated with light.
But then again the quiet will fall,
and so must the moon.

Pier Fiedorowicz, Grade 5
Eton School, WA

Angel in the Night

It was a very stormy night,
Praying for it to stop.
Cried so hard, I was only 8
A big bash of thunder,
Crying even harder
Then, something touched my hair.
Wondering if it was mom,
Seeing the most beautiful face
I wasn't scared anymore
Soon I fell asleep,
Dreaming of angels!

Kaela Schober, Grade 5
Lewis & Clark Elementary School, OR

Mice

Mice,
nice, fast,
running, squeaking, weird
nice to me always,
rodents.

Willam Skylar Decker, Grade 6
Sequoia Village School, AZ

Red

If I was the color red,
I would be a bright balloon
In a toddler's hand
An apple on the teacher's desk
A toolbox in a man's garage
A shirt for my mom

Chase Johnson, Grade 4
East Evergreen Elementary School, MT

What a Life

What a life I have
It's hard, easy, and always crazy
Running, falling is my life
My parents are cool
But they hate the school
Jogging, tripping is my life
My brothers are mean
But they try to be clean
Walking, kicking is my life
What a life I have

Austin Robinson, Grade 6
Fox Creek Jr High School, AZ

Spring

Daisies and blossoms
Grow high to the blue sky
Tulips and roses
Grow out of the green bare ground
Flowers shining in the sun

Lauren Duda, Grade 4
Copper Canyon Elementary School, AZ

Storm

The wind is howling
Like a wolf calling to the moon
Thunder booms and flashes
Lightning crashes down
A saguaro goes to the ground
Another bolt hits a tree
Forest fires come
All the trees are dead
The land is charred
As black as coal
Everything is in ashes
It all happened before me
I couldn't do anything
I'm tortured for life

Zachary Olson, Grade 6
Fox Creek Jr High School, AZ

Blue House

A blue house cozy and warm,
Hot, colorful, flames in a fireplace,
Drinks with spicy food that is so good,
A lot of friends talking.

Outside is like a big cocoon,
It sits upon wet clean grass,
With flowers on the front porch
Green moss is on flower baskets.

Big barn with huge doors,
A little shed with chickens,
Cows wandering in a green field,
Brown horses wandering too.

Little woodpeckers, blue jays with voices,
They like to sing out loud,
Sing a pretty song,
That never stops a sound.

We heard something,
Bright lightning was very crooked,
Covering my ears,
Thunder seemed so loud.

Salena Mays, Grade 5
Lewis & Clark Elementary School, OR

Fat Cat

There once was fat cat,
who knew a really small rat,
who had a really big hat.
That rat sat, and sat on a flat mat.
Now the cat liked that flat mat,
so that was the end of the rat
with the really big hat.

Austin McRae, Grade 6
Thomas Jefferson Charter School, ID

The Lonely Tree House

The lonely tree house sits there day and night
With an inner happiness that won't lose the fight
The children used to play in it
But now they're grown and ready to take flight
But once again all the children are back
Watching the lonely tree house
Recalling old memories and all those things.

Sukhmani Ghuman, Grade 5
Spring Creek Country Day School, CO

Beautiful Heaven

Heaven is all white with roads and sidewalks made of gold,
The beautiful angels sing with praise,
There is astonishingly, wonderful days,
Heaven is a place you would always want to be day and night,
Mostly all because of the beautiful sight,
The angels and people laughing, and skipping around
Is a wonderful, praising, and joyful sound

Sarah Archuleta, Grade 5
Cuba Elementary School, NM

Just Playing the Game

Just five minutes left!
We were playing basketball,
It gave me butterflies in my stomach,
Because the players wow, they were so tall.

Courtney Khal, Grade 6
Mt Olive Lutheran School, NV

Alone

silent and still
a rose waits tonight
alone in the deep shadows of the night
waiting for the moment that light overcomes darkness
in which the rose will be warm
and glow its deep red

still and silent
alone in the deep shadows
a rose waits tonight

Keifer Pehowic, Grade 6
Eagle Point Middle School, OR

Ocean Breeze

As I walk through the sandy beach,
The ocean talks to me,
It sways as if showing me its new dress,
I walk in the water and the seaweed hugs me

We talk for hours as the sun is falling asleep,
The water sings me a lullaby,
And I wander off to another world,
As the light slowly dims,
I say my last good-byes.

Nicole Palmer, Grade 6
Pope John XXIII Catholic School Community, AZ

False Cover

The ting,
        ting
             tinging of the symbol
                          echoes,
                               echoes,
off the chestnut walls.
The steady rhythm of the snare
provides a graceful "snap"
shimmering, shining, blue cover surround
my drums, illuminating the dark basement walls.
Boom!
      Boom!
            The bass drum thunders,
like a giant, dancing in the rain.
Amazing such beauty can make so much noise!

Hunter Ashburn, Grade 5
Greenwood Elementary School, CO

Fight or Flight

Stand, before you run
It's not a game,
It's not very fun
Your heart starts pounding
Your blood is rushing
Your eyes turn red
Then your bones start crushing
You're as stiff as an oak
And ready to cringe,
Waiting for the chance to get revenge
You're scared and afraid, that you might die
So look that beast straight in the eye
The danger has come,
While you're still there
It's life and death
With the shift of the air

Hunter Hedequist, Grade 6
Colbert Elementary School, WA

What Could It Be?

Lives at altitudes of 20,000 feet.
What could it be?
Stalking its prey by the moon.
Not knowing the meaning of fear.
Doing anything to survive.
Its glinting coat shining in the moon.
There aren't very many left what could it be?
Thinking of its plans.
Thick fur to keep it warm.
Has more than a score of spots.
Long tail to keep it warm.
What could it be?
    A snow leopard stalking by the moon.

Ethan Strassman, Grade 4
Acacia Elementary School, AZ

Weather

If I stand in the rain,
I get wet!
If I stand in the sun,
I get burned!
If I stand in the snow,
I get cold!
If I stand in the hail,
I get hurt!

Why can't I stand in the rain,
And have my cares washed away?
Why can't I stand in the sun,
And have my lunch cooked instead of me?
Why can't I stand in the snow,
And have my ice cream freeze, not me?
Why can't I stand in the hail,
And have my sores healed, instead of opened?

Why can't the weather agree with me?

Amy Gigger, Grade 5
Gate City Elementary School, ID

Man on the Moon

Is there really a man on the moon?
Does he live in a deep, deep crater?
What does he eat for breakfast and lunch?
Does he have his very own waiter?

What does he wear each day?
Or are there even days?
Are there any alien friends?
Does he always stargaze?

These are some of the many questions
That stray in my mind through the days
I wonder if there is a man on the moon
Who dances in the sun's rays

Rachael Eckersley, Grade 6
Bright Beginnings School, AZ

Ode to My Dog

Little dog,
You are the object of my praise
You are trustworthy and kind
Sometimes you are crazy
You chase birds, but it's fine
Sometimes you play
Your white and brown spots are a beautiful sight
Your flowing long ears are silky
You are graceful when you run
When you leap up the steps to our house
You romp like a tiger
Then you loyally go to sleep
Oh, favorite dog of mine

Vanessa Palomares, Grade 5
Mary Blair Elementary School, CO

The Prom

My brother Travis is waiting for a call, from a certain girl,
and if you want to know her name, well it is Katie.
Then she called, said she could go, boy was Travis happy!
Then he got his car keys, and jumped into his car,
then he drove to Katie's house and proudly took her to the prom.
Then they got there and ran inside, and danced their hearts away.
Then the prom was over, they were tired anyway.
So Travis took Katie home and told her good night,
and so Travis drove away.

Dallas Tanner, Grade 5
Sally Mauro Elementary School, UT

Hills with Water

The clouds are flowing of the rocks.
There are green leaves growing over the rocks like the trees in the forest.
The sky is cloudy like smoke.
There are blue rocks as blue as the sky.
The shadows in the air are hopping from rocks.
There is moss on the rocks like a field of grass growing.
There are flowers creeping out of the trees.
There are birds chirping like the wind blows.
The water is flying down the river.

Randi Garmann, Grade 5
Sally Mauro Elementary School, UT

Pig

I am a pink, and black and white spotted piggy
I wonder if I am a normal pig compared to my brothers and sisters
I hear all my brothers and sisters squealing
I want to become a normal pig like all the others
I am a unique pig
I pretend like I'm an ordinary pig
I worry that everyone will treat me differently
I cry because I am different
I am a pig with white and black spots
I understand that I am different than the others
I say that I am still a pig even though I have spots
I dream that one day I will become normal
I hope I get to become a regular pig
I am a pink, and black and white spotted piggy

Alfredo Rodriguez, Grade 6
Wallace Elementary School, AZ

Lucky

My dad gave me a Corvette my mom gave me a candy bar
My sister gave me 3 new hats I knew this was a con

My uncle gave me a golf set my aunt gave me a rat
I knew this was two good to be true am I in a dream, was I hit by a bat?

I heard some knocking at my door I knew this was a dream,
but then my dad came in and said, "Ready for some ice cream?"

Mike Gibbens, Grade 6
Spring Creek Elementary School, WY

My Perfect Buddy

My perfect buddy would
Be as sweet as candy.
My perfect buddy would
Not be shy.

My perfect buddy would
Bring out the best of me.
My perfect buddy would
Never lie.

My perfect buddy would
Push me to try new, and good things.
My perfect buddy can
Be a guy.

My perfect buddy would
Be my best friend.
My perfect buddy wouldn't
Be me, myself, and I.

Perfect buddy wherever you are,
I dream of you every night.
Haydee Jimenez, Grade 6
Somerton Middle School, AZ

I Am From

I am from the noise of babies
Crying at night.
From the noise of barking dogs
And meowing cats.
I am from the smell of perfume
In the early morning
From a house full of love
And noisy kids
I am from the smell of dinner cooking
On Thanksgiving Day
From the weekdays
We play games
I am from my grandpa's logging truck
In the fall
From the snowy mountains
In winter
I am from a family
That cares about me
Harley Long, Grade 4
Grass Valley Elementary School, NV

Sally

Outside,
Free like the wind,
Sniffing the nature of
Curious thought,
Thinking of what lies in her future
Clawing an old tree.
Raileena Cozza, Grade 5
Acme Elementary School, WA

Rushing River

A little creek
Coming from a mountain,
Flowing like a river,
Flowing in a stream.
Joins the rushing river
To flow out to the sea.
Angela Froschauer, Grade 5
Lister Elementary School, WA

My Brother's Cast

I went to class,
I hope I pass,
and when I got home
I went on the phone.
I had a blast,
then I just heard
my brother had a cast.
Amanda Adams, Grade 5
Bennett Elementary School, NV

Fear

As I wait at night,
I sense fear is near.
As a door is opening,
I wait…
praying and hoping
that no one bad came in.
As I am silently crying,
I feel fear creeping up my spine.
Someone is coming…
My heart is thumping…
It's just…
Mom and Dad coming to say goodnight.

(Author's note: If you don't get over
your fears, you will always be afraid.)
Dustin Prince, Grade 5
Frontier Valley Elementary School, CO

Freeze

For the crime I used my flashlight
I was good and did the learning
The suspect escaped at night
He was bad and did the burning

I put a message on a dove
The crime was solved by the boss
I was careful and put on my glove
The suspect put poison in the sauce

The suspect was put into jail
I solved the second crime
He did not receive any of his mail
It was solved on time
Katy Vavivoda, Grade 6
Blaine Middle School, WA

Giant on a Cliff

Moving very slowly,
A giant on a cliff.
Silent, cold and rough it is,
What it isn't is small and quick.

You would want to slide down it,
But be careful if you do,
Bring a brake to stop,
Because it's hard to do.

It is a giant ice cube,
Made of water and cold.
It is like a giant,
Big, strong, and bold.
Glaciers.
Eric Willmore, Grade 5
Barratt School, UT

Flowers

Flowers, flowers everywhere
On the floor, and in my hair.
They smell so nice
Like a pie slice.
When the night comes they drift away.
As I wake
The flowers are gone,
I sing a lovely song.
Leslie Kelly, Grade 5
St Mary's School, ID

I Hate That Man

I hate that man that lives next door.
He plays the flute.
I hate *that* more.
His hair is purple,
His face is blue,
How would you like a man like that
To live next door to you?
Ruxandra Ionescu, Grade 4
Eureka Elementary School, MT

Mirage in the Desert

In a beautiful desert
On a blazing hot day
At the crack of dawn
A snappy little puddle appears
A palm tree shows
Fish jumping
Sun shining
A path leading to the water
Seagulls flying out above
Walking toward the water
Suddenly it's gone
Sad and burning
Lizzie Martin, Grade 6
Robert Frost Elementary School, OR

Flying on an Eagle's Wings

Flying on an eagle's wings,
We hit a draft and go fast,
But that will never last,
Because we keep on going,
Not stopping to rest,
Because life is like a wheel,
That time can't even stop,
So the eagle's wings and I keep on going,
Without a drop,
And the sky blue above us,
And the ground brown below us,
We lock on our target,
And when we get there,
We do the same,
And turn back again,
And go through the air,
Flying so bravely,
On the wings of an eagle
Having no fear,
This is the way I like it,
And that will never change.

Casey Campbell, Grade 5
La Veta Elementary School, CO

I'm Home

It's just me and my family now,
all alone,
sitting in our car.
I see my house,
I see my friends,
all in smiles upside down.
When I look at the sky,
I feel like it…
bluer and bluer,
more and more.
But now,
all I see are little dots
of friends,
and a small square of my old living.
Time seems so little
that in a sudden minute or two,
I see very large pentagons,
white at the top,
and gray in the rest.
I say to myself,
"I'm home."

Abbey Pint, Grade 5
Frontier Valley Elementary School, CO

Coyotes

Skinny, mangy, gaunt
Yellow eyes piercing the night
Hunting for its meal

Derek Kellams, Grade 5
St Cyril Elementary School, AZ

White

White is the color of clouds,
But is a puffy cotton ball
Moving from place to place.

White dashes through the sky,
Running through the fields,
Climbing to the top,
And covers itself in snow.

White reaches from the mountains,
And always stands out.

White is normal.

Jasmine Green, Grade 6
Patton Middle School, OR

Strumming

I sat on a stool
At school
They sat on the ground
Children all around
To hear a beautiful strumming sound.

Chaz Denny, Grade 5
Whiteriver Elementary School, AZ

Birthdays

Lots of gifts
We talk
Celebrate with my family and friends
A new age
A big cake
Food
Lots of eating
My special day
We play games
We dance
Have pizza
Celebrate the good times

Kristen Pough, Grade 6
South Middle School, CO

Problems

When I was 3 years old
I moved to Arizona
We've been through a lot since then
I've moved a thousand times
Been through many fights
Lost my father figure
And never got another
I've pretty much moved on
But still miss the old days
Wish I felt I was a part of a family
I wish nothing had changed

Tessa Fusko, Grade 6
Fox Creek Jr High School, AZ

Flying

Flying
An awesome thrill
A great way to travel
Like on the wings of a bird
Soaring

Kalene White, Grade 6
Heath Middle School, CO

March

M any kinds of flowers
A lmost always warm
R un in the grass
C an lie in the sun, if warm
H ave fun outside

Bethany Parker, Grade 5
Cottonwood Elementary School, CO

10 Little Monkeys

10 little monkeys swung on a vine
1 fell off and then there were 9
9 little monkeys ate fish bait
1 threw up and then there were 8

8 little monkeys joking about Heaven
1 believed and then there were 7
7 little monkeys playing with sticks
1 got hit and then there were 6

6 little monkeys messing with a beehive
1 was chased and then there were 5
5 little monkeys thought they could soar
1 fell hard and then there were 4

4 little monkeys chasing bees
1 got stung and then there were 3
3 little monkeys went to the zoo
1 got caught and then there were 2

2 little monkeys ate a ton
1 got full and then there was 1
1 little monkey saying "All done"
He got bored and then there were none

Samantha Thorne, Grade 6
Walt Clark Middle School, CO

War and Peace

War
Angry, black
Fighting, shooting, heartbreaking
Hate, rage, calm, silence
Caring, loving, relaxing
Warm, steady
Peace

Salem Tewelde, Grade 4
Aurora Quest Academy, CO

The Beach

Waves creep onto the beach.
They tickle between my toes.
My hands burn on the HOT, dry sand.
The crisp morning breeze comes brushing against my face.
The fish in the sea are awakening.
The crabs on the beach are coming out of their shells.
They are all now awake, which means I now have to go to sleep.

Cheyenne Branum, Grade 4
Gold Canyon Elementary School, AZ

Platypus of the Zoo

Why are they all staring at me?
Have I broken a law?
A city code,
made a baby bawl?

Is it my bill?
My beaver tail?
My otter body,
that may have given them a chill?

Maybe they're amazed
at my spectacular features?
At my hybrid cross
between 4 creatures?

I wonder if they're jealous of me?
Angry at me, or that they envy me?

But can't they see?
I want to go home where no one is staring at me!

Jake Bradshaw, Grade 6
East Middle School, CO

Fun, Fun, Fun

Stayed up all night, my eyes are dead.
Feels like someone pulled them out of my head.
Watched a lot of movies, including *Top Gun.*
"Come on everybody, let's have more fun."

Went to the beach, played in the sand.
Dug a great big hole with my two bare hands.
Somebody tripped and fell inside.
"Someone get him out, before high tide."

Got in the car and drove around.
The scream of the engine is a cool sound.
Racin' down the highway, in the new Corvette.
Speedin' along, as fast as we could get.

We slowed to a stop, to look around.
Nobody in sight, not the slightest sound.
Looks like our day is over, it's finally done.
It was the best day ever, havin' Fun, Fun, Fun.

Jake Ramacher, Grade 6
St Joseph School, WA

Snickers

S weet
N ice
I t's only satisfying if you eat it
C runchy peanuts
K icks higher than any other candy bar
E xcellent
R ich
S atisfying

Celia Harrington, Grade 5
St Mary's School, ID

Number the Stars

N azis come to Denmark
U ncle Henrik opens the casket
M ama takes Ellen and Anne-Marie to Gillelje
B irte, Anne-Marie's "aunt" did not exist
E llen finally saw her mom and dad again
R emember the magnificent fireworks

T ivoli Gardens is closed now
H eavy feet come into the bedroom
E llen had to take off her necklace

S ecrets were spread
T ears flowed down when Lise died
A re the soldiers going to take over?
R eady Anne-Marie asked Ellen as they ran
S he glanced at Ellen, motionless

Paytne Hinger, Grade 5
Kingman Academy of Learning, AZ

Together as a Beach

Ocean, my calm, blue mother
You wash away my sadness
You take away my heartaches
You bring a melancholy feeling inside
But that is soon gone with the wind
As you bathe over my sorrows
Covering them with a joy
A joy above all others
You are cool when a breeze goes over you
You are warm when the golden sun rests upon you
I can feel you and touch you
You are willing to stay by me
When I need you most
Without you
I am just the rough and hot sand
Waiting to be washed over and smoothed out
With you I am an entire beach
With cool and smooth sand
Together we bring bliss
That no other beach can bring

Lubaba Ahmed, Grade 5
Kyrene De Las Brisas School, AZ

Have You Ever Wondered?

Have you ever wondered what love is like
You just have to wait
Have you ever wondered what kindness is like
you just have to wait
Have you ever wondered what hatred was like
well you don't want to wait
Have you ever wondered what cheating is like
well you don't want to wait
Have you ever wondered what forgiveness is like
well…It already happened.

Marinna Hunt, Grade 6
Fox Creek Jr High School, AZ

Goodnight

The sun says goodnight
With a wave of its rays.
So many different colors,
Red, orange, yellow, pink, and violet,
Like a rainbow of colors shining just for me.
I don't want this day to be over,
For I do not know what tomorrow will bring.
I pray it will bring the same cheer,
The same happiness, friendship, and love.
But ending each day is sad for a girl like me,
For each day is as precious as a human life.
As the light fades beneath the hillside,
And the moon says hello,
I miss all the beautiful colors,
As the sun says goodbye.

Moriah Prescia, Grade 6
Connect Charter School, CO

The Sunflower

Sorrow, sadness, weeping, loss,
Mending the wounded, mourning the lost,
Fire, wind, sirens, water,
Flames, gone,
Lost, lost, lost,
Gone, gone, gone,
Things lost,
Gone forever,
The spirit,
But,
The sunflower that remained,
Hope,
For all to see,
The light,
At the end, of the storm,
Forever shining,
For all to see,
Angels come,
Mend the broken,
Help the sorrow,
For all to see.

Rebecca K. Roskowski, Grade 6
East Middle School, CO

Pot of Gold

At the end of every rainbow a shiny pot shall lay,
but when a person gets up close it lightly fades away.
No mortal eye can see it's just the leprechauns and me,
when you touch it something happens they want to dance with glee.
They hide in the meadows as you can see
They sometimes hide in the bushes or the trees.

They tap their sticks of magic then a rainbow appears,
They step into the colored light and reappear
with all the animals like the birds, the bees, and the deer.
One leprechaun starts to step up and say:
"I wish you all luck on St. Patrick's Day."

Chase Pryor, Grade 5
Sally Mauro Elementary School, UT

My Garden

The roses are in full bloom.
Blissful breezes waft through the trees making their leaves rustle and sway.
Intricate spider webs glitter with early morning dew.
The water in the birdbath gleams and ripples.
Sparrows chirp in ecstasy as they feel the start of spring.
Lush, green grass waves in the gentle wind.
The silence is that of movement everywhere.
The rosemary's sweet aroma has a bitter tang, but it still smells delicious.
My garden is an amazing place of peace and serenity.

Charlotte E. Moore, Grade 4
Eton School, WA

Senses

To feel is to know,
To see is to witness worldly things,
To smell is to fill your soul with fragrance,
To taste is to be in a different world,
To hear is to except a compliment or to discard hurtful remarks,
These things are what make us ourselves,
The way we perceive things is what makes us each unique,
We all have used our senses in one way or another,
That might be how we are all here right now,
We are always using our senses and trying new things,
Every moment that we blink or take a breath of air…

Ellie McCoy, Grade 6
Vikan Middle School, CO

SUV Quad

On a hot sunny day.
At sunrise.
Snakes and lizards fighting in the sand.
Hot sandy wind the hot breeze on my face.
Hearing the motor go tic-tic-tic to put the Quad in 4-wheel drive.
Jumping in the air flying and the Quad grinding its motor.
I park my SUV, a cold glass of water now I'm freshened up.
My parents say I have to go in, I tell them I'm coming.
Just one more jump so I jump and I land;
I can't believe it, I land a superman!!

Daniel Gutierrez, Grade 6
Fox Creek Jr High School, AZ

Imprisonment

Out of my bedroom window,
Past the side of the house,
Into the woods,
Onto the railroad tracks,
Through the rushing river,
Upon one more yard,
Across the lonesome house,
Inside the clean window sill,
Among the yielding carpet,
Opening a bedroom door,
Around a clothes strewn floor,
Through a blanket made fort,
Under a desk,
Near a closet door,
Together you will find my friend and I giggling,
As I relate my story on how I escaped…IMPRISONMENT.

Lindsay Stadeli, Grade 6
Robert Frost Elementary School, OR

I Am From

I am from the fresh breeze of the mountainside.
I am from a meow outside my window.
I am from a garage bigger than my house.
I am from plants that didn't get enough water.
I am from a loud brother.
I am from a noisy house.
I am from learning to play the keyboard.
I am from the noise of an alarm clock
And my mom on the computer when I wake up in the morning.
I am from a brother and a sister.

Abigail Miller, Grade 4
Evergreen Elementary School, OR

Golden Hope

Hope is gold like a ring
And also like a sun
It reminds me of trust
It makes me feel kind
It makes me want to help those less fortunate

Mike Mickelson, Grade 6
Walt Clark Middle School, CO

Kittens*

Kittens are babies, small and cute
Kittens are little teddy bears, cute as can be.
They will give you a little wet kiss,
but if they see a dog they will hiss.
A kitten is a little mouse, tiny and quiet
Kittens are lambs, fluffy as can be.
They're a ball of fur
and when you pet them they purr.

Haley McCrary, Grade 4
Roy Moore Elementary School, CO
*Dedicated to my cat, Angel.

Chocolate

I have a bear named Chocolate.
He is a special bear because
he can do special things.
He can scare the monsters and
the bad dreams away.
For, when I don't have him I get a fright,
I even wet the bed at night.
Then he comes back to do his job
of protecting me.
Without giving me a fright.
For, I love it when Chocolate
my teddy bear is there.

Kylynn Jorgensen, Grade 6
Meridian Middle School, ID

The Night

While I look out, of the window,
I see the deep, dark sky,
while it blows through my hair,
with a cool breeze.

While it's dark,
I fall in a deep, deep, sleep,
and fall into my dream.
I dream of the sky, and in my dream
the colors of the sky, are blue, purple, green.

When it's dark,
while I am in bed,
I can hear the wind,
Blow in the night.

Stars shine in their brightness,
And they say,
"Fall into a deep sleep,
we will glow in the night."

When it's twelve o'clock midnight,
I look out and I see,
Brightness from the stars.

Alma Oxereok, Grade 5
Williwaw Elementary School, AK

Protists

Animal-like protists there are many different kinds.
Zooflagellates, sporazoans, ciliates, sarcodines.
They all move in different ways flagella, psuedopods, cilia.
Some can help ya some can kill ya

Plant-like protists also have many kinds.
Euglenas, diatoms, and dinoflagellates oh my!
They all make their own food which makes them autotrouphs.
Protists are important and we couldn't live without them.

Mackenzie Hahn, Grade 6
Pope John XXIII Catholic School Community, AZ

Spring

Spring starts soon,
snow slowly subsides.
Seagulls start soaring over Seattle,
and sunflowers sprout from soft soil.

Smart students still have school
but soon spring-break will stop by.
Spring-break sounds so cool and
Summer is still on its way!

Adrienne Wang, Grade 4
Eton School, WA

The Rodeo

Boy, that horse in the rodeo sure is great
The rider on that horse is Cowgirl Kate

That horse sure can chase cows
After the show, Cowgirl Kate bows

Cowgirl Kate comes back the next day
First she needs to give her horse hay

Cowgirl Kate says, "Good-bye"
Her horse sure did fly

Alex Peters, Grade 4
Mound Valley Rural School, NV

When Summer Comes

Oh how I love to go to the beach
when the sun is shining bright!
Wind in my hair, sand in my toes
I find it such a delight!
With my shovel and pail
I build my dreams,
of castles, rivers and such.
I can spend all day just playing there,
and never find it too much.
So until I'm told it's time to go
when the sun slips down the sky,
I'll run and play and dream of the day
I will never have to say good bye.

Alicia Pole, Grade 4
River HomeLink Program, WA

Me (The Shark)

Lonely, scavenging, a shark,
A shark, which is just like me.
Most sharks don't become friends,
I can relate.
Most sharks look for something,
I can relate.
So now you can see,
The shark inside me.

Braden Carlson, Grade 6
Walt Clark Middle School, CO

A Friend Is Like an Angel

A best friend keeps your secrets,
a best friend tells you theirs.
You remember what they tell you,
And your best friend really cares!

When you're scared and lonely,
Or you don't know what to do,
Your best friend is always there,
Looking after you.

Like an angel earns their wings,
Like they really know!
A best friend earns your gratitude
although it might not show!

My best friend is the BEST
She has all of these things.
She will help with anything,
I think…I know she has her wings.

Jennee Martinez, Grade 5
Sally Mauro Elementary School, UT

Poverty

In the U.S.A.,
It's there every day,
In Africa's streets,
It'll be with you in heartbeats,
Everywhere you walk,
These people never talk,
They sleep on stoops,
When they wake they droop,
These places never get attention,
They always had a good intention,
These things are poverty stricken,
You must quicken,
Before you are scared,
By poverty's unimpaired,
Ways of putting you on the street,
Poverty can't be beat.

Katie Stoner, Grade 6
Uplands Elementary School, OR

Why Do I…

I do not understand
Why there are onions
Why cows moo
Why the sky is blue
But most of all I do not understand
What is snow?
Because I live in Arizona
What I understand most
Are kids
Because I am one

Bryce Corning, Grade 5
Copper Creek Elementary School, AZ

Friends

There are times when you're alone
And you think no one knows
You hide a feeling deep inside
Hoping no one will find
You will ignore them
But they know
You insult them
But it shows
A friend doesn't just let it slide
They hold on tight and won't let go

Michelle Page, Grade 6
Fox Creek Jr High School, AZ

Colorful Leaves

The crying wind blows
Colorful leaves in a swirl
Giving them a ride.

Cinthya Espinoza, Grade 4
Jackpot Combined School, NV

Little Kitty

Missy is a kitty who's adventurous,
Who gets in sticky situations;
Climbing, playing, rolling, running.
She'll one day run nation to nation!

Emily Norris, Grade 6
Mt Olive Lutheran School, NV

Dream

Dream Dream
All the day
Dream Dream
Dream away

Dream of dragons
Dream of knights
Dream of fairies
Dream of sprites

You could dream that you could fly
Up away fly so high
You could even touch the sky
It is great to fly so high

Dream you could soar in outer space
Find someone else than the human race
Go to the moon and jump around
Even make one huge bound

Dream Dream
All the night
Dream Dream
And make yourself bright

Adam Hall, Grade 5
Blanding School, UT

Where the Panda Clouds Dwell

I once flew
where the Panda Clouds dwell
If you look closely
and truly believe
you can see their faces
emerge from the clouds
gazing at you with big, adorable eyes

They live in hermitage
above the land
cut off from cities and towns
Where they peacefully roll
through the sky
in perfect harmony with the world

The large prod the small along
with their snouts
ever patient
like a mother aiding her cubs
It makes you wonder
maybe we could learn a thing or two
if we all paid a visit
to where the Panda Clouds dwell

Daniel Karbon, Grade 4
Kyrene De Las Brisas School, AZ

Birds

Pretend you are a glossy bird.
Moving in the wind oh so swiftly.
Eating anything your stomach pleases.
Going house to house yard to yard any time you want
Flying anywhere your wings will take you;
Moving to a new tree to make a fabulous new home.
Dodging cars and people time to time.
Having tremendous loads of fun.
Trying to stay away from your horrible predators.

Katie Boucher, Grade 6
Midway Middle School, ID

My Dog Tigger

my dog tigger was a digger
he would dig here and there
one day he stuck his nose in a hole and he pulled out a mole
and long behold in the hole he found some gold.

James Welty, Grade 6
Coffenberry Middle School, OR

Excitement

Excitement is the feeling you find,
When it feels like the sun has come out in your mind,
And you just want to go out and jump for joy,
With so much energy like a mechanical play toy,
Being excited will make you believe,
That the sad feelings inside you will very soon leave.

Sheridan Rosner, Grade 6
Bright Beginnings School, AZ

A Magical World*

Smelling flowers in the soft breeze
Swimming in the stream so clear and blue

Diamond water all around me
Shining in the sun so hot and red

You might wonder how I found it
Well 'twas a cute and white striped tiger

It had spoken in my scared thoughts
Saying "Come with me, I mean no harm."

Laura Bergsma, Grade 4
Eton School, WA
*Sung to the tune of "Deck the Halls"

Little Mexican Puerco

I am a little Mexican puerco
I wonder why they feed me tacos and beans and burritos
I hear mariachi on dia del los muertos
I want to eat my food
I am a little Mexican puerco

I pretend that I am a little American pig
I feel happy all the time
I touch the rocky soil in the pen
I worry about being killed for my meat
I cry when they don't feed me
I am a little Mexican puerco

I understand a foreign language
I say I like rolling in the mud
I dream about going to a nice American farm
I try to be happy not sad
I hope I go to America
I am a little Mexican pig

Edgar Ramon Sandoval, Grade 6
Wallace Elementary School, AZ

Science

This poem is on Fungus
Fungus is everywhere among us
Forms of fungus are,
take not they aren't far,
Yeast, mold, and mushrooms too
Some mushrooms are poisonous and deadly to you

Animals, watch out for hypea
If it get you will pay a high fee
A fruiting body sticks out of it
Then in a while the fungus hits
That is the end of it
The animal and my poem.

Mary Ahern, Grade 6
Pope John XXIII Catholic School Community, AZ

The Building

The building was as tall as a mountain,
But as sturdy as the ground that we walk on.
Windows as dark as an empty moon night.
As quiet as a mouse.
In a quiet city
There it rests.

Austin Lehrke, Grade 4
Fulton Elementary School, CO

A Dream

I want to go to bed with my very sleepy head
resting on a pillow dreaming of the willow

I want to sail through the air with my hair
flailing behind not in a bind

I want to go Africa eating eggs with paprika
going on a safari wearing an Indian sari

I want to win an Oscar on a movie about a far
away place winning a NASCAR race

I want to write a book fight captain hook
sail a boat ride on a Thanksgiving float

I want to go to Rome see the famous dome
eat a talking chocolate bar sail off to mars

I want to write poetry about a willow tree
now that is done I am going to bed for more fun
Madeleine Kehl, Grade 6
St Anne School, WA

Alien Vacation

Two aliens went for a vacation last summer,
But it was quite a bummer,
They tried to surf,
And landed up on the turf.
They had no fun on the islands,
So they decided to go to the highlands,
Halfway through their flight,
In the middle of the night,
One of the crewmen,
Noticed they weren't human,
And really roared.
So they were thrown overboard,
They had not liked the plane,
And one ate the other's brain.
He hit the ground the next day,
And wanted to play,
So he went into a grocery store,
And fell asleep in a drawer,
Please do not wail,
This is but part of the tale.

Nick Kubasti, Grade 6
Washington Middle School, WA

I Am Not Old…

I am not an old guy with a cane.
I don't wonder if I'll die tomorrow.
I don't hear the pulse of my heart through a machine.
I don't feel a cane in my hand.
I don't want to be young again.
I am not an old guy with a cane.

I don't pretend to be young and playing games again.
I don't feel like taking random naps.
I don't touch the alarm to call some body to help me up from the floor.
I don't worry about who will get my things when I die.
I don't cry about wanting to redo my life.
I am not an old guy with a cane.

I don't understand what canes are for.
I don't say, "Is that you?" to a lamp sitting in the corner
    because of my horrible eyesight.
I don't dream about being 12 years old again.
I don't try to look young.
I don't hope they find a good place to bury me.
I am not an old guy with a cane.

Andrew LaFountain, Grade 6
Cadwallader Middle School, NV

There Is a Reason

You shall never be alone, but may feel alone.
The spirit of love will always guide you.
When you feel lonely,
You shall remember those who love you
And that shall bring a smile of memory back.
Just look outside at all the birds and all the squirrels and remember
How nice it is to smell the sweet smell of a good new day.
There is a reason for everything that happens.

Katie Howell, Grade 4
Durham Elementary School, OR

If I Were in Charge of the World

If I were in the charge of the world I would cancel the Teletubies
I would also cancel *Barney*
And I would cancel all the bad TV shows

If I were in the charge of the world there'd be more chocolate for everyone
There'd be cures for cancer
And everyone would be happy all the time
If I were in charge of the world you wouldn't have bad grades
You wouldn't have wars
You wouldn't even have school every day
If I were in the charge of the world a tomato would be a vegetable
And a person who forgot to be nice to everyone all the time
You would be able to yell
In charge of the world

Caity Bagwell, Grade 6
Walt Clark Middle School, CO

Fly High

Birds flying in the sky,
bird flying low and high,
flying, fly way up high.
All kinds of different birds chirping everywhere.
A bird tells another bird,
"let's go fly, let's fly low, let's fly high,
any way we'll have to make it fast
'cause if you don't, you might get crazy before we start.
So let's go fly, fly high and low,
anyway we go is up, up, up high."

Jessa Baisden, Grade 4
Acme Elementary School, WA

Golfing

As I approach the first tee
The crowd roars,
Not for me of course,
But what do I care?
I go up, swing, and hit the ball
It curves around the tree,
I walk up and see
That the ball is in a hazard,
I can still hit, but a very risky shot
I take a 5-iron, and hit through the trees
Unfortunately the ball lands in the bunker,
I plant my feet, and I hit the ball
It goes for a 25 foot putt,
I bend down, read the putt,
It's breaking 1 cup to the left,
Stand up,
Putt,
The ball rolls, rolls, and rolls
Breaks left and goes in the hole,
We go into a tiebreaker, and I win
I'm about to pick up the prize money, then I wake up.

Michael Schaloum, Grade 5
West Mercer Elementary School, WA

Inside a Computer's Mind

Click!
That's better. So what do they want me to do?
Type? Surf the Internet?
Huh? What's their wish?
I'm theirs to command.
Playing a game! My favorite!
Oh, man a storm. I hate these.
It means I have to go to bed (AKA getting turned off).
I'm not tired though.
Z.
Z.
ZZZZZZZZZZ
Black.

Talitha Trippel, Grade 5
South Side Elementary School, WY

The Me No One Has Ever Seen

I am a tough girl that loves soccer.
I wonder if we have a second life after death.
I hear ripples of blood going to a beating heart.
I see another dimension of the world.
I want one day a husband that will take care of me.
I am a tough girl that loves soccer.

I pretend that I'm a famous rock star that everyone loves.
I feel people hurting other people for no reason.
I touch water from a different point of view.
I worry that someone close to me might die.
I cry when I see orphan children crying.
I am a tough girl that loves soccer.

I understand that life is not fair.
I say everyone deserves respect.
I dream to be a pro soccer player some day.
I try to be the best I can be.
I hope life will be long and happy.
I am a tough girl that loves soccer.

Nicole Franco, Grade 6
H Guy Child School, UT

Seasons Pass

Spring's last rain has waved its goodbye,
Summer is walking up the road.
The blazing sun smiles at me,
Telling me that the heat will be fine.

Summer has been squashed,
By Fall's rains of leaves.
Happy, colorful trees,
Grass-stained knees,
Whispering to me in the wind.

Winter has unleashed itself on fall,
Fall retreats from the winter's cruelness.
It cries in dismay,
But winter says it's here to stay.

Winter has been washed away,
By spring's torrential downpours.
He yells at citizens;
            Thunder roars loudly
But what? Summer hasn't had his say.

Kevin Cabano, Grade 6
Pope John XXIII Catholic School Community, AZ

Red

Red is the color of reading,
The color of apples shimmering shades of red,
Red is the smell of candles,
The incredible sight of the fire's fierce flames,
Red is warmth.

Corey Caulkins, Grade 4
Hunters Glen Elementary School, CO

The Wind

Sun shines upon us
The freshness so clean
The breeze on my face
Trees swing and sway from the wind
So amazing when they dance!

Meghan Hinckley, Grade 4
Copper Canyon Elementary School, AZ

My Name

My name is inside
When it's called, it sticks
Like a magnet
'Til I find its echoing call.
It's soothing to hear.
It calms me down,
It's like magic.
When someone calls it,
My heart races with excitement.
It calls in a whisper,
Or a shout,
And then I know it is mine.

Emily Boyd, Grade 4
Brush Creek Elementary School, CO

Man on the Moon

I'm a quilt of silver strands.
Golden waves of the vast ocean,
And the desert's shifting sands.
I am full of motion.

Hidden in the night sky,
Hidden in ruin I'm like your face.
I'm still there when you die,
But another will take my place.

I'm the cyclone in the clouds
Covered in the shadow of shrouds.

Logan Buzzell, Grade 6
Morgan Middle School, WA

The Bluebird

In the brightness of the morning,
the bluebird sits.

Waiting,
for the breeze that may blow by.
Perched,
upon a branch outside my window.

Chirping,
happily as neighbor families fly by,
wishing they were her own,
the bluebird.

Erin Ford, Grade 6
Mrachek Middle School, CO

Oregon Coast

Like sand everywhere
Like ocean water splashing on your feet
Like salt in your mouth
Like smelling the fish market by the dock
Like the smell of salt everywhere
Like finding seashells on the sandy beach

Amber Peterson, Grade 6
Walt Clark Middle School, CO

Why

Why is there pain?
Why do we act vain?
Why do we put people down?
All it does is leave a frown.
Why do we die?
Just so God can see a tear in your eye?
It's hard to understand but you need to.

Marco Mahaffey, Grade 6
St Patrick's Catholic School, WA

How Not to Clean Your Room!

I can't I have homework,
I would get lost in my clothes.
I have to go to a friend's house,
You don't look well,
I'm hungry,
I don't want to,
I'm playing video games,
I don't feel like it,
Look a monkey,
Bathroom!
Earthquake
Ahhh I'm Hit!
OK fine!
I hate cleaning my room!

Anthony Hinkson, Grade 5
St Patrick's Catholic School, WA

The Eraser

Erasing
Erasin
Erasi
Eras
Era
Er
E

Emma Koltun-Baker, Grade 4
Mesa Elementary School, CO

Frost

white, cold, and frosty
dark, wet shadows of the trees
the frost on a hill

Olivia Taitt, Grade 4
Scenic Park Elementary School, AK

Alone

Alone,
All alone
In a dark room,
With feelings to burn.
The sun outside
The darkness creeps in
I hear laughs and cries
From another world.
They come closer,
And closer.
I stand as still as stone,
Afraid of being
Alone
All alone.

Rachel Khadivi, Grade 6
Hazelwood Elementary School, WA

Roller Coaster

Roller coasters
Their heights
Their jerking turns
They make noise as
Loud as the roar
Of a plane.

You go upside down
They're so frightfully
High because of the
Screechy fast moving
Cart.

It has horrible
Screaming and
Yelling it gives
You a headache
So that you're exhausted,
Dizzy, and excited once
In a while.

Cameron Shaw, Grade 5
Barratt School, UT

Davis

One day my friend got cancer
everybody mourned
nobody knew the answer

Near Christmas day
we all said hey Davis!
but the unhappy day grew near

then it happened
it was sudden
but it happened

Luke DuChesne, Grade 5
Elger Bay Elementary School, WA

If I Were a Sunflower

If I were a sunflower, I would be sprouting.
From the seed I go, up and up.
All around me turns green, animals scurry past me as I spring.
Still up, and up I go.
I start to grow leaves and I see others too.
I dance in the rain as it washes down my face.
As I grow taller, I can see the break of dawn,
sunlight washes over me, drying me off like a towel.
As I bud out, I spread my arms out and shout,
as spring is here, and as I droop, fall is near.
As my leaves fall all golden and brown.
My fun is over, until next year
I wake, waiting for the sun to take me up.
"The time has come," the sun will say,
and puts me back until some other day.

Nathan Harris, Grade 4
Double Eagle Elementary School, NM

Hope

The rain is falling fast from the sky.
I look out the window and I begin to cry.
Everything is washing away.
I sit and pray that it will all go away.
Suddenly it becomes the most beautiful day.
I am filled with joy, happiness, and glee,
but maybe next time I should let things be.

Shianne Hale, Grade 6
Sequoia Village School, AZ

Why I Hate P.E.

P.E. is hard because they make us run
I am slow at running
And I don't like the sun
It won't make me stunning
I'd rather be playing wall-ball
Or go in class and do some graphing
I'd rather be in a bathroom stall
Or be with my friends laughing
If they made us run less
Or let us play tag
I would have less stress
Or I wouldn't have to make myself drag
Teacher, if you let us have more free time
Then I will do anything you say like run, jump or climb.

Areeba Moten, Grade 4
Rogers Elementary School, NV

Black

Black is the darkness that is in my mind
Black is the gun shots of war
And the death of screaming children
Black is the hate in the eyes of dissimilar people
As I sit in the dark alone and afraid
I think of black

Casey Lawson, Grade 6
Robert Frost Elementary School, OR

Forest Fire

I started my growth from a single spark
And began to spread from the very start.
I feasted on the duff and bottom of oaks
Stretching upwards as I woke.

As I reached the crown of the trees
I saw that I was finally free.
Then, I was smothered, gone, and dead
For rangers thought I had no more to be said.

The rangers thought that I was bad
Though I was just helping out a tad.
I told myself that I'd be back
When the time is right for another whack.

Madison Nikkel, Grade 6
Beacon Country Day School, CO

Condi Rice

Condi Rice is a happy lass,
    with skills, smarts, and plenty of sass.
Born in Alabama in 1952,
    she makes life better for me and you.

She witnessed segregation in the first hand,
    it was a major problem in our land.
She's a concert pianist and much much more,
    people that have met her say she's not a bore.

She was an advisor to the president you know,
    she made him look good, she made him glow.
The Secretary of state is what she is today,
    she really is impressive, she'd take your breath away.

Aidan Hinshaw, Grade 6
Rogers Adventist School, WA

California Beach Breeze

The dry sand is hot
The wet sand is coolish warm
I jump in the water
I feel the seaweed brush up against my legs
I splash my way out of the water
I get some soda and fruit snacks
I sit on my beach towel
I take a sip
I take a bite
Then I get a big bucket and dig for sand crabs
with my companions
I feel the crabs between my toes
After we let the critters go
I take a boogie board
Then it's face plant world
I will never forget!!

Kelli Timpano, Grade 5
Frontier Valley Elementary School, CO

Dreams

Dreams flow into your mind,
As waves onto a beach.

They paint colorful ideas
That are finally set free.
No more confined
Than a newborn butterfly.

They dance in your mind,
Not caring their order.
Happy to finally be set free
From their daytime chamber.

Cat Zagona-Prizio, Grade 6
Southern Hills Middle School, CO

Trees

Trees are good.
They're terrific.
They're fantastic.
They're great.
They're fun to climb.
They're tall.
They're short.
They're all sizes.
There are all kinds.
They're trees.

Hailey Ladeau, Grade 6
Syracuse School, UT

Basketball

The ball feels bumpy, I bounce it,
The sound goes
Boom, boom, boom

I feel nervous,
When I shoot, My hands are sweaty.
When I shoot, I get goose bumps,
When I shoot I get excited.

I go up to the line,
My two feet are on the line,
I get ready,
I bend my knees
And then
Then
Then

I throw the ball and it keeps going
Going
Going
It goes around the hoop
And…Swish
It goes through the hoop.
I score

Togafiti Manu, Grade 5
Williwaw Elementary School, AK

Blue

Blue is my happy color it can mean sadness to others such as you.
Blue is the color of the endless sky.
Blue also happens to be the color of my mother's eyes.
Blue comes in all different shades.
I think it's one of the prettiest colors God has ever made.

Malinda Lovell, Grade 6
Walt Clark Middle School, CO

Bad Day

I woke up in the morning and hit my knee on my bed,
I was having a terrible hair day as it flopped around my head.
I walked into the kitchen and poured some cereal into a bowl,
But as I lifted up the milk, it all leaked out through a hole.
So I ate my cereal dry and rushed off to catch the bus,
But as I got there, the bus was already gone with a trailing puff of dust.
I sighed and started to walk to school,
But as I was walking past the Johnson's house I tripped and fell into their pool.
I walked into the classroom soaking wet with water,
I tried to make a good excuse for being late but thought "Why bother?"
At lunch I pulled out a sandwich covered in mold,
I also pulled out tomato soup that was now ice-cold.
During 5th period, I accidentally belched in class,
And while running a relay in P.E. I came in very last.
As I boarded the bus to go home,
I was hit in the head with someone's ice cream cone.
I walked into my house and Mom asked me if my day went well
Not wanting to be embarrassed, I lied and said "Just swell."

Amber McFarland, Grade 6
Meridian Middle School, ID

Baby Angels

Are babies really the angels of the world
watching us play in the meadows of a forgotten valley?

Are babies the love of every mother and father
who will cradle their baby until she is in the land of dreams resting?

Are the babies in the world
catching our wishes, hopes, and dreams,
holding on to them waiting?

Are they in the soft clouds
playing hopscotch, and painting?

These are the wonders of the world,
secrets untold, waiting to be opened and revealed.

Lindsey Wilson, Grade 6
Badger Road Elementary School, AK

Red, Yellow, White, Tan

If I were the color yellow, I would be the bright sun warming you when it's cold.
If white, I would be the fluffy clouds in the sky.
If tan, I would be the teddy bear you squeeze when you are sad.
If the color red, I would be the smile of someone who really cares.

Ashley Ferguson, Grade 4
East Evergreen Elementary School, MT

The Invisible Girl

She is invisible.
A whisper in the wind, a shadow on the wall.
She is waiting, hear her call.
She is nothing. A thought in your mind,
or a figure in your dreams.
She is not there or so it seems.
Forever she stands in the pouring rain,
feeling nothing but sadness and pain.
She looks in the eyes of fear
and in the dark she sheds a tear.
To you she is nothing just a girl in the hall.
You think of her once and then not at all.
The pain in her heart no one can mend.
To you she is just a girl, forever searching for a friend.

Christa Hubbard, Grade 6
Eagle Point Middle School, OR

The Sun

Sustaining life on Earth
Preserving plants' lives
Providing energy for living things
Keeping humans and animals healthy and alive

Giving the planet warmth
Providing light when it's needed most
Causing a powerful force of weather
One of the key factors for survival
The Sun

Causing heat exhaustion
Creating horrible sunburn
Killing many plants
Stealing precious water by evaporation

Developing skin cancer
Destroying thousands because of ultraviolet radiation
Harming helpless animals
A huge killer around the world
The Sun

Nick Fillhouer, Grade 6
Hidden Hills Elementary School, AZ

Pretend

Pretend you are a fuzzy ferret.
Running around the house happily.
Eating all the time.
Growing longer and furrier every few weeks.
Leaping out of your bath like a frog.
Sleeping whenever you want during the day.
Sneaking up on any and everyone in sight.
Playing with a colorful ball.
Having to go to the mean vet once a month.

MaKayla Call, Grade 6
Midway Middle School, ID

Autumn

Rainbows of color lying on the ground
Snowstorms ready to happen
Trees as bare as skeletons
Squirrels stuffing themselves for hibernation
Children hoping for the snow
Beautiful season

Shea Baxter, Grade 4
Lincoln Elementary School, AZ

Indian Eagle

The eagle is as proud as an Indian chief.
The man is as strong as a grizzly bear in a meadow.
The markings are as strange as a monkey.
The man is as brave as a lion.
His pelt is as soft as a cloud.
His eyes as strong as hawks.
His feathers as pretty as a flower.
His face as stern as a statue.

Daniel Atwood, Grade 5
Sally Mauro Elementary School, UT

Plays

I was waiting behind a big maroon curtain.
What is going on I'm not certain.
It is my turn to go on stage.
I hear the audience quietly trying to engage.
I feel the spotlight shining bright.
All of the smiles in the audience are a wonderful sight.
When I go on stage the microphone turns on with a cling.
Then I open my mouth and start to sing.

Bridget Stapleton, Grade 4
Colbert Elementary School, WA

Cafeteria Food

Food at our cafeteria is lousy,
but we have to eat it every day,
just the smell of it makes me drowsy,
"I'm gonna puke," I hear everyone say.
The cheese sticks I would not dare,
to try or even touch,
because sometimes I do find a hair,
it's deadly, very much.
The meatballs bounce off the walls,
they're alive I tell you it's true,
they're horrifying in every way,
they taste like a rotten shoe.
The fries are as hard as a stick,
and taste like uncooked dough,
most of them make me sick,
they're disturbing, that is so.
Don't get me started on the pizza,
I can barely stand just looking,
Even though it truly tastes like dirt,
it's better than my mom's cooking.

Kayla Matino, Grade 5
Escuela Bilingüe Pioneer Elementary School, CO

The Horse
The horse does a prance
In the lush, green, open space
He wants to show off
Sarah Darst, Grade 5
Sequoia Village School, AZ

My Flowers Are
My flowers are

in many colors
a symbol of love
a sign of beauty
a gift to bees
a sweet smell
a sign of happiness
the sunshine
bringing color to the sky

These are what my flowers are
Conner Neilsen, Grade 4
The Meadows School, NV

Another World
Anything can happen here
Climb up trees that grow
You can jump off a towering cliff
Or float high, the Earth below

Imagination rules over you
A twisted world, it may seem
Out of place, but just right
Asleep in your dream
Madeleine Colvin, Grade 6
Eton School, WA

There Is a Ghost Inside Me
There is a ghost inside me
and I don't know why
there is a ghost inside me
that I cannot stop
It's deep inside me
and it will not let go
It's down in my soul
taken me over
It tells me the wrong thing to do
I don't know why I listen
Because it gets me in trouble
It even sometimes
gets me mad
it tries to control me
this little ghost inside me
I try to stop it
But this ghost will live on forever
Thomanisha M. Ivra, Grade 6
South Middle School, CO

White Snow
White is the ground
A big blanket of soft snow
Falling soundless.
Lydia Gabriel, Grade 6
Hamilton Middle School, MT

The Christmas Tree
The tiny little Christmas tree
Alone out on the lawn
The snowflakes in the air fly free,
With the sun, they soon are gone.
Karsten Card, Grade 5
Reid School, UT

Waves
The wind is blowing
icy cold, when will the sun come
To melt all the snow?
Erin Loranger, Grade 6
Hamilton Middle School, MT

Football
There's 10 seconds left
We have the ball
I leap I bound
To the other end
I score I spin
We win! We win!
We're happy they're sad
We're good they're bad
We shake hands
We've done real well
Everyone is very swell
We're done it's the season's end
There's another season around the bend
Garrett Adams, Grade 6
Corpus Christi School, CO

The Dolphin Within
The Dolphin inside me
swims freely in my soul
doing flips, spins, and twirls
having fun among the shoal

The Dolphin inside me
has a spirit that can't be broken
wild, reckless, and free
it won't be broken

As you can see
I am wild and reckless
I am my own person
I am not helpless
Brooke Freitag, Grade 6
Walt Clark Middle School, CO

Where Am I?
Where am I?
The field is rusty orange
Where am I?
There seems to be no end
Where am I?
The twilight is compressing
Where am I?
The wind is pushing me to go
Where am I?
Am I alone
Where am I?
Are there others
Where am I?
Only time will tell
Chloe Jagelski, Grade 6
East Middle School, CO

Spring Rainfall
Dripity drop
Dripity drop
Says the rain on the sidewalk

Trickling down the pipe
Leooo
Leooo
Leooo

Exploding like fireworks
Then disappearing
Upon the dark
Gray sky
Caley Powell, Grade 4
Trails West Elementary School, CO

Ants
There once was a group of ants,
Who loved to walk — not dance,
They were walking one day,
In what they thought was some hay,
But actually was a pair of pants!
Glen Lowell, Grade 6
St Cyril Elementary School, AZ

When Joey Died...
Joey died when he was four.
He was really close.
I miss him a lot.
I will always know he will
Be in my dreams.
I'll be happy when we're
Together again.
I know that he is
Watching over me.
Haleigh Smith, Grade 6
Hazelwood Elementary School, WA

The Ocean

As I was walking on the ocean shore, I feel the shivering water.
The soft, brown sand is like brown sugar.
The wispy wind makes my hair fly like a bird.
I see the deep, blue ocean swimming in the sky.
I also see the sun setting over the ocean like a lemon.
I hear the waves crashing onto the shore like two pans hitting.
I taste the salty water as it hits my tongue.
I smell the fresh air; it's as fresh as a newly bloomed flower.

Jerrica Salazar, Grade 5
Sally Mauro Elementary School, UT

My Heart

My doctor said surgery is what I need
I was very nervous indeed.
The doctor said the hole in my heart
Needed fixing to give me a new start.
My room was right by the helipad,
At nights it was really bad.
All the nurses were friendly, all said; "Hello"
At dinner time they brought me Jell-O.
I healed up really fast,
Now the scar is all that remains from this painful past.

Spencer Fuller, Grade 6
Altara School, UT

Sawmill Canyon

In Sawmill Canyon waterfalls slither down like a snake.
Trees shake in the wind.
Nature's sounds echo through the canyon.
The wind smacks you across the face.
At night the bird's song puts nature to sleep.

Jake Hurt, Grade 4
Great Expectations Academy, AZ

The Garden of Eden

The soft smell of lavender
Such a sweet smell of green,
Peeling bark and a scent of fur
A piney, piney scent,
Such smells entice my nose
Stoop low, sniff a rose

Birds are rejoicing, all the joy in the world
All the cheeps and tweets make a symphony,
Crunch, crunch, leaves under foot
I love these sounds
All around

Blooming buds are cherry red
Like a wave crashing out,
Leaves are a gentle living green
Hanging like tears from branches,
My eyes are drinking in the day
I'm glad I'm here anyway

Lucy Banta, Grade 5
Lyons Elementary School, CO

Moonlight

Moonlight shining in the sky
I often wonder why?
It glows and glows 'till morning,
Only it knows when to continue
It lights the night and shines on and on
Just like a bright light in the atmosphere
It is the light of the night
And never leaves your sight in the hours of darkness.

Madison Luick, Grade 5
Uplands Elementary School, OR

The too Tiny Pencil

Once there was a pencil made of all wood
A golden brownish color and a little pink hood.
He was used so much he just kept getting smaller
From too hard a clutch. He wanted to be taller!

The pencil was just too tiny he lived in a blue box shining
He wished when he was sad — he could simply go flying.

One day, the little pencil
Sat on the desk and started to whistle.
He thought to himself:
'Life is a waste, I'm so tiny,
I'll probably die in a day.'

The pencil now looking sad and depressed
Prepared his life for his last breath.
But suddenly the pencil stopped and thought
'I don't need wealth
Just my health.

I don't need to be taller
I could even be smaller
I look around and see
I'm just happy to be me!'

Maekena Hall, Grade 6
Corvallis Waldorf School, OR

Goodbye

It's the end of the year
Wipe away your tear
We have grown so close
We're going to miss each other the most
School has just flown by
We have to say goodbye
We might see each other in seventh grade
Hopefully our friendships don't fade
So, it's almost summer
Oh what a bummer!
See you next year
It is pretty near

Kristina Dunlap, Grade 6
East Middle School, CO

Pup

Running wild
as if the wind
hopping as a bunny
jumping for butterflies
fleeing from human hands
who stop the freedom,
a sailing boat
in the vast prairie of blue
playing with its wild friends
and tumbling all around
free from evil grasp,
out in the sun's rays
until the day is done.
Freedom dwindles
captivity grows
running to no avail
he's a caught deer.
Nighttime is here!

Luke Haresnape, Grade 6
Columbia City Elementary School, OR

Maui

Hot, humid weather
Beautiful blue ocean views
Fun to go surfing!

Sammie Knight, Grade 4
Copper Canyon Elementary School, AZ

Life

Life,
What is it?
Is it a color, or a shape,
What meaning does it have?
How much do you have to pay for it?
Is it priceless, or does it cost a lot.
You choose,
It's your life.

Kristine Kumar, Grade 6
Hazelwood Elementary School, WA

A Dry Dirt Road

Quiet as a cat
Sleeping in the sun
A bird sings
The other responds
Still again
A car passes
Dust flies
Still again
A leaf falls
Sways in the air
Still again
Again and again
Still

Elliott Noell, Grade 6
Whatcom Day Academy, WA

The Heart Stealer

The heart stealer has a dark monster in him.
He gets your hopes up and your heart filled with love
then destroys it like ripping my soul out of my body with his bare hand.
Even speaking his name makes me feel like an invisible man is jumping into my body
and blows me up from the inside.
He blocks me out of his life every day
and he keeps my brother in like a lock.
This monster is my dad
and he's never going back in my life.

Marchus Lewis, Grade 5
Amelia Maldonado Elementary School, AZ

A Friend

The Quiet,
The Wind,
The Leaves
I'm looking around the tall, green, straw grass.
There I see my friend, horse looking at me,
up over the fence I go getting ready to jump, glide onto her rump.
We jump we leap we creep around we get ready to ride,
I pull the grass,
to feed to my friend,
We sit.
I give her something to eat or she might eat the street!
She looks around I smile,
There is the sun, setting.
She lets me up, she lets me jump, on, on, and on we go…
We run towards the sun it is somewhat fun.
Off down the hills we all disappear leaving behind,
The Quiet,
The Wind,
The Leaves.

Chloe Westgate, Grade 5
West Mercer Elementary School, WA

The Sun

When the sun rises it shines on the mountains with glistening wonder.
Reflecting off the snow with pure white power.
Shining with blinding light.
Slowly setting, painting clouds with orange and purple.
Steadily falling behind the mountains.
Then rising the next day, with the same toughness and tenacity.

Jonathan Vall, Grade 6
Corpus Christi School, CO

Sudden Silence

The silence of cold arms and hands as the wind makes them shiver.
The silence of when you first open a library door.
The silence of a child as they doze off to a peaceful slumber.
The sudden silence before a baby is born,
And a new life begins.

Caitlin Elliott, Grade 6
Badger Road Elementary School, AK

Same

I get whacked all the time,
My dad gets whacked,
My mom gets whacked,
My sister gets whacked,
It seems everyone who is my color gets whacked,
I want never to be whacked again,
If it was over, my family would be free,
That depends if they should win,
Then my family would be free,
I am tired of being whacked,
I sometimes feel blood on my back,
I am not yours to command,
I am not your dog, cow, or horse,
I am a human,
I am the same as you,
As you are the same as me,
We are brothers, one is not higher,
We are the same,
I would never whack you,
So why do you whack me?
I am a human, humans do not get whacked.

Jesse Koehler, Grade 5
Santa Fe School for the Arts, NM

America

In America we respect freedom
In America we expect freedom
In America we live and die for freedom
In America we need to appreciate freedom

Freedom means choosing our own religion
Freedom means choosing what to do
Freedom means the right to love life
Freedom means something not to be abused

Sean Madden, Grade 6
Pope John XXIII Catholic School Community, AZ

My Dessert Decorating Plan

As I pull out the steaming hot metal pan.
Of my steaming hot oven, oh man!
As I look at the steaming hot pan.
I discover my dessert decoration plan.

As I pull out my delicious looking dessert.
I decide to put the squeezable pink fluffy goodness on first.
The little chocolate sprinkles will go next
Then, I will eat the rest!

As I plunge my fork into my completion.
It quickly consumes my affection.
I decide it is cooked to perfection.
A second bite will win my election.

Tyler Reaser, Grade 6
Pope John XXIII Catholic School Community, AZ

My Father

Like the beginning of time
He was there, your buddy, your friend, your Father.
From the beginning, and will always be.

Like a teacher, patient, kind, and wise.
He'll guide you and instruct you
Through life's mysterious ways.

Like the chosen lamb, a sacrifice for my sins.
Like stains washed away,
I am not worthy of His grace!

Kaitlyn Weber, Grade 6
Walt Clark Middle School, CO

My Dad, My Hero

Hi Dad — I was thinking of your today
I wish you didn't live so far away
Maybe I will write you…maybe tomorrow
I am so excited because every summer you come this way
I still have my X-box so we can play
MY DAD, MY HERO

Mom told me something about you, I can't believe it's real
Part of me is gone now, I don't know how to feel
It's like God gave me you, like to borrow
I wish somebody, anybody can tell me why
Because I didn't even get a hug or kiss goodbye
MY CRAZIEST DAD, MY BEST HERO

I was told I was your shining star
And I know you didn't mean to leave me in this pain or sorrow
Now you're my 'Daddy Guardian Angel' and won't be too far
I love you Dad and will forever miss MY HERO

Stacey Plumage, Grade 6
Harlem Elementary School, MT

Spring

spring-o-spring, that lovely spring
the perfect time for birds to sing
lots of laughter, lots of fun, lots of playing in the sun.

Julie Soto, Grade 6
Avenue B School, AZ

What Goes on at the Beach

What goes on at the beach on the beach.
In my lounge chair.
Toward the water.
Beyond the waves.
Underneath the water the dolphins play.
Through the seaweed they dash.
Past the sharks they swam.
Near the top of the water.
Over the waves they jumped.
Out in the water I see two dolphins playing in the ocean.

Taylor Picard, Grade 6
Fox Creek Jr High School, AZ

Ancient Wing

It had teeth like rock
and
feathers as soft as a sock.

With feathered wings it could
glide away
from predatory things.

It could outrun
the clock
and had eyes like a hawk.

It fed on dragonflies
as it flew through
the skies.

Archaeopteryx is the first bird
and
that can be assured.

Khalil Shariati, Grade 6
Sedona Charter School, AZ

The Perfect Shot

I was there,
Playing the game.
I could not hear the yelling.
I turned around,
I looked at the basket,
An open shot.
10, 9, 8,
My heartbeats,
7, 6, 5,
The ball slips out of my hands.
4, 3, 2,
The ball hits the backboard.
A perfect shot!
The ball goes in!
The whistle blows!
The crowd cheers!
I did it!
My teammates pick me up!
They cheer.
But I,
Just smile.

Katie Burbank, Grade 5
Home Choice Academy, WA

The Night Sky

The lights so high
Shone above the night sky
And to the light circles that swirls
In the bright moony night
With the moon shining brightly

Steven Hickman, Grade 6
Morgan Middle School, WA

Seyoum

Seyoum,
My grandpa died before I was born.
Heard many stories about him,
Doctors didn't know anything,
Was an officer in Ethiopia,
Had eight children.
Seyoum, my grandpa died.

Yophtahe Seyoum, Grade 6
Hazelwood Elementary School, WA

Dog Friend

A short while ago
I lost a good friend
I'll always love her
No matter how it ends.

She died with a simple shot
That my dad had to make
I cried 'till I was tired
And it wasn't a fake!

I knew she had to go
But couldn't let her leave
I know that she loves me
That's something I'll always believe.

Brianna Burlingame, Grade 6
Enterprise Middle School, WA

The Annoying Sisters

We go to our friends just to get away
from our sisters.
Because they're so annoying we can't
stand them at all.
So that's why we go to our friends.

Jared Nielsen, Grade 5
Sally Mauro Elementary School, UT

Passion

passion
what is it?
where do you get it?
how do you use it?

the truth is
it's right there
right there in front of you
like your shadow
waiting
waiting
for you to catch it
so get it
it's right there
get it while you've got it

Gem Boehm-Reifenkugel, Grade 6
Sedona Charter School, AZ

Every Heart

Every heart has a beat
Every heart has a sound
It will not retreat
It may get lost but will get found

Every heart has a light
That shines within
It's so bright
It can repent a sin

Every heart has a song
You just have to listen
It's so strong
It'll make you shine or glisten

Christina Marie O'Claray, Grade 6
Harlem Elementary School, MT

Speak to the Moon

Creature of the night
howling at the night sky's moon
speaking to it with grace.

Brittany West, Grade 6
Hamilton Middle School, MT

Sunny/Cloudy

Sunny
Playing, sunbathing
Sunburn, games, heat
Clearer, hotter, raining, colder
Windy, lightning, thunder
Scaring, darker
Cloudy

Darian Genzmer, Grade 4
Jackpot Combined School, NV

Inside the Wind

Blowing through,
I am a jaguar,
Roaring so loudly everyone feels it.
I and my siblings
Pad through the crowd,
Some batting at coats,
Others running through the air.
Mischievously we tangle flags,
Causing them to flap harder,
Us playing as a kitten plays with yarn.
We pounce on people full force,
Often causing them to attempt
To push against us.
They have no success,
Until we grow tired and die down.
We breeze through slowly,
Happy to settle and rest for another time.

Naomi Bishop, Grade 6
Eagleview Middle School, CO

Up to the Cabin

Toward the blue water
Beneath the white snow
Along the rushing riverbed
Near the yellow flowers
Over the grassy hills
Through the green trees
Across the green grass
Beyond the blue sky and the shining stars
Above the birds in the night sky
Up to the cabin on the grassy hill.

Mitchell Thierman, Grade 6
Fox Creek Jr High School, AZ

Snowstorm

A white blanket falls to the ground,
A blank sheet of paper covers the town.
Calm and peaceful I sit by the blazing fire,
I'm wrapped in a cave of blankets.
My cat is a ball just cuddled in my lap.
The hot chocolate is a swirl of great joy in my cup.
I love a snowstorm.

Erin Rayne, Grade 4
Roy Moore Elementary School, CO

Racism

Racism is a quadrilateral
Each side is a different race
All sides are not equal on a quadrilateral
We are all different
That doesn't stop me from liking other people
Racism is a circle
It will never stop
A circle has no end
It just keeps going and going
Racism is a rectangle
Two of the sides are the same
The other sides are different
One of the two sides thinks they are better; nobody is better
Everybody should like all shapes
Everybody should like all people
Racism is like all shapes; don't be a racist

Hannah Levine, Grade 4
Rowland Hall-St Mark's School, UT

The Earth

As the Earth spins 'round and 'round
The day turns into night.
The seasons change, the years go by
Half the world is quiet through the silence of the night.

Night is day and what was day is now night
You're entering a different world
Either dreams or real life
The Earth spins and life goes on.

Carly Robertson, Grade 5
Candalaria Elementary School, OR

The Airport

On my way to the airport, as far as I could see,
Planes flying to and from, looking straight at me.
I'm sprinting through this place
Like running to home base.
I look up at the clock,
As I feel a great shock.
It's time for me to board,
I'm not at my gate, good lord!
My eyes start to water and I begin to sweat,
My knees shake and I commence to fret.
I finally found my gate,
But it was a little too late.

Jalyn Vigil, Grade 5
Colbert Elementary School, WA

Jack-o-Lantern

Jack-o-lantern shining bright,
In the shadows of the night,
On Halloween's eve you smile till dawn,
And till the last stars are gone,
Then your candle dies down and you decide to rest,
But still you look your best,
Before long you will be shriveled and dry
But the spirit inside you will never die,
You will rot and be thrown away soon,
But you don't mind because you go to dance with the moon,
The moon that glows bright as bright as your smile,
And comes out on Halloween.

Grace Welch-Zaricor, Grade 6
St Cyril Elementary School, AZ

Yosemite

I wondered as I looked around
About the treasure I had found
A place right by the stream
I felt like I was in a dream.

The stream's water was rushing by
It was in a hurry, I didn't know why.
The mountain stood like a purple sentry,
Not allowing any entry.

The trees covered me like an umbrella
So silent if you asked them something,
They wouldn't tell a fella',

I wondered as I looked around
About the treasure I had found.
The thread of water that was a waterfall.
The sound was like a thundering call.
Yosemite soothes me with a motherly touch,
And I still miss it very much.

Aumkar Dixit, Grade 6
Southern Hills Middle School, CO

Wishes

If I had 3 wishes,
There would be no dirty dishes,
Then I'd have 2 wishes left,
I would wish for no theft,
I had 3 wishes, now I have one,
After my wish my wishes are done.

Chelsie Denton, Grade 6
Eagle Point Middle School, OR

Life

Life is a valuable thing.
Do not waste it,
Use it wisely,
Otherwise you'll be sorry.
First you're a flea,
Then you're a tick.
And then a fly, an ant and a bug.
Then a spider, a fish, and a mouse.
Then a mole, a rat, a hamster.
Then you become a cat and a dog.
Finally a baby, and then you grow.
If you commit suicide,
Before you die from age,
You are very foolish because,
Then you turn into a flea again.

Grace Samtani, Grade 5
Copper Creek Elementary School, AZ

Red

Red is the color
Of a hot fire,
The mother of pink
And the face of a liar.

Red is the color
Of a juicy cherry,
The Huskers jersey
And ripe strawberry.

Red is the color
Of blood shot eyes,
An apple's peal
And the morning sunrise.

Red is the color
Of a fiery flame,
The color I turn
When I am to blame.

Red is the color
Of yummy apple sauce,
The color of a rose
And spicy spaghetti sauce.

Logan Hurt, Grade 6
Kendallvue Elementary School, CO

Hermit Crab Express

Oh dear Clumsy Joe!
Where in the world did you go?
You forgot your shell.

Sophie Forslund, Grade 6
Hamilton Middle School, MT

Harry and Draco

Harry Potter
brave, friendly
daring, loving, caring
famous, powerful, pathetic, cruel
hating, demanding, bullying
mean, selfish
Draco Malfoy

Yahaira Garcia, Grade 6
Fox Creek Jr High School, AZ

Acting

I get to be someone new,
for a day.
I can erase my life and start over,
for a while.
No person,
no being,
no one
will know
who I am
when I act.

Lottie MacAulay, Grade 5
West Mercer Elementary School, WA

Sawfish

Sawfish
scary, freaky
swimming, sneaking, creeping
Swimming and looking for its prey
sharp nose

Darrian Myatt, Grade 6
Fox Creek Jr High School, AZ

Summer

I love summer
I hear a drummer
When I'm at the parade
And no more grades
The fresh evening air
Oh, it's so fair
In the summer I eat ice cream
It's so good I scream
Summer is like a dove
Beautiful with love
Summer is the best season
That's my reason

Sara Leffingwell, Grade 4
Shields Valley Elementary School, MT

Earth

The world is a place
where humans live.
You creatures out there
may call it Earth.
The world turns,
spins,
sleeps,
and takes sun baths.

Nathan Mars, Grade 5
Carrolls Elementary School, WA

Tweet Friends

Birds, birds
See them fly
See them way up in the sky
You can hear them
Beat their wings
When they take off
In the spring
When they land
In their nest
They eat all the mosquito pests
But then again
They are our friends
So treat them like a special friend

Raime Drake, Grade 4
Grass Valley Elementary School, NV

Snakes

Arizona is home to snakes in the sand
Snakes slivering in the steaming sand
Trying to catch their pry
Trying to hide from their enemies.

Casey Friedt, Grade 5
Kingman Academy of Learning, AZ

The Bright Shiny Sun

The sun is bright,
The sun is yellow,
The sun is big,
Like a big bright circle

A big, yellow thing.
So bright and shiny,
And never stops,
All day and night

The sun shines so brightly.
That's what we should do.

So make your life,
Like the bright, shiny sun

Freda Ireigbe, Grade 4
Christian Faith School, WA

Cheating

When you look back what do you remember?
A short glance is all it took
When remembering why did you look?
A dishonest move got you here
But why are all your records clear?
Without anyone knowing without anyone caring
Why was someone else sharing?
Guilt has now begun
But you still won
Why are people snickering?
Why are people comparing?
Why did you cheat, here comes the heat

Kathleen Callahan, Grade 6
Pope John XXIII Catholic School Community, AZ

My Flowers Are

My flowers are

sunflowers and daisies
a symbol of Aphrodite's beauty
a symbol of the nature in the spring
a symbol of romance
a bug club
what makes Heaven the happiest place ever
as pretty as the moon
as bright as Heaven on a gloomy, rainy day

This is what my flowers are.

Jacqueline Adams, Grade 4
The Meadows School, NV

Winter in Utah

Winters in Utah are snowy and gay,
In the mornings we eat breakfast and go out to play.

If I peek from a bush, I see deer all around,
I watch from a distance, and do not make a sound.

When we're throwing snowballs, in an igloo I hide,
Then later, we hop on a sled and go for a ride.

The freshly fallen snow, I try to catch,
Half an hour later falls another new batch.

Snow angels are awesome, and snowmen too,
But if I make them too long, I could get the flu.

I was born in Utah and left five years ago,
I had so much fun with all that snow.

I think of the good times I had back then,
And I hope to have winter there soon again.

Anisa Abdul-Quadir, Grade 4
Phoenix Metro Islamic School, AZ

Ode to Hula

Koo-ie, Awayhay, and Ka-holo
Are steps that have lasted through many generations
And the dance that I do now
I feel my skirt shifting from side to side
Like palm trees swaying on a
Tropical breeze
With my bare feet stepping lightly through
The warm, dry, sand
In unison we step, together
Graceful hands tell
The story
There are lots of girls with chocolatey skin
But not me
I am freckles, fair skin, and blonde hair
But I still dance with those
Who love, value, cherish, and treasure,
The dance that we all call
Hula

Lacey Jones, Grade 5
Barratt School, UT

Inside-Outside

Inside and outside I'm a lot alike
but my outside is a little different as you see.

My outside wears pretty nice clothes
and is a medium height too
thin golden blond hair,
with light freckles scattered everywhere
pretty good looking
but don't really care.

My inside is different but fairly the same.

A professional gymnast
twisting and turning flying through the air,
long, long hair everywhere
my face as soft as a cloud
perfection everywhere
my feet are pointed as I land
a perfect ten wins for me.

Erin Mihalchick, Grade 6
Walt Clark Middle School, CO

Summer

It is summertime
The bugs scampering away from the heat
The flowers with a joyful face
And same with me

It's the swimming season
The water is yelling at me to get in
The sun is jumping on me
Until fall comes running.

Hannah Krebs, Grade 6
Pope John XXIII Catholic School Community, AZ

If I Were the Color...

If I were the color red, I would be a sly fox nestled in her den with her cubs.
If green, I would be the calm spring grass sprouting up from a brown earth.
If I were copper, I would be a lucky penny waiting to be picked up by a person so I could spread my luck.
If gold, I would be a 24-karat ring wrapped up for my mother.
If I were brown, I would be the long sturdy trunk of a tree.
If silver, I would be a silent winter's moon.
If purple, I would be a field of light colored pansies, waiting to be picked and carried to a house to be put in a vase.
If I were the color blue, I would be the dark midnight sky.
If I were black, I would be an immense crow flying through the dawn sky, or his reflection on the sea.

Kayleigh Pollack, Grade 4
East Evergreen Elementary School, MT

My Magic Box

I will put in my box, the silence of the world when the snow falls outdoors
The pitter patter of the rain as it cascades down from the sky
The jingling noise my cat's or dog's collar makes when they dart over to me.

I will put in my box, the warm feeling of sand between my toes as I amble down the beach
The wonderful world I go into as I read a marvelous new novel
The emptiness in my stomach when I first try something new.

I will put in my box, the excitement of winning our basketball game
Of driving down the court on a fast break
Of shooting a basket and hearing the crowd applaud.

I will put in my box, the sensation of jumping into a lagoon when the water first touches my skin
The remembrance of the marvelous times in Mexico with my cousins
The joy of seeing one of my best friends for the first time in weeks.

I will put in my box, the sweet scent of cookies straight out of the oven
The wondrous aroma of walking into my house while pasta and meat sauce is cooking
Walking outside after a rainstorm to inhale the freshness of the air.

I will be in my box, until the orange sky of the sunrise comes to reclaim me
When I allow myself to be transported out of the world of dreams
Back to the world of humans, the world of school.

Kelsey J. Hunt, Grade 5
Mesa Elementary School, CO

Pugs

Pugs, pugs, pugs
Pugs are like great big balls of hugs
Pugs, pugs, pugs
Pugs have a short and stubby nose and it is cute
Pugs, pugs, pugs
Pugs have the cutest little face and big body
Pugs, pugs, pugs
Pugs have big eyes, little ears, small nose, and just don't seem to match head to body,
    but have a huge heart for loving you
Pugs, pugs, pugs
Pugs may look different, but I can guarantee that you will fall in love with their adorable face
Pugs, pugs, pugs
I love pugs, and so should you
Pugs, pugs, pugs

Samantha Stapleton, Grade 6
The Colorado Springs School, CO

Blue

Blue is the sound of distant water flowing.
Blue is a flower,
Blue is the sky.
Blue is soft and light.
Blue is how you feel when a friend moves away.
Water skiing and sky diving are blue.
Listen to the wind, it is blue.
Florida is blue.
The salty sea water is blue.
Blue is a sweet little pond.
Blue is all around us.
Check behind you!

Katie Johnson, Grade 6
Patton Middle School, OR

I Am

I am an outgoing girl that loves to sing!
I wonder if I will ever sing for money!
I hear all of my fans screaming!
I see myself singing and dancing on stage!
I am an outgoing girl that loves to sing!

I pretend to hear my number 1 hit song on the radio!
I feel that if I try hard I can accomplish all of my dreams!
I touch the microphone in my hands!
I worry that I will not make it very far!
I cry that my fans might forget my hits!
I am an outgoing girl that loves to sing!

I understand this dream will be a lot of work!
I say that no matter what I will make it!
I dream that all of the fame, cameras, and lights will be on me!
I try my best to be all that I can be!
I hope that one day these things will all come true!
I am an outgoing girl that loves to sing!

Vanessa Manning, Grade 6
Cadwallader Middle School, NV

Note Book

My note book holds all my dreams my life my wishes
In my note book I can write what I want to in the night
I can write my stories too and read it when I'm feeling blue

Madelyn Bloom, Grade 5
West Mercer Elementary School, WA

The Ocean Waves

The rocks are as brown as fudge brownies.
The sunset is as beautiful as Mrs. Barker.
The sand is as smooth as lotion.
The island is as big as the world.
The waves are as powerful as a stampede.
The sunshine is as bright as a light bulb.
The water is as blue as the sky.
The mist is like rain on a rainy day.

Alicia Ruiz, Grade 5
Sally Mauro Elementary School, UT

Orcas and Dolphins Plus Whales

O ceans are what I call home
R ushing to catch my prey
C atching and eating my food
A mazing animals is what we are
S wimming in my big blue home

D olphins love to dive and play
O h! The glory of having fun
L oving to play and tease my friends
P laying all day long
H appy life I have until I die
I n Heaven I shall go when I die
N o one will bring me back to life, but God
S wimming in the big ocean after death

W atching over them
H aving lots of fun
A time where you can go anywhere
L eaping out of the water is what I love to do
E ating the gooey, yummy fish
S wimming and having fun is what it is all about!

Alexzandra Luna, Grade 5
Gold Canyon Elementary School, AZ

Holidays

At the beach on a mat I lay.
On an awesome, amazing day.
During the morning sun.
Seagulls fly on a greedy run.
My brother, playing in the sea
Is the only thing I see.
As my parents enjoy the view
The sea looks like a shade of blue
And that's all I'll say on this little place
As I go on my adventures and at my pace.

Zachary Hing, Grade 6
Fox Creek Jr High School, AZ

Soccer

Your body goes numb as you run across
the blades of grass, the rain feeling hot,
the mud covered all over you, the ball
gets kicked your way and as your foot
touched the ball the world stops,
it's just you, the ball, and the goal,
everyone is still but you, you can't stop,
the beat of the ball controls you, your rushing heart
clonking around your body, then you take a kick,
intense feeling takes control of your mind, you can
feel the ball hitting the net.

You won.

Ashley Putman, Grade 6
Acme Elementary School, WA

White

White is the color
Of pure and clean,
It lacks any hues
As a ghost can't, be seen.

White is the color
Of snow and ice,
Eggs, cream, and sugar
My favorite is white rice.

White is the color
Of a brides lacy veil,
A fluffy cloud
My skin, when I'm pale.

White is the color
Of a beautiful pearl,
An actor's teeth
And Grandma's curl.

White is the color
Of a white rose,
Lilies and daisies
Sunblock on my nose.

Cassie Ault, Grade 6
Kendallvue Elementary School, CO

Amanda Martinez

A thletic
M artinez family member
A rizona fan
N oisy
D isneyland is the bomb
A muses people

M illionaire (future)
A ctive
R eliable
T raveler
I ntelligent
N oble
E njoys piano
Z any

Amanda Martinez, Grade 5
St Cyril Elementary School, AZ

My Dog

He sleeps like a log
And he eats like a hog
He is always mean
He is never clean
He is always my dog

Tyler England, Grade 5
Hafen Elementary School, NV

We Still Live Free

We still live free,
In the land we love,
Because of the army,
We have harmony.

Let freedom ring,
In our hearts,
Forever they will sing,
Let's let freedom ring.

Alex Hammond, Grade 4
Cokeville Elementary School, WY

Chocolate

C hewy
H aving a creamy taste
O bscenely good
C ocoa
O h, so yummy
L ooking for more
A sking for more
T antalizing flavor
E very bite as good as the last

Katie Smallcomb, Grade 6
Heath Middle School, CO

Run

I run and run, as fast as I can.
I should probably go back,
'cause I don't have a plan.
I have no clue where I'm going,
as the wind starts a'blowing.
It's starting to get cold.
At least I'm self-controlled,
'cause I'm tempted to go home.
The wind continues to blow.
Then it starts to snow,
so I head back,
with my coat and my backpack,
and run.

Alex Bracht, Grade 5
Frontier Valley Elementary School, CO

Who Am I?

Who am I?
I do not use a cane,
But I am a little vain.
I love the color pink,
but I hate to fix sinks.
Fashion is my passion,
but your biggest clue yet
is that my name starts with
an S and it rhymes with banana.

Savanna Hoover, Grade 6
Meridian Middle School, ID

Basketball/Baseball

Basketball
Tiring, strategical
Passing, shooting, playing
Hoops, court, diamond, bases
Batting, throwing, catching
Running, skidding
Baseball

Skye JV Daco Lewis, Grade 6
Hazelwood Elementary School, WA

Oceans with Dolphins

O ver joyful
C lean
E very day
A lways
N eedful
S wimming

W ith
I ntelligent
T hings
H ere and there

D olphins
O ver powerful
L eading ships away
P rocessed
H eavily
I n a way
N eedful swimming
S wimming away from me.

Jenica Scott, Grade 4
Gold Canyon Elementary School, AZ

A Piece of Fall

Leaves,
Changing colors,
Dangling from the branches,
Falling

Families,
Strolling on the path,
Blowing out the candles,
Laughing

Holidays,
Labor Day and Halloween,
Coming and going,
Celebrate

Have some fun!
It's fall.

Amy Weintraub, Grade 5
Spring Creek Country Day School, CO

Landon

L oves to play soccer
A nd likes every kind of car almost
N ice to everybody
D oes good in mechanical work
O ften helps around the house
N ever gets in too much trouble

Landon Bovero, Grade 6
H Guy Child School, UT

Winter Engulfed by Spring

Lemon circle rises in the navy sky causing sunny weather.
Distinct figures can be seen now that the mist is gone.
Glamorous flowers blooming are beautiful in the spring.
This all happens now that winter is engulfed by spring.

Perfumed air blossoms along with the flowers.
Fragrance of the dew seems to lift many spirits.
Aromatic flowers coat the air with fresh new scents.
This all happens now that winter is engulfed by spring.

Tangy fruit from the spring weather tickles taste buds.
Delicious hot eggs come straight from the boiling pot.
Sugary candies give children sweet delighted mouths.
This all happens now that winter is engulfed by spring.

Cracking leaves are no longer around the yard.
Riots are caused by gleeful children playing.
Clamors are made when animals emerge from hibernation.
This all happens now that winter is engulfed by spring.

Warm air caresses our skin in the spring.
Silky petals are rubbed between many fingers.
Slippery ice is melted away from the weather change.
This all happens now that winter is engulfed by spring.

Matthew Savas, Grade 6
Bella Vista Elementary School, UT

Time Goes By

Have you ever stopped to think about your accomplishments?
Or just how you were going to win the race to the finish line?
Life's not a race, do take it slow,
That's the time you will feel a special glow
If you don't live life to the fullest you will regret,
Sitting at home just watching your TV set.
Don't rush through an important project, just make things right
I promise if you do this, it will provide a bright light.
Have you ever told yourself, I'll do it tomorrow,
But what if tomorrow never comes, not realizing your sorrow.
Do things when you have a chance,
Get up and do a nice dance.
Dance just the right speed, not too fast,
Because you need enough time to make the music last.

Madison Blau, Grade 6
The Hebrew Academy, NV

My Worst Day Ever

Today I had a horrible day,
I lost my homework, so I couldn't play.
And after that I missed the bus,
And after the bus went my dog Gus.
Finally I got to school really late,
I screamed, "This is the kind of thing I hate!"
Then after school the second bell rang,
And then my mind began to hang,
Around the thought that being home would be nice,
I could sit around and snack on rice.
I could also relax and watch TV.
When I'm at home I can just be me.

Kyle Sanowski, Grade 6
Hidden Hills Elementary School, AZ

My Brother

While I am relaxing in the living room
My little brother is in the worst place of all
the room of torture, the room of doom —
school with math and even worse English
and I can't believe I am saying this word
because it's so horrible — Science

Tony Castillo, Grade 4
Jackpot Combined School, NV

Fire/Water

Fire
Burning, warmth
Spreading, devouring, hot
Glowing, shining, reflecting
Pure, flowing, deep, indigo
Water

Miguel Bencomo, Grade 5
Escuela Bilingüe Pioneer Elementary School, CO

Red

Red is more than a color, yellow and green.
It's like having a friend or jumping in leaves.
Red is like love or the closing of day,
it's like nothing I've ever seen before
and that's what I'll say.
For now I just guess I'll leave it at that,
but there is more to red,
than I can say in a day.

Lacy McKinley, Grade 5
Sangre De Cristo Elementary School, CO

Rainy Day

A fog
Worms
Umbrellas
Pitter-patter noise
Wet wet wet
Puddles

Madeleine Crouch, Grade 6
Horizons K-8 Alternative Charter School, CO

Everything That God Created

Everything that God created;
From me to you,
Or even the animals in the zoo,
Were all created by God.
Everything that passes by and by
Were all created by God.

He doesn't like it when you feel sad or mad,
But He loves it when you feel happy and glad!
He'll love it when you do something good,
But if you do something bad,
I'll bet He'll be sad.

But all the things that you did
That were bad,
Ask him for forgiveness,
Because I bet you'll be glad that you did that.

Jennifer Hahn, Grade 6
Green Valley Christian School, NV

Kittens

K ind to each other
I rresistible to everyone
T hey are very sweet
T ogether they run and run
E very day they wake up early and play
N ever will they run out of curiosity
S oft as a pillow

Brooklyn Larson, Grade 4
Conestoga Elementary School, WY

If I Could Grant a Wish for You

If I could grant a wish for you,
There would be so many things I could do.

May all your worries disappear.
May you never know fear.

May candy be a fruit to eat.
May your room always be neat.

May you grow strong and wise.
May you never tell lies.

May you always have peace and joy.
May you always have your favorite toy.

May the sun always shine your way.
May you always think before you say.

May you live a wonderful life.
May you have a faithful husband or wife.

Bella Lucareli, Grade 6
Walt Clark Middle School, CO

Riot at the Hyatt

Sunday April 2nd there was a riot at the Denver Hyatt.
The Avalanche had a fashion show at the Hyatt.
Another part of the riot at the Hyatt, Children's Hospital was in the fashion show.
The hockey players did us a special favor.
Photo ops and signing our tops.
The time came for the fashion show we stood by our players row, by row.
On stage, on stage, we all go for the fabulous Avalanche fashion show.
Photographers shot pictures galore.
The crowd applauded more, more.
Child Hospital ambassadors soared, soared
As their family and friends roared, roared.

Dominic Harden, Grade 6
Corpus Christi School, CO

If I Were the Colors

If I were the color red, I would be a heart pounding in someone's chest.
If the color green, I would be a piece of grass floating in the wind.
If I were the color white, I would be a dove gliding into the sky.
If blue, I would be a bluebird finding food for her babies.

Meagan Nelson, Grade 4
East Evergreen Elementary School, MT

Purple and Green

If I were the color purple,
I would be a small flower growing in Mrs. Mitchell's backyard.
Each day she would tell me how her day went.
I would be a crayon coloring a winter sunset,
Marshmallows floating in hot chocolate,
A car zooming through town passing everyone.

If I were the color green, I would be the grass, the stem,
and the leaves of the little purple flower in Mrs. Mitchell's backyard.
A fourth grader's poetry folder full of all kinds of poems.
An emerald in a silver ring.
I would be a leprechaun leaving candy everywhere.

Skyla Komeotis, Grade 4
East Evergreen Elementary School, MT

Love

Love is something we all need.
Without it we are locked in a cage of darkness and hatred.
You share your hatred with others.
Finally someone unlocks your cage with love, releasing you into the light.
Your heart is warm with happiness and laughter.
You share your happiness with others.
You know that someone loves you and cares for you, you are complete.

Sarah Ireland, Grade 5
Coyote Springs Elementary School, AZ

A Dog

A dog is truly the world's greatest gift.
A dog can be your aid, your companion, or even your savior.
A dog will stay by your side always, no matter who you are or who you become.
A dog is surely, "man's best friend."

Matthew Zeller, Grade 6
Meridian Middle School, ID

A Shimmering Christmas Tree

There once was a shimmering Christmas tree.
Filling the snow covered house with glee.
It was perched with presents in a heap.
I'm telling you, don't peep.
Christmas cheer, presents here,
And a shimmering Christmas tree is the key.

Jacklynn Janae Spoklie, Grade 6
Midway Middle School, ID

Memories and Thoughts

When you think about someone you love
From morning till night.
It makes you feel really bright
And think their birthright was always right.
It makes them wander
So far away
In the deep dark starlight
And the oh so bright sunlight
That downright daylight and midnight
Will always feel right
When someone who loves you
Is always thinking of you
From morning till night
With only thoughts
And memories for now
Till the time we meet
In either the bright sunlight
Or the deep dark starlight
For now only thinking of you
Is all I can do.

Natasha Archuleta, Grade 6
Corpus Christi School, CO

Books

Books are fun,
Books are boring,
Sometimes they'll just leave you snoring.
When you read them they're probably good,
You like to read them and you should.
So take a book,
And have a look,
It should be fantastic.

Kyle Carr, Grade 4
Meadow Point Elementary School, CO

Mirror

Shiny and mysterious.
Duplicate, follow, show.
When I just stood in front of the mirror,
Mirror tells everyone's outside, but to me it was a mood-teller,
Inside of me and answer of my heart.
Looking, reflecting, glinting.
Bright and colorful
Mirror is my mood.

Claire Yang, Grade 5
Eton School, WA

Magnificence of Nature

A startling predator swoops into sight
Glistening wings of gold shimmer in the sun
In piercing eyes I see determination
A wickedly curved beak receives gifts of survival
Claws grasp and clutch the weak and helpless prey
A powerful body slices silently through the air
And still, I acknowledge this beautiful creature
As a spirit of survival

Nola Basey, Grade 5
Lyons Elementary School, CO

Morning Bell Rush

The morning bell rush is very fast,
It's like a roller coaster ride.
The morning bell rush doesn't go down,
But it's like a giant slide.

The morning bell rush is very tricky,
We all try to fit through one door.
The morning bell rush is so much fun,
I want to go some more.

The morning bell rush is so exciting,
I'm getting sucked into a black hole.
The morning bell rush is the reason,
I come early to school.

The morning bell rush is pretty dangerous,
There's teachers on the spot.
The last thing about the morning bell rush is,
Some kids make it and some do not.

Olivia Claridge, Grade 6
Spring Creek Elementary School, WY

Be You

White, black
Jewish, Christian
No matter who you are or what religion
Why, why discrimination?
Why not appreciation?
Why, why is everyone different?
Why be the same?
Why play the same game?
Why, why worry?
Why run around in a hurry?
We need to relax.
Not run around like maniacs!
Why, why do people feel left out?
Why not run around with friends and shout?
Be different, be kind
speak your mind.
Be you, not them, be yourself.

Keely Lewis, Grade 6
Cadwallader Middle School, NV

The Only One on Earth
He is big and brown,
He is nice and cuddly.
He sleeps on the foot of the bed,
He is also smart and funny.
He jumps like a kangaroo,
He is the only one of his kind
My dog Cujo
Chris Hanson, Grade 6
Monforton School, MT

Dolphins
Dolphins are:
exciting, fun, gentle,
happy, intelligent, jumpful, kind,
leapful, magnificent, neat, outstanding,
quite rubbery,
loud.
Deisha Morgan, Grade 6
Sequoia Village School, AZ

Sister
Sister
Pretty, energetic
Talking, sleeping, driving
Phones, boys, TVs, malls
Eating, laughing, smiling
Funny, outgoing
Chloe!
Kyra Cundall, Grade 6
Greybull Middle School, WY

Sky King
The graceful eagle glides through the air,
his glistening plumage shines so fair.

Majesty and power regal,
is held by this mighty eagle.

On freedoms wings does he reside,
beautiful, fierce, full of pride.

The all-time king of the marine sky,
may the eagle always fly.

Through the darkened hours of night,
the eagle brings liberty, truth, and light.

Coasting through that expanse of blue,
fly on eagle, fly on true.

Soaring through that plain of sky,
fly you eagle, fly you high.
Ethan Schow, Grade 5
Gate City Elementary School, ID

Cassidy
C ool
A ll-Star
S weet
S mart
I mportant
D etective
Y oung.
Jessica Caswell, Grade 4
Acme Elementary School, WA

Kelly
Kelly is my dog,
he is afraid of many things,
He is afraid of fog,
When he's tired he likes to cling.

Kelly is very active,
he knows how to fetch,
he can make messes that are massive,
he also knows how to catch.

My dog is liver and white,
Kelly is a springer spaniel,
he loves to bite,
his middle name is Daniel.

My dog is lots of fun,
He likes to run in the sun.
Ciara Thornhill, Grade 5
St Patrick's Catholic School, WA

Loneliness
One day I stood here
Paralyzed forever
I try to stretch
My feet would not move
They're planted to the ground.
Loneliness.
I have no friends in sight
Tears come rolling down
Being like a tree with no wind
My voice is gone.
Nobody knows.
Ruby Brady, Grade 5
Carrolls Elementary School, WA

Tinkerbell
Tinkerbell
Stubborn, adorable
Flies, glistens, dazzles
Has attitude, big time
Fairy
Ashlee Henson, Grade 5
Cottonwood Elementary School, CO

The Majestic Giraffe
The giraffe,
Tall and majestic
Reaching over the
Height of the elephant
Towering over humans.
Bravely a young child
Walks over to the giraffe pit
She strokes the majestic
Animal's long nose,
The tall giraffe seems to have
A hint of a smile on its long
Majestic face.
Ian Gorrell, Grade 6
Grant Middle School, NM

My Flowers
My flowers are
unique
beautiful
different shapes and sizes
colorful
plants of gold and silver
symbols of peace
like the moon and stars
the color of the rainbow
as bright as the sun can be
tastes like ripe strawberries

These are my flowers.
Eric Hirsberg, Grade 4
The Meadows School, NV

Useless Things
A school without teachers
A church without preachers
A needle without thread
A pencil without lead

A jacket without a zip
A person without a hip
A dog without fur
A cat without a purr

A book without words
A pair of wings without birds
A pair of glasses without a lens
A person without friends

A sun without heat
A person without feet
A shoe without a sole
A soup without a bowl
Heather Deringer, Grade 6
Walt Clark Middle School, CO

Recovering from Cold Winter

You would begin to see the sunny day coming.
It is gleaming behind the thick ashen clouds,
Appearing so high bright in the sky.
Spring cleaning will be taking place soon.

Birds will be heard chirping and peeping.
The wind will swish at the gleaming sun,
Frogs croaking and cows mooing at spring.
Spring cleaning will be taking place soon.

Fragrant flowers will be found and smelled.
Trees will smell fresh and piney at the morning,
While the grass will be damp and mildewed.
Spring cleaning will be taking place soon.

You can touch the cool prickly grass at morning,
That will soon be warm and dry at the afternoon.
Also the feathery and fuzzy birds flying around.
Spring cleaning will be taking place soon.

You will start to eat a warm, buttery toast,
Then, eating some ripe, juicy, apples and other fruits.
Those are just a bit of spring.
Spring cleaning will be taking place soon.

Jinno Guevara, Grade 6
Bella Vista Elementary School, UT

Arizona

In Arizona there are many deserts.
How I love walking in the squishy yet hard sand,
While gazing upon a beautiful, dry cactus as
I take a sip of ice cold water.
After it's done raining, I breathe in fresh air
As I walk on the muddy sand.
How I love living in Arizona!

Stephanie Petroff, Grade 5
Gold Canyon Elementary School, AZ

Fluttering Butterfly

Fluttering butterfly,
Fluttering butterfly,
Thank you for coming by.
You flutter and flutter all day long,
and finally you find the flower where you belong.
You're sweet and pretty,
And when I hold you, I don't feel fritty.
You wonder why?
Because you're soft, that's why.
Your wings are made up of a different color.
Red, blue, and the color of butter.
So now you know I like you.
So come on by so I don't feel blue.

Joshua De Lauder, Grade 6
Avenue B School, AZ

Cortez

My life changed when the men came.
They came in great ships with voluminous sails.
They were different.
Their skin was as white as a majestic heron's feather.
They came on great beasts,
As tall as the buffalo.
We offered their leader
A noble sacrifice
And he refused it violently
Then they attacked us
We had as much of a chance
As a weasel against a bear
And we were defeated.

Spencer Connor, Grade 6
Southern Hills Middle School, CO

Romance

Romance wears red lace.
Creamy milk chocolate sinks down my throat.
The scent of beautiful red roses fills the air
as they bloom from the rich soil.
Church bells ring from the distance,
while in Alaska the Northern Lights glow
on a warm summer night.

Lexi Long, Grade 6
Lolo Elementary School, MT

My Sister

I love my sister, she is very kind to me.
She loves me, even though we have hard times,
we still love each other.
She listens to me.
She trusts me.
I trust her.
She looks out for me.
I look out for her.
I love my sister!

Ataya Nielsen, Grade 6
Meridian Middle School, ID

There Are Some Melancholy Things

Sad things, sad things
Many things make me sad
Losing I hate it because it is not what I wanted

Sometimes I do something bad
but my parents shouldn't have to yell as you
can tell I hate it

Losing a very close friend or something
out of my life, I would just hate it

I hate sad movies 'cause some are not good
Sad things, sad things I hate sad things

Cameron Hemenway, Grade 5
Greenwood Elementary School, CO

Leaning on My Window

Leaning on my window
I see people in the fields
Motorcycles on the road
Their hair blowing in the wind
I see tulips blooming in the gardens
Children playing in the park
I see skateboarders doing tricks
Birds singing on tree branches
So much to see!
Leaning on my window.

James Gonzales, Grade 6
Washington Intermediate School, CO

The Flag

The flag has many stars.
Stripes going across.
Blue, red, white.
Red, white, and blue it does not matter
what order you say the colors.
The stripes, the stars, and the colors
all mean freedom.

Jessica Shubin, Grade 6
Eagle Point Middle School, OR

Vampire

I have a need
The need to feed
A child of the night
To live in fright

With fangs so sharp
And eyes so black
And I can turn into a bat

Sunlight burns so I don't go
To me you are very, very low

Sweet and tart, that's
How you will taste
So you better go run,
Yes, run in haste

Layla Farahani, Grade 6
Bright Beginnings School, AZ

I Wonder Why

I wonder why people aren't nice first…
It could be they are scared,
It could be they are mean,
It could be they are superior,
It could be they are not taught,
It could be they are cold-hearted,
It could be they are rude,
It could be they are unintelligent,
It could be they are without faith.

Jarrett Moffitt, Grade 4
Copper Canyon Elementary School, AZ

Who

Monica
Weird, athletic, funny and nice
Lover of soccer, snowboarding and guinea pigs.
Who feels sad when it's snowing, not being with friends and not playing soccer.
Who needs soccer, music and a great book.
Who gives smiles, good passes in soccer and quick note passing in class.
Who fears too much make up, hairspray and love.
Who would like to have more soccer, *Napoleon Dynamite* movies and less school.
Who dreams of being a pro soccer player, living in Italy and having a nice car.
Penfield

Monica Penfield, Grade 6
H Guy Child School, UT

The Storm

The way it blows.
The way it pitter-patters.
The way it thumps.
The way it crashes.
The way it lights up the whole night sky.
I like how the wind blows.
I like how the rain pitter-patters against my window.
I like the white blanket on the grass that waits for me in the morning.
The earth is energized from its drink.

Dominique LaRosa, Grade 4
Frontier Valley Elementary School, CO

If I Were the Colors

If I were the color yellow, I would be the sun warming a bird's egg
A bee flying in a hive
If I were the color white, I would be the moon making the earth cold
If I were black, I would be a total eclipse darkening the night sky

Hunter Frishkorn, Grade 4
East Evergreen Elementary School, MT

All About Kelly Morrison

I used to be a small one year old, but now I am 10 1/2 years old
I used to hate green olives, but now I think they are delicious
I used to despise the color grey, but now it is a decent color
I used to be a slow, wobbly runner, but now I am faster
I used to like furry, fluffy cats, but now I absolutely don't like them
I used to be extremely short, but now I am taller
I used to want a small, cute puppy, but now I have a big, playful dog
I used to hate mindless video games, but now I play them every day
I used to like bobbling head toys, but now I prefer stuffed animals
I used to not do homework, but now I do my homework almost perfect
I used to stay inside being lazy, but now I go outside more often
I used to have a small desk, but now it is much bigger
I used to like soothing country music, but now I enjoy hip-hop
I used to love chewy chocolate, but now I don't enjoy it as much
I used to be really clueless, but now I know what to do
I used to be afraid of pulling my tooth out, but now I pull it out easily

Kelly Morrison, Grade 5
Wheeler Elementary School, AZ

Finola — (My Dog)

She greets me with excitement when I walk through the door
Rolls on her back and scoots across the floor
Barks at anything or anyone she sees
When I sit down on a chair, she puts her paws on my knees
Fluffy, black and white
Is cute as can be
When you walk through my door…you will see!

How she runs around in our two-story house
As light as a feather, quiet as a mouse
When she falls down the stairs,
Or does something bad
You can't hear her, or tell that she's doing it…
Isn't that sad!?

Madelyn Burns, Grade 5
Windsor Charter Academy, CO

Devil

D is for devil which with tries to persuade.
E is for elephant which stomps all around.
V is for vein which pumps your blood.
I is for Irish with his big pot of gold.
L is for loopy like my sister.

Gabe Hamontree, Grade 5
Thomas Edison Charter School, UT

Jessie

J oyful
E nergetic
S hoe lover
S pazzy
I rish
E njoys bike riding

H ates getting up early
A ppreciates friends
W orks hard in school
O versleeps on weekends
R eads large books
T hinks dark chocolate should be a food group
H appy almost every day

Jessica Haworth, Grade 6
St Cyril Elementary School, AZ

Sunset

I watch you as you move away and cast your reddish glow
In the sky or on the water way, way down below
So wonderful and silent, you make jaws drop
And suddenly the moon appears way up top
You're almost gone as we say goodbye
And now the stars begin to fly
We loved you as you retreated back
Here comes darkness, here comes
Black.

Evie VanderWende, Grade 4
Wilson Elementary School, WA

Las Vegas

Past the long Vegas road
Between the tall casinos
Around me people stand
With a twinkle in my eye
Without crying I stand there laughing
Across the road I see people singing
With looking down I see the lights on the road
Upon my cheek a tear runs down
By the time I get home I will be sad
Until I go there again I will be happy

Monique Chavez, Grade 6
Fox Creek Jr High School, AZ

Math

Math is fun to do! Adding, subtracting, multiplying
dividing, whichever's best for you!

Easy to learn, easy to do, you'll love it, too!

Numbers get bigger, numbers get smaller.
It also makes you smart!

Jacob loves it, Nick loves it, I love it, too!

Nicholas Lakosky, Grade 4
Acacia Elementary School, AZ

Arizona

Drip, drop,
Drip drop,
Goes the sweat from my face,
The beams, the lasers of sun on my face.
My hat isn't working,
I don't think anything will.
There is no shade in this overheated place,
The burns, the scars on my skin and my face.
There is nowhere,
I repeat nowhere to go,
I would give just about anything for a little bit of snow.

Sean Casey, Grade 5
West Mercer Elementary School, WA

Ecosystems

E arthquakes shake
C actus nowhere to be found
O rganisms everywhere around
S andy shores as far as I can see
Y ellowstone Park's with long wet grass
S oil soft and soaked
T rees grow all over
E stuaries full of life
M igrating animals move south
S unshine makes it all live

Sarah Ann Budny, Grade 5
Hafen Elementary School, NV

Spring Is Coming

The trees are growing
the daffodils are blooming
spring is coming
Matthew Zabiliski, Grade 4
St Thomas the Apostle School, AZ

Shark Desert

Out of the wind
appeared the magical
shark desert,

the sand rolls
as the ocean,
the great dunes
crash down as waves,

dorsal fin rocks
drift around
searching for
a catch,

The sand spins around biting,
the heat pierces your skin
like shark teeth,

The scarce clouds
swim around in the sky
The desert
was as if it
were a shark.

Kyler Johnson, Grade 4
Kyrene De Las Brisas School, AZ

Christmas Is

Christmas is glorious
The Christmas tree's day
Presents so wondrous
All on display

Christmas is a spiritual thing
A day for family
The church bells ring
Time passing so merrily
Claudia Kosylak, Grade 6
Washington Intermediate School, CO

Girl in 5th Grade

There once was a girl in fifth grade
She was in a fancy parade
She tripped on a float
And fell in a moat
Now her destination is made
Sarah Hefferan, Grade 5
Copper Creek Elementary School, AZ

I Remember Lots of Things

I remember what I used to like,
but maybe I still do.
Or when I went on splash mountain,
the animals singing zip-a-de-do.

I remember walking to the beach,
with my friends across the street.
And when we went sun tanning,
the sun screen tickled on our feet.

I remember when my friend and I used
to buy friendship rings.
But gee I remember lots of things.
Emma DuChesne, Grade 5
Elger Bay Elementary School, WA

The Tiger

In the sun the tiger slumbers,
Dreaming of chases he remembers.
If you are looking at the beast,
You can tell he is dreaming of feasts.
Suddenly the sun is replaced,
And he awakes.
I wish I was far away,
So I don't become his prey.
Lora Collison, Grade 5
Firwood Elementary School, OR

Moon

Our dreams are guarded
by the Moon
he gives us a heads up
that it's time to sleep soon
He is the guardian
of the night
you can tell by his light
Guardian of my dreams
Cameron Von Halle, Grade 4
Scenic Park Elementary School, AK

One Day of Spring

It smells like dew
The grass is green
The sky is blue
Flowers blooming
To give off a great smell
Trees are green
And fresh as well
As the day ends
And the moon comes up
As the day ends
The last day of spring
Juliana Provencio, Grade 5
St Cyril Elementary School, AZ

Tears

He cries like a lost traveler
Alone in the woods
Like the wind on a stormy day
Out at sea.

He cries tears of loneliness
Out in the cold, dark dead of night.

Tears like the rain
In a fiery rainstorm
Like a starving child,
The baby lamb cries for its mother.
Elizabeth Fischer, Grade 5
Colbert Elementary School, WA

Silence on the Move

Silence is a shadow in the darkness,
silence is an old fashioned movie,
silence is a ninja about to attack,
silence is me.
Greg Spear, Grade 6
Badger Road Elementary School, AK

My Love for Soccer

Soccer, how do I love thee?
Let me count the ways.
Grass below and sky above
Outdoors in the bright sun
It is tense until the whistle blows.
Then, CHAOS explodes!
Running, sprinting, yelling, screaming
I give all I have on the field
Suddenly, one, two, three blows
The game is over, we have won!
Parents cheer, little kids run
Faces covered in Popsicle sweets
They hug me and say "Good job"
But all I can do is say "Thank you"
Then I go home and take a nap
When I am asleep, I think
How my life would be without
The love of soccer at my feet.
Emilia Zamora, Grade 5
St Cyril Elementary School, AZ

Friends and Family

Small little drops of tear
Shedding from the human flesh
in a small quiet oasis.
Love is in the air
Loving friend and family
Sharing and caring
Destini Hutchins, Grade 5
Hafen Elementary School, NV

In Winter

outside in the winter breeze
there is no one out in the cold
just the rush of wind laughs and laughs

the creek of wood sounds
the air as one door flies through the air
and all the children come through care of the parents

Synjon Lyons-Mandel, Grade 6
Walt Clark Middle School, CO

Everlasting Battle

Light is supposed to triumph over dark,
yet when light appears dark fights.
Why is this the ending?
Why does dark fight
yet light fights too.
Will light ever prevail?
For the dark is greedy
and power hungry,
so he scampers space
in search of power.
Shall they fight forever,
never to love again,
for all eternity?
Why is it dark fights
at the glimpse of light?
Does light intimidate him?
It not why does dark fight in anger?
Does your symbol of light,
remind him of a sin he committed,
long, long ago?
Why, why must you fight forever?

Chris Graves, Grade 6
Khalsa Montessori Elementary School, AZ

The Wind

             d
                n
                   i
      The   w
It flows gracefully and so sweetly
It brings the pride and effect of the o   e   n
                                        c   a
It makes the world go quiet
Then whistles a HAPPY tune in my ear
I feel as if I'm
              carried
                 across
                    the
                       sea
To a far off land
Where no one can find me.

Claire Surber, Grade 4
Olympic Range Carden Academy, WA

What Happens?

I wonder what happens when I pass away?
What will it be like?
When will I go?
Do I even know if I'll have a nose?
Will I go up?
Or will I go down?
Will I be happy, sad, mad, or all three?
Will there be colors or will it be blank?
Will I know everything and everyone?
Or will I still have to go to school?
Will any of these things ever really happen?
What will happen when I'm gone?

Desiree Ranshaw, Grade 6
Pope John XXIII Catholic School Community, AZ

Misunderstood Marsupial

I am a bear that is misunderstood,
Because I'd sleep all day long if I could.
In fact I am not a bear at all,
For if I was I'd be much too small.
I live down under in the outback; it's true,
I live right by my cousin kangaroo.
We carry our babies in pouches you see,
This makes hunting much easier way up in a tree.
You might call me boring or stupid or lazy;
But if I smell eucalyptus,
Watch out, I'll go crazy!
So if this poem gave you a scare,
Don't worry it's just me…the Koala Bear!!

Alex Ryan, Grade 6
Morgan Middle School, WA

Death

Death, dark and endless,
Or bright and infinite, peaceful or restless.

That is death.
Death is a word that has many meanings,
The end of life,
The start of a new one,
The start of pain
Or the end of problems.

Death is the most important thing in our lives;
Because, without death
No life would be.

Itzel Ramirez, Grade 6
Somerton Middle School, AZ

White

White is the color of snow that fills my heart with delight.
White is the color of hope that fills my heart with light.
White is the color of peace that makes my heart take flight,
And sends my heart soaring all through the night.

Enolie Perez, Grade 4
Jackpot Combined School, NV

Find the Seasons

Summer
Bathe in golden light.
Run through emerald grass,
Drink icy lemonade,
Look for autumn.

Autumn
Watch leaves fall,
Jump in piles of color
Breathe in crisp air.
Look for winter.

Winter
Stroll through hills of white,
Feel ice flowers touch your face,
Gulp hot chocolate by a fire,
Look for spring.

Spring
Wait for green buds to open,
Sit in new grass,
Climb to the tops of trees,
Find the seasons.

Melanie Schaffer, Grade 6
Southern Hills Middle School, CO

Music Dessert

Music is my ear chocolate.
I devour it like a cookie.
The instruments are my gummy worms,
the guitar wiggles into my ear.
The rhythm is my ice cream,
as my soul melts.
The flow is my cake,
with its spongy goodness.
Music is my ear chocolate.
Music is my dessert.

Katie Hughes, Grade 6
Walker Middle School, OR

Making Milk

The cows produce milk
And graze in the long thick grass
Making the best milk

Josh Lyman, Grade 4
West Woodland School, WA

Sun

The sun rises
like a loaf of bread.
It sits on the horizon
waiting to bake,
now it is time
for it to go to sleep.

Carly Reid, Grade 5
Gold Canyon Elementary School, AZ

Cold Night

The trees hide their faces in their leaves as the cold night creeps up on the forest.
The busy squirrels scouring the ground for nuts, scamper back
to their warm home to hide from the cold night.
The lone wolf that howls on the hillside stops his sad song
to run away from the night, now wishing he wasn't alone.
The wild stallions that gallop so freely and the old toad that lives in the pond,
run to escape the cold, dark night.
As the night whisks through the forest things grow silent.
As the time grows near, the night runs away.
The sun is up and is here to stay.
The trees stretch their branches and stand up tall.
The squirrels run around blissfully, chasing their own shadows.
The stallions gallop once again letting the warm sunshine kiss their shiny coats.

Monica Lopez, Grade 5
Eton School, WA

Waterfalls

Waterfalls sprinkle into a pond of serenity
It falls until infinity

Leading to an unknown world where anything can happen
Looking like diamonds falling in

I wish I knew the mystery
Of how you fall so rapidly, yet so gracefully, and your ancient history

You peacefully glide into the pond
You and the rivers share a tight bond

When the sun sets you glimmer like jewels
Into shimmering pools

When the sun rises you reflect the light
Sparkling oh so bright

You rush down with a booming sound
You know what no one else has found

When the day is done you give the animals a sweet song
To go to sleep for the night so long

Abby Peters, Grade 5
Foothills Elementary School, CO

I'm Ready

Sometimes people are lucky you see
They find someone who has not only changed their brain but who they are yet to be
Sometimes people have help to reach for the sky
Sometimes people need help to fly
Ms. Anderson and Mrs. Zeitler are two teachers I had
Leaving them will indeed make me so sad
Also Mrs. Reed and Mrs. Kraus are teachers who too changed my years
When I leave them I will be crying countless tears
After taking test after test
I now am ready to go on and do my best.

Renee Tesarek, Grade 5
Gibson Elementary School, NV

Life Is Like a Road

Life's journey's like a road,
you never know what's around the corner,
bumps and potholes are problems that can be avoided

Life is like an egg, it's very fragile
one small crack may ruin your breakfast
and in turn your entire day

Life is like dominos, when one falls it can
cause a horrible chain reaction. Your actions in life
can effect others, be cautious.

Life is like the weather
many days are rainy or gloomy
but there's always a sunny day to come.

Tomorrow is never the same as the day before
Live each day to the fullest

Brittney Knapp, Grade 5
Elger Bay Elementary School, WA

The Angry King

One fine day a starving king sat down to eat,
But on his plate appeared a baseball cleat.
"Get this junk from under my nose,
It belongs on someone's toes!"

He jumped up and down and threw a fit,
Although none could solve it.
The cooks were puzzled who had switched his turkey meat,
With someone's baseball cleat.

Then the knight saw a baseball star,
Running yet he hadn't gone far.
In his hand was some turkey meat,
Then he saw his two bare feet.

The king was enraged when he saw who,
Had switched his meal with a baseball shoe.
They had a fight,
It lasted all day and all night.

Then, "STOP!" yelled the king, "something is not right,
I just lost my appetite."

Brigham Larsen, Grade 5
Gate City Elementary School, ID

Horses

H yper and fast, graceful and beautiful.
O ne foot after the other, they run so fast.
R eally mysterious, majestic and muscular.
S o powerful and strong, soft and kind.
E normous and intelligent, tall, sweet and soft.
S un so hot beats down upon their shiny black backs.

Natasha Hunter, Grade 4
Conestoga Elementary School, WY

The Thing

When I was walking home one day,
Something big and fat blocked my way
I didn't even know what to say,
So I just stepped aside and went my way.

When I was walking to the store one night,
I met something furry and white
What a fright it gave me that night!

When I'm afraid and I turn white,
I like to pull covers over my head tight
It might look like a funny sight,
But that's how I do things
When I'm full of fright.

Jeremy Watson, Grade 5
Oak Creek Elementary School, OR

Matthew

You came to school one day
You looked like a girl that day
You sat in the corner all shy and not talking,
A few months later I talked to you while we were walking
I said "hello!" to you and I figured
That you were all configured
You were a boy and I didn't know
But you were still a kind fellow
Even though you were a little deranged
Thinking back now, we were both strange!

Keoki Warford, Grade 6
Hidden Creek Elementary School, WA

Dirty Dirt

It waits for someone to plant a sturdy tree
or a sweet-smelling flower where the dirt is,
But there is no one in sight.
If they do plant a flower or tree,
it will try its hardest to help it grow.
It hears something, something that
sounds like an oink, then a growl.
It strains to hear the sound as soft as the ocean waves
washing up on the beach.
The sound is coming this way!
It's a pack of wolves chasing a wild boar.
In the end the wolves win, but the boar tried its hardest.
Years pass, and there are weeds in the dirt.
It hopes that someone will pull them.
And now there are people, people that
have trees to plant.
They look the dirt over swiftly,
and don't notice the good things.
But they see the weeds
and walk away.

Jared Curtis, Grade 5
Barratt School, UT

Spring

The grass is starting to turn green,
The flowers are blowing nice and sweet,
The trees are turning green.
Berries are growing on berry bushes,
Apples are hanging from my apple tree,
Worms are crawling in my apples,
That are hanging on my apple tree.

Jonathon Tankersley, Grade 4
McCormick Elementary School, NM

Hurricane Katrina

Ever since Hurricane Katrina happened,
The world has changed.
People died
    and went to the sky.
Some survived
    wishing they could hide.
Women lost their babies,
And some men lost their ladies.
People drown
With a frown.
People tried not to cry
For the people who died.
They try to make that possible,
But it was too impossible.
All those people wish it was a nightmare,
But it was the real world.
The world has changed
When Hurricane Katrina
Went to the city of New Orleans.

Nayeli Castro, Grade 6
Somerton Middle School, AZ

Beyond This Door

Beyond this door
Are many worlds to explore.
I can't wait to dive in
But not to see a perilous fin.

When I go underwater it is the best
When I find that treasure chest.
But I don't go where it's dark
I might see a shark.

Wyatt Bryan, Grade 4
Larkspur Elementary School, CO

Football

Football
Three dimension
Throw it far
Soft on your hands
Fun

Colin Flannery, Grade 5
Copper Creek Elementary School, AZ

Sad

Tears
running
down my
face, My heart
pumping like a race,
Fingers clutched in a fist,
Wishes turning into mist,
Face turning red, Blood
boiling in my head,
Almost wish I was
dead.

TaylorEve M. Allan, Grade 5
Thomas Edison Charter School, UT

Up in the Morning

Up in the morning,
Have to take my bath
Then straight to school, and
English, science, and math.
The tardy bell rang,
My homework's done.
I have nothing to do,
Today should be fun.
Then all of a sudden
My teacher yells out,
Here's more work,
And without a doubt,
My day turns dark.
More work to do
My happiness leaves,
This makes me blue.
But I know it's good,
And I have a yearn,
I'll do my homework
And I will learn.

Zach Ugarriza, Grade 6
Meridian Middle School, ID

Fire

Fire
Hot, bright
Crackling, burning, sputtering
The world's greatest invention
Light

Zane Nelson, Grade 6
Cascade Middle School, WA

Oh Brother

My brother is mentally numb.
He sucks on his big thumb.
Every day and night,
He's not very bright!

Kyle Kelly, Grade 5
Hafen Elementary School, NV

Rainbow Appears

Wind blows very hard,
Starts to rain with big clouds there,
Then the rainbow comes.

Pooja Jaradi, Grade 6
Hazelwood Elementary School, WA

My Tree

In the meadow lies a tree,
That reaches to the sky.
It's hidden from all who can see,
And I know it's all mine.
My tree is thicker than all trees,
Taller than them too.
My tree tells me a lot of stories,
That I never knew.
I tell my tree all of my secrets,
I tell it all my thoughts.
I whisper to it to calm it down,
I comfort it a lot.
I like to get into its branches,
And doze off for a nap.
As I dream my tree holds me,
On its leafy lap.
We share a lot of special moments,
In the winter and in spring.
And every time I visit it,
I say, "I love you tree."

Braidy Mills, Grade 5
Sally Mauro Elementary School, UT

The Rat with the Big Hat

Once there was a rat
That had a big hat.
That rat with the big hat
Also had a big bat.

He found a cat
And hit it with the bat.
And that
Was the end of that!

Tyler Penner, Grade 6
Thomas Jefferson Charter School, ID

Movies

Movies, movies,
I love movies,
Some short,
Some long,
Some humorous,
Some action-filled,
Movies, movies,
I love movies.

Byron Judah, Grade 4
Colbert Elementary School, WA

The Friend I Lost

The friend I lost I loved,
The friend I lost loved me.
She helped me with my work,
She cut my hair and styled it.
My aunt and her friend went for a drive.
A truck hit them.
She died instantly.
Her friend got one broken leg
and was in the hospital for a couple weeks.
Her funeral was the saddest thing I have ever been to.

Bryce Dahl, Grade 6
Lolo Elementary School, MT

Soccer

Whooo the whistle blows
captains called, shaking hands, flipping coins,
we call that side, you get that.
Your team gets the kick now go back.
They run to the team
to tell them the news.
Coaches pump the spirits
high, positions placed 1,2,3, tweet, the game begins.
Later the game goes on.
Still last quarter 7 to 9.
The keeper misses 7 to 10.
The crowd goes wild, off-sides, penalty, foul,
person down, bad call
coaches yell 11-11 take the kick, pass, keeper misses
Yes's, cries, no's, and smiles
it's an emotional game when soccer is played
just about to kick the ball
when three whistles blows the game is done
it was exciting for everyone.

Ali Feathers, Grade 4
Acacia Elementary School, AZ

Light Is Shining!

You are trapped
no way to get out
free no more.
Trapped —
no light to show you the way.
The light is your life
hold onto it.
There is still light,
but you cannot see it.
The light is your heart
believe and you will have wings to fly.
No more will you be trapped
the light has called you,
listen to your heart.
Now fly to the wind for your life awaits you.

Geylee Chapman, Grade 5
Sangre De Cristo Elementary School, CO

To Be or Not to Be

"To be or not to be?" Asked the little boy to his weary father.
"To ask or not to ask?" he replied to his mischievous son.
The boy could not answer that one.
"To be or not to be?" He asked his tired mother.
"To do or not to do?" She said with a smile.
He knew this would take a while.
"To be or not to be?" The boy asked his friend Tommy.
"To speak or not to speak?" He said while skipping away.
This the boy could not say.
To be or not to be, is a question you just may
Have a conflict with someday.

Katie McGinnis, Grade 6
St Cyril Elementary School, AZ

Indian Chief

I smell fresh venison cooking on an open fire,
I hear a young squaw call to her children,
I feel the soft green grass,
I see the gentle eagle fly across the bright blue sky,
I taste the firm juicy apple.

Logan Escobar, Grade 5
Gold Canyon Elementary School, AZ

The Beach

When I go to the beach,
I feel the hot sun beating down on my tender skin,
making it as rosy red as a ripe cherry.
The cool of the shade and the heat rays from the sun
make for a competitive day.
Little waves with their soft, white hands,
brushing against my legs.
Millions of grains of sand laid before my feet,
like a soft towel coming out fresh and warm from the dryer.
The beach is a peaceful place.

Samantha Divelbiss, Grade 6
Connect Charter School, CO

I Want

Instead of sausage, bacon, and eggs with cheese
I want some cookies…oh please, please!
Or ice cream with a lollipop on top!
Maybe some cupcakes shaped like soda pop.
I want a shake with gummy bears inside.
I like it when the cream and pie collide.
Give me some frosting on top of a cake.
Give me candy that will give me a toothache.
I'd like a popsicle filled with ice cream.
That will make my frozen head scream.
I want some brownies filled with cookie dough.
Come on hurry up, don't be slow.
I don't care for veggies and fruit!
I want some cookies shaped like a flute.
What, what is that you say, I have a birthday party?
Well I surely don't want to be tardy.

Karly Rede, Grade 5
St Cyril Elementary School, AZ

Snow Is a Magic Land

Snow is sparkling on the ground and on the trees,
it's like a galaxy.
I go down a hill on my magic sled,
then I fall in a snowy land.
Brrr, I'm cold
I go home and say good bye
Magic Land.

Emma Hatfield, Grade 4
Hunters Glen Elementary School, CO

Tears

Tears
Sob. Cry
I don't know why.
Am I sad?
All I hear is
titter tatter
splish splash
titter tatter
could this day get any badder?
I want to YELL I want to SHOUT
I want to THROW things all about!
CRASH BANG BOOM
I send things soaring through the room
my eyes are sore
I want to ROAR
my eyelids slowly close
the room begins to decompose
silence silence
that's all I hear
there there not to fear
she gently wipes away my tears

Makella Brems, Grade 5
Diamond Canyon Elementary School, AZ

Snowflake

A beautiful fluffy cloud,
Soaring down from the black mystical sky,

Landing in my mouth,
Melting…melting,
Until there is nothing more, like a minty
white breath strip,

They heavily drift while shining like a
milky diamond…laying on the neck of a child
looking at his future in the free falling white flowers
dancing like a champion ballet dancer,

Caressing on my rosy red cheek,
Like my mom's eyelashes when she give
me a butterfly kiss.

Shane Caye, Grade 6
Lolo Elementary School, MT

Apathy

As the early dawn sun casts down golden rays,
She sat and thought of the mysteries of the world.
Why blue jays and blackbirds sang to herald the day,
Yet owls and whippoorwills serenaded the Moon.
How horses and dogs could sense your fear,
And cats could see through the veil of night.
But she thought that the greatest perplexity of them all
Was how all the creatures of the earth were so in tune with one another,
Yet we are ignorant, misunderstanding, and cruel.
How we take creatures, who know more of this earth than a warm home,
And put them in cages,
Their life in our apathetic hands.

Haley Manda, Grade 6
Gate City Elementary School, ID

Stephanie

Nice, caring, trustworthy
Who wishes to make a difference of which she will be proud.
Who dreams of becoming a singer.
Who wants to help the sick and the poor.
Who wonders what is there in the future for her.
Who fears death.
Who is afraid of people getting divorced.
Who wants to see her father happy again.
Who believes in God.
Who loves her family and friends.
Who loves to play soccer.
Who loves to go on trips especially family trips.
Who loves more than anything in the world her father
    that has been with her and is showing her the way of life.
Who plans to be a faithful wife.
Who plans to live the good life.
Who plans not to disappoint her parents.
Whose final destination is to reach adulthood with peace, happiness,
    and God by her side.

Stephanie Arciga, Grade 6
Patton Middle School, OR

Fork

A fork has many friends
But they're all jammed into one drawer
They talk day in and day out
But then one of the forks gets taken away
To get a facial
Getting food shoved into their faces
Then once they're done getting their facials
They get put in a sink where they can sit there for days
Next they get put in this machine that people call a "dishwasher"
It sprays them with soap and water
It gets really hot and steamy, they can't see anything
Once it's over people put them tight back with their friends.

Andrea Cody, Grade 6
Walt Clark Middle School, CO

My Mother

My mother is my mother that's why
I love her. I love her for having all
my brothers I love her for having me and
my sister. I know in my own mind
she's the great mother. I also love her
for going through tough times with me,
my brother and my father and whenever
I get a chance I run up to her and hug her.
I love my mother hopefully she will live
long enough to see me be a kind and
loving mother just like her. My mother.

Eva Egurrola, Grade 6
Avenue B School, AZ

Season by Season

Winter. Icy. Wet.
Crystal ice daggers of isolation drip down from caves.
Flakes of frozen water coat the ground one by one.

Spring. Thaws out the icy name of death.
Birds sing. Seeds grow.
Flowers bloom petal by petal

Summer. The synonym of heat.
Shade is the ultimate factor of survival now.
Shade brings joy creature by creature.

Fall. Flames.
Fire burns all around you yet you feel cool.
As each leaf changes color by color.

And as each season goes by
The world is changing
Season by season.

Patrick Michaelsen, Grade 5
Kyrene De Las Brisas School, AZ

List

Gorgeous views of the scenic lake
Teal, shiny fish leaping back and forth
Waves splashing side to side
Creating thundering crashes here and there
With the calm, peaceful mountains
Hardly visible hiding in the colorful sunset
Late in the evening with the bright white clouds
While I'm dreaming, lying on the green grass plains

Bhavani Kotha, Grade 4
Eton School, WA

Smith, Myth, Jog, Bog

Cheryl Barrel Smith,
She carried around a myth.
And when she went to go on a jog,
Of course, she had to do it around a bog.

Lindsey Paricio, Grade 4
Trails West Elementary School, CO

The Jackrabbit

A jackrabbit scurries through the air
Telling the other jackrabbits to beware
For a coyote follows close in pursuit looking for a snack
Not far behind him is the rest of the pack
The rabbit tells the rest of his friends to go hide
He promised luck would be on his side
He took off running across the floor
Behind him is the coyote who is maddened even more
The rabbit zooms and zips
The coyote right on his hips
Then the rabbit runs south
Just when the coyote was opening his mouth
It was too late for the coyote to see
So, he ran right into a Palo Verde tree
All the rabbits cheered and shouted
That brave jackrabbit was never doubted

Amelia Rosenberg, Grade 6
St Cyril Elementary School, AZ

My Upside Down World

My world's upside down,
Not right side up.
My shirt is on backwards;
My hair's sticking up.
Uh oh, here we go,
I can't feel my toes.
Oh, how I wish
My world was
Right side up;
For I can't find
My gardening stuff.
My flowers are wilting;
I can't find my peas.
Oh, someone please help me,
Please help me, peas!

Kelsey Tegan Dunlap, Grade 5
Edmonds Homeschool Resource Center, WA

Gray

Gray is the stormy clouds rolling across the lightning sky,
The strong wind is gray blowing by,
Gray is the beat of rain fallin' on the hard floor,
Gray is the emptiness without an open door,
A tornado is gray whipping like a belt across the plains,
A sadness inside you filled with pains,
An Arabian is gray galloping on a field that has no memories,
A dead rose is gray with the last drop of red falls off with ease,
Gray is the mist that hovers above the ground,
A hawk that screeches and a mouse without an open sound,
A rainy day that never stops,
A foggy day that never drops,
Gray is the color of impatience.

Dunia Baghdanov, Grade 6
Robert Frost Elementary School, OR

Slaves

Slaves
No shoes
And
Ripped clothes
Scared

Not free
And
Worked all day
And night
No
Reading
No writing

They don't have fun
At all
Mad
Sad
Don't run away
Or
You might be killed

Slaves
Viviana De Santiago Valle, Grade 4
Emerald Elementary School, CO

Hospital

Helping people from all the world
On the run the doctor goes
Saving people is their goal
People visiting their relatives
In a hurry the doctor goes
To every room in the hospital
Awesome! They saved people
Leaving the hospital
The ambulance goes again.
Stephaney Moreno, Grade 6
Fox Creek Jr High School, AZ

War

Although war is bad
It also has some good.
The men and women who protect us
Soldiers be thy name.
But for the families
And the soldiers that suffer
Their bodies may die,
But their souls will never,
For their soul goes to Heaven
And joins our Father.
So war is white and black
And the red, white, and blue.
Mark Monahan, Grade 6
Walt Clark Middle School, CO

I Am Happiness

I am happiness.
You know me for kindness.
My mother is love.
My father is caring.
I was born in respect.
I live in your hearts.
My friend is responsibility
We love to laugh.
My enemy is anger,
Because we never get along.
I am happiness.
Daniel Calaway, Grade 5
Desert View Academy, AZ

Spring

Spring is now here.
The stream is very clear.
Gardens have a lot of flowers.
Earth has a lot of showers.
Kaysheba, Grade 5
Whiteriver Elementary School, AZ

Below the Sea

Below the sea I like to swim
Beneath the water, crabs fight to win
Above the dolphins like to play
In water, fish are bright as day
Among the fish in the deep blue
from far away seals talk to you
Beside you swims a big blue whale
Behind he hits with his big tail
Up I go the day is done
Toward land I look I had so much fun
Lauren Burgess, Grade 6
Fox Creek Jr High School, AZ

Blazing Arizona

B eautiful scenery
L uscious mountains
A ncient artifacts
Z esty spices
I lluminating sunrises
N atural wonder
G rand Canyon

A mazing cacti
R attlesnakes
I ndian country
Z ippy roadrunners
O range skies
N ational monuments
A dventurous trails
Daniela Acosta, Grade 5
St Cyril Elementary School, AZ

Hi, My Name's Taylor

No one can buy my name.
It's deep inside me.
It's who I am.
It's too late.
I've had it since birth.
When someone
Calls it,
Whispers it,
Shouts it,
It cryfully whines
And begs
To look at the announcer.
When I see it on drawings,
It shows who I am.
Hi, I'm Taylor.
Taylor Denning, Grade 4
Brush Creek Elementary School, CO

Golden Dream Forest

golden dream moon
is magical from the sight
glazed with snow

high as you can see
the mountains are snowy white
with purple and blue

the trees whistle through
in the golden fall you hear
the trees whispering.
Samuel Less, Grade 6
Walt Clark Middle School, CO

First Time Ever

I shut my eyes tight
Then start to move forward
I'm frozen with fright
I slowly move backwards
I feel a gently push
I start to open my eyes
Then hear a crunch, a squoosh
And see to my surprise
A sparkling hill of snow
That shines and glistens and glows
I make half a triangle with my skis
And start to make my way down
Soon I'm flying past the trees
And making too much sound
I tumble, tumble
And soon can see
My grandpa smiling
Back at me
Elaine Kelly, Grade 6
Monforton School, MT

Brush College Creek

The pure water streams down
Down into the pond that waits below
The huge log that sits on top of the banks
Holding them up so they don't cave in.

The dim light casts shadows along the shallows
Making the sun dance off of the top.

Running water
Like tapping shoes upon a stage
Almost silent
I hear a gentle tearing noise
As a leaf floats down to find a new home.

I think to myself how long will this place be here?
In this place where everything is peaceful
But how come I feel slightly sad.

Jamie Foglesong, Grade 6
Walker Middle School, OR

Angels

Angels high in heaven watching over you,
Granting all your wishes making them come true.
For life is just a lesson for all of us to learn,
Just a simple little question to help us take our turn.
Spirits on the high watching from above,
Hoping all your wishes are made with care and love.
For this is just a lesson from me to the world,
Just a simple little question they'll answer in return.

Daniel Sutley, Grade 6
Eureka Elementary School, MT

Johnny Park

Like lonely wilderness
away from regular civilization.
Like clear blue skies and lush green grass.
Like brown dirt trails
some muddy, some dry.

Like birds in the trees
singing merrily to each other.
Like cars and trucks
out of sight and out of earshot.
Like clear bustling rivers
gurgling all the time.

Like cold air on my face
always refreshing me.
Like the shining sun
warming my body when I'm out of the shade.
Like knowing that I'm free
the best feeling inside of me!

Chance Conner, Grade 6
Walt Clark Middle School, CO

Candle Day

I brought my sandals and we're making candles.
Hey, look at that pouch.
I wish I could crouch. Ouch!
I wish it was colder and we were making holders.

Frances Lindner, Grade 4
B A Winans School, MT

Greek Myths

Greek myths are sometimes funny!
But sometimes they are sad.
Greek myths can make you sad or glad or mad!
In Greek myths there are fights
In them are also flights
There are heroes and villains and gods in all their might!
Zeus then Hera, Ares god of war, Aphrodite goddess of love,
Hephaethus fire guy, Hermes with Demeter at his side.
Poseidon, Athena, Apollo, Artimas and Hestia.
And at last comes Dionysus. Hey!!!

Hunter Knudsen, Grade 5
Windsor School, UT

Guess Who?

I am a crazy kid who likes skateboarding.
I wonder what I will look like in the future.
I hear alien ships landing on Earth.
I see me a pro skateboarder in the future.
I want world peace.
I am a crazy kid who likes skateboarding.

I pretend I'm the greatest person alive.
I feel good.
I touch the universe and all that's in it.
I worry about my family when they're hurt.
I cry when I get majorly hurt or break a bone.
I am a crazy kid who likes skateboarding.

I understand that drugs can hurt you.
I say never do drugs.
I dream to be a millionaire.
I try to be nice to family and friends.
I hope one of my family members never dies.
I am a crazy kid who likes skateboarding.

Jose Virgen, Grade 6
H Guy Child School, UT

The Sunset Ocean

The water is like cerulean diamonds glistening in the sun
and the sun is pineapple yellow, bright and juicy.
The pink and purple sky is being whipped smooth and silky.
The clouds are horsetails in the wind that cover part of the sun.
The air is salty and sweet and the water is cold
and wet like snow melting in my hands.
The sound of the waves rippling blow are eyes watching me
and the ocean is a silky blanket.

Deidra Wilstead, Grade 5
Sally Mauro Elementary School, UT

Stars

When the sun fades away
And night comes again
The sky is filled
With dots of bright light
That dance, sparkle, and fly
In the dark black night sky
If you wait long enough,
And look at the lights,
Sometimes they look back,
Twinkling and winking
Staring down at the Earth
Yet once again the sun will rise
The black sky will change to blue
And all the little dots of light
Will fade away
Waiting for another night
Clarissa Cooper, Grade 6
East Middle School, CO

Tempo of Time

I am changing,
The dog is playing,
And the years are going by.

The clock is ticking,
Time isn't stopping,
And I see myself grow over time.

Why, I say,
With a wondering sigh,
Why is time going by?

Because the clocks tick tock,
The tempo doesn't stop,
And the seconds keep going by.
Kendra Berry, Grade 6
Washington Middle School, WA

Maui

The waves bubble with rage
as off the island lifts the haze.
Tropical birds fly
in bright and sunny skies.
The sand is very soft
if you run it flies aloft.
Sunrises light up the sky
while rainbows glitter up high.
Katherine Gray, Grade 4
Eton School, WA

Rope 'Em Cowboy

Back up in the box.
Throw that rope around the neck.
Dally. Stop. Calf caught.
Hannah Burlingham, Grade 6
Hamilton Middle School, MT

Brown

If I were the color brown, I would be a rattlesnake hunting for my prey in the desert
If green, I would be grass blowing gently
If I were blue, I would be the waves in the enormous ocean of Oregon
If red, I would be a heart beating very fast
If I were gold, I would be a gold coin
Dallas Elrod, Grade 4
East Evergreen Elementary School, MT

An Ode to Backpacks

As I walk to school my backpack rests,
tightly clinging to my shoulders as a small infant might do.
I think of the books it holds the burden it carries for me.

Now I think we are our own backpacks
Carrying the textbooks of life.

At some moments I wish I were my backpack
Laying loose on a chair my zipper zipped tightly
Keeping my knowledge deep down inside
Unaware of all life passing 'round me
My straps, a bit worn from clinging to my carrier.

Only at some moments I wish I were my backpack
At other moments
The thought of being squished
Between human and seat
And then there's the washing machine
It's all just too vile.

Whether it's fun or it's hard
Whether it's light or it's heavy
I believe a backpack is the best gift of all
So if it's mine or it's yours here's an ode to backpacks all over the world
Amanda Greene, Grade 5
Barratt School, UT

Anonymous and Annoying

Oh, the things that bug me things I cannot stand.
Millions of them, but only five you will understand.

Girls with hair as dark as blood, and to add more of it a mullet too.
With hair longer than a meter stick!

Spiders. Flies. Two words. Nasty words. Words that make me quiver, and shiver.
Spiders with their long hairy legs exploring the wall. Heads. Anything they please.
Flies buzzing around like an out of tune guitar.
Why did God create these things?
No one knows but it creeps me out from head to toe.

CSAP, a stressing time. During CSAP you are like a mime.
You can't talk, or move about how you please. Complete silence.

Please, anything but slamming doors. I'd rather kiss a thousand boars.
Beds in hotels are always a mess. Bed bugs galore! I would rather sleep in a bath tub!
Leena Kaye, Grade 5
Greenwood Elementary School, CO

Spring Emerges Bringing All Life Forth

I hear the chirping of birds arriving home
Listening to the hum of all life growing back
The whisper of the breeze beckons the warmth
Spring emerges bringing all life with it

Bright and pleasant is the world around me
Clean from the grasp of winter's cold
Calm and at peace is nature at last
Spring emerges bringing all life with it

Fresh and dewy is the scent of outdoors
Fragrant and luscious are the flowers renewed
Sweet and tempting aromas drift about me
Spring emerges bringing all life with it

Ripe and sweet are goods freshly picked
Sugary candies are abundant and at hand
Light yet filling dishes are prepared at the table
Spring emerges bringing all life with it

Damp is the earth in the early hours of dawn
Cool is the breeze on my face
Fragile are the new plants bursting forth every more
Spring emerges bringing all life with it

Abby Schwendiman, Grade 6
Bella Vista Elementary School, UT

Little Babies

Babies are a precious gift
They are so tiny and cute
Infants are one of God's wonderful creations
When they look at you with big eyes
You can feel your heart melt
They are so trusting to break that would be awful
I love babies very much
I think they are the most innocent things on this Earth

Emily Scott, Grade 6
Mohawk Valley School, AZ

Camp Sight

Once I found a camp site
Far into the trees
The trees seem to talk
Swish, swish, swoosh
There was a little hut made out of logs
It came peeking out of the hill
It had a small home feeling
A couch, a kitchen, it's part of an army base
I pictured a face at the door
It said, "come to me, I am home"
In a little fire ring
I had some hot dogs cooking
Tsssss, hissss, tsssss
For there I plan to go

Alexander C. Gaddis, Grade 4
Brush Creek Elementary School, CO

Blue

Blue is the sky that hangs above us,
The waves whispering in the sea,
Blue is the sadness that clings above me,
But in some ways makes me happy,
Blue is like the glossy lake with no one swimming,
The fish swimming in the dazzling sea,
Blue is like the cool winter breeze,
The snowflakes frolicking,
Blue is the moon that brightens the night,
The wonderful color of the sea,
Blue is the color that inspires me,
The brightness of the sea,
Blue is the color of the butterflies wings,
The color that everyone sings,
Blue is the color of eyes I dream.

Kjersten Holliday, Grade 6
Robert Frost Elementary School, OR

Light and Dark

A speck of sand consumed in darkness
Alone in the emptiness.
No longer will it endure Eternal loneliness
For now is the time of creation.
Light expanding within that grain
Illuminating space
Beginning the first second of life.
Radiant clouds of dust swarm upon the vast area.
Transparent clouds
Condense into clumps drifting aimlessly.
A luster emerges from its sleep within the clumps
Positioning itself
Inferno nearly devouring the white dwarf
Mass penetrating its own confinement
Heat grasping the outer rim
Time frozen
Luminescent star tearing through time
Engulfing light from nearby giants
Burst of light escaping the consumer
A nursery of newborns
Replaces the dark reality of reincarnation

Manbir Wazir, Grade 5
Khalsa Montessori Elementary School, AZ

The Moon

Thy moon glides across thy spacious skies,
Gleaming with talent to catch thy eyes.
Natural night light to a fawn,
Arrives by sunset, leaves by dawn.
Accompanied with glittery stars,
Asteroids and even Mars;
O, thy moon, never worn
You slip away from me by morn.

Aline Diaz, Grade 5
Jane D Hull Elementary School, AZ

The Last Bull Ride

The crowd waits with baited breath,
hoping,
just hoping
they young rider will not be thrown.
He sits tall on the huge brown bull,
waiting for the buzzer to go off,
it does, and so does the bull
1,2,3,4,5,6,7,8,9,10 seconds go by,
but to the young man they are like
Hours,
Days,
and weeks
the buzzer sounds again,
the young man jumps off and runs
for joy,
happiness and enthrallment
he has lived his dream.

Kaitlyn Bernier, Grade 5
Scenic Park Elementary School, AK

The Car

Something flashes,
polished steel,
tinted windows,
spinning wheels,
making marks upon the road,
of tire tracks,
like secret codes.
Shining metal,
darkened glass,
fleeing wheels,
far too fast.
It has everything
but grace;
painting fear on a mustangs' face.
Rolling wheels,
take away
the modern monster of today…

Molly McGinnis, Grade 5
Calvert Home School, ID

Under Pressure

I have the ball. I move toward the hoop.
People all around…watching, waiting.
They get closer. What do I do?
Sweat is running down my
face. So much pressure, so
little time. I jump. I hear a
swoosh. The crowd, they
scream. Scream with joy.
No more pressure.
So much time.

Joseph Rothlin, Grade 6
St Joseph School, WA

High Mountains

Rocks appear
as dark, misty,
rough,
hard
stones.
The pink
shining pillars
look beautiful.
This valuable
glowing top
shows everyone
how large
it seems.
See
the delightful sky
looking
over
the mountains.

Umar Templeton, Grade 4
Audubon Elementary School, CO

My Friend

Meaghan
Pretty, fun
Playing, loving, caring
Basketball, football, dog-lover, kind
Joking, running, sleeping
Charming, beautiful
Friend

Chelsea Nipper, Grade 5
Copper Creek Elementary School, AZ

Miss B.*

I have a teacher she's so mean
She won't even let us sing
Each time we go to P.E.
She holds us back 'til a quarter to three
And when we go P.E.'s all done
As you see we have no fun
Math really is no help
Each time I do it I want to yelp
You see I want to change schools
But to my parents it's against the rules
Writing time is a bore
Because my hand gets really sore
Recess time is the best
'Cause then our brain can get a rest
The homework she gives us is a pain
Each time I do it I have a migraine
I would rather be insane
Than go to Miss B., who is a pain

Anjelica Chandler, Grade 5
Thomas Edison Charter School, UT
*Dedicated to Miss Bidstrup

Cry of the Moon

An eerie song
Of a nocturnal chant
A wild wailing
Dominating the moonlight
A pride that shadows
A worrier limping
The agony sealed
Deliberate wounds
A rhythm of blood
Dripping down
A primordial beast's face
Undulating on the ground
The rays of the moon
As the woods of fury
Become the silent of all

Cassie Eaton, Grade 6
Liberty Middle School, CO

Yellow Is…

a warm, fuzzy baby chick
the morning sun shining on my face
huge helium balloons
my cute little golden puppy
a field of tulips

Christina Rash, Grade 5
Wheeler Elementary School, AZ

Kitten

K ind, cute, and cuddly.
I rresistible and small.
T hey like to scratch.
T hey like milk a lot.
E ating meat all the time
N apping all the time.

Alex Carson, Grade 4
Conestoga Elementary School, WY

Zoo*

Going to the zoo
To see a cockatoo
The birdhouse is quite warm
With feathery charm
Polly parrot squawks
She really cannot talk
Oh what fun it is to feed the birds
The penguins are delights
Birdie smells, birdie smells
I say what the hay
Oh what fun it is to fly
Too bad you're in a cage
Yeah

Marcel Colvin, Grade 4
Eton School, WA
*Sung to the tune of Jingle Bells

What Makes That Feeling?

What makes me scared?
Being alone in the dark,
Thinking the Boogie Man is real,
And if other things are real,
Watching scary movies,
Thinking if the things in scary movies are real.
What makes me cry?
Thinking I'm less than my little and big sister,
My parents yelling at each other,
My love life.
What makes me lonely?
Having no friends,
When nobody talks or hangs out with me,
Being alone in the world.

Elizabeth Nguyen, Grade 6
Hazelwood Elementary School, WA

What If

What if you lived in a zoo?
The cows went nay the horses went moo
What if you had a pet monkey?
That took all your clothes
And ate your new puppy
What if one night you got much taller?
And your hat didn't fit because your hair got longer
What if your mom got a diamond ring?
And she got mad because you let it drop with a cling
What if you told a lie to your brother?
Then he got mad because you used all the butter
What if you read a book where everything was upside down?
Then you realized it was as real as a clown
What if one day you had a spelling bee?
Then you realized that you had not studied at all?
What if that happened to you?
What if that happened to me?
WHAT IF

Sawyer Smith, Grade 4
Rowland Hall-St Mark's School, UT

Love Is Everywhere

Love is everywhere,
No matter where you are;
Some people love dogs,
Some people love cats
Some people love each other,
But love is all that counts
Some people love birds,
Some birds love other birds,
Some dogs love cats
Some cats love dogs,
No matter what you are
Love only counts

Kali Komer, Grade 6
Pope John XXIII Catholic School Community, AZ

I Am From…

I am from fighting with my brother.
I am from the pollution of Modesto, California.
I am from the swallowing of a penny.
I am from being in a police car.
I am from not knowing a sister.
I am from meeting outrageous friends.
I am from madness and gladness.
I am from small apartments.
I am from departing and meeting friends.
I am from deodorant.
I am from hating and loving.
I am from the Raiders.
I am from wrestling with my uncle.
I am from slamming the door on my uncle.
I am from petting my dog.
I am from loving my whole family.

Bruce Arnett, Grade 5
Evergreen Elementary School, OR

Creature

As a rugged jagged creature climbed,
With helium light paws,
Still used razor tipped claws,
To feel at home in his new environment

As a rugged jagged mountain he challenged,
He made his rugged body,
Fit in with the rugged world,
And so lived the rugged little creature

Ty Clark, Grade 6
Pope John XXIII Catholic School Community, AZ

Sun and Wind

Sun
Hot, yellow
Burning, beaming, steaming
Sky, high, cold, white
Hurrying, fast, rushing
Blowy, brrr
Wind

Andre Aragón, Grade 5
Escuela Bilingüe Pioneer Elementary School, CO

Seasons

Snow in the field and trees without leaves
Snowflakes falling and fog covering the buildings
Wind making grass shake and cars going by
Snow crunching as I walk through the snowy field
Relaxed and cold in the middle of winter,
I feel like time has stopped.
Pine needles and blossoms on a small plum tree
Roses beginning to bloom, patch of grass filled with clover
A tree covered with bright green leaves
School has ended and summertime has begun.

Matthew Pride, Grade 4
Lincoln Elementary School, AZ

My Baby Brother Dylan
I have a baby brother,
He's really hard to leave,
When he cries his heart out,
It's one of my big peeves,
When he wakes up,
In the morning gleam,
He gives me a hug and a kiss,
He's a cup of love it seems,
When it's time for breakfast,
He sits up with a smile,
'Cuz every time he eats something,
It's always in a pile,
When breakfast is over,
It's time for fun and play
But when It's time for the school bus,
The fun is done,
And big sis is gone for the day.
Vanessa Fallin, Grade 4
Gause Intermediate School, WA

The Hourglass
The hourglass rolls on by.
Sometimes it wishes it could fly,
high above the sky again and again
it's all it's ever been,
is an hourglass wasted in time.
Bryce Mintz, Grade 6
Meridian Middle School, ID

My Life
As I walk the path
Of my life surrounded
By trees as straight as a knife

The trees as quiet as
Can be everything seems
So still to me

I'm here for a time
For a reason
For a purpose

The path may be crooked
Or straight each is different each
With a clean slate

Which path will I take is
The unknown whichever I travel
I'm not alone

As I walk the path of
My life
Trinity Frazee, Grade 6
Barbara Bush Elementary School, AZ

My Grandmother
A pale ghost afraid of colored faces
The sneaky fox in the fairy tale of old
The youthful eyes in the wrinkled face
Generous woman who just loves to talk
A child who was forced to be tough
My beloved grandmother who teases me
My savior, my angel, my blissful hope
Emma Glavish, Grade 6
Cascade Middle School, WA

Spider
Black and orange
Black as coal
Orange as a pumpkin
Big and hairy
With long legs
With orange stripes
With a web as big as a door.
Riley Richardson, Grade 4
Wilson Elementary School, WA

People
A person,
shapes and sizes,
lives and grows,
slowly,
an individual.
Sarah Murphy, Grade 6
Fox Creek Jr High School, AZ

The Sun Will Come
Waiting here for the sun to come
Faith to rise, hope to run
Looking out my big glass window
Waiting for the sun to come
Doodle on the clouds above
Wishing that you'll see a dove
The sign of peace, will clear the skies
So the sun can soon rise
Without the peace
The sun won't show
So back to bed we there by go
Hoping that the sun will shed
Whether or not our souls are pure
Tells when the sun will appear
Now it's time for the sun to rise
Up, up it goes…now it's day
Now it waits with open ears
For someone to say
Thank you sun for the day
Now here, so come again
Now that you know our souls are pure
Katie Bryant, Grade 6
Barbara Bush Elementary School, AZ

Butterflies
Red, blue, pink butterflies
Flying above the tall grasses
Lady bugs and spiders hiding within
— Landing on pedals of daisies,
Red, blue, pink butterflies
How beautiful!
Mary Beckham, Grade 6
Wallace Elementary School, AZ

Roses
A rose is not but a rose
But when watered and fed
It grows and grows
Until it is dead

They flourish in the field
Like a bright road sign
Their colors say yield
Aren't I divine?
Jamie Ryerson, Grade 5
Towne Meadows Elementary School, AZ

Me
Jessica
Caring, curious, honest, nice
Sister of Alex
Learner, smiles, hard worker
Joy when singing
Hot cocoa every day
Friendship, encouragement, laughter
Hunger, pain, ghost
Grandparents
Cheyenne
Woyak
Jessica Woyak, Grade 6
Miller Elementary School, WY

My Flowers Are
My flowers are

unique, daisies
a beauty of life
colorful
what makes people's eyes glow
a symbol of happiness
as pretty as the moon
as bright as the sun
peace on Earth
as sweet as chocolate
joy to my garden

These are my flowers.
Anjali Daulat, Grade 4
The Meadows School, NV

Never Again

I woke up this morning and saw rain pouring.
I could also hear my sister snoring.
The whole morning was boring.

I finally awoke completely with a thunderclap.
So I got ready and changed in a snap.
When I got home from school I was so worn out I took a nap.

I was so tired that day
I made a vow.
Never again will I stay up all night.
Not even if a show gives you a good fright.
Will I keep my promise?
I don't know how.

Viviana Torres, Grade 6
Somerton Middle School, AZ

Soccer

S erious concentration is needed.
O bedience to your coach and players.
C ritical thinking is needed to keep up with the game.
C reate plays to help score goals.
E veryone needs to participate even the coach and fans.
R ely on your team to help you get through hard times.

Connor Brown, Grade 6
St Cyril Elementary School, AZ

Hockey for You!

H acking the puck for a icing
O ver and under the other players' sticks
C areful not to lose the movement
K icking hard to skate
E very player tries their best
Y elling and cheering your team on

I t's time to win
S peeding down for a pass

T ripping all opposing teams
H elping your teammates with a check
E rasing the other team's lead

S peeding up the ice
P roceeding to the other net
O ver the slashing stick
R eady for a goal
T earing the puck away from the group

F aster and faster you skate
O n the ice for short shifts
R acing for the points

M eeting a player face to face
E lation! We won

Preston Franck, Grade 6
Monforton School, MT

Seasons

When I look through my hard glassed window
and I see the stormy, hard blowing snow rushing down,
I feel a cold strike of shiver going straight down my body
and through my veins.
As I lay back down in the hot as lava morning
I stream to the air as the breeze
comes wishing through my hair.

Kaylen Solomon, Grade 4
Acme Elementary School, WA

Skiing

When you ski you need to turn, stop, and slow way down
To avoid hitting the ground.
You definitely don't want to hit a tree,
Or fall and injure your knee.
If you go down a hill that's steep
And it seems frightening, please do not weep,
Just take big "S" turns and you'll be fine,
When I did that my skiing experience was divine!

Kayla Newby, Grade 6
Desert Mountain School, AZ

Sunrise

Sunrise is beautiful and calm
Not too dark and not too light.
Sunrise is not too cold
or not too hot.
Sunrise is so colorful
with your red, pink, and orange.
That's what sunrise is all about.

Nicolas Molina, Grade 5
Sangre De Cristo Elementary School, CO

Dream Builder

I write a message on the sand
To the golden fish in the silver sea…
A message that hunters will understand!
Soon the great fish will belong to me.
For though the fish may ride the waves,
The power of this wish I cast into the silver sea
Will catch the golden fish.

Julia Nguyen, Grade 5
Fulton Elementary School, CO

My Dream

In my dream I scream!!
I was beaned by a ball!
I was mad I was sad
Tears came out of my eyes
I tried not to cry
I saw no one, the world was blank like a plank
My dad woke me up, I felt better!

Andy Charles Kinn, Grade 6
St Anne School, WA

Pain

Pain will sometimes drive you insane
When you're in pain you will never feel the same
So listen closely I ain't playing games
You might feel pain when someone calls you names
Or if someone breaks your heart someone you loved from the start
You never wanna part or someone you loved died you feel all this hurt inside
Because you thought they would always be by your side
But now they are gone you try to move on but everything goes wrong
Or you might have gotten a bad grade on a test you might be upset 'cause you're not the best.
So you're confidence just becomes less and less.
You might think you are not that cool so you just feel like a fool.
Pain it's not a wonderful thing but you can overcome pain just know you're not lame.
So don't be ashamed just remember not everyone is the same.
　　　　PAIN

Deven Williams, Grade 6
Jenkins Middle School, CO

Praying Mantis

Quickly, with strong, green arms, a green blur flies from his egg sack and grasps his prey.
Delicately he hides his food in a radiant marigold so no other ravenous insect will find it.
Then, he flies swiftly, like a falcon, in search of a place to live.
Landing on a creamy narcissus, he claims it for his own.
But a dark shadow creeps forward and tackles the extremely large insect.
The beautiful flower is already occupied by a ferocious family of spiders, darker than midnight.
Seeing the red hourglass on their stomachs, the mantis tries to look for a safer place to dwell.
The gigantic, multicolored insect lands on a tea rose so softly that the petals do not even sway.
Even so, an inhabitant detects the mantis' approach.
With a flurry of wings, a wasp flies out of the harmless looking flower and stings the bulky mantis many times.
Tattered and torn, the mantis flies back to the uninhabited marigold.
He has finally found a home.

Molly Cole, Grade 6
Colbert Elementary School, WA

One Small Knight

The knight said bravely to his men; "We must attack today!
Our enemy is getting close, I think they're on the way!"
The men they yelled and stomped and screamed and hyped themselves all up,
But no one noticed one small knight, as quiet as a pup.
He didn't want to go to war, he didn't see the point
Of stabbing swords through peoples' heads and dismantling their joints.
He trudged behind the other knights looking sad and grim
Until another man looked back, and finally noticed him.
"What the heck is going on?" The other knight cried out.
"The time is here, the time is now! Don't sit around and pout!"
"Buy why fight?" the small knight said, "When instead there can be love?
Things instead like rainbows and flowers and angels from up above!"
"This is all nonsense!" the other shouted, and pushed the small knight on
To where they would fight and kill and destroy, and probably be dead by dawn.
But when they got there and the field was bare
Except for the enemy's knights, they just gave up and all went home, forgetting about the fights.
What made both sides just stop, you ask? And leave without a shout?
Well, while they were arguing with that one small knight, they had forgotten what the fight was about.

Kenzie Yoshimura, Grade 6
Hood River Middle School, OR

Little Kid Life

Seeing myself in a Santa suit
With the smell of dry grass, leaves
And cotton surrounding my little kid life

I am also warm in my hood
Stepping on grass and some wood
With a street and a house in the back
I wonder what's for snack

I see my mom taking this picture
But I want to know why am I in this suit
My tot life was sweet and I sure loved to leap
But it's over and I loved it

Mark Ault, Grade 6
Walt Clark Middle School, CO

Black and White

Black is the child
White is the child
Red is the swing set that they used to not share

Black is the man
White is the man
Brown is the bench that they used to not share

Black are the people
White are the people
Blue and green is the Earth that they now share

Julia D'Amico, Grade 6
Southern Hills Middle School, CO

Goodbye Dravon*

Dravon I'll remember your smile and your laugh;
your cuteness and all
I will never forget the love that we share
and I will forget someday
the day we lost your beautiful face

Bethany Hernandez, Grade 5
Sequoia Village School, AZ
*Dedicated to Dravon Reed Hutton

Writing Stories

I am a champion of writing stories
You can spread your imagination beyond its limit.
Making it go up, down, right and left
You put it on paper and let it amaze everyone.

I think like characters that I create
I pretend I'm there and what I would do.
If the character is sad or happy, I am too.
That's how I write stories.
You can do it too.

Andrea Boettcher, Grade 4
Acacia Elementary School, AZ

Trust

Trust, to feel trust is to know it's okay,
To listen to someone with more than your ears,
To feel as if people can depend on you as you depend on them,
To look more carefully than usual this is to feel trust.

Makayla Dean, Grade 6
Hidden Creek Elementary School, WA

No Time

There is no time,
I have to go!
I'm going to be late,
When the first bell rings.

Get out of my face,
I'm like in a race.
So, get out of my way
or I'll push you away.

I really like to push,
Especially, when I'm in a rush.
So, I'm here, there, and all over the place.
You better not make me late!
Or you will be sorry.

No time, no time.
I have to hurry!
I better wake up early,
Or there is never time.

Ashlee Montoya, Grade 6
Spring Creek Elementary School, WY

Four Seasons

Seasons come seasons go
All our fun blown away
No more swimming
No more making snowmen
No more jumping in the leaves
No more flowers
It feels like they will never come again
But now we wait for the next four seasons

Taylor O'Hara, Grade 6
Fox Creek Jr High School, AZ

Blue

Blue is the sky, and my favorite color,
And blue is soft.
Blue is the taste of cotton candy.
Chocolate chip cookies and Reeses smell blue.
Games make me feel blue.
Blue is the sound of eating and talking
Blue is ice cream, clouds, and the ocean.
Fishing is blue.
Crying is also blue.
Blue is the sound of success.

Trent Dashney, Grade 6
Patton Middle School, OR

Forest

I see trees
It tastes like sap
It smells like cedar
It sounds like rustling leaves
It feels like jagged rocks
Forest

Sara Anderson, Grade 6
Heath Middle School, CO

Little Puppy

My little snuggle puppy
Oh you just went for a walk
Come to me, warm up on my lap
Sleep little snuggle puppy
Lick my hand, lick my face
Play around all over the place
It's time for fun, time for games
For this you don't have to be tame
Oh puppy, I love what you do
My little snuggle puppy I love you.

Mallory Thorp, Grade 5
Lister Elementary School, WA

Blue Is…

as peaceful as the bottom of the ocean
the beautiful brightness of the sky
blueberry pie and the color of my tongue
the warmth of my room
the joy of a bluebird singing

Emma Perry, Grade 5
Wheeler Elementary School, AZ

Doll

My grandma once gave me
A beautiful doll
Its face as fragile as porcelain
It was made by her
With silky soft fabric as green as dill
It held a small handkerchief
Made from lace
To touch it makes my hands tingle
She had a small beauty mark
Upon her face
The reason I love it
Is because she had it
And she gave it to me
Now it sits
Upon my dresser
Starring blindly
Into the darkness
Bat, bat, batting
Her eyelashes

Katie Andrews, Grade 4
Brush Creek Elementary School, CO

Winter

As I ready to step outside,
I look at the picture before me.
Snow glistens on the ground
as it reflects the sun's rays.
No one has been out yet;
no one to disturb this perfect picture,
to disturb lonely, yet comforting, silence;
silence that fills the air.
Evergreens sway back and forth
under the weight of sparkling branches;
glistening, shining, beckoning.
Do I step into the untouched,
and break the silence?
Or do I leave the picture
untouched and unbroken
for others to feel like me?

Dara Mysliwiec, Grade 6
Connect Charter School, CO

Colors

I have a small hamster named Bear
He has a lot of hair
He is very fat
Afraid of that cat
When it chases him he gets a big scare

Danielle Schulz, Grade 6
Bright Beginnings School, AZ

Fourth of July

Fourth of July
The crackle of red, white, and blue
The smell of fire sparklers
The ooo, aaah of people after the set off
The warming of your hot dog
Fourth of July

Kelsey Wood, Grade 4
Coal Creek Elementary School, CO

Collecting

Collecting for
seven years,
twelve boxes
that equals,
all full of rocks,
gems, crystals,
and minerals.
All this filling
my room
and the rest.
Someday I hope
to become a
famous geologist.

William Laborin, Grade 4
Acacia Elementary School, AZ

Today Is My Lucky Day

Today is my lucky day,
my brother is off shoveling hay.
I'm all alone in the house,
not bothered even by a mouse.
I'm gonna have a party night,
then I'm gonna start a fight.
Once my parents come home,
they're gonna lock me in a dome.
As I sit alone in my dome,
I wish I could go to Rome.

Jared Banta, Grade 6
Cedar Ridge School, UT

Cheetah Sky

At night
cheetahs stalk the stars
and hunt the planets.
In the day
they pounce
on the sun.

Kiley Barz, Grade 4
Wilson Elementary School, WA

Penguin Dreams

Penguin, Penguin flying high
flying high into the sky.
This may not be what it seems
but that's what a penguin dreams.

Brock Holmes, Grade 6
Hamilton Middle School, MT

Dino

That odd looking dino
That looks like a rhino
Sat by the water one day
Eating green leaves
Said T-rex, that terrible beast
Has not taste in the least.
As T-rex picked up a lizard
And ate it.

Brady Ulrich, Grade 4
Summit Elementary School, UT

Fire and Ice

Fire is powerful and strong
Ice is cool and beautiful
Spark, flame, bonfire, inferno
Crystal, flake, icicle, glacier
Warm, hot, burn
Cool, cold, freeze
Fire, ice, meet defeat
Wood, water.

Micah Brady, Grade 5
St Mary's School, ID

Dogs

About dogs is a fun feeling
past my knees is how tall they are
Inside they come sometimes like a person walking in
Outside they stay so they can play with each other
Until night falls then inside they come to sleep so no more fun

Monique Rubio, Grade 6
Fox Creek Jr High School, AZ

Pink Pig

I am a pink piggy
I hear many animals in the farm
I want to be free
I am a pink piggy

I feel really happy to be a little cuddly pig
I touch the dirt in my hooves when I walk
I cry oink! oink!
I am a pink piggy

I understand that I have to be in a farm
I dream to have parents, mine were killed
I try to not be sad
I hope I get to see my new family
I am a pink piggy

Haydee Solorio, Grade 6
Wallace Elementary School, AZ

Examples

Example is leadership on a low caring day
Example is a leap of faith on the way
Example is teaching others how to play
Example is teaching others how to have a good day.

Examples are one for love
Examples are like flying like a dove
Examples are like giving nightmares a shove
Examples are lights from above.

Examples are for what?
You and all and haute and haute.

Dallon Lines, Grade 5
Discovery Plus Academy, AZ

The People Zoo

If you were to visit a people zoo,
on display would be people like you.
Dark skinned, light skinned,
tall, short, fat, thin.
But there's still more about the people zoo,
there's cafes and a gift shop too.
Animals of all kinds would come to stare,
at all the people locked up in there.
If you were to visit a people zoo
you'd be locked up and stared at too.

Wyatt Estes, Grade 4
Spring Creek Elementary School, WY

Spike

I'm so soft
So soft indeed
I can play tag
I can climb trees
I can cuddle and snuggle
With that kid I see
So don't you come and bother me please
'Cause I'll be asleep
In perfect peace

JC Hanson, Grade 6
Cottonwood School, MT

Zoom In

In the Big Picture you can see a lot
Not a lot of detail on the far side
But you can see a lot around you
Look at the things around you
You can tell it is far, but beautiful

Go closer up you can see the detail
Up on the surface you can also sense what is underneath
You can see less around you but it is better
Look at the details that you see what it feels like
Look at the things that matter

Close up you can see every little detail
Every seam, every little cut
You can't see a lot around you but it is better
You can see everything in another way
Little things make the difference

Alyssa Hancock, Grade 6
Blanco Elementary School, NM

Washington, D.C.

The capitol of our nation,
Stretching out like freedom itself,
Housing memories of the great people
Who helped shape this country.

Like indentations to run fingers over,
Instilling terrible, or wonderful scenes
in the mind's eye.

Like dedicated people who work
so hard
to become who they are and
to bring peace and justice.

Like the astral feeling
of what the eternal flame really is,
for the ones who feel the pain, the sorrow, and the joy,
that resides in Washington, D.C.

Jasmine Schafer, Grade 6
Walt Clark Middle School, CO

I Am From...

I am from Blackfoot and Cherokee.
I am from meeting and Bible.
I am from sawmill and sawdust.
I am from Grant's Pass and California.
I am from *Boomerang* and *Flintstones*.

I am from nail-in-foot and dog bite.
I am from baseball and football.
I am from fixing things and stacking wood.
I am from Rozy and Cheetow.
I am from candy bars and cookies.
I am from Hot Wheels and bikes.

I am Matthew Tyler Dominguez.
Matthew Tyler Dominguez, Grade 5
Evergreen Elementary School, OR

Living the Life

What happens when you have all the fame?
Does it become a big pain?
Do people want your autograph?
Do they want your photograph?
Does the paparazzi often annoy you?
Do you often want to sue?
Does fame bring money to buy jewels?
Does fame bring money for people to drool?
Do you get to sing lots of games?
Will your life ever be the same?
Courtney Ferguson, Grade 6
Blaine Middle School, WA

I Am...

I am thankful and hopeful
I wonder if I will ever travel to Hawaii
I hear Hawaii coming closer to Washington
I see myself swimming with turtles
I want to be able to live with my aunts.
I am thankful and hopeful

I pretend to be a teacher
I feel that my aunts are taking care of me
I touch an imaginary turtle in my sleep.
I worry that some body will take my brother and I.
I cry when I hear my mom's favorite song
I am thankful and hopeful

I understand getting to Hawaii costs money
I say I will get to Hawaii some day
I dream about at 4.0 G.P.A.
I try to keep my G.P.A. at least at a 3.0.
I hope college is an option for me.
I am thankful and hopeful.
Anthoni L. Pryor-Brooks, Grade 6
East Valley Intermediate School, WA

The Day Will Come for a Change

The day will come for a change
Six long tiring years pass without knowing
Pass
One day is all it takes to clear it up
One
I can feel it bubbling inside me with a rage and pain
The time will come for a change
Change
If one day is all it takes
One
Why didn't it happen six years ago
Why
I need a change, a change, one change
One
The time will come for a change, it will come
The time grows rougher, the times get stronger
I get weaker and weaker I get
I cry, I cry, I cry day after day after day I get weaker
I wait day after day after day I wait
I know it will come no longer hate no longer pain no longer suffering

The Day Will Come for Change!!
Guadalupe Avalos, Grade 6
South Middle School, CO

In the Forest

I can see the sap frozen in time
I hum as the soft green light shines down upon me
I can hear the gentle breeze passing through every leaf on the trees
The chirping of bird's songs
Rings throughout the forest
I can taste the perfume from the
Sweet flowers in the air
Pine and cedar fills the air
It feels like nature is a part of me
I know this is the place for me.

Ben Sechrest, Grade 5
Eton School, WA

Dishes

Dishes to the ceiling dishes to the wall,
my my, I think all the dishes just might fall.
I'm quite tired because you see,
the stacks of dishes are taller than me.
I'm surrounded by these horrible things,
they pop up out of nowhere just as if they were horrible jumping beans.
They jump to the left, and they jump to the right,
they might even jump out of sight.
Then all of a sudden...
BANG! BOOM! BASH! Oh, no, I just took a deep breath and then...
CRASH, goes the dishes!

Rebecca Toland, Grade 6
Meridian Middle School, ID

Candy

Sweet and Sour,
mostly sweet
I love candy, what a treat!

Gummy, crunchy, sour too
I love candy,
How 'bout you?

Candy, candy
Sugar cane
made with sugar
not whole grain

Well, DUH
Don't be Healthy about it!
River Dougherty, Grade 4
Lyons Elementary School, CO

Dancing Snow

Twirling, swirling,
'Round, and 'round,
Seems you never,
Hit the ground.
Clumps and drifts,
Of pure white,
Few pieces survive,
Dancing down to the floor,
Now it's ended,
There's no more!
Alyssa Thompson, Grade 5
Frederick Elementary School, CO

Love

Love is good, love is kind,
Every heart God tries to find
Love is everywhere
We can feel it in the air
Love is golden
don't let it be broken
God has love for you and love for me
God loves you can't you see?
Amanda Blake, Grade 6
Walt Clark Middle School, CO

Christmas

C heering friends in the night
H elping Santa working bright
R eindeer flying in twilight
I ce castles hard and tough
S anta's workers making toys rough
T ingling bells on ringing reins
M erry elves eating candy canes
A merry holiday with cheers
S leigh bells ringing in New Years
Jacob Schmidt, Grade 4
Grass Valley Elementary School, NV

Monkey Groove!

Once there was a weird animal,
I think that his name was Daniel.
He is one cool monkey,
That is sort of funky,
That is why he's such a scoundrel.
Cameo Gillum, Grade 5
Hafen Elementary School, NV

Puppies Poem

Puppies are like dancing flowers
Can't be blamed for being cowards
Man's best friend and my friend too
Plenty of treats for me and you
Kassie Whisenant, Grade 5
Grantsdale School, MT

The Lady Fair

Behind the fallen tree of old,
I saw a lady fair.
She stood there with a golden ring
And light brown flowing hair.
She beckoned me to come to her
And share my secrets there.
I whispered them into her ear
And quickly walked away.
She stared at me with bright blue eyes,
Begging me to stay.
I stared into her eyes with fear,
sensing evil play.
Alas, I had been fooled
By her lure,
And now it was time to pay.
Shelby Thompson, Grade 6
Eureka Middle School, MT

Bad Day

I woke up at nine
and felt fine
Until I realized I was late
School was at eight
Then I felt sick
like my brother Nick
I told my mom
and she went off like a bomb
So I went out the door
Half touching the floor
Justin Sloan, Grade 5
Frontier Valley Elementary School, CO

Snow and the Ocean Clouds

Snow is like a blanket
covering a mountain.
The ocean is like the sky.
Clouds are like the snow.
Andrew Skyberg, Grade 4
Wilson Elementary School, WA

Ocean

Waves crash on the shore,
Water glitters in the sunshine
Waves wash me away.
Zachary Cannon, Grade 5
Cottonwood Elementary School, CO

Friends

F un
R eliable
I ntelligent
E asy going
N ever let you down
D etermined
S illy
Tiffany Polson, Grade 6
Conestoga Elementary School, WY

Fat Man from New York

There was a fat man from New York
Who loved to eat beef and pork
He went to the deli
To fill his big belly
And there he ate with a spoon and fork
Chris Anger, Grade 4
St Thomas the Apostle School, AZ

The Game

About the softball game,
Across the town is where we play,
Before it is the end of the day,
At 7:30 the game begins,
But everyone knows we will win,
Beside third base is where I stand,
Inside my glove the ball should land,
Down the line is where I run,
For hitting the ball is lots of fun,
Around 9 is when it ends,
"Until next time" I say to my friends.
Misi Cummings, Grade 6
Fox Creek Jr High School, AZ

Long Nose Frank

There once was a girl with a long nose
It was as big as a garden hose
She had a cough
Then her nose fell off
Now they call her beautiful Rose.
Cierra Stater, Grade 6
Fox Creek Jr High School, AZ

Small Bug

Down in the tall grass
a small bug wanders around
looking for his home.
Christi Spiel, Grade 5
Ammon Elementary School, ID

Day to Night
Day
hot, sunny
walking, running, shouting,
sun, moon, cold, cloudy
sleeping, snoring, calming
quiet, dark
Night
Kael Bristle, Grade 6
Fox Creek Jr High School, AZ

My Flowers Are
My flowers are

dancers in the wind
powerful
full of life
to stop and smell
very sweet
joy even to Hades
the prettiest of them all
never lonely
the brightness of my day
the miracle of my life
peaceful as Mother Earth
what makes the birds sing

These are my flowers.
Chynna Campbell, Grade 4
The Meadows School, NV

In a Field
In a field,
Butterflies flutter
up, down, all around
playing with each other,
making no sound.
Grasshoppers hop
springing here, springing there
they never stop
bouncing everywhere
Bees buzz by flowers
gathering pollen
soon there'll be showers
so there's no time for stallin'
The tree blows
in the breeze
the creek flows
with joyful ease
the sun is setting,
dark has come
everything's resting,
with a gentle hum
Heather Seacrest, Grade 6
East Middle School, CO

Skiing
jumping, floating through the air
going fast, but you don't care
when I stop with a flop
as I get up I see
people laughing at me
but I don't care
I am the best one there
Charlie Airhart, Grade 6
Monforton School, MT

Why Did I Have to Die?
Why did I have to die?
Why did I have to eat that pie?
Why did I have to choke?
Why did I have to tell that joke?
Why did I have to drown?
Why did I have to go to the pound?
Why did I have to fall on that pin?
Why did I have to grow a big fin?
I guess I'll never know.
Christian Ashliman, Grade 5
Thomas Edison Charter School, UT

Sadie the Dino
There was a dino her name was Sadie,
She was a lady,
Sadie loved to fly a kite,
She loved to fly it at night,
Sadie enjoyed ice cream,
She liked the color green.
Rebekah Maughan, Grade 4
Summit Elementary School, UT

The Dog
As I was walking down the street,
I saw a dog I wanted to meet.
I stopped to say hello to him,
and as his tail wagged, I began to grin.
His fur was soft and white,
I wanted to hug him with all my might.
His eyes were as blue as the sky,
you just couldn't pass him by.
I had to get going to school,
but bringing a dog was against the rule.
I started walking down the street
I looked down and he was at my feet.
As I arrived at school,
he began to drool.
So I took him home that day,
to ask if he could stay.
But Mom said, "No Way!"
Get rid of him within a day.
Saige Wickstrom, Grade 6
Meridian Middle School, ID

Ocean/Desert
Ocean
Cold, salty
Swaying, waving, breezing
Wet, humorous, hot, windy
Dying, drying, heating
Waterless, burning
Desert
Bernardo Aguirre, Grade 5
St Cyril Elementary School, AZ

Crazy Hair Day
Today is crazy hair day
So nobody should go away
Some people like their hair purple
Some people want it blue
But whatever you are wearing
It is up to you
Patricia McClinton, Grade 4
Mills Elementary School, OR

The Desert
The gila monster
Hiding behind the cactus
Tackling his prey
Jake Rundell, Grade 5
Kingman Academy of Learning, AZ

Fourth of July
Fourth of July
Red, white, and blue fireworks
Burnt flares laying on the ground
Stinging sounds of fireworks in your ear
Cold ice cream on your tongue
Sparklers flickering high
Fourth of July
Aida Neitenbach, Grade 4
Coal Creek Elementary School, CO

My Lovely Ocean Waters
A lonely beach
On a sunny day
A sunset
Seagulls flying over my head
Winds lightly blowing
Waves gently crashing
Birds feed over the water
As I run through the sand
Boats appear in the horizon
Children play in the water
We lay in the sand
On the long lazy summer
I will be sad when it's time to end
Savannah Short, Grade 6
Fox Creek Jr High School, AZ

Magical World

When I was a young girl
I turned a knob to a magical world
I saw horses grazing in the beautiful wind field.
As I looked across my heart began to yield.
When my dream was over, I awoke very sad.
Longing to go back where my spirit was glad.

Kendra Gearhard, Grade 4
Larkspur Elementary School, CO

Winter Storm

W hite snow is falling fast
I dream of snowflakes twirling by
N othing's better than that cold icy feeling
T he glorious icy days
E verything so delicate and soft
R ain turns to

S now and spirals fast
T he moaning wind blows
O n top of old snow new snow falls
R emember to dress warm
M emories go past as every flake gets bigger

Veronika Reidel, Grade 6
Heath Middle School, CO

Hope

The mirage of happiness shining in the sky
bringing love and faith to all that are too shy
Keeping the wondrous feeling of love
keeps truth and faith flying like a dove
Makes all souls fly
helps all little bluebirds reach the sky
Bringing light when it is dark
helping people make their mark
Changing the mood of a young one's heart
making no hearts break apart
The feeling of faith when sorrow is here
hope keeps it away when it is near
What is it?
whatever it is hope deletes it

Ariel Edwards, Grade 6
Gate City Elementary School, ID

The Dream

Shadows on the wall
A yell down the hall
It is such a scare
But then I see something there
Is it an angel I see?
It's coming closer to me
Then it stops and flies up into the air
It comes to me and brushes its hands through my hair.
I wake and standing there
Was my mother brushing her hand through my hair.

Donny Naylor, Grade 6
Eagle Point Middle School, OR

Somebody or Nobody?

Somebody's turn out to be a real nobody.
Nobody's become somebody.
Who is who?
Which is which?
Only God knows.

Are all somebody's nobody?
Are all nobody's somebody?
What is what?
Which is which?
Only God knows.

Who's a somebody?
Who's a nobody?
Who is who?
Which is which?
Only God knows.

Who am I?
Who are you?
Only God knows.

Alexis A. Vaughn, Grade 5
Aurora Quest Academy, CO

Dogs Are Cute

I do not understand why most boys like pink
Why time goes fast when it is fun
Why kids (we) have to study so hard
But most of all I do not understand
Why other countries speak different languages
Because it is hard to learn
What I understand most
Is dogs are sooooo cute
Because I have a lovely dog at my house

Mayu Iizawa, Grade 5
Copper Creek Elementary School, AZ

The Hunt

The breeze felt cool on my face
My gun rested solidly by my knees
The deer had vanished with nary a trace
We thought they were by the trees.
We moved out, packed up and walked
Kept our guns ready in case they should appear
Crested the hill and stopped
There were the deer
We crawled down the steep slope
Adrenaline rushing through our veins
The deer sprang away in a lope
We rose up and shot, a deer fell down with no pain.
The hunt was mostly over,
The deer lay majestically dead in the clover.

Erik Lillquist, Grade 6
Morgan Middle School, WA

He Made Me

You broke your point and made me fail the test.
He put down A for B and C for D.
Pencil it is all your fault.
That's how Mom I got a 3.
It wasn't me he made me.
He said he for she and she for he.
Please Mom don't ground me.
He got into my mind and stole my brain.
He made me Mom he made me.

Austin Clark, Grade 5
Colbert Elementary School, WA

Regret

If my tears could wash away deceptions,
Then the very world would be clean,
If regret could make my rights my wrongs,
The righteousness of the world would be seen.

But alas, wishes cannot make things a right,
Regret can only unfold,
A path I shall not take again,
A future I shall not hold.

Sins that cannot be undone,
Follies that age and grow,
The deathly heartbeat of my life,
Is the punishment I will know.

But those whom I have sinned against,
Evil plans against me vow,
With wicked pleasure, Revenge licks her lips,
Two souls she has captured now!

Kaitlyn Meska, Grade 6
Pinnacle Charter School, CO

The Last World

A place of rural peace
spreading from sea to sea

Forest, woods, meadows
restricted by Nature's force: the last world

One place shrouded in mystery
the only place left
the sea…gold with the last sun's help

Caves unentered by all: the last world

Beauty never to be seen
one galaxy, in another universe…all else gone

The last world of beauty

Gabe Fine, Grade 4
Bromwell Elementary School, CO

Eternal Motion

On the Banks of Infinity
There lies the Forest of Forever,
Deep within the Forest of Forever resides the Town of Evermore,
Under the Town of Evermore there is an Endless Tunnel,
In the Endless Tunnel a branch pathway leads to the Eternal Sea,
In the middle of the Eternal Sea a boat sails to its shifting destination,
Never ending, never stopping the boat sails on infinitely.

Alexander Lash, Grade 6
Thomas Jefferson Charter School, ID

My Brothers

My brothers are great, and they are special.
My brothers are all special in their own way
My brother Chris is the oldest in my family, and very smart.
My brother Matt is the second oldest in my family, and very interesting.
My brother Robert is the third oldest in my family, and really funny.
My brother Nick is the youngest in my family, and he is nice.
My brothers are the best, and very special to me.

Joanna Chandler, Grade 5
Sangre De Cristo Elementary School, CO

Cave Creek

Cave Creek is a place where beautiful things grow.
Like trees, plants and some other things too.
When you walk around, you hear the leaves crack.
Then when you lay down you feel the smoothness of the grass.
Then when you're scorching you can splash some water on your face.
Then the day is over.

Jesse Hunter, Grade 4
Great Expectations Academy, AZ

TAD

TAD are the initials of someone whom I like.
I can't believe I'm saying this normally I'm uptight.
At night I see his face during the day I think of him.
He knows me I know him and yet he does not notice me.
I do my hair, I do my nails but he still does not see
That I like him and he might like me if he would look
And try to see the part of me that isn't seen.
So now you know do you see that I like him and he might like me.

Kaitlyn Combs, Grade 6
Meridian Middle School, ID

Queen of Heaven

Hera, queen of all the gods and goddesses of Greece,
Lived atop Mount Olympus.
Daughter of the Titans, Cronus and Rhea,
She was beautiful but jealous and vengeful, proud and bad-tempered.
She could help others with their marriages
But did not possess the power to make her own marriage to Zeus a happy one.
She needed a faithful husband and feared her rivals.
She wanted her children to be happy and to stop Zeus's roving eye.
She asked for nothing but the destruction of the mighty Hercules
And her husband home at the hearth with her alone.

Bryonna McKinney, Grade 4
East Valley Academy, AZ

When I Get on the Field

When I get on the field I think
where are my parents to give me a wink.
I wait 'til the ref blows his whistle
now I can't wait to shoot the ball like a missile.
Then the ball gets passed to me
I bounce the ball with my knee.
The defense comes and wants the ball
I feel like I'm a wall.
Now I shoot I hope I score
my shot goes in the net's core.
Then the ref blows his whistle loud
now I smile proud.
We won the game
soon the other team walks away in shame.

Maddison Ackiss, Grade 5
University Park Elementary School, AK

I Am From…

I am from Texas and Oregon.
I am from Christmas and Thanksgiving.
I am from Irish and German.
I am from chicken strips and manicottis.
I am from Leo and Pearl.

I am from cooking and drawing.
I am from ice skating and roller-blading.
I am from surgery on my foot and burn on my leg.
I am from *That's So Raven* and *Gilmore Girls*.
I am from beautician and electrician.

I am Hannah Marie Brook Kanig.

Hannah Marie Brook Kanig, Grade 5
Evergreen Elementary School, OR

Confetti Easter

Spring rains are invisible
droplets of water gingerly landing on soil to sprout
fruits and vegetables that feed the galaxy.
Spring sports make a benefit to sock you
with bruises on your knees and on your cranium.
Spring light leaves you in the evening and
greets you in the morning.
Spring vacation is full of swimming,
laughing, and jogging but ends you with
the Washington Assessment of Student Learning
Spring flowers grow to leave a mysterious
scent wandering through the spring air.
Spring fruits are delicious for the
whole season and are my favorite food.
In spring I throw confetti eggs at my
absolutely ridiculous godbrothers.

Marcelina Santana, Grade 4
Skyline Elementary School, WA

On Top of My Dad's Head

On top of my dad's head there is no hair
On top of my dad's head you will find it bare
On top of my dad's head you will find nothing there
On top of my dad's head you will say where is his hair.

William Allen Peterson II, Grade 4
Gause Intermediate School, WA

Blue Is Everywhere

Blue like the ocean,
Blue like the sky.
Blue like the tears that fall from my eyes.
Blue like water,
Blue like my pen.
Blue like rain spots where water has been.
Blue like dresses,
Blue like that bag.
Blue like the color on the American Flag.
Blue like a kite,
Blue like a pool.
Blue like sunglasses that look really cool.
Blue like a blue jay,
Blue like a bass.
Blue like the dew on morning grass.
Blue like a flower,
Blue like a whale.
Blue like that couch with much detail.
Blue is here,
Blue is there.
The color blue is everywhere!

Kelly Peyton, Grade 6
Bright Beginnings School, AZ

Alone

You think you're alone
But you really don't know.
There's times when you're going to blow.
It feels like no one cares.
You might have a brother or maybe a sister
Wondering, do you get less attention than them?
When you get a four wheeler
You have to share it
But didn't your parents say it's yours?
People think that you have a black hole
Everybody thinks you don't care about anything
You always have a frown on your face.
People talk about you
You think they're being mean to you
But is that what they're doing?
It feels like the world's against you.
On your shoulder you carry a chip
Why don't you brush it off?
If you stop hibernating in the house
Maybe go outside
You might see the world differently.

Tehvyn West, Grade 5
Lewis & Clark Elementary School, OR

Clouds
Fuzzy and fluffy
Coming when it's rain or shine
Clouds are fun to see
Karlie Coleman, Grade 5
Gold Canyon Elementary School, AZ

The Oak
My favorite place
Is a tree
Towering above the world.

I curl up in the oak's branches
Accepting the comforting embrace.

Even though I'm flying,
I feel solidness and security.

My favorite place
Is a tree
Towering above the world.
Kaziah White, Grade 6
Southern Hills Middle School, CO

Ode to the Moon
He glistens above me
During the night,
His face is scarred
From bits of rock that
Drive into his body.
He captures the ocean
And raises the tides
He circles above us
Like a hawk does a mouse.
The moon is a monarch,
A master of minds,
He can be very shy,
Hiding half, none, or
All of his face.
The light he gives off
Reminds me of pearly-white steel,
He resembles a lantern
With many black patches.
He just stays up,
rising and setting,
Over and over again.
Dallin Day, Grade 5
Barratt School, UT

Spring Making Its Way
Spring is now coming
good thing it is not snowing
flowers are blooming
Lizzie Pomeroy, Grade 4
St Thomas the Apostle School, AZ

Dolphins
Dolphins
Blue, slippery
Frisky, keen, clever
Exciting, interesting, awesome, playful
Porpoise
Ana Cook, Grade 5
Cokeville Elementary School, WY

Snow Is Fun
S nowflake
N ice
O utside
W ater

I ce
S hower

F reezing
U mbrella
N umb
Jesse Li, Grade 5
St Mary's School, ID

My Grandpa
My grandpa was so close to me,
He even gave me a nickname,
He always called me Big Bird.
We always wrestled.
When my dad told me that he died,
I cried and cried all through the night.
I still remember him just the same,
I wish he was still alive today,
I have so many memories in my heart,
But in the end I always miss him!
Shana Henderson, Grade 6
Hazelwood Elementary School, WA

While the Autumn Winds Blow
Leaves will fall, colors will glow
People will feast
While the autumn winds blow.

The autumn winds blow
As cold as a crow
And the colors
Put on an autumny show.

Rivers will flow
While the autumn winds blow
A tune in your ear
And suddenly…
Snow.
Haydon Ekstrom, Grade 6
Kingman Academy of Learning, AZ

Ned in Bed
There once was a boy named Ned
Who was always restless in bed
He tried to count sheep
But his clock would go "beep!"
Then his cat would jump on his head
Calvin DeMore-Mack, Grade 4
St Thomas the Apostle School, AZ

Recipe for Love
Add a quart of hugs,
Sprinkle on some sugar,
Add a pound of kisses,
Add some happiness too.
Add a little spice,
Then pour it in a bowl.
Stir it with a spoon.
Put it in the oven for 36 seconds.
Take it out.
What does it look like?
It's shaped like a heart!
Ariana Argomaniz, Grade 5
Desert View Academy, AZ

White Lion Moon
Creeping in the dark shadows of the sky,
White lion moon comes passing by,
When morning comes she leaps behind,
Just anything that she might find,
For it is orange lion's time to prowl.
Brynn Campbell, Grade 4
Wilson Elementary School, WA

Rain in Maine
Flowing through the sky
Down and down
Hits the ground
Splatters all around
My, oh my, oh my
Playing in the wet grass
While it lasts
Faster and faster
Making a disaster
My, oh my, oh my
Brett Stuard, Grade 4
Grass Valley Elementary School, NV

Cheerful
Cheerful is to be happy.
To not be sad.
To be jumping with joy.
To not be mad.
This is to be cheerful.
Crysta Hardy, Grade 6
Hidden Creek Elementary School, WA

August 19, 2005 — One of the Best Days of My Life

I was excited, I was giddy,
The gun went off
I started running
Of course uphill, I needed to walk
Huffing and puffing all around me
Different people, from different places
Some were quicker, some were not
Time went fast, so did I

Almost there, just 3 more miles
Nature gets angry, I get wild
I am cold, I am thirsty and I am a little afraid
It is not fun out here, but there is the top
I feel the thunder is coming,
I get scared and I start running
"Praise the Lord" there is the finish,
In 4 hours 45 minutes

Joshua Randono, Grade 6
Corpus Christi School, CO

I Am From…

I am from Italian and Indian.
I am from New York and Orange County.
I am from Shop Smart and graduating.
I am from Christmas and Halloween.
I am from BET and Spongebob.

I am from football and basketball.
I am from swimming and camping.
I am from skweekers and bootsie.
I am from "leave me alone" and "Why won't she stop crying?"

I am from potatoes and spaghetti.
I am from remote cars and trampoline.

I am Elizabeth M. Jenkins.

Elizabeth M. Jenkins, Grade 5
Evergreen Elementary School, OR

Life

Life is like a river,
Like a stream that flows.
The Lord is the only one
That understands and really knows.

It has its twists and turns
And rocks with which it collides
But always understand
God is at your side.

We will have times of majesty
And we will have times of hurt,
But whatever it is
We should look at life for what it's worth.

Matthew S. Lychock, Grade 6
Green Valley Christian School, NV

Pretend You Are…

Pretend you are a pink bunny slipper.
Chucked under the bottomless pit they call a bed.
Crashing very painfully into a solid brick wall.
Frolicking on a snowy Christmas Day.
Forced to swallow five disgusting toes for, it seems, forever.
Having very hot cocoa spilled on your plastic, emerald eyes.
Slammed into the cold, despised washing machine.
Drowning slower than somebody's grandma.
Losing your consciousness as quick as you can open presents.
Waking up only to do the whole darn thing over again.

Sarah Wood, Grade 6
Midway Middle School, ID

The Sea

The sea is a pretty place,
a diamond on someone's finger.
Suddenly, the current rolling faster, faster.
The sea is a loud horn blowing,
when the storm is over it's as quiet as a mouse.
Colorful ballerinas dance,
when the sun sets upon it.
The dolphins jump, the fish swim
the whales glide like airplanes.
What a beautiful sight!

Saige Snyder, Grade 4
Roy Moore Elementary School, CO

The Dog

Inside the big pen
A retriever jumps for joy
Can I please get this one?
I hope it's a boy!

Once we took him home
He begged to go outside
When I let him out
He rolled over on his side.

Sleeping on my bed
Keeping me really warm
Like a little blanket
While outside is a storm.

In the morning we go outside
He has really grown a lot
Outside we are playing
It is really hot.

Now he can't sleep on my bed
I am really cold
I have no more of my dog keeping me warm
Because he is too big and old.

Carly Hayes, Grade 6
Enterprise Middle School, WA

My Friends
Always loving, always caring
Even if she is bearing
To leave my house, leave my life
Slice our friendship with a knife
We get in fights
It really bites
But we still get together
We still stick together
Our friendship still lasts
Our years together have past
But we keep going
And we keep showing
What our friendship can do
Now we will show you
Hannah Rose, Grade 6
Morgan Middle School, WA

Spring
Butterflies flutter
bees are pollinating too
lots of flowers bloom
Kirwan Kennedy, Grade 4
St Thomas the Apostle School, AZ

Friend
I am filled with sorrow,
Because I lost my friend
To a fatal accident
She lost her life for someone else's.

I'm here to tell you
For what she did
She lost her own life
To save my OWN.
Darith Ambriz, Grade 6
Somerton Middle School, AZ

Moms
M akes me laugh
O verly happy
M oms are so nice
S ees the good in her kids.
Alix Wedmore, Grade 6
Fox Creek Jr High School, AZ

The Heart
The heart loves
The heart is big
The heart can change
The heart can be seen
The heart can be drawn
And it can grow
Kristin Cook, Grade 4
Christian Faith School, WA

My Secret Place
Deep in the willows
Where the river flows
And the flowers mellow
But nobody knows…

I only hear the quiet
Like the river flowing
Never any riot
I sit solemnly knowing.

When the sun sets slightly
The stars shine above
I start off quietly
For this is the place I love.
Sydney Moody, Grade 5
Gold Canyon Elementary School, AZ

Have You Ever Felt
Have you ever felt
    when nobody loves you.

Have you ever felt
    when somebody is talking
    behind your back.

Have you ever felt
    when people don't care
    about you.

Have you ever felt
    when friends don't care
    about you.

Well I have friends who
    think that. But everybody…
    loves her and forever we
    will love!
Katrina Ruiz, Grade 6
St Vincent de Paul School, AZ

Sadness
When you passed away I was
sad,
upset,
mad,
angry,
disappointed,
and I couldn't believe
that you were gone out of my life.
I stand here today and say that
I will never forget you because
I love you!
Jesse Slott, Grade 5
Edgewater Elementary School, CO

The Day I Got My Freedom!
Whip, whip
They whip us like
A piece of trash
They treat us like
I'm a piece of dirt
like we have no life or no souls.
We work so long
so we can get freedom
Our souls weep every night for life,
We are losing our dignity,
Very fast please God
Oh help us please
Put me out of my misery
My veins are losing power
My feet are so blistering
Rose from the hard raped weeds
What's that I see they're setting me free,
Free at last free at last
Thank God oh Mighty
I'm free at last
Ashlee Radney, Grade 5
Greenwood Elementary School, CO

Groundhog Day
Groundhog day
Groundhogs sticking out
Pancakes cooking
Squeaks of groundhogs
A perfect dinner
My warm pillow
Groundhog day
Henry Maloney, Grade 4
Coal Creek Elementary School, CO

The Fight
A passion for rage
captured within
one savage beast
let loose
by a continuous
hatred
the silence
broken by
a fierce snarl
two creatures
fighting 'til the end
flesh torn
and bones crushed
until there was a
champion
no witnesses
to the finishing of one.
Brittany Klein, Grade 6
Liberty Middle School, CO

White

What do you see when you see the color white?
Most see death, emptiness, loneliness.
But I see heaven.
I see angels, clouds, the Holy God.
I see singing, praising, rejoicing.
I see happiness, laughter, and joy.
I see children, adults, grandparents.
I see Him.

Michaela Ferguson, Grade 6
Walt Clark Middle School, CO

Beautiful

Beautiful as can be,
but you hide so no one can see.
Because they all laugh in jealousy.
But slowly if devoured you become ugly and mean,
for no one has seen what beauty you had
but just made you mad.
Their evilness made you ugly,
but only one has seen your change
and noticed your beauty,
that one is me.

Brandon Harrison, Grade 6
Green Valley Christian School, NV

The Ocean Vacation

The wind whistled a musical tune,
While the cat leaped up on a flowing loom.
Outside stars shine like smiles
The ocean calls me into the night.

Out on the horizon
The sun gleams blindly bright
Just like a candle on a pitch-black night.
The ocean calls me into the morning

I walk down to the sand
And wriggle my feet down into the deep.
My toes bury themselves into cool sand,
All of the sudden a wave comes up
Unburying my toes from the deep!

That's what the ocean does to me.

Alma Jensen, Grade 5
Spring Creek Country Day School, CO

Blue

If I were the color blue, I would be the waves in the ocean
The rain falling from the sky
A bright truck driving down the highway
The clear sky during the day
I would be the glistening water in an immense lake

Austin McGrew, Grade 4
East Evergreen Elementary School, MT

Katrina

Some men saw the wave
And evacuated brave
Though millions of people didn't make it
No one tried to fake it

Oh when we remember that tragic day
When the people screamed to say
Where's my baby, where's my dog?
Could they be floating on a log?

Day and night the people searched
Looking for their house of birch
Filled with mud and leaves and twigs
And the houses smelled like pigs

People wept and lied and cheated
Trying to get the things they needed
They stole plates and food and diapers too
Trying to get their mourning through

Katrina you're courageous your waves are big and round
The people started screaming as you headed toward their town
As the water started rising and the people scurried about
Oh Katrina you make the people shout!!

Sara Ballard, Grade 6
Eagleridge Enrichment Program, AZ

My Flower Is

My flower is

    made of stained glass
    the brightness of the moon
    hope beyond any other
    peace for all to have
    a colored sun
    what made the angels sing
    what brings Persephone back from Hades
    what makes criers laugh
    what makes the sun come out
    a never ending source of light

That is what my flower is.

Maxwell Tolan, Grade 4
The Meadows School, NV

Olympic Dreams

Going to the Olympics would be great,
The gold medal would be on my plate.
On the soccer team is where I would be,
When we won we shouted with glee.
The refs came over and announced our win,
I looked at my team, and on their face was a grin.
The refs came over with medals of gold,
Then my mom said, "wake up," and I did as I was told.

Nick Tobey, Grade 6
Bradford Intermediate School, CO

Beautiful Star

Beautiful star,
    twinkling in the sky.
You don't know how
I wish you were mine.

To put you in my hand
and use you as my
sleeping light.

I feel happy
when you come
to visit me at night.

Alicia Gonzalez, Grade 4
Lewis E. Rowe Elementary School, NV

Camping

As we back our camper
Avoiding the trees,
While welcomed by
A cooling breeze

As we hike up
Towards the tippy-top,
My feet so tired
Can't jump nor hop

As we drive down the road
Watching the eagles soar
We drive by the cabin —
Looking gift store

When I get home
I tell the story,
Of camping
And its glory

I love camping!

Dylan Tibbetts, Grade 4
Colbert Elementary School, WA

Horseback

Against the horse's brown saddle,
Beyond the green flowing hills,
Past the woods of white trees,
Down the dusty tan path,
Behind the silver stallion,
About to quickly gallop,
Until he slows to a canter,
Across the old wooden pilgrim homes,
Into the flowing crystal waters,
Past the woods of pure green spruce,
Upon the horse's brown saddle.

Kaitlin Porter, Grade 6
Fox Creek Jr High School, AZ

Room

Floor
Hardwood, tile
Stunning, shining, impressing
Hard, smooth, high, beamed
Breathtaking, towering, soaring
Shelter, roof
Ceiling

Logan Bohlender, Grade 6
Heath Middle School, CO

Rescue

Hit. Beat. Yell. Hurt.
A neighbor calls the police.
The police come and arrest.
Drop the rescue to safety.
A shelter for abused pets.
They feed, water, groom, and play.
Success.
Up for adoption, who will save?
Only a few days left.
A family comes to look for a pet.
Their kid sees the gentle old mutt,
That has been waiting for a while.
They take him home,
Another rescue to a good home.

Romy Witz, Grade 5
West Mercer Elementary School, WA

When I Grow Up

Someday soon when I grow up,
I'll have a job to do.
I'll write a book,
Or be a cook,
Or work inside a zoo.

I might want to drive a bus
Or teach children to read.
I'll load a train,
Or fly a plane,
Or plant a little seed.

I might want to fight a fire
Or be a doctor, too.
I'll build a house,
Or sew a blouse,
Or sail the ocean blue.

So many jobs that I might choose.
I wonder what I'll be.
I'll work and learn,
'Till it's my turn
To find a job for me!

Mary Lou Hill, Grade 5
Wallace Elementary School, AZ

So Lonely

So lonely
dark and cold
silent nights
sleepy kids
starving ways
crying silently in the night
people say "what" a way
to spend the night so lonely and gray
alone at night

Candice Moore, Grade 6
Fox Creek Jr High School, AZ

Brown Bear

A little brown bear
sleeps quietly in his den
waiting for the spring

Mackenzie Guzman, Grade 5
Ammon Elementary School, ID

Mama Love

M aternal
A great role model
M agnificent
A chieving tons

L oving
O pen minded
V aluable
E fficient

Sarah Jablonski, Grade 5
Gold Canyon Elementary School, AZ

The Moon

Above all the land,
Out in the night,
Underneath lay sleeping children,
Against the clear black sky,
Out of reach
Among the stars
Up is the moon

Meagan McBride, Grade 5
Cottonwood Elementary School, CO

The Storm

The ocean roared,
A seagull soared.
The rocks smashed,
As my sailboat crashed.
On the beach at night,
I could not find light.
What I should be aware of first,
Is to quench my thirst.

Varun Chandorkar, Grade 4
Eton School, WA

God's Children

We are God's children of night and day.
He shall still love us for whatever comes our way.
When the sun is bright
Or when the stars are in the night,
He shall still love us.
He loves us for who we are,
Not how we look or what we do,
But what's inside our great big heart.
We love Him too just the same
For what's inside of Him today.

Rebecca Paul, Grade 6
St Cyril Elementary School, AZ

The Mysterious Creature

As I walked home from school today
And went outside to play
I thought I saw someone follow me
Like a stalker in the tree
I walked a little faster
Then faster then faster
Until I was at my friend's yard
Where she set up some playing cards
We were to play a game
But then I thought the mysterious creature had came
I looked and I looked
I soon became hooked
On finding this mysterious creature
I decided to tell my mom, who is a teacher
She said it was nothing, nothing at all
It wasn't a stalker or even a ball
My shadow it was
And following people is what it does

Becca Libby, Grade 6
Colbert Elementary School, WA

My First Horse

I just started riding lessons
I can't wait to trot, canter, and jump fences.
As I walk up to the barn
Or maybe it was called a farm
There were many, many courses
Then I came across the horses
One was jumpy another casual
Soon I came to one who was natural
I picked her and her name was Snapple
Just for a snack I gave her an apple
When I was done I went on her back
Which was easy except the riding that I lack
I wanted left but she turned right
And when I wanted to stop she would bite
It was mad at me I could tell
Because she threw me into a well
The next thing was that I was rammed into a tree
But I felt much better after she nuzzled me

Emily Cukurs, Grade 6
Meridian Middle School, ID

I Wonder Why Clouds Make Pictures in the Sky

I wonder why clouds make pictures in the sky.
I lie on the ground and watch them go by.
Sometimes they make patterns and shapes on their way.
Forming outlines of pictures that stay through the day.

I can pick out a large polar bear,
skating away with puffy white hair.
Then I see the shape of a butterfly,
slowly clumsily swooping by.

A sparkly unicorn staggers along,
poking other animals in their silent song.
A magic dragon way up there,
gracefully floats without a care.

An enormous elephant sloppily leaps by,
dancing as if it is going to fly.
There's an alligator tumbling through the air.
What's he doing way up there?

I close my eyes to think about why.
I open them up again to a clear sky.
I'll do it again another day,
when fluffy white clouds come back to stay.

Tristen Clark, Grade 5
Gate City Elementary School, ID

Sadness

Sadness is when
you lost a loved one
when you cry
you cry until no more
I now know how you feel
I lost my great-grandma
all the memories
all the fun times
I feel sorry for you
because you didn't just lost your grandma
you lost the thing you need most —
a brother to play with
a sister to fight with
a mom to tell you what to wear,
and a grandma to tell you stories
like my great-grandma
I miss her a lot
and you probably miss your family
but you have a dad
to protect you and
to read to you

Kyle VanDyk, Grade 6
Acme Elementary School, WA

Bird in the Tree

Eyes straight forward,
Black as can be,
Staring at me,
Bird in the tree.

Beak straight forward,
Sharp as can be,
Chirping at me,
Bird in the tree.

Claws straight forward,
Strong as can be,
Pointing at me,
Bird in the tree.

Feathers straight forward,
Colorful as can be,
Shining at me,
Bird in the tree.

Leaves pointing everywhere,
Wood stronger than me,
Towering over me,
The tree with a bird.

Will Wolf, Grade 6
Pope John XXIII Catholic School Community, AZ

10 Little Frogs

10 little frogs swimming along
one was mine and then there were 9
9 little frogs sitting on a log
one was bait and then there were 8

8 little frogs lying around
one went to Heaven and then there were 7
7 little frogs sitting in a pond
one ate too many Trix and then there were 6

6 little frogs sitting on a lily pad
one did a dive and then there were 5
5 little frogs lying about
one went home to do a chore and then there were 4

4 little frogs hopping around
one got free and then there were 3
3 little frogs on a sidewalk
one got smashed by a shoe and then there were 2

2 little frogs doing the backstroke
one had too much fun and then there was 1
1 little frog swimming by
a fish snuck up and now well there's none.

Katie Ayres, Grade 6
Walt Clark Middle School, CO

My Magic Box

I will put in my box
A cat that is wild like a panther in the forests of Africa.
Her name is Kisa.

I will put in my box
enough Legos to build another Eiffel Tower,
in every color of the rainbow.

I will put in my box
an arcade full of games: Gameboy, PlayStation 2 and DS.
Games that will pass the time,
or take me to faraway lands without even leaving the house.

I will put in my box
a lot of family photos.
They will be images frozen in time like a caveman in an iceberg.

Jeremy Starr, Grade 5
Mesa Elementary School, CO

Why

Why is the sun so far away and the mist so cold?
Why does the moon follow us and the clouds water?
The sun is far away so we can have light above us not beside us.
The mist is cold because the wind follows it.
The moon follows us because it keeps an eye on us.
The clouds water because Heaven above is crying.
Why did God make Earth, and why did He make mankind?
Only God can answer those questions and nobody else.

Kendra Ross, Grade 4
Lahontan Elementary School, NV

My Love for Eternity

When troubles bring you down and you don't know what to do,
Just look inside your heart and you'll know that I love you!
Everyone has a destiny to find,
Looking in your eyes I have found mine.
You're all I ever wanted, you're all I ever needed.
I will be yours always, and you'll have my love for eternity.

Kelsey McMillian, Grade 6
Saghalie Jr High School, WA

The World of Loss

The cold chill, the one I always get when fear comes calling,
The unbearable heat, that burns through my heart and soul,
The blood chilling scream, like ones I've heard in horror movies,
The lifeless air, the one that has no thoughts of oxygen,
I try to breathe, but the air pulls me in, slowly sucking my life,
The minutes pass, but years are taken from me with every second,
I sense her corpse, that used to be a lively body, that is now lying
on a cold gray ground,
I sense the end, coming closer and closer,
But it's worth it just to see her again.

Corrina A. Leatherwood, Grade 5
Santa Fe School for the Arts, NM

Plums

Plums
delicious, juicy
squirting, rolling, bouncing
friends to my mouth
Fruits
Kaylee Kauffman, Grade 5
Sequoia Village School, AZ

Sneaky

Desert
Brown ground
Swimming and biking
I live here
Nevada
Zonia Avila, Grade 4
Jackpot Combined School, NV

Camping

camping with my brother,
what a great joy,
the sun, the fish
the wide open space,
the fresh air,
the birds chirping their peaceful song,
the squirrels climbing feet
scattering all over the trees,
the silent wind granting our wishes,
and the mist rushing through the air,
camping…
what a great joy!
Becca L. Weatherby, Grade 4
Scenic Park Elementary School, AK

Waterfalls

Sparkling rushing waterfalls
Rolling down tall rocky cliffs
Splashing on slippery rocks

Into a refreshing pool of glittery water
The sound is comforting and calming
Looking at the peaceful waterfall

Almost like diamonds falling down
The breeze blowing water on my face
I enjoy the view of the waterfall
Kayla Moredock, Grade 6
Wallace Elementary School, AZ

The Squirrel

A fuzzy squirrel
eating a delicious nut
in the lush forest.
J.T. Fraser, Grade 6
St Joseph School, WA

Nice Person

I am a nice person and helper.
I wonder if unicorns exist.
I hear rainbows talking.
I see a unicorn.
I want a dog.
I am a nice person and helper.

I pretend I'm flying the sky.
I feel like a banker
I touch the sky.
I worry about life.
I cry at funerals.
I am a nice person and helper.

I understand worries.
I say sound is good.
I dream of dogs.
I try to cry.
I hope I can help the world.
I am a nice person and helper.
Jeff Hart, Grade 6
H Guy Child School, UT

The Point

Waiting, I'm not sure
Why, or where but just
Waiting, if we all die
Waiting, the question will
Never be answered

The big question we
Ask, what is the meaning
The point of our short lives?
Maybe we all seek
The big question

Some say there is no
Point to life while
Others say life is a
Very powerful thing
While death is a whole other subject.
Elicia James, Grade 5
Lewis & Clark Elementary School, OR

Liftoff!

Soaring to the sky
Hurrying to the moon
Using all the rockets
Trying to accelerate
Trying to survive
Landing on the moon
Excitement all around.
Vincent Villegas, Grade 6
Fox Creek Jr High School, AZ

Despondency

Pandemonium spread
With the eerie sound of
Inevitable destruction.
Habitats vanished;
Animals died.
The dominant species
Of sentient beings,
Smothered the animals' homelands
For their own,
Selfish purposes.
A treacherous misdemeanor,
Leading to be
A barbarous felony.
The animals' futile attempts
To save their territory,
Watching it crash and burn,
Torturing their souls.
All that was left for the animals,
Was a chasm of rage,
And a melancholy memory.
Andrei Ramos, Grade 6
Liberty Middle School, CO

A Chip of the Rainbow

A masked intruder's eye
The wings of a butterfly
Like a colored moth
Shiny piece of candy for a kid's cough
What am I?
Abby Hall, Grade 6
Morgan Middle School, WA

Storm

Rain, revenge crashing down.
Chewing up houses like a dog.
It's fast, deadly, cruel.
Taking homes, family, pets from all.

All hope this day will end,
And stop before tomorrow.
For people have crops to grow,
And seeds to plant.

Winds start to die,
Waves start to shrink.
This hurricane will soon be done.
And we'll be safe.

It's taken so many lives,
And flooded so many towns.
Yet next time we'll be ready.
And we'll have a place to hide.
Duncan Adams, Grade 5
Lewis & Clark Elementary School, OR

Flip-Flops
There was a triceratops
Of which I knew
Who had a pair of flip-flops
A very noisy shoe
Shelby Nielsen, Grade 4
Summit Elementary School, UT

The Whatchamadoodle
If I had a million dollars,
I'll tell you what I'd do.
If I had a million dollars,
I'd start to run a zoo.
And to the zoo I'd bring,
A very peculiar thing.
Its pet is a poodle,
It likes to eat noodles.
The thing, it is called, a
Whatchamadoodle.
The Whatchamadoodle is very rare,
It has a ton of purple hair.
Yes, that life would be very good,
Except if that strange animal should,
Get very, very disgusted with noodles.
And then, only then, the
Whatchamadoodle,
I think he would, maybe he might,
Pick me up and take a bite.
Kahlie Taylor, Grade 6
Towne Meadows, AZ

Our Flag Free
The flag represents our nation Free
The flag is the fruit on our liberty
The flag is the gift of our Nation United
The flag is how we stay delighted
Clarissa Story, Grade 6
H Guy Child School, UT

Too Old
I hate you
you little dumb thing
in the tub
you feel and smell
just like a giant stink bug
though you feel
and look different
with big and bright eyes
though I still don't like you
with your big surprise
we use to have some
quite big luck
but now
I'm too old
for a little rubber duck
Ronny Enciso, Grade 4
Windsor School, UT

Monkeys
I like monkeys,
they're so cool,
they're not fools,
a lot are in Africa,
not a lot in America,
monkeys are way up high,
and I do not lie!
Adela Traeger, Grade 5
Sequoia Village School, AZ

Sand Castle
It's strong and sturdy.
But yet very dirty.
I built it once before,
But the ocean washed it away
By the end of the day
My sand castle was huge,
Big and strong with a mote
To keep the water at bay
But it did not work, no way!!
Austin April, Grade 4
Colbert Elementary School, WA

I Am
I am a big, fat, pink pig
I wonder if I will ever get skinny
I hear other pigs squealing
I want to live somewhere else
I am a big, fat, pink pig.

I pretend I can fly
I feel the gooey mud in my hooves
I touch my food with my tongue
I worry if I will ever die
I cry when my stomach hurts from eating
I am a big, fat, pink pig.

I understand I will not fly
I say I can do anything
I dream I will meet my parents
I try to talk
I hope I will be able to fly
I am a big, fat, pink pig.
Camille Aspa, Grade 6
Wallace Elementary School, AZ

Christmas Eve
Christmas Eve
Presents
Fresh baked cookies
Jingle bells
Gingerbread cookies
Sparkling white snow
Christmas Eve
Dana Bakke, Grade 4
Coal Creek Elementary School, CO

Cactus Blossoms
Tiny light pink buds
Blooming in the warm sunlight
Soon to be ripe fruit
Olivia Kerwin, Grade 6
St Cyril Elementary School, AZ

The Fourth of July
An American Celebration
With colorful fireworks
Joyful cheering children
With their faces glowing
Proud American colors
People singing the National Anthem
Praising this country
And then
After the sun is gone
Everyone watches the beautiful fireworks
BOOM!!!
As they light the sky
Katelynn Garner, Grade 6
Fruitland Middle School, ID

School vs Home
School
desk, chairs
learning, writing, teaching
Students, paper, pencils, learning
cleaning, annoying, climbing
big, grass
Home
Derian Vidales, Grade 4
Amesse Elementary School, CO

Social Studies
What's Social Studies?
It's fun to play in the school.
We read in textbooks.
Brittney Motto, Grade 6
Hamilton Middle School, MT

Dogs
Loyal and loving
Friendly and fun
I'm soft and playful
My obedience never fails
I'll play like a puppy
For you.

I'm an old dog now
I can jump and soar no more
But I'll always be
Loving and loyal
Friendly and fun
For you.
Kayla Todd, Grade 5
Uplands Elementary School, OR

Fall Colors

In the fall, leaves on the trees change colors. The leaves change from green, to orange, to yellow, to brown. In the winter, the leaves fall off the trees. So in the spring, the fresh leaves will grow back again. Birds will sing, and crickets will chirp and chatter. The sun will shine on the misty ground and tree roots will suck up what was once snow. Animals will be born and the Earth will be brought back to life once more.

Robbin Hemperley, Grade 4
Great Expectations Academy, AZ

In My Heart Forever

I will never forget, the times we spent
The laughs we shared, the rules we bent
I will never forget your smile, your laugh is fresh in my mind
Your voice I can hear in the wind, wherever I go, your face I can always find
That phone call I got, was the worst one ever
The conversation that was shared is still fresh in my mind
It was your mom, and she didn't sound happy
For all eternity it seemed she was bound, to one emotion, of strong sadness and tears
And in a few seconds, my whole world turned upside down
She told me that there had been an accident, it had been the drunk driver's fault
Your sister survived, and the driver survived, but you had not
I felt hot tears fill my eyes, I felt like part of me had died, I felt like I would never smile again
I didn't know what to do
Those first few weeks were unbearable, whenever I tried to do something
My mind would turn back to you, and I would cry
At your funeral, I was scared and sad, everything was a blur, I couldn't stand to be there
I called my mom to come pick me up, I just couldn't be there, I just couldn't do it
But whenever your song came on the radio, or I ate your favorite food
Whenever I did things we usually would do together, I would cry
Eventually, I moved on, I learned to deal with it, and to accept what had happened
I learned that it was not the end

Meghan Sandoval, Grade 6
Barbara Bush Elementary School, AZ

Hurricane

It seems like only yesterday I was a child of play. The clouds drifted so steadily that time was passing by too quickly. They darkened in sadness and tears of rain pounded the ground like strokes of evil were upon them. Thunder roared over the city like a beating of drums. Flashes of lightning hastened to the city only to destroy. God knew something was wrong, something to cry about. Animals ran lightning flashed. This was no ordinary storm it was a hurricane. God was punishing us we all knew. The power went off, children crying. Trees falling down in flames. Thunder lightning shocks of terror. Frightening people in their sleep. Screams in the night. Fire here fire there our city was being destroyed. Everything was in chaos. No more trees no more grass no more anything. Houses were breaking down the streets were flooding. Everything that was perfect is in the water. We had disobeyed God now we must listen.

Alexia Riveros, Grade 6
St Cyril Elementary School, AZ

Eagle's Spirit

I feel the warm wind against my soft feathers as I soar across the sky.
I look down and see a canyon carved by the river, untamed as the spirit of the eagle.
I look up and see the sky, a prairie, a range of open blue.
I swoop, I dive, I grasp a fish from the clear, rushing water.
Gliding up I feel the wriggling fish in my talons.
Landing on a nearby branch I feast on my prize.
Come dance the west wing and sail off the mountain tops,
Glide through the canyons and the river's heart.
And all those who free me and all who believe in me cherish the freedom of the eagle that I see.

Sophie Zega, Grade 6
Hood River Middle School, OR

What Are My Flowers?

What are my flowers?
   Special
   Symbols of beauty
   Bright like the sun
   Breezy like the wind
   Sweet like honey
   Shine like the midnight moon and stars
   Bring joy to the darkest souls on Earth
   Relax the heart
   Make the wind lose its breath
   Bring light to darkness
   Bring hope to people in need
   Give personality to shyness

That is what my flowers are.

Daria Butler, Grade 4
The Meadows School, NV

Have You Ever...

Have you ever
heard the city sounds,
the cars and sirens?

Have you ever
seen what life could be like
without
all of that

Just take a moment and
think
about the natural things the Earth has to offer

Which would you rather have
Buses, smoke and pollution,
or
happiness, peace and care

Have You Ever?...

Sabrina Janssen, Grade 5
Edgewater Elementary School, CO

Hunting

A mazing **B** ouncing **C** oyotes
D eer **E** legantly **F** lee
G razing **H** elplessly
I ncredible **J** oyful **K** ick
L eaping **M** adly
N oisy **O** rdeal
P atience
Q uite **R** emarkable **S** tories
T ramping **U** nder **V** arious **W** eather
X tremely **Y** outhful **Z** igzag

Shay Goettemoeller, Grade 6
Denton Elementary School, MT

Starry Night*

Diamonds shining in the dark night, a black that sucks me in.
Different emotions that I feel, go 'round and 'round and 'round again.
They circle the wheel and now I'm scared, but then again I'm happy.
The lights of the stars above, twinkle a great big song.
So gentle this unheard song is,
The better that I feel.
The breeze flows my way,
It sweeps me off my feet.
The stars they sing, the wind it blows high above the world.
Are they the enemy?
Are they the friend?
It pulls me up, the sky so magnificent sucks me in.
Twirl and twirl and twirl I spin,
The black hole makes me go.
I open my mouth to scream so loud, but only silence comes out.
I try again and it happens again,
All I can do is watch.
Black and blue and green and red, are the colors that blur.
As I watch it bestows on me,
The gift of returning home.
I never did tell a soul, of this adventure never told!

Irma Aganovic, Grade 6
Omar D Blair Edison Charter School, CO
*For those who live in the dark.

Mom

My mother shows me unconditional love.
A fallen angel from above.
When I wake up to the sound of her voice,
It is as if there are no worries in the world.
Her genuine goodness overflows.
I love her personality the best because she has a passion for everything.
She makes me feel so happy and carefree.
My mom inspires me to be the best person I can be.

Aaron Catucci, Grade 5
Mullan Road Elementary School, WA

Cassandra

Cassandra, the Trojan princess,
Daughter to King Priam and Queen Hecuba,
Sister to brave Hector and foolish Paris,
Beautiful and loyal priestess who loved Apollo —
Loved her family and devoted herself to the gods.
Blessed with the gift of foresight,
Cursed because nobody believed her predictions —
Cassandra could not save her beloved city of Troy from the Greeks.
She would have nightmares about the large wooden horse her whole life long.
Taken slave by the Greek King Agamemnon,
She was forced to go to the strange land of Greece with him
But her fate did not change.
When she warned Agamemnon that his wife Clytemnestra plotted to kill him,
He listened not — and was slain.
Still, Cassandra's gifts brought no delight and she longed for the impossible —
One glimpse of her family and her home.

Ariana Young, Grade 4
East Valley Academy, AZ

Sunday
Sunday
Fun, cheerful day
Pray, worship, singing, rest day
When I awake I just play
Funday

Play day
Very joyful
Learning about Jesus
I know God loves me a lot
You too
Jake Scott, Grade 5
Olympic Range Garden Academy, WA

I Have a Feeling
I have a warm feeling
Of Grandma's cookies
The squeak of snow on my feet
The welcoming dog who jumps on me
The whiff of air from my childhood
The warm feeling of a hug
The warm fuzzy mittens covered in snow
Kids playing and laughing
Building snowmen with friends
Laughing all the time
Cody Mitchell, Grade 4
Grass Valley Elementary School, NV

Buddy
Buddy was my bird,
When he got out of his cage he would
Fly to me,
Get on my shoulder,
He had green, blue, yellow, orange
Color all over his body,
He was noisy sometimes,
He would fly everywhere to find me,
Buddy died last year then I was sad,
But I had to let him go from my life.
J.J. Granberg, Grade 6
Hazelwood Elementary School, WA

Dreaming
When I am
Dreaming I set
Off to the mountains
And soar up to the walls
Of the mountain, and see as
If there is a gleaming power-filled
Tower in the darkened sky, when I am

Dreaming
Sutter Davies, Grade 4
New Emerson School, CO

Tax Day, Tax Day, Tax Day
Why is it so hard,
the people can't open a jar

now everyone is scared of the bank,
they wish it could shake

they're not even eating their meal,
and they make me feel ill

make it end,
let the people spend

That's how Tax Day is so scary.
Kemberly Mejia, Grade 5
Bennett Elementary School, NV

Beautiful Creature
Horse
wise wild
enlightening understanding
mustang mare stallion colt
walking trotting loping
Western English
Tonto
Eleanor Mueller, Grade 5
Eton School, WA

Red
Red is the color
Of the velvet I wear,
Bright a a laser
And some kids' hair.

Red is the color
Of the planet Mars,
Red as an apple
And red as sports cars.

Red is the color
Of a fireman's hose,
Back of a lizard
And the tip of my freezing nose.

Red is the color
Of a clown's mop,
Color of strawberries
And red means stop.

Red is the color
Of our flag's stripes
Bright as a grading pen
And raspberries ripe.
Nick Tyo, Grade 6
Kendallvue Elementary School, CO

Blue
Blue means unhappy,
Like a deep dark mysterious ocean,
With creatures all alone

It is also like a raindrop,
Falling and falling,
Pounding, beating the ground,
Until it is gone,
Washed away by the rain

It brings a tear from my heart,
Straight to my eyes,
It makes me feel,
Like I want to
Die.
Nicole Hlavacek, Grade 6
Walt Clark Middle School, CO

Me
Adriana
Bossy, silly, happy, crazy
Sister of Marc and Ashley
Lover of discipline and focus
Excitement in riding
Spring every day
Friendship, teamwork
Encouragement
Death, pain, bombers
Peace
Cheyenne
Meadowcroft
Adriana Meadowcroft, Grade 6
Miller Elementary School, WY

I Am From
I am from the sandy shores
Of the Pacific Ocean

From the heartwarming sunsets
Each day

I am from the little dogs
Leaping about in happiness

From the brownies that tempt me
When I enter the house

I am from the family gathering
Of noisy love

From the raccoons to the deer
The park is where I come from
Khyra Cooley, Grade 4
Grass Valley Elementary School, NV

Minor Feelings for War

My feelings are down,
Gone away,
Gone.
Not living,
But growing,
Growing into a painful sight.
Easier to touch,
And feel.
Becoming saddened,
Mournful.
Why should we fight for a terrible thing called war?
Having more people cry,
For their loved ones.
Why?

Caleb Johnstun, Grade 5
Lewis & Clark Elementary School, OR

N'aaya and N'aishdiya

N'aaya, I love your food.
N'aishdiya, I love your tenderness and care.
You have both been there in my times of need
I'll be here for you in your times of need too.
You will always be my parents no matter what.
Do not forget we are family, nothing will tear us apart.
N'aaya, you never gave up on me.
You believe I can do anything if I just try hard enough.
N'aishdiya, you always knew me more than anybody else.
We are family and our love will never be broken.
I love you Mom and Dad.

Miranda Chino, Grade 6
Sky City Community School, NM

The River's Edge

There is something so peaceful
along the river's edge.
The soft sound of water
runs through my head.
The gently cry of a chickadee
gives me peace of mind.
The freezing cold water
stops me dead in my tracks.
The swish and flick of my rod
sharply fills the silence
of the frigid air.
When my fly hits the water
it sends out a small ripple.
When the bait is taken under,
I see and feel
the rod start to bend.
The trout squirms and struggles
in desperation to be free.
When I take the hook from it's mouth
and place it in the water
it swims away and brings a smile to my face.

Jackson Goodman, Grade 6
Monforton School, MT

Madness

The last leaf on the tree, flitted down to earth
Then came winter, the death to all birth
It was like a dream, the day you left me
Or maybe a nightmare, blinded by what I see
Your love became myth, your words were lost
My happiness disappeared, your touch turned to frost
I faded away, heart turned to stone
Went cold as the snow, killed by everything I've known
I created the chasm, between my mind and reality
Standing on the edge, at the brink of my sanity
I'm dying, missing your love
Rotting away, no light from above
Falling into hell, I cannot hold on any longer
Losing control, the pain's grip is growing stronger
I'm crying, falling into space
I'm screaming, my life has fled without a trace

Dora Holland, Grade 6
Columbia Falls Jr High School, MT

Hiccups

Hiccups are so infuriating
I get them all the time
Then I hold my breath and what do you know
It never works
Everyone's looking at me from the eerie sounding hiccups
Man it's so thwarting
All the kids are giving me ways to end my hiccups
I try to listen to all of them
I'm so infuriated none of the ideas work
Smoke is impending out my ears
My eyes are turning bright fire red
Then I noticed something very pleasant
My hiccups had vanished!

Samantha Lopez, Grade 6
Desert Mountain School, AZ

Index